The tabla is the most important and popular drum in North Indian classical music. This book aims to increase our understanding of the Lucknow tabla-playing tradition by showing what distinguishes it from other styles both musically and technically and by analysing the processes involved in composition and improvisation. In conjunction with the musical discussion James Kippen considers the socio-musical development of Lucknow from the late eighteenth century to the present day and analyses several important aspects of the lives of a particular group of hereditary musicians connected with Lucknow who specialise in the tabla. He investigates the scope for music-making in Lucknow today, the social relationships of the musicians and the controversial topic of political intrigue, perceptions of, and attitudes towards, musical change, and institutionalised methods of musical instruction. The author shows that the individuality of the Lucknow tradition is linked to the individuality of the cultural climate that sustained it through most of the late eighteenth and nineteenth centuries and that the disappearance of that climate along with the demise of princely patronage and the increased control of the State during the twentieth century have contributed to Lucknow's position as a cultural backwater where the older traditions struggle to survive alongside new ones that cater to the tastes of modern Indian audiences.

James Kippen has illustrated his book with notations which for the first time facilitate a technical reconstruction of pieces as they are played. An accompanying cassette provides recorded examples of the pieces discussed.

The Tabla of Lucknow

A cultural analysis of a musical tradition

James Kippen

MANOHAR
2005

First published by Cambridge University Press, 1988
Reprinted with a new preface, 2005

ISBN 81-7304-574-7

Published by
Ajay Kumar Jain for
Manohar Publishers & Distributors
4753/23 Ansari Road, Daryaganj
New Delhi 110002

Distributed in South Asia by
FOUNDATION BOOKS
4381/4, Ansari Road
Daryaganj, New Delhi 110 002
and its branches at Mumbai, Hyderabad, Bangalore, Chennai, Kolkata

Printed at
Lordson Publishers Pvt. Ltd.
Delhi 110007

This book is dedicated to the memory of my father, Alexander Kippen (1904–80), who knew Lucknow long before I did and whose tales of India first inspired my interest, and to Ustad Afaq Husain Khan who made this study possible.

Contents

Plates, charts and maps

Plates

Charts

Maps

Preface to the second printing

As a prelude to writing this new preface to Manohar's reprinting of my book, I did something I hadn't done since 1988: I read this work from cover to cover. It brought back to me many very vivid memories as well as startling reminders of the rapid pace of change. *The Tabla of Lucknow* preserves in its pages a world that has all but disappeared. Most importantly, Afaq Husain Khan, doyen of the Lucknow tabla tradition and the character central to this study, died from an apparent heart attack on 18 February 1990, at the age of fifty-nine. Many other personalities whose words, ideas, and influences can be felt throughout the book have also passed away, including, early in 1997, Akbar Husain 'Ballu' Khan of the so-called Kothiwal tabla tradition. Lucknow today is a different city: in barely a generation it has more than doubled in size: its sprawl, crowding, pollution and traffic woes are a sharp reminder of the inexorable march of urban 'progress'. Technological change has come swiftly too: whereas it proved virtually impossible to place a telephone call from one part of the city to another when I conducted my primary fieldwork, I am now able to contact people by e-mail or reach them on their mobile phones as they stroll through the labyrinths of the Chowk Bazaar. Moreover, instead of the single television channel broadcasting just a few hours each day, Lucknowis choose from dozens of channels that, in style and content, resemble the dross of North American commercial television. Perhaps it is a trait peculiar to Lucknowis, and to honorary Lucknowis like me, that we are tricked by the city's crumbling charms into becoming maudlin and wistful, longing for the refinement and elegance of a past era, always believing we were witnesses to *The Last Phase of an Oriental Culture.*[1]

This book documents Lucknow, its culture, its music, and specifically the influences that have shaped a particular kind of tabla playing. Although it relates to the early 1980s, it also carries broader messages relevant to the present. This is a book about decline: decline of a family tradition, of a music culture, of an ethos. Nowadays, when anyone with impunity can call himself an *ustad* or *pandit*, where audiences are largely undiscriminating and musicians sing and play without depth, without *ras* ('juice', emotional essence), we begin to realize that the qualities most connoisseurs cherish belonged to a world that has been devalued by modern bourgeois ideals in India. That was a world of traditional, hereditary occupational specialization built around strong family and clan networks of musicians sustained economically by a wealthy social elite. At the root of all of that, I would venture to argue, were the courtesans and the tabla and *sarangi* players that both taught and accompanied them. From at least the eighteenth century to the present day, great instrumentalists and singers have emerged from their ranks. These networks established identity and order, both socially and musically, and my guess is they also constituted critical audiences for their communities' music, thus ensuring continuity, coherence, and quality control.

Recent studies have continued the exploration of these key musical communities. The remarkable work of Lowell Lybarger[2] in Lahore documents aspects of a quasi-feudal society

[1] I refer here to the translated title of Abdul Halim Sharar's famous writings on Lucknow.

[2] Lowell H. Lybarger, 'The Tabla Solo Repertoire of Pakistani Panjab: An Ethnomusicological Perspective.' Unpublished Ph.D. thesis, University of Toronto, 2003.

in which musicians in contemporary Pakistan are as marginalized as they once were in pre-Independence India, and where there are few if any non-hereditary musicians. The social networks of musicians in Lahore thus remain intact, and one may still witness elaborate, ritualized social behaviour in the key events where musicians play for other musicians. Such behaviour enacts the internal hierarchies through which streams of knowledge—*silsilas*—have been passed down, and recognizes and honours authority and skill. The wonderful study of *sarangi* culture by Nicolas Magriel[3] suggests these customs are not yet dead in India, though they have clearly become entirely peripheral to mainstream Hindustani music culture. Moreover, his accounts of training for young children show precisely why heredity and early immersion in a musical environment are crucial to the transmission of this difficult and esoteric music. Amelia Maciszewski's penetrating research into the remnants of courtesan culture[4] provides yet another example of a community dispossessed of its musical livelihood by the sweeping changes that transformed Indian society during the late-nineteenth and twentieth centuries. Margaret Walker's forthcoming study of *kathak* dance[5] will, like these other works, help us to place in perspective the radical shift in thinking that has attempted to distance the present from what mainstream India considers unwelcome elements of the past. I look forward to further enlightening publications from these and other scholars in the future, and to dispelling some more of the revisionist myths endemic to most contemporary views of Hindustani music's evolution.

The Lucknow tabla tradition is now in the capable hands of Ilmas Husain Khan, the son of Afaq Husain. He is an excellent musician, and the repository of a wealth of social and musical information. The more I learn through my research and my practice the better equipped I become to ask him pertinent questions and elicit fascinating information. Our collaboration on an article reassessing Robert S. Gottlieb's transcription and analysis of Ilmas's grandfather's tabla solo performance from 1971 proved to be a richly rewarding experience, and I think the result has added a further layer to our understanding of traditional Lucknow tabla playing.[6] Should Ilmas resist compromising the integrity of his musical knowledge then it remains to be seen how far into the future his family tradition will survive. Such preservation may come at a personal cost, since it runs counter to current trends in tabla playing that pander to popular tastes for the bland and homogeneous. In any event, I am heartened that so many people have continued to push for a reprint of this book, and I am grateful that my work has helped bring attention to the Lucknow tabla tradition by according it the respect it richly deserves.

Toronto JK
January 2004

[3] Nicolas Magriel, 'Sarangi Style in North Indian Art Music.' Unpublished Ph.D. thesis, School of Oriental and African Studies, University of London, 2001.

[4] Amelia Maciszewski, 'Gendered stories, gendered styles: Contemporary Hindusthani music as discourse, attitudes, and practice.' Unpublished Ph.D. thesis, University of Texas, Austin, 1998. See also her 'Multiple Voices, Multiple Selves: Song Style and North Indian Women's Identity.' *Asian Music*, 32 (2), Spring/Summer 2001, pp. 1-40.

[5] Margaret Walker, 'Kathak Dance: a Critical History.' Forthcoming Ph.D. thesis, University of Toronto, 2004.

[6] 'Wajid Revisited: A Reassessment of Robert Gottlieb's Transcription and Analysis of a Tabla Solo by Wajid Hussain Khan of Lucknow.' *Asian Music*, 33 (2) Spring/Summer 2002, pp. 111-74.

Preface

The tabla is the most commonly played drum set in North Indian classical music. It is the instrument most frequently used to accompany vocal, instrumental and dance musics, where its primary function is to maintain the metric cycles in which compositions are set. However, tabla players are also soloists in their own right, and many have vast repertoires of elaborate compositions some of which have been handed down orally from father to son over seven or eight generations. Until this century, tabla knowledge was the domain of families of hereditary occupational specialists, commonly known as *gharānās*. Six *gharānās* are widely recognised: those of Delhi, Lucknow, Ajrara, Farukkhabad, Punjab and Benares. Increasingly, non-hereditary musicians are being recruited as tabla knowledge is more widely disseminated, helped in part by India's music schools, colleges and universities.

Some tabla traditions, in particular those of Delhi and Benares, have received considerably more attention than others in the literature. By contrast, the musics of Ajrara and Lucknow are little known either inside or outside India. Furthermore, most tabla studies have concentrated largely on descriptions of drum strokes and the repertoire, whilst information provided on tabla musicians has tended to be anecdotal and non-analytical. However, Daniel Neuman's anthropological work *The Life of Music in North India* (1980) has given an important lead by helping to shift the focus of Indian music studies to the musicians themselves. My own work may be viewed as an attempt to tread the middle path. My aim has been to understand the tabla playing of Lucknow: to learn what distinguishes it from other styles both technically and musically, to identify the scope of its repertoire, and to investigate its dynamism in terms of the processes involved in composition and improvisation. But since the creation and performance of music are the acts of individuals whose sensibilities are shaped by the culture of a particular time and place, it is vital to relate any musical analysis to its wider cultural context. Therefore, this is also a study of the lives of those musicians who create and perform the tabla music of Lucknow: how they earn a living, how they organise themselves socially and interact with other individuals or groups of musicians, how they perceive the music world about them, how they transmit their music, and how they perceive and respond to musical change.

Essentially, I relied upon the social anthropological method of participant observation in order to carry out this investigation. This involved learning the tabla (which I had studied before and in which I was greatly interested) with the intention of becoming, as far as possible, a performer. This approach was invaluable as it not only gave me an opportunity to document both the music and the teaching and learning processes but it also afforded me tremendous insights into how the tabla players of Lucknow viewed their world. Additionally, I collected hundreds of hours of taped interviews with several key informants and nearly one hundred casual informants. I also made trips to other centres of music in North India in order to observe how they differed from Lucknow and to compare notes with other researchers in this field.

This book is based on work submitted for a Ph.D. at The Queen's University of Belfast in 1985, supported by a grant from the Social Science Research Council of the United Kingdom (now the Economic and Social Research Council). Fieldwork was carried out in two periods: sixteen months in 1980–2 and four months in 1982–3. Further periods of fieldwork – in 1983–4 funded by the National Centre for Performing Arts (Bombay), and in 1986 as part of ongoing postdoctoral research supported by the Leverhulme Trust – provided me with opportunities to gather further information.

It would be impossible to thank all those who were kind enough to assist me in the collection of data and the preparation of this book. To all my informants and advisers I extend my deepest gratitude. However, nothing would have been possible without the co-operation of the character central to this study: the head of the Lucknow tabla *gharānā*, Ustad Afaq Husain Khan. As my teacher and guide, I owe to him my understanding of the music and my ability to play the tabla. I only hope that others may have an opportunity to experience as I did the degree of love and affection possible in the relationship between a master and his disciple. Others I should especially like to thank are as follows: Sri Bhupal Ray Choudhuri and the late Ustad Habib Raza Khan, both of Calcutta, who generously shared their knowledge with me; Ilmas Husain Khan, Probir Kumar Mittra, Pankaj Kumar Chowdhury, Christian 'Layal' Lacourieux and Gilles Bourquin, my closest *gurū-bhāʾīs*, whose friendship and assistance not only made my life in Lucknow easier but also happier; Dr S. S. Awasthi and Mr V. P. Mathur, who kindly gave their permission to observe classes at the Bhatkhande Music College of Lucknow; Mrs Saeeda Manzoor, who taught me Urdu and provided me with a home whenever I needed it; Saiyed Farhad Husain, who also taught me Urdu and provided me with an insight into the bygone days of Lucknow; my friends Bernard and Andreine Bel and Jim 'Wasiuddin' Arnold, with whom I shared many ideas; and finally Professor John Blacking, Dr John Baily, Dr Richard Widdess, Dr Neil Sorrell and my wife Dr Annette Sanger for their helpful comments on parts or all of the text.

Throughout the text I have used the twenty-four hour clock for times of the day. The exchange rate for Indian rupees during my periods of fieldwork fluctuated between fourteen and eighteen rupees to one pound sterling (nine to twelve rupees to one US dollar).

Terminology, transliteration and translation

All indigenous terminology has been italicised throughout, including the spoken representations (*bols*) of tabla music that appear within a body of text. *Bols* separated from the text as musical illustrations or examples are not italicised, and they represent the most accurate transliteration possible of these sounds as spoken by my informants. As notations they are prescriptive: they are not represenatative of any single performance but rather are derived from the basic material common to a great many renditions collected during my lessons over a period of nearly three years.

The system of transliteration I have employed derives from that used in Platt's *A Dictionary of Urdu, Classical Hindi and English* (1977). Essentially, this utilises diacritical marks for three distinct purposes: firstly to elongate the vowels *ā*, *ī* and *ū*; secondly, to modify the pronunciation of certain consonants such as the retroflex *ṭ*, *ḍ* and *ṛ*, and the nasalised *ṅ*; and thirdly, to differentiate between consonants pronounced identically in Urdu but spelt differently in the Nastaliq (Perso-Arabic) script owing to their distinctiveness in the original Arabic. To give just one example, the sound *z* can also be transliterated as *ẕ*, *ẓ* and *z̤* depending on the spelling of the work in which it occurs. I have, however, made three alterations to Platts's system: the vowel *ĕ* a truncated form of the elongated *e*, has been replaced by the short vowel *i*, which is more commonly used in colloquial Urdu speech; the diacritical mark has been omitted from the unaspirated palatal *c* as I believe it to be unnecessary; and the guttural fricative *g* has been substituted by the underlined compound letter g͟h owing to its commonly accepted usage in certain words with wide currency, such as *g͟hazal*.

The calligraphy used for poetic fragments quoted in Chapter 6 is my own, and I accept full responsibility for any deficiences. Similarly, all translations from the Urdu and Hindi (about 75 per cent of the reported speech of my informants) are mine. I would like, however, to acknowledge the generous assistance of Mr Ralph Russell, who advised me in the translation of difficult passages of Urdu poetry.

The organology and nomenclature of the tabla

Plate 1. The tabla

The tabla comprises two tuned drums which are played horizontally with the hands. The *dāhinā* (lit. right hand; also called *dāyāṅ* or tabla) is a slightly flared, closed cylindrical drum carved from a solid block of wood (*kāṭ*), the narrower end of which is partly hollowed and is covered with a composite head (*puṛī*). It stands between 24cm. and 29cm. in height and has a diameter at the neck of between 12cm. and 15cm. The *bāyāṅ* (lit. left hand; also called *duggī*) is a modified hemispherical kettle drum commonly made of copper, brass or clay. It stands between 22cm. and 28cm. in height, and its slightly narrowed neck, also covered with a composite head, measures between 20cm. and 23cm. in diameter. Each head is made from a circular piece of treated goat skin partly covered by a second skin that is trimmed away to form a rim (*kinār* or *cāṅṭī*) around its circumference. The lower skin, whose central portion is left exposed, is called the *maidān* (also *lav*). Both skins are laced to a ring (*gajrā*, *pagṛī* or *siṅgār*) that fits tightly over the neck. Black spots (*siyāhī*) 7cm. in diameter made of paste and iron filings, centrally placed on the *dāhinā* and eccentrically on the *bāyāṅ*, give the drums pitch and resonance. (Taken together, the *maidān* and *siyāhī* of the *dāhinā* are often termed the *sūr*.) The heads are laced with hide thongs (*baddhī*), and the *dāhinā* is tuneable by a combination of adjusting a number of cylindrical wooden wedges (*gaṭṭā*) to increase or decrease the general tension of the head and by tapping and *gajrā* with a small hammer (*hathauṛī*) for finer tuning. The *dāhinā* is tuned to the first, fourth or fifth degree of the scale in use, while the *bāyāṅ* is pitched at an imprecise low note that the player can modify, by wrist position and pressure, in order to add inflexion to the 'voice' of the drums. Both drums are placed upon rings (*īṅḍwī* or *adhār*) that provide stability during playing.

More than one name attaches to a number of the tabla's constituent parts, and no consensus of opinion exists as to a 'correct' set of terms. In each case above, I have given the names used by tabla players of the Lucknow tradition first, followed by their most common alternatives. Throughout this book I have retained the Lucknow terminology.

An explanation of the notational system used for tabla

Indian drum and dance musics may be represented orally by attributing syllables to each stroke or step. These syllables are generally called *bols*, from the Hindi/Urdu verb *bolnā* meaning 'to speak'. In many drumming systems, including that of tabla, the word *bol* also refers to the articulation of the stroke itself.

Many notational systems have been employed by musicians and scholars for Indian drumming, all of which attempt, in one way or another, to organise written representations of these syllables on paper. Unfortunately, few have been systematic in their presentation of rhythm and even fewer have been able to cope with the fact that there is not necessarily a one-to-one correlation between strokes and syllables. Joshi (1981) has listed no fewer than thirteen different ways of playing the sequence *ghiṛanga*, all of which are largely dependent upon factors such as style and musical context. A number of solutions to these problems have involved the use of modified staff notation, grids and symbols, but it appears that greater clarity has only been achieved at the expense of greater complexity. I feel there is a need, therefore, for a new notational system that aims both to avoid ambiguity while being uncomplicated.

The system I have proposed provides for the prescriptive notation of the rhythms and strokes used in tabla playing by means of a layout of phonetically written syllables and a limited set of symbols. With a view to minimising the amount of visual information, no attempt has been made to indicate dynamics or timbre, nor have delicate inflections of the *bāyāṅ's* voice been codified.

Layout

The essential organising principle of the notation is the grouping of all *bols* to be said or played within one beat (*mātrā*) and the spatial separation of one group from another. The groups are then set out in a manner that is symbolic of the *tāl* (metric cycle) in which the overall piece is designed to be played. *Tāls* are structurally subdivided into smaller sections (*vibhāgs*) that may or may not contain an equal number of *mātrās*. The notation places each *vibhāg* on a separate line preceded by symbols that denote whether or not the first *mātrā* or a *vibhāg* is stressed (*tālī* – lit. clap) or unstressed (*k͟hālī – lit. empty*). *The tālīs* of a *tāl* are numbered in sequence while the *k͟hālī* (usually one, but sometimes more) is marked by a zero. In accordance with most Indian notational systems, an x replaces the number 1, a convention which serves to emphasise the importance of the initial *mātrā* (*sam*) of the cycle (*āvartan*). (An x also replaces a zero if, as in *rūpak tāl*, the *āvartan* begins with a *k͟hālī vibhāg*.) Thus, when tabulated for added clarity, the layout of, for example, *jhaptāl* (ten *mātrās* subdivided into four unequal *vibhāgs*) is x dhī nā

2 dhī dhī nā

o tī nā

3 dhī dhī nā

In instances where the number of *bols* is too great to fit comfortably on one line, the *vibhāg* is split and the second part indented to avoid confusion.

Rhythm

The notation of rhythm is achieved by means of dividing the *mātrā* into a number of equal parts. These parts are separated by single space. The following are divisions of two, three and four respectively:

dhi ṭe

dhā ti ṭe

dhī nā dhā tit

Each part may contain more than one *bol*, thus:

dhāti ṭedhā

tira kiṭa taka

kiṛanaga tirakiṭa takataka tirakiṭa

And a *mātrā* may comprise subdivisions that contain varying numbers of *bols*, thus:

dhā kiṭa

dhā dinagina dinagina

kiṛa naga tī nā

A pause is indicated by a dash, the value of which is equivalent to one *bol* in the context of how that *mātrā* has been divided. For example:

– dhā

dhā – na

dhā –dhā –ta kiṭa

kiṛanaga tirakiṭa takatā– –

Additional devices

There are a number of instances where *bols* that are regularly played are by convention never spoken. These have been enclosed within square brackets, thus: *dhā dhā[ge] dhī nā*. Furthermore, certain *bols* may be optional and their inclusion simply results in an alternative version of a piece. These have been enclosed within rounded brackets, thus: *dhā(gena) dhāgedhin*.

Structurally, some pieces contain sections designed to be repeated three times as a cadential device. These are known as *tihā'īs*. Vertical bars delimit what is to be repeated, as in:

| kṛa dhā tī ghin - ta dhā |

Care should be taken that in instances where a bar falls within a *mātrā*, as in this case, the foregoing subdivisions are clearly indicated in order to avoid mistakes in interpretation. Note that this example should not be read:

| kṛa dhā tī ghin - ta dhā - |

If a piece, or section of a piece, that contains a *tihā'ī* is in turn to be played three times, as in the *cakkardār* or *tihā'ī kī tihā'ī* (the *tihā'ī* of a *tihā'ī*), then large square brackets enclose the material to be repeated, as in the following:

[| dhāti ṭedhā gena dhāge tīna kīna dhā | -]

Stroke symbols

In certain kinds of illustration it is clearly unnecessary to include indications of exactly how a stroke is to be played. However, in cases where this is required, I have used a limited set of symbols aimed at defining which fingers are to strike which parts of the tabla. As many pieces include much repetition, an attempt has been made to restrict the use of symbols to initial statements of themes or blocks of material in order to leave notations as uncluttered as possible.

Above and below syllables are symbols that refer to strokes on the high-pitched *dāhinā* and the low-pitched *bāyāṅ* respectively. These symbols are constructed from simple and familiar signs and shapes, and act as mnemonic devices to indicate whether or not a stroke allows the drum to resonate. Resonating strokes (produced by ricocheting the fingers off the skins) are depicted by shapes whose lines enclose space (which may perhaps be thought of as a resonating chamber): circles, squares and triangles. Non-resonating strokes (produced by damping the skin with the palm or fingers) are depicted by signs whose lines do not enclose space, such as X, +, > and V. At another symbolic level, some shapes suggest the fingering and position of a stroke. However, in cases where essentially the same stroke may be fingered in several different ways, numbers qualify which fingers are to be used, from 1 for the index finger up to 4 for the little finger.

For the following descriptions, strokes are referred to by only one name, though most may be called several different names. Additional information on alternative syllables and precise descriptions of motor movements will be furnished in Chapter 7. (Because pieces illustrated in this book include all but a small number of rarely used strokes, this system may be taken as fairly comprehensive.) The diagrams depict the three portions of the drumhead (the ***kinār***, the ***maidān***, and the shaded *siyāhī*) as viewed from the player's perspective. The black areas signify the positions where the palm or main fingers strike the drum. Supporting fingers that touch the skins are not illustrated.

Resonating strokes on the *dāhinā*

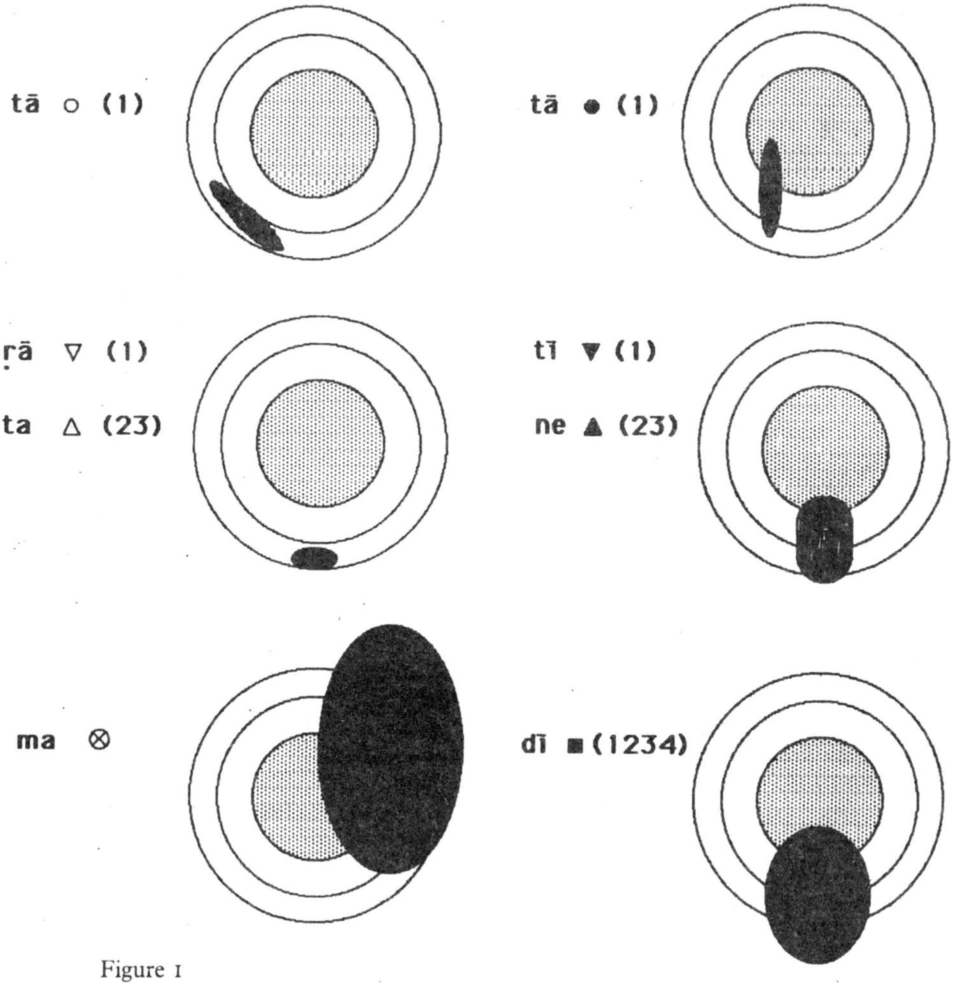

Figure 1

The two strokes known as *tā* as played on the *kinār* and *sūr* are arguably the most important in tabla playing. Circles indicate these strokes: a white circle for *tā* on the *kinār*, the white part of the drumhead, and a black circle for *tā* on the *sūr*, where the black *siyāhī* is situated. The same colour associations are used for the four strokes depicted by triangles. When the apex of the triangle points downwards (i.e. the direction a stroke takes) it signifies that one finger is used, as in *ṛā* and *tī*; when two corners of the triangle are downmost, two fingers are used, as in *ta* and *ne*. A black square indicates the stroke *dī*, which is articulated on the *sūr* with all four fingers. The uncommon stroke *ma*, used only in the *pakhāwaj*-derived combination *dhuma*, has been given a symbol that expresses its semi-resonating quality, a cross superimposed on a circle.

Non-resonating strokes on the *dāhinā*

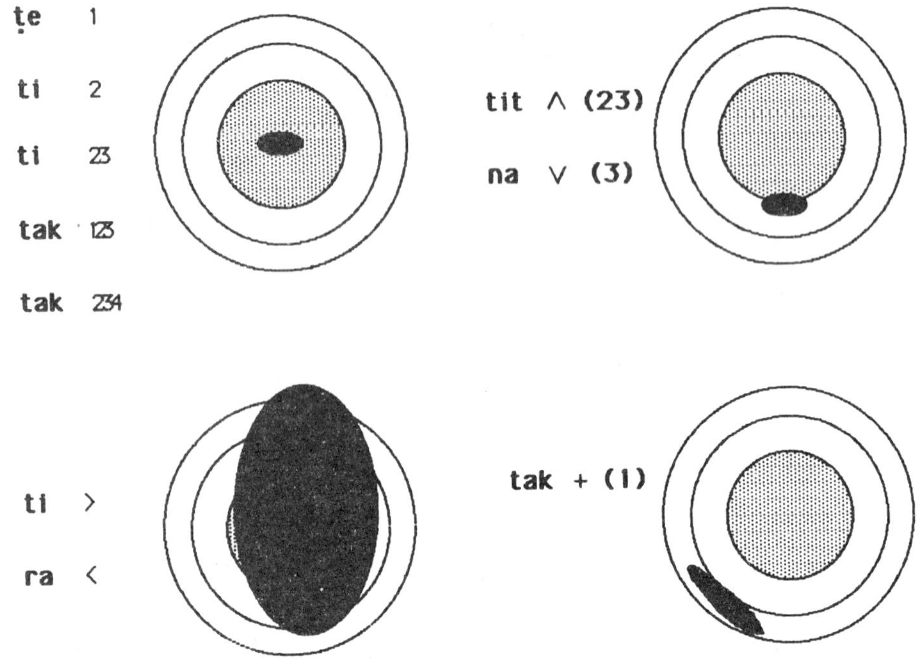

Figure 2

The various strokes played on the centre of the *siyāhī* have been differentiated by numbers referring to the fingers used to play them. Symbols are used for the other strokes. For example, *tit* and *na* are given incomplete triangles: again the direction of the triangle signifies the number of fingers to be used. With *ti* and *ra*, strokes using the outer and inner halves of the palm, essentially the same symbol is rotated to become an arrowhead pointing to the side of the downturned palm to be used on the skin. Lastly, the unusual stroke *tak*, where the finger 'sticks' to the *kinār* to produce a sharp click (it is often referred to as *capaknewālā tā* – the *tā* that 'sticks'), is notated with a +.

Resonating strokes on the *bāyāṅ*

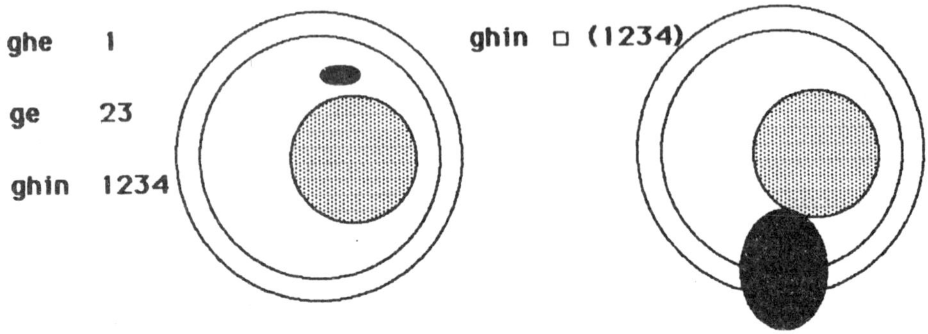

Figure 3

Numbers are used to differentiate between the various fingerings of resonating *bāyāṅ* strokes except for one *pakhāwaj*-inspired stroke in which all four fingers hit that portion of the *bāyāṅ* nearest the player. Owing to its technical similarity to *dī* on the *dāhinā*, this stroke is indicated with a square: here with a white square since the fingers do not touch the *siyāhī*.

Non-resonating strokes on the *bāyāṅ*

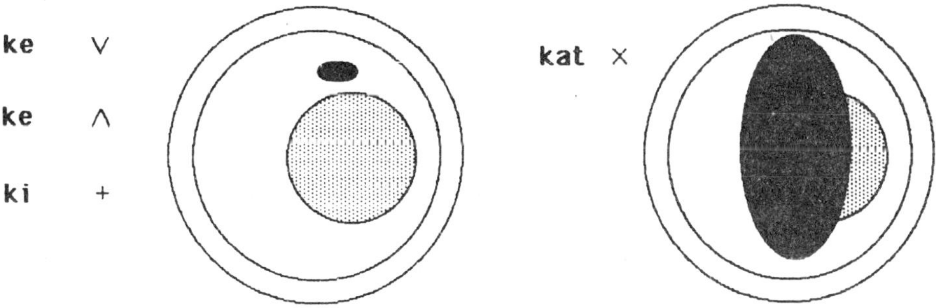

Figure 4

Usually, *kat*, as played with the flattened palm, is by far the most prominent of non-resonating *bāyāṅ* strokes, here depicted by an X. However, in some playing styles, in particular that of Lucknow, two other forms of this stroke are equally important, for they function as the non-resonating counterparts of *ghe* and *ge* respectively. V and Λ are once more used to differentiate between *ke* as played with one finger and *ke* with two fingers. Additionally, *ki*, a finger flick which produces a sharp click, is indicated by a + owing to its similarity to *tak* on the *dāhinā*.

Additional symbols

Occasionally, one hand may cross to perform a stroke on the opposite drumhead. In practice, it is usually the *bāyāṅ* hand that strikes the *dāhinā* (references to the left and right hands have been avoided because a number of players reverse their drums and play the *dāhinā* left-handed). Thus the letter B – for *bāyāṅ* hand – is entered above the symbol:

```
  B   B
▽ ▽ ▽ ▽
naga naga
```

More unusually, two strokes are played on the same drum. Here the symbol for the stroke to be played with the opposite hand appears above the other:

```
B
△
▽
nā
```

Short 'grace-note' strokes subsidiary to a main stroke appear with a slur. These are implied in syllables where the consonants *k* or *t* precede *ṛ* or *r* with no intervening short vowel:

```
 V          ‿23 1
kra         tra
x‿
```

Once a resonating *bāyāṅ* stroke has been played, its sound may be rearticulated not by restriking but by pushing the heel of the hand sharply forward to produce an instant rise in pitch. This rise in pitch to another level has been symbolised by a /:

```
 o
dhā - ge
 1  / 23
```

Lastly, a dash is used to indicate that no stroke is to be played despite being implied by a syllable. This is sometimes the case with resonating strokes on the *bāyāṅ* that are implied by the phoneme *dh*, thus:

```
>  <   >  <
dhira dhira
 1      –
```

A notation

The following is a sample taken from the notations that appear in the last chapter of this book. It is illustrated on the accompanying cassette as Example 36. For those readers less familiar with tabla music who might wish to see a Western approximation of its rhythm and sound, a simplified version has been added in modified staff notation. Resonating and non-resonating sounds are indicated by circles and crosses respectively.

```
       ▼  o          V  o           o  2 1         V  o
X     dhī nā        kiṛa naga      tā tiṭe        kiṛa naga
       23            V       Λ      V              V       Λ

       2 1   V       o    o         2 1   V        o
2     tira kiṭa     taka tā        tira kiṭa      tā  –
             ×         ×                 ×

       o  o                            Λ            o
0     tā dhā       – | ghin          –  ta         dhā  – |
          1            23                           1
```

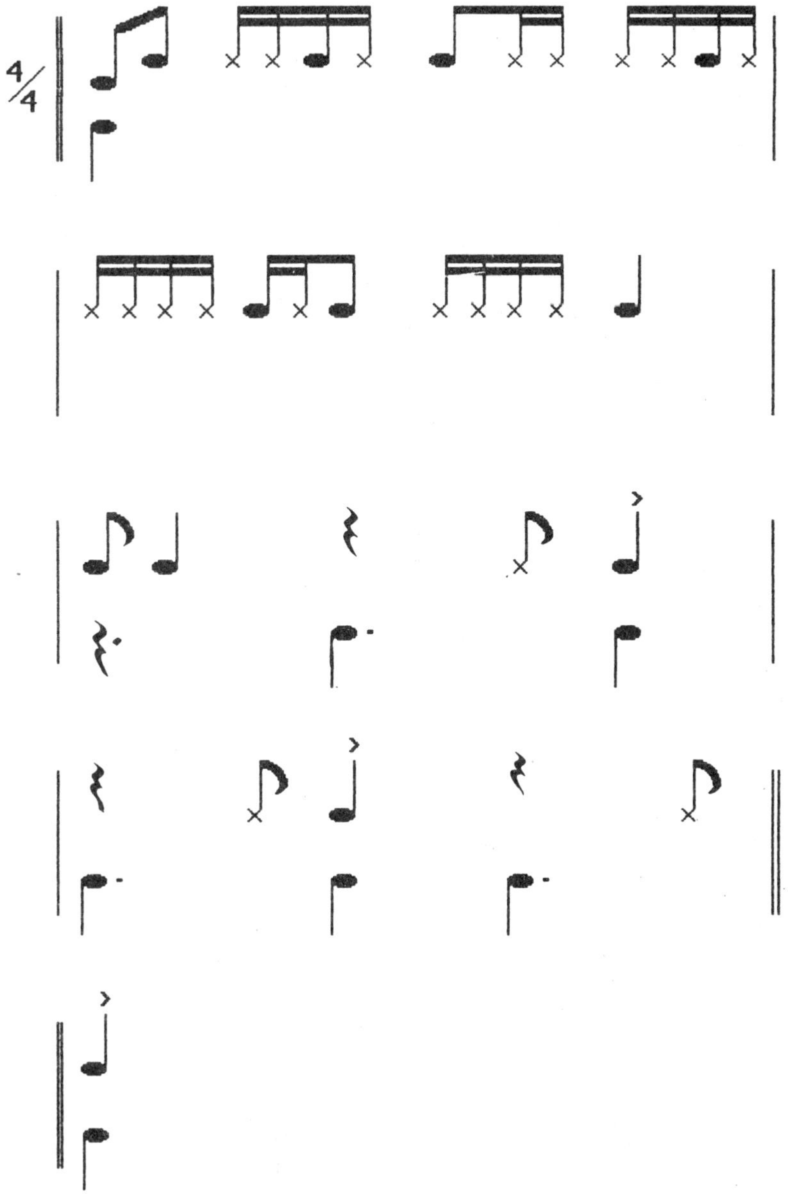
4/4

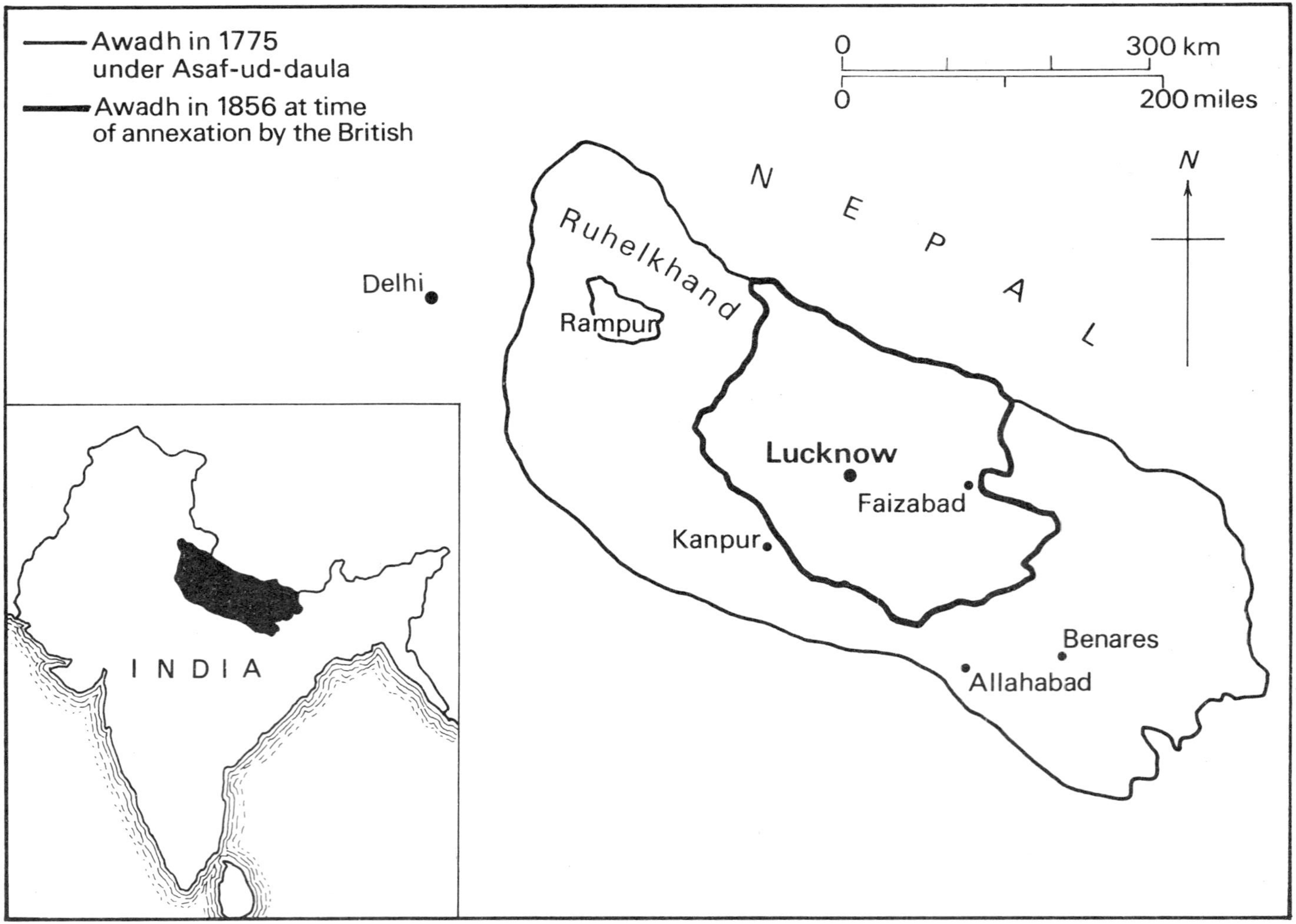

Map 1. Awadh in 1775 and 1856

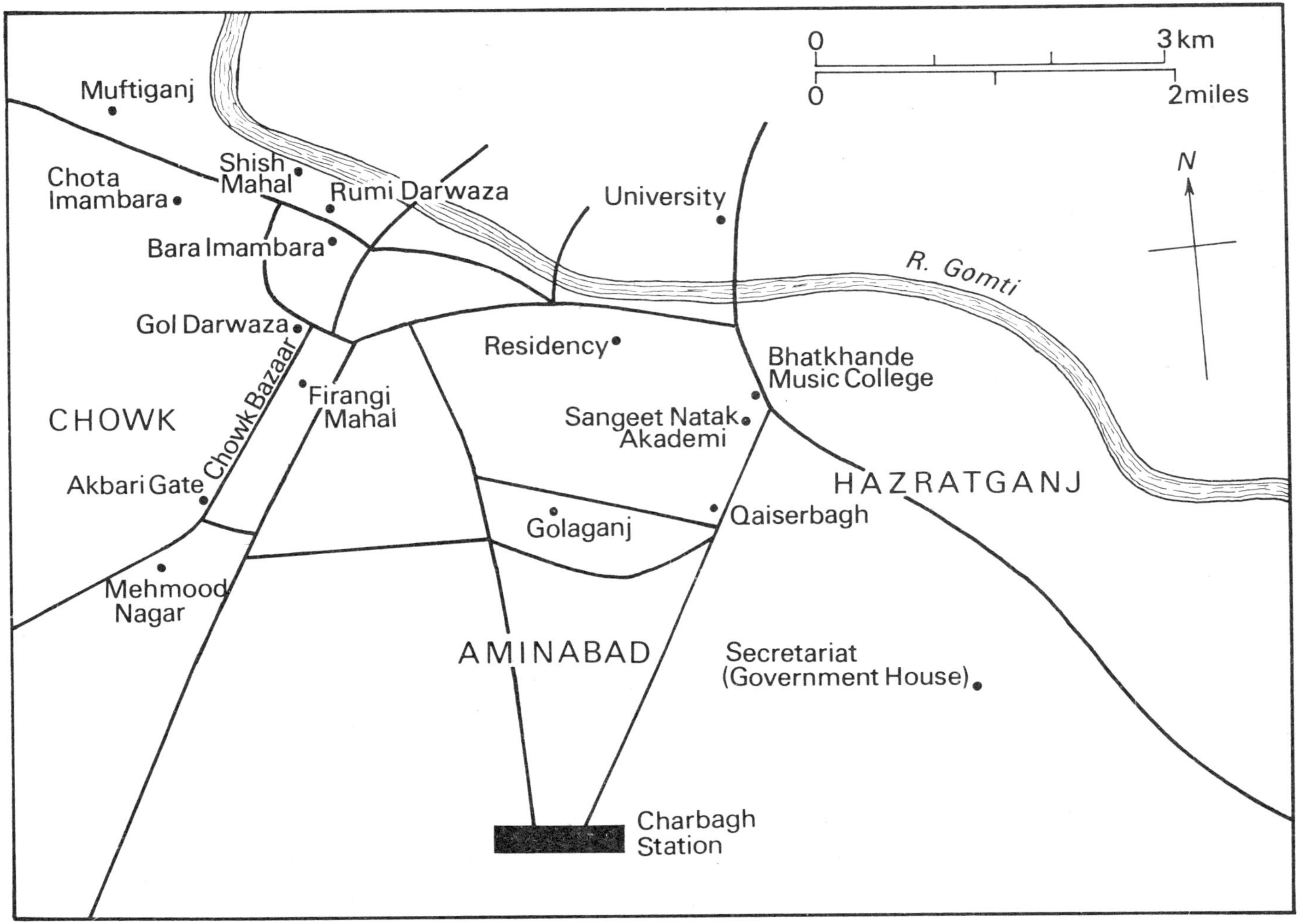

Map 2. City of Lucknow

1 *An introduction to Lucknow*

The history of the city

'Ah! What a beautiful sight', I said to my Urdu teacher, Saiyed Farhad Husain, who, with his long white beard, *sherwānī* coat, and pointed *ṭopī* somewhat reminiscent of the caps worn by Urdu poets of old, was accompanying me on an evening stroll through the old city of Lucknow in the heart of the Gangetic plains of North India. All around us were the silhouettes of vast domes and minarets that rose above parapets punctuated by towers and gates through whose pointed arches scores of rickshaws and cycles, their bells constantly ringing, were being skilfully guided. The still, warm air at sunset was filled with the mellifluous tones of a dozen *mu'azzins*, each calling the faithful to prayer from surrounding mosques. Yet this picturesque scene was in reality an illusion, for not even the encroaching dusk could totally conceal scarred and broken masonry everywhere. 'Hae hae!', sighed my companion as he surveyed the horizon with a graceful sweep of his hand, 'but you should have seen it when I was a boy!' He described how, during his own lifetime of some eighty years, he had witnessed so many beautiful though sorely neglected buildings crumble, finally to collapse or be demolished, and how the city that was once renowned for its gardens had lost them one by one. Yet even in the early twentieth century, when Farhad Husain was a boy, Lucknow was but a remnant of former days. It had suffered the devastation and ruin of a British onslaught aimed at crushing a revolt and breaking a siege which had become the most celebrated symbol of rebellion in British India: the Indian Mutiny and the Siege of Lucknow of 1857 and 1858. William Russell, correspondent of *The Times* newspaper, was perhaps the last person to see Lucknow in pristine condition, for with him were the British regiments waiting to advance on the city in order to wrest it from the hands of the rebels. His panoramic view from atop Dilkhusha Palace just to the east of the city on 3 March 1858 inspired the following entry in *My Indian Mutiny Diary* (1957: 57–8):

> A vision of palaces, minars, domes azure and golden, cupolas, colonnades, long facades of fair perspective in pillar and column, terraced roofs – all rising up amid a calm still ocean of the brightest verdure. Look for miles and miles away, and still the ocean spreads, and the towers of the fairy-city gleam in its midst. Spires of gold glitter in the sun. Turrets and gilded spheres shine like constellations. There is nothing mean or squalid to be seen. There is a city more vast than Paris, as it seems, and more brilliant, lying before us. Is this a city in Oudh? Is this the capital of a semibarbarous race, erected by a corrupt, effete, and degraded dynasty? I confess I felt inclined to rub my eyes again and again.

All this was soon to change, for the initial looting and ransacking of the palaces by the troops whom Russell was accompanying, and the subsequent dynamiting of large tracts of the city by the new British government, were devasting blows from which Lucknow has never recovered.

The region known as Awadh, written Oudh or Oude by the British, was, according to

Hindu mythology, awarded by Ram to his brother Lakshman after the conquest of Sri Lanka. A settlement was established on a hill situated on the south bank of the river Gomti. The site is still know as Lakshman Tila, on which in the late seventeenth century, the Emperor Aurangzeb built an imposing mosque, the Shah Pir Muhammad Hill mosque. The settlement had grown steadily to become the seat of a governor when the Emperor Akbar divided India into twelve provinces in 1590. As a provincial capital, the city enjoyed a period of growth, and much of what now constitutes the old city of Lucknow, the Chowk, dates from this time. By the mid-seventeenth century Lucknow was known as a major centre for trade and Islamic teaching.

In 1720, Saadat Khan, a Shiite Muslim from Nishapur in the north of Persia, was appointed as *naẓīm*, or governor, of Awadh by the Mogul Emperor Muhammad Shah. The post was a reward for services rendered in battle. Saadat Khan, otherwise known as Burhan-ul-Mulk, set up his capital not in Lucknow but in Faizabad, building up the latter into a formidable fortress until his death from poisoning in 1739. Saadat Khan's successor, his nephew and son-in-law Safdar Jang (1739–54), was the first governor to be designated a *nawāb* (later *nawāb wazīr* or vizier). The new title carried with it the status of viceroy although sovereignty was firmly retained by the Mogul Emperor in Delhi (Pemble 1977: 4). Nevertheless, this succession was representative of a new dynasty in the making.

Nawab Shuja-ud-daula (1754–75) spent much of the first half of his rule in Lucknow. He joined battle with the British at Baksar (or Buxar) in Bihar in 1765, but defeat merely proved he could do nothing to prevent the inexorable movement towards the domination of India by the British East India Company. The gradual collapse of the Mogul system was creating an ever-increasing power vacuum which the opportunist British were eager to fill. As victors at Baksar, they forced Shuja-ud-daula to forfeit one-third of the revenue of his territory. In return the Company would establish a military presence, so guaranteeing Awadh's nominal independence from the imperial Mogul court in Delhi.

With independence and security thus ensured, Shuja-ud-daula moved back to Faizabad, where he embarked upon a rebuilding scheme that was to develop the fortress into a bustling, crowded city and an irresistible attraction for thousands of emigrants from the crumbling imperial capital, Delhi. The military was still very much in evidence, but in that short period of time the city became known as a centre of wealth and fashion. Furthermore, the Nawab was very fond of music and dance, and consequently many courtesans, dancers, singers and instrumental musicians also made their way from Delhi to Faizabad. Delhi had been replaced as the major centre of patronage for the arts in North India.

Nawab Asaf-ud-daula acceded in 1775 and immediately transferred his court to Lucknow. A *nawāb* remembered fondly to this day by Lucknowis for his generosity and liberality (Oldenburg 1984: 16), Asaf-ud-daula's potential as a great patron drew a large number of people from Faizabad who evidently surmised that there were considerable benefits to be enjoyed by keeping in contact with the court. Those disenchanted with the socio-political situation in Delhi who had not hitherto been enticed by fashionable Faizabad under Shuja-ud-daula were quick to make their way to Lucknow, for the new capital promised to be an even greater centre of wealth and splendour. Indeed, so great was Asaf-ud-daula's patronage that it has been said he became more famous throughout India than the Mogul Emperor himself (Hay 1939: 14).

The British, ever intent on extending their sphere of influence, saw yet another opportun-

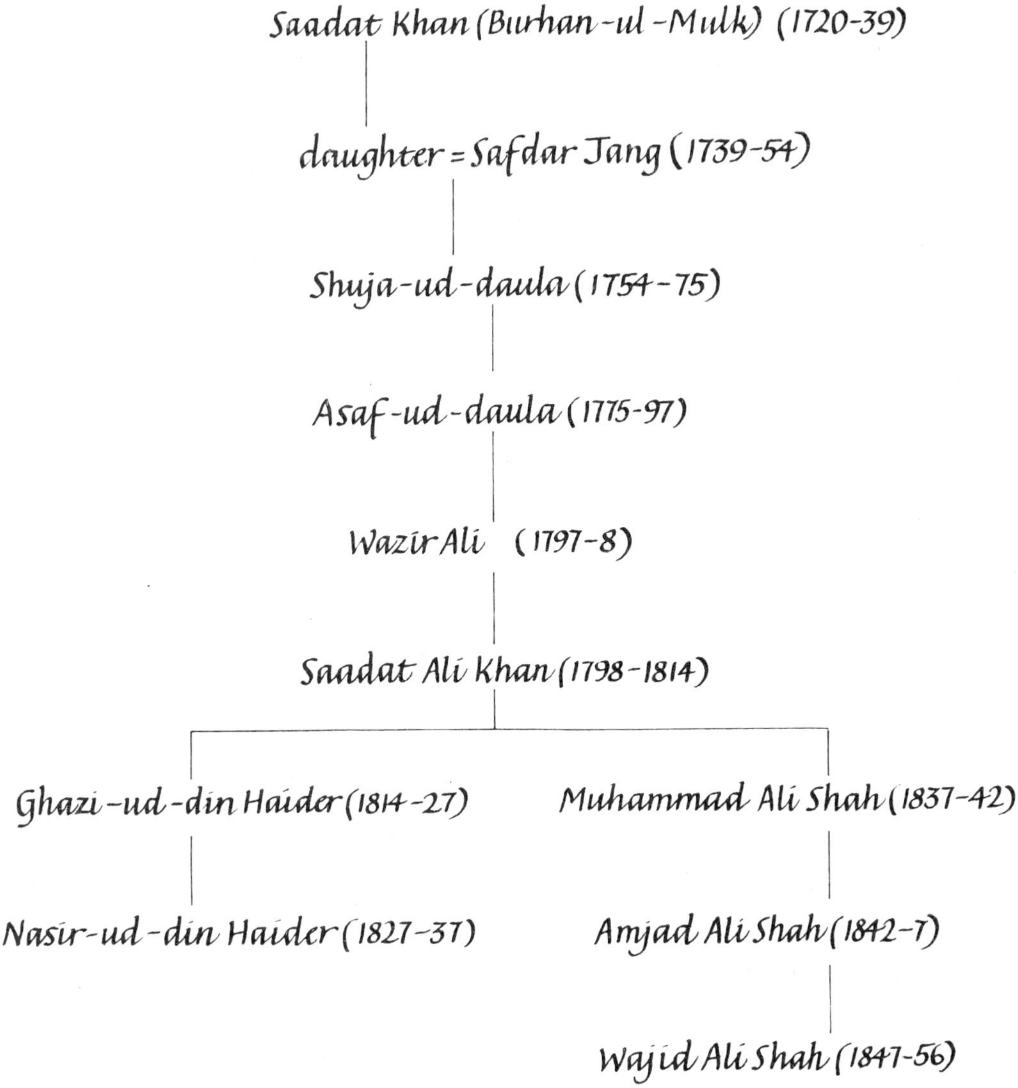
Saadat Khan (Burhan-ul-Mulk) (1720-39)
daughter = Safdar Jang (1739-54)
Shuja-ud-daula (1754-75)
Asaf-ud-daula (1775-97)
Wazir Ali (1797-8)
Saadat Ali Khan (1798-1814)
Ghazi-ud-din Haider (1814-27)
Muhammad Ali Shah (1837-42)
Nasir-ud-din Haider (1827-37)
Amjad Ali Shah (1842-7)
Wajid Ali Shah (1847-56)

Chart 1. The *nawābs* of Awadh

ity to increase their administrative authority over the region, this time by limiting the Nawab's army, a feat easily achieved as Asaf-ud-daula maintained little interest in military affairs. As a reward for his friendship and co-operation the British extended Awadh to incorporate Ruhelkhand to the north-west, making the Nawab the nominal ruler of a territory roughly equivalent in size to modern-day Uttar Pradesh (see Map 1).

Freed of the need to spend much of his revenue on defence, Asaf-ud-daula embarked on a massive project of construction aimed at creating a city of magnificence and splendour unrivalled elsewhere in India. Many of the great palaces and mosques of Lucknow date from this time, as do numerous elaborate residences and religious meeting places called *imāmbāṛās*. The Asafi or Bara (Great) Imambara complex, complete with a vast mosque, was constructed in 1784 at a cost of two million rupees. The visible splendour of the city increased and with it the decadence of a life of unmitigated luxury and affluence. For instance, one of the more celebrated excesses of the court of Asaf-ud-daula was the wealth lavished on the wedding of the Nawab's son and successor, Wazir Ali, in 1795. In the procession, 1,200 elephants paraded through the city, and the heir to the throne wore a robe onto which jewels worth two million rupees had been sewn (Sharar 1975: 47).

Following the death of Asaf-ud-daula in 1797, the British demonstrated their total control over the court by deposing Wazir Ali, who had occupied the throne for less than a year. More acceptable to the British was Saadat Ali Khan (1798–1814), who was seen not only as a good administrator but also as a more sympathetic ally. In return for promotion, Saadat Ali was forced to sign a treaty yielding half the territory of Awadh to the British and formally ending its independence. Although this gained the Nawab many enemies among his own people, the British guaranteed his security by maintaining a strong and permanent military presence in the city itself.

The remaining five *nawābs* of Awadh were known more for their extravagance and self-indulgence than for their administrative prowess. For example, an extraordinary and unquestionably exaggerated account of the frivolous amusements of Nasir-ud-din Haider (1827–37), evidently written with the full intention of shocking a British audience, appeared under the title *The Private Life of an Eastern King*, by William Knighton, in 1855. Michael Edwardes's book *The Orchid House: Splendours and Miseries of the Kingdom of Oudh, 1827–1857* (1960) covers much the same ground. These accounts represent just a small part of the damning evidence against what William Russell called an 'effete and degraded dynasty'. However, more recent studies of the role of the British in Awadh up to and beyond annexation in 1856, such as the survey of *nawābī* architecture by Llewellyn-Jones (1985) and Oldenburg's (1984) analysis of the early years of colonial Lucknow, paint a different picture. The *nawābs* were of course little more than puppets in the hands of the Residents appointed by the British East India Company who, though perhaps morally outraged, manipulated and blackmailed the *nawābs*, and encouraged their seemingly eccentric behaviour, because they believed it distracted them from having any designs on political power.

What had in practice been a monarchy for almost one hundred years became so in theory when in 1819 the British bestowed upon Nawab Ghazi-ud-din Haider the title 'King of Awadh'. From Ghazi-ud-din (1814–27) onwards, the *nawābs* shared a tremendous zest for religious ceremony. Their courts were dominated by Shiah religious observations and superstitions, which dictated, for example, that one should wait for an auspicious moment, to

Plate 2. The Asafi or Bara Imambara complex

be determined astrologically, before setting out on a journey. Wet gram was hand-fed to donkeys in the belief that it was a cure for smallpox, and expectant mothers were kept awake for fear that sleep would damage the unborn child (Hasan 1983). The courts were also teeming with courtesans and musicians, and the *nawābs* gave full vent to their passion for music, dance and poetry. They continued the beautification of Lucknow by adding palaces and mosques, the most notable of which were built under Muhammad Ali Shah (1837–42) and Wajid Ali Shah (1847–56). The city was greatly extended under Amjad Ali Shah (1842–7), who built the fashionable areas of Aminabad and Hazratganj (see Map 2). The *nawābī* love of the European style of architecture came out particularly strongly in the new areas of the city (for a full account, see Llewellyn-Jones 1985), leading Bishop Heber (1828) to liken Lucknow to Dresden. The most lavish patronge of the arts, particularly of music and dance, was offered by Ghazi-ud-din Haider, Nasir-ud-din Haider, and not least by the last and most notorious King of Awadh, Wajid Ali Shah.

Wajid Ali Shah is traditionally known for his unbridled pursuit of pleasure and amusement, though an excellent and sympathetic study of his life by G. D. Bhatnagar (1968) suggests he was in fact a much misunderstood character. Wajid Ali spent most of his time in the company of courtesans and musicians, some of whom came to wield considerable administrative power (Miner 1981: 218). He learned music from them and was himself an accomplished dancer and poet. His poetry unashamedly describes in detail events that occurred in his various love affairs, descriptions which earned him the censure of many because he 'had no hesitation in showing shamefully low taste and in using obscene language' (Sharar 1975: 64). As a religious zealot he donned black to head the sombre processions of the Shiites, while as a frivolous actor he would take female roles in plays (Hay 1939: 54–5) or become an ash-covered yogi at the public fairs held in his palace complex at Qaiser Bagh (Sharar 1975: 64).

The British Governor-General, Lord Dalhousie (1848–56), had already annexed a large number of states in India, and he saw in the decadent behaviour of Wajid Ali Shah and his court a plausible excuse to add Awadh to his list of appropriated territories. The British took over the complete administration of the kingdom in 1856 (see Map 1) by sending an armed force to Lucknow and by issuing the King with the instruction that Awadh was no longer under his rule. Intending to plead with Queen Victoria in London for reinstatement, Wajid Ali Shah departed from Lucknow with his retinue to travel to Calcutta, from where members of his family left for a royal audience in England. During their absence, new and momentous events shook Lucknow and the deposed King was never to see the city again. He remained until his death in 1887 in Matiya Burj, Calcutta, pursuing his eccentricities and fulfilling his taste for the arts and luxurious living.

There was, among many of India's subjects, general dissatisfaction with the rapid expansion of British rule. In 1857 an incident involving the grease used for the cartridges of the new Enfield rifle (the Hindus and Muslims thought they were being forced to use the fat of their taboo animals, the cow and pig respectively) sparked off a mutiny of many of the European-trained native soldiers, the sepoys. Fighting was fierce in Lucknow and British troops quartered in the city were forced to barricade themselves and their families within the grounds of the Residency, dynamiting a number of *nawābī* palaces as they retreated. This was the beginning of the famous Siege of Lucknow, which was to last nearly five months. Although the relief of the Siege was effected late in November 1857, it was not until March

Plate 3. Inside the labyrinth of the Asafi Imambara

Plate 4. The Husainabad Imambara

1858 that the British, after heavy bombardment of the city, finally recaptured Lucknow, using the largest British army in Indian history to that date.

Following the restoration of order in the city, large-scale demolition was ordered to make Lucknow defensible from further riot and insurrection. A tract of land on the south bank of the river Gomti, 500 yards wide and some four miles long, was flattened and cleared of all buildings save the Residency complex and a number of the larger palaces and religious buildings (Oldenburg 1984: 29–42). Entire residential districts (*mohallas*) disappeared, resulting in the displacement of up to a third of the population. Furthermore, wide roads were driven through densely populated and labyrinthine areas to the south of this new wasteland, thus providing the city with a network of arteries along which the British could swiftly move their forces to nip any uprising in the bud.

After the Mutiny, those members of the court aristocracy who remained in Lucknow after the departure of Wajid Ali Shah were never really rehabilitated, and in their place a new order of nobility was created from the ranks of the local rulers, the landowners and tax-collectors, known as *zamīndārs* and *tāluqdārs*. This was an attempt by the British actively to enlist the support of that class which exercised greatest control over the general mass of the Indian people (Spear 1978: 147–8). From the *tāluqdār* class, several maharajas were created who were given a stronger hand in the administration of local power in the districts of Awadh. Music and dance continued to be patronised by the new nobility in much the same way as they had been under the *nawābs* whom the new order had replaced. The British policy of Westernisation, which precipitated an upsurge in English education, was initially slow to take hold, but by the twentieth century it had effected the transference of power and

Plate 5. Detail of the calligraphic inlay decorating the Husainabad Imambara

influence to the Westernised, middle classes. Patronage of the arts, too, gradually shifted from the maharajas and *tāluqdārs* to the middle classes, a transition completed by Independence in 1947.

Lucknow remained a provincial capital until 1877, when Awadh was amalgamated with the North Western Provinces, renamed the United Provinces in 1902. The seat of government of the province, which had been moved to Allahabad, shifted back to Lucknow in 1921 and remained there with the creation of Uttar Pradesh after Independence in 1947. The establishment of the Muslim state of Pakistan that same year saw an exodus from the city of a large number of Muslims. Most families were split by Partition, though many people waited several years before making the decision to leave India.

As the capital of the largest state (in terms of population) of the Republic of India, Lucknow had an estimated population of 1,200,000 in 1981, a figure that indicates rapid growth since Independence. The ninety or so years of British rule saw the figure remain relatively constant: 253,729 in 1881, and 274,659 in 1931 (quoted in Neuman 1978: 199). This represents something of a decrease in population in comparison with the *nawābī* era, when Lucknow had an estimated population of 300,000 in 1800 (Llewellyn-Jones 1985: 12–13) and may have reached as many as half a million by 1858 (Pemble 1977: 3). There is no evidence to suggest that the religious make-up of Lucknow's inhabitants has ever been significantly different from that stated for 1971: 68 per cent Hindu and 29 per cent Muslim (Saxena 1973: 2). Shiite Muslims are in the minority in India (possibly amounting to between

Plate 6. The Sat Khande

10 and 15 per cent), but have traditionally been strongly represented in Lucknow as a result of the Persian heritage of the courts and the large Persian population that followed to settle there. Shiites account for about 40 per cent of Muslims in the city and a state of tension and antagonism exists between Shiite and Sunni communities, who, for the most part, live in separate and exclusive quarters. Riots are frequent between members of the two sects and the religious processions of the Shiites during Muharram (a period of mourning) frequently provoke violent clashes. Curfews are a regular occurrence, and the state government has banned the processions, a ban which many defy.

As is typical of any administrative centre, Lucknow is a city of petty bureaucrats and government office workers. 'Negligible industrial expansion' (Saxena 1973: 1) and the absence of big companies have meant that Lucknow has been slow to modernise its infrastructure of roads and new buildings. The city is still known primarily for its arts and crafts, and one can see, tucked away in the tiny shops of the narrow alleyways of the old city, all manner of jewellery, pottery, enamelware, embroidered cloth, and cloth of gold and silver. Some shops are scented with the *ʿiṭr* (attar) perfume they sell in a hundred varieties. In others can be seen stacks of paper kites of various colours and sizes, and still one can buy delicious sweets made purely from ground almonds and saffron.

The tourist board of Uttar Pradesh would still like to promote Lucknow as a site of architectural monuments. The city is advertised through pictures of such impressive structures as the Rumi Darwaza, built by Asaf-ud-daula in 1784, a huge, elaborate gate said to be modelled on one of the original gateways to Constantinople. But like most of Lucknow's historical buildings, the Rumi Darwaza is neglected and crumbling, a situation made worse by the fact that it stands astride a main thoroughfare used constantly by heavy trucks and overloaded buses. Few buildings that survived the events of 1858 have been maintained or restored, and all around, deterioration and decay bring dismay to the few old Lucknowis, like my Urdu teacher, who remember the way things used to be.

The culture of the city

The culture of Lucknow is a heritage shared by Muslim and Hindu families whose histories have been intertwined with the history of the city itself. It derives from a strongly Persianised court culture which developed a refined taste in manners, speech, entertainments and the arts. The abundant patronage of the arts in general, and of music and dance in particular, made the city famous throughout India. Music and dance will be dealt with in the next section. I would like to cover in this section some of the other cultural features that distinguish Lucknow.

Lucknow is known as the 'City of Adab', or manners. The idea is often characterised in pictures of a gentleman immaculately dressed in a long silk *kurta* (shirt), embroidered waistcoat, *cūrīdār* pyjamas (trousers that fit tightly round the calf and which are gathered in layers of rings at the ankles) and *ṭopī* (hat), inclining gracefully as he raises his right hand to make a salaam, paying his respects in short, delicate waves back and forth in front of his nose. A synonym for the 'City of Adab' is the 'City of Pahle Āp', which literally means 'after you'. This has been coined from the famous joke about two gentlemen of Lucknow who, in their efforts to show the greatest courtesy and politeness to each other by repeating *pahle āp*, allow the train they intended to board to pull out of the station. As a guest of a Lucknowi, one will

Plate 7. The Rumi Darwaza

always hear the words *Āp takalluf na kījiye*, imploring one to be informal and not to stand on ceremony. The irony is that its use has become for most a ceremonious formality in itself.

The *ṭawā'ifs*, or courtesans, were, like the geishas of Japan, experts in highly refined and cultured behaviour as well as being great exponents of the arts. They were patronised by the rich and powerful social elite and were a permanent feature of the courts of the *nawābs* of Awadh. *Ṭawā'ifs* have been much maligned by the more puritanical middle classes of this century, who have identified them as cheap prostitutes. But this is being unfair to the real courtesans, who were among the most loyal of women and had prolonged relationships, in stark contrast to ordinary prostitutes and 'dancing girls' (Sethi 1983). In order that they might learn the most refined manners and social graces, the children of the Lucknow nobility were sent to *tawā'ifs* for instruction.

The rules and principles of social conduct were clearly defined. Examples of these feature in Sharar's book *Lucknow: The Last Phase of an Oriental Culture* (first published as a series of articles in the Lucknow journal *Dil Gudaz* between 1913 and about 1921), many of which I find still to be in common use, especially those which deal with how one should meet and conduct oneself with visitors (Sharar 1975: 194):

> If an equal with whom you are not well acquainted, or an elderly or venerable person, came to the house, he was given the seat of honour with the *gau* [large barrel-shaped cushion] behind him. Everyone else joined a large or small circle around him, according to the numbers present, and sat with him respectfully. Anyone to whom he spoke would join his hands together and answer with complete humility. It was considered a social misdemeanour to talk too much or to raise one's voice to a higher level than his.

Many cultural features of Lucknow are inextricably connected with the Urdu language. Kripalani (1975: 307) observed that 'under the patronage of the Mughals and later of the Lucknow Court and society, [Urdu] developed a highly polished, sophisticated, and urbane form which has made it different from every other Indian language and given it an elegance and vigour all its own'. He also notes that the word 'Urdu' is derived from the Turkish *Ordu*, meaning 'army' or 'camp', from which also comes the English word 'horde'. Indeed, Urdu was spoken by soldiers of the Mogul armies and is a hybridised form of Persian, which was the court language of the Moguls, and the local languages of North and North-West India. It developed as a literary language in the independent Muslim Kingdoms of the Deccan of Central-South India in the sixteenth and seventeenth centuries, where the Perso-Arabic script was adapted for use. After the conquest of the Deccan by the Mogul Emperor Aurangzeb in the late seventeenth century, Urdu spread back to the North, where it gained in popularity under the patronage of the courts of Delhi and Lucknow. It came to be used not only by Muslims, but by many of the educated Hindu families of North India and was eventually adopted by the British as a language of administration.

The official language of the courts of Lucknow, as of the Mogul Empire and the early days of the British administration in India, was Persian. Many poets chose to write their verse in both Persian and Urdu, reaching a high level of proficiency in the former despite having the latter as a mother tongue. The courtiers and nobility of Lucknow, being Shiite Muslims eager to retain cultural links with Persia, with which they identified and to which they traced their ancestry, retained the use of the Persian language long after it had fallen into disuse elsewhere in India. Sharar (1975: 100) writes of a time around the middle of the last century, though I was frequently assured this was still the case right up until the early twentieth century, when 'every child could speak Persian, when ghazals [poems] were on the lips of all, even the uneducated, the courtesans and bazaar workers, and when even a *bhand* [entertainer] would jest in Persian'.

Consequently the Urdu of Lucknow was coloured with Persian vocabulary and idiom, the greater use of which came to be a sign of the user's education, good-breeding and manners. This is still the case today, especially among Shiites. Although only a few members of the older generation speak Persian, people still regard the mastery of even a few phrases as a mark of distinction and social advancement, and therefore many aspire to learn the language.

Lucknow Urdu is extremely polite and highly expressive. The politest form of address, the second person plural *āp* is nearly always used. I observed that many parents invariably refrained from using other forms of address, even when speaking to their own children. The *āp* form is almost always used for a senior third person who is present. This caused me much confusion at first. When I came to use elsewhere what I had learned in Lucknow, I found that those who understood the idioms were enthralled, often embarking immediately on a conversation in praise of Lucknow Urdu. More often than not, those who did not understand found the language esoteric, and demanded explanations. Once, when I was ill, I remember being very puzzled when a friend asked me for how long I would be 'looking after this parrot' (*Yeh ṭoṭā kab tak pāliyegā?*). He explained that parrots were thought to be a nuisance to look after, and therefore his question was an idiomatic way of enquiring about how long I would have to put up with the inconvenience of being ill. I was also assured by two elderly gentlemen that unless one was conversant with Lucknow Urdu, in particular the Urdu spoken by women in certain areas of the old city and rarely heard nowadays called *rekhtī*, the ambiguities and subtleties present in the language of novels, such as the famous *Umrao Jan Ada* (translated as *The Courtesan of Lucknow*), would go unnoticed.

Umrao Jan Ada, by Mirza Ruswa, is arguably the greatest novel in the Urdu language. However, prose fiction only became an important genre of Urdu literature after about 1870. Poetry has always dominated Urdu literature, and the *ghazal* has always been the most important and widely employed form of poetic composition. The only accurate definition of a *ghazal* is, as with other types of poetic composition in Urdu, one which defines the form and not the content. It is a short poem of between five and ten couplets set in one of a variety of metres. The first two lines of the first couplet rhyme aa and thereafter the second line of each couplet rhymes with those of the first couplet (ba, ca, da, etc.). By convention the pen-name, or *takhallus*, of the poet is incorporated into the final couplet. In content the *ghazal*'s couplets may deal with a variety of ideas, not necessarily related, but usually concerning love, or *ʿishq*, of which there are two kinds: the mystic love for God, known as *haqīqī*, or 'real', and the earthly love for a man or woman, which is termed *majāzī*, or 'symbolic' (and not the other way round). In order to reflect both types of love, a poet may be intentionally ambiguous in what he writes. The *ghazal* was originally successful because of social circumstances which are still largely prevalent today and may well be the reason the form has remained popular. In a society of arranged marriages where falling in love was looked on with horror, illicit love for a boy, a courtesan, or an engaged or married girl, could be expressed in obscure and ambiguous verse.

The *ghazal* first appeared in about 1730, and the major poets of the eighteenth century were Mir, Sauda and Mir Hasan, who flourished in the Mogul courts of Delhi (see Russell and

Islam 1969). Towards the end of the eighteenth century the nobles of the rival court at Lucknow were offering alternative patronage, and many great poets of the Mogul courts, including the three mentioned above, were enticed to Lucknow. In general, the Delhi poets were not happy in Lucknow, where stylistic refinement was in far greater demand than refinement of content. This provoked Mir to write (quoted in Pemble 1977: 26):

> One ruined Delhi is worth ten Lucknows.
> I should have died there, not come here to weep.

Poets recite their *g͟hazals*, as they have always done, at a gathering called a *mushāʿara*. In response to *g͟hazals* delivered in *taḥt-ul-lafẓ* (declamatory) or *tarannum* (sung) style, the audience shows its appreciation, indifference or disapproval. An element of competition is always present (Russell 1969: 22; Qureshi 1969: 425-6). I attended many *mushāʿaras*, ranging from vast symposia of thirty or forty poets and an audience numbering well over a thousand to small, drawing-room gatherings where a few friends listened to each other's latest literary efforts. I found that most educated Lucknowis could remember and recite from a small repertoire of *g͟hazals*, and I was encouraged to do the same, receiving constant requests for the lines of Ghalib, Mir and Momin I knew by heart. A knowledge of *g͟hazals* seemed essential to anyone engaged in conversation, as relevant and explanatory lines of poetry would frequently be used to articulate ideas.

Lucknow's unique contribution to Urdu literature, however, lay in the longer poetic forms. Sauda, who, having left Delhi for Lucknow, enjoyed the patronage of Asaf-ud-daula, excelled at the *qaṣīda*, a long eulogy requiring a considerable technical mastery of form. But the Persian forms, the *maṣnawī* and the *marṣiya*, best expressed the Persianised culture and Shiah religion of the court. The *maṣnawī* is always concerned with love, but the custom was to be precise and detailed, giving, for example, a clear picture of the social background to any situation. Other forms, such as the *g͟hazal*, are very imprecise and obscure in this respect. The *marṣiya* is a lament dealing with any incident from the life of the Prophet Muhammad's grandson, Husain, especially with his martyrdom, an event of the greatest significance for Shiites. As in other areas where there are Shiite communities, it is recited mostly during the month of Muharram and is so emotionally charged that it brings groans and wails from those congregated. An assembly of this kind is termed a *majlis* and usually takes place in the *imāmbāṛās*, though many are held in private homes. The most celebrated exponents of the *marṣiya* form were Dabir and Mir Anis. Mir Anis also made an art of the recitation of the *marṣiya* which involved the subtlest of gestures, facial expressions and inflections (Sharar 1975: 84).

Turning away from the language and literature of Lucknow, I shall now describe a number of other features which have characterised the culture of the city. A favourite pastime of Lucknowis was the preparation, presentation and tasting of food, in all of which they are reported to have excelled. The best cooks in India came from the kitchens of the Lucknow nobility (Sharar 1975: 165). Sharar relates several examples, of which two are particularly memorable. In one, pieces of meat from a *pulāʾo* (rice dish) would be fashioned to look just like chickens and cooked with such care that the shapes would not disintegrate. They were placed on plates on which the rice had been arranged to look like grain. Each guest was then presented with a plate on which it appeared that a bird was pecking away at grain. Another example describes a dish which appeared to be a raw pumpkin. Having been successfully fooled, its recipient then found it not only to have been properly cooked but also to be the most delicious thing ever tasted (Sharar 1975: 162–3).

The *nawābs* developed a taste for animal combat, and tigers, cheetahs, leopards, camels, rhinoceroses, stags and rams were made to fight for the court's entertainment. Elephants, too, charged and butted each other with such terrific impact that it is said the noise could be heard for miles around. Cock-fighting was a particular favourite; in fact almost any type of bird was made to fight, not least the quail.

Contests of all kinds were invented in human combat too. Men expertly wielding sticks, swords, spears and cudgels engaged in martial arts, almost all of which have become obsolete. The most famous form was called *bā̃nk* and could either be fought in contests or used purely for self-defence. It involved the use of knives, as well as holds and throws similar to those used in Japanese aikido. A small number of people still practise *bā̃nk* today. My Urdu teacher, Saiyed Farhad Husain, is one. He would often prove that in spite of his eighty years he could still hurl me across a room and pin me down in knots.

Kite-flying and kite-fighting are diversions in which Lucknowis were, and still are, renowned for their expertise. Few people remain untouched by the passion displayed for this hobby. As a boy, my tabla teacher, when not found practising his instrument, would be out in the parks fighting with his kites. The evening skies over the old city are speckled with hundreds of entangled kites. The string is impregnated with secret compounds comprising substances like ground glass and crushed eggshell, and he who cuts his opponent's strings, leaving his own kite flying aloft, is the winner.

It is beyond the scope of this book to give more than a brief outline of the cultural features which characterise Lucknow. For a complete and detailed study, Sharar's *Lucknow: The Last Phase of an Oriental Culture* (1975) is invaluable, as is the more recent *Qadeem Lucknow ki Akhiri Bahar* by Mirza Jafar Husain (1981). But despite the fact that Sharar, writing in the early twentieth century, was describing what he felt to be the end of an era, there are nevertheless a number of facets of that culture surviving today which serve to give those people whose families have been historically connected with the city a strong sense of identity.

The history of music in Lucknow

The development of music in Lucknow was originally linked with the court, in which musicians and dancers found a new source of patronage to replace that of the Mogul courts of Delhi. Miner (1981: 150) states that following the death of the Emperor Muhammad Shah in 1748, musicians 'began to move away to other courts which were emerging as prosperous cultural centers'. Furthermore, Miner suggests that these emigrants took with them new musical forms and instruments, in particular the recently developed *sitār*. But it was in fact to Faizabad that musicians and dancers were initially drawn, enticed by its reputation as a new and fashionable metropolis under the patronage of Nawab Shuja-ud-daula.

Hakim Mohammad Karam Imam has provided us with the main source of information on music during the *nawābī* period. A courtier of Wajid Ali Shah, he wrote the *Maʿdanul Moosiqui* a few years after the deposal, in 1856, of the King. He asserts (1959: 17) that the main influx of musicians to Lucknow was in 1775, when, on the accession of Nawab Asaf-ud-daula, 'they shifted from Faizabad to Lucknow along with the Capital'. The new ruler, keen to indulge in his favourite passions, began spending lavishly both on the city's architectural development and on the arts and entertainment. The prospects of patronage were now even greater than they had been under Shuja-ud-daula and many of Delhi's musicians who had not been tempted to migrate earlier now did so.

It was sometime during this period that Miyan Bakhshu Khan, the forefather of my *ustād* (teacher or master) and founder of the Lucknow tabla *gharānā* (tradition), came from Delhi to settle in Lucknow. My *ustād*, Afaq Husain Khan, told me that his ancestor was employed in the service of Shuja-ud-daula, but he later showed deference to an elder of the family, Habib Raza Khan, who was in no doubt that Bakhshu Khan had arrived from Delhi in the reign of Asaf-ud-daula. Could it therefore be that both are correct: that Bakhsuji, as he is also known, was indeed initially employed at Faizabad before moving to Lucknow in the entourage of Asaf-ud-daula? Unfortunately no documentary evidence has ever been uncovered that would clarify points like these, and so as regards certain features in the history of Indian music we are left in the not unfamiliar realm of conjecture.

Hirendra Kumar Ganguli, a celebrated teacher from Calcutta, has claimed that Bakhshu Khan invented the tabla and many of the strokes used in playing it. According to Stewart (1974: 6–7), the tabla is more likely to have developed in Delhi at an earlier date as a hybridised instrument whose form was most probably based on existing drums, particularly the *pakhāwaj* and the *naqqāra*. She bases her assumption both on the pictorial evidence of Mogul-style miniatures showing the hemispherical drum pairs of the prototypal tabla, as well as on genealogical evidence concerning the tabla performance practices of members of the Delhi *gharānā* which stretch back to the second quarter of the eighteenth century. Of the drummers entering Lucknow in 1775, it must therefore be assumed that there were indeed a number of tabla players in addition to players of other drums, such as the *pakhāwaj*, the *ḍholak* and the *naqqāra*. From Imam's descriptions it is clear that many drummers were proficient on more than one instrument. One illustration of this concerns Aghawan Naqqarchi of Unnao, who 'was an adept in playing Tabla and Naqqara' (Imam 1959: 26).

Sharar (1975: 134) reports that Shuja-ud-daula took musicians and courtesans with him on journeys. It appears that Asaf-ud-daula followed suit by taking with him on hunting expeditions 'dancing women and boys, singers, musicians' (Pemble 1977: 15). And from a history of Asaf-ud-daula written in 1804, Pemble (1977: 14–15) quotes the following description of a scene at the wedding procession of Wazir Ali in 1795:

> On each side of the procession, in front of the line of elephants, were dancing girls richly dressed [and] carried on platforms supported by men called bearers, who danced as we went along. All these platforms were covered with gold and silver cloths; and there were two musicians on each platform. The number of these platforms was about a hundred on each side of the procession.

It is clear, therefore, that a large number of musicians had found security and patronage in the court at Lucknow. Meer (1980: 118) notes that 'For them the decadent period of the princely courts was a glorious one', and I have also noticed how many musicians today still romantically refer back to that kind of security, regarding it as an ideal situation and one they would dearly love to see revived.

But what of the paradox of music flourishing in a Muslim society? Music is widely held to be contrary to Islamic law, though Sufis have always used music in order to attain ecstatic and divine inspiration. It is, however, an extremely controversial subject, due in part to the fact that there is no mention of any word directly signifying the concept of music in the Koran (see Roy Choudhury 1957: 46). As was the case with the Emperor Akbar, the *nawābs* of Awadh had been influenced by the indigenous musical traditions of India, and they sought to unite Hindus and Muslims by encouraging music to prosper. Shiah religious law is arguably more narrow-minded than orthodox Sunni law, but even so a type of religious music peculiar to the Shiites, called *soz*, was to become an important part of music in Lucknow.

The performance of *soz*, called *soz-k͟hwānī*, 'was begun by Shias in India to keep fresh the memory of the martyrdom of the Prophet's family' (Sharar 1975: 147) and is still practised today. It is performed during a period of mourning lasting two months and eight days beginning with Muharram, during which the playing or singing of music is strictly prohibited. *Soz* is set in a musical framework but it would be in violation of Islamic principles to describe it as music, just as it would be incorrect for the same reason to describe as music the 'call to prayer' or the incantation of the Koran. *Soz* is never 'sung' (*gānā*), rather it is 'read' (*paṛhnā*); the word *k͟hwānī* also implies reading or recitation. The texts of *soz* are specially composed *marṣiyas*, but are generally shorter than their poetic counterparts, containing perhaps only a dozen verses. The verses are set in the framework of a melodic composition which is based on a *rāg* (melodic 'mode'), and the *soz-k͟hwān*, or *soz*-reader, 'reads' the composition with an unembellished voice, accompanied by disciples who vocalise the drone (the use of drone instruments, for example the *tānpūrā*, being prohibited). Although several different performance styles exist, the general effect has been described by Syed Fida Husain, an informant particularly knowledgeable about the subject, as 'like the delivery of a *dhrupad* [i.e. austere] ... without *tān* or *palṭā* [i.e. rapid, melismatic sequences of notes]'.

Many *soz* compositions are old, dating from at least the early nineteenth century. Others are newly composed by the *soz-k͟hwān* himself. The *soz-k͟hwān* is paid a small sum by those who invite him to perform at a *majlis*, and I was informed that several *soz-k͟hwāns* are retained on a small monthly salary by the organisations responsible for two of the largest *imāmbāṛās* in Lucknow, where *soz* can be heard throughout Muharram.

Soz was more widely performed during the *nawābī* era. Many famous classical vocalists of the period, such as Nasir Khan (mentioned by Sharar (1975: 148) to be a descendant of Tansen) and 'Siri' (Mad) Haideri Khan, became experts, presumably because they were forbidden to sing any other type of music for more than two months. Women, too, perfected the art of *soz-k͟hwānī* although I was told no female performers now remain in Lucknow.

Somewhat related to *soz* is another form of recitation called *mātam*, which is also 'read', not 'sung'. Consisting of perhaps three to five verses, *mātam* is shorter than *soz* and is performed in groups of any number upwards of ten, sometimes reaching a hundred or more. A doleful melody is 'read' by a leader and echoed by the chorus while all the time a steady rhythm is provided by the beating of breasts. *Mātam* is more commonly performed by women who gather in small local groups for a *majlis* each Thursday evening throughout the year, and daily during the period of Muharram. Men gather on the important religious occasions of the year in large groups called *anjumans* (societies), and their performance is far more intense, emotional and frenzied.

Not all the *nawābs* of Awadh were equally kindly disposed towards music. Muhammad Ali Shah and Amjad Ali Shah had little time for it. Saadat Ali Khan also took little interest and Imam (1959: 17) tells us that during his reign many musicians migrated from Lucknow, though he fails to indicate where they went. One may assume that they migrated to rival courts, as there was evidently a tradition of going on musical tours of other centres of patronage (Miner 1981: 196–7). Other *nawābs* more than made up for this dearth of interest. The aforementioned Haideri Khan lived at the time of Ghazi-ud-din Haider and was reputed to have been one of the greatest musicians of the period. A famous story concerning Haideri Khan and the King is reproduced in Sharar (1975: 135–6), but the following is a slightly different version given by Saiyed Farhad Husain. The main points of the story, however, remain the same.

In the days of Ghazi-ud-din Haider lived a musician whose name was Haideri Khan. He would never sing for money, and in spite of many invitations by the nobles of Lucknow, Haideri Khan would never visit them. He told the nobles that if they wished to hear his performance they should go to his house where he would entertain them.

Ghazi-ud-din Haider was an irate and cynical man. One day he sent his servant to summon Haideri Khan. At that time the *wazīr* [Prime Minister] of Lucknow was Agha Mir. Agha Mir was a wide-awake man who kept his ear to the ground. He knew the life of Haideri Khan would be foreshortened when the King learned that the singer had refused to attend court. He told the servant not to relate Haideri Khan's words to anyone in court unless Agha Mir himself was present.

It so happened that Agha Mir was present before Ghazi-ud-din Haider when the servant came. The King asked why the servant had failed to bring Haideri Khan with him. The servant said:

'If the King wishes to listen to Haideri Khan's music, he is to go to the latter's hut, sit on a *carpā'ī* [bed], and smoke a cheap *huqqa* [hookah]. Only then may the King hear him.'

The King was enraged and immediately ordered Haideri Khan to be beheaded. Agha Mir then stood up and with folded hands said:

'Haideri Khan is mad. He is called Siri [Mad] Haideri Khan because he refuses money and never performs to any rich man. And in history it will be written that the King, Ghazi-ud-din Haider, killed a madman because he would not come to the *darbār* [court].'

So the life of Haideri Khan was saved.

One day, some time later, the King was going along in his *havādār*, a palanquin with no roof, accompanied by some nobles. All were in plain dress. Someone recognized the figure of the great singer and exclaimed: 'There goes Haideri Khan!' The King stopped his *havādār*, and went over to the singer and asked:

Amāṅ, Haideri Khan! [*Amāṅ* is the equivalent of the old English 'Mercy!'] Won't you come to my house and perform for me?'

Haideri Khan said 'Why not?', because he thought the King, who was in plain dress, was just an ordinary man in the street. So Haideri Khan accompanied the King, but when they neared the palace he was all aghast and didn't know what to do. As he had given his word he attended the court that day and, with a silver voice, sang. Everyone enjoyed that. Then at midnight Haideri Khan was asked to perform *sohni*, which is a *rāginī* [melodic 'mode'] that brings tears to the eyes and fills man with sadness. Haideri Khan started singing. Soon the King and the nobles were in tears. The King wanted to listen to the piece a second time. He said to Haideri Khan: 'Sing that again and if you don't you will be beheaded!'

Haideri Khan was very angry. He didn't know what to do, but he was in the *darbār*. He proceeded to sing at such a pitch and intensity that, in the court and even outside the court, everyone was transfixed by his performance. Following this, the King said:

'Haideri Khan! Whatever you want from me, all you have to do is ask for it and I shall grant it.'

Haideri Khan said: 'I need nothing'.

The King asked a second time, and again a third. Then Haideri Khan said: 'But you would not give me what I want.'

The King replied that, as he had given his word, he would certainly grant it. Haideri Khan then said:

'I would only ask you for one thing. I would ask that you never call me here again.' He went on: 'If you die, Awadh will have another king. But if I die, India would have no other musician of my greatness.'

This is the story of Haideri Khan.

Music continued to be popular under Nasir-ud-din Haider, but it reached a peak under the patronage of Wajid Ali Shah, a king who preferred the company of courtesans, dancers and musicians to that of his ministers and advisers. In order to demonstrate the influence some musicians may have enjoyed in the court, Edwardes (1960: 155) quotes from Sleeman's *A Journey through the Kingdom of Oude, in 1849–1850*:

the most powerful favourites were two eunuchs, two fiddlers [Neuman (1980: 171) has suggested the most likely theory that these were *sārāṅgī* players], 'two poetasters, and the Minister and his creatures. The Minister could not stand a moment without the eunuchs, fiddlers and poets, and he is obliged to acquiesce in all the orders given by the King for their benefit. The fiddlers have the control over administration of civil justice, public buildings, etc. The Minister has the land revenue; and all are making enormous fortunes.'

Further evidence is given by Miner (1981: 218), who refers to the fortune amassed by the singer and *sitār* player, Ghulam Raza, who at one stage was appointed Deputy Prime Minister to the King.

Wajid Ali Shah himself had been taught music and dance, and so was not only a patron but a performer in his own right. Sharar (1975: 138) writes that the King's toes would twitch rhythmically in his sleep, and I was told that he lost the power of hearing in one ear because, as a child, he was struck by his teacher for incessantly tapping his feet during an Urdu and Persian lesson. There is a legend that Bindadin Maharaj, the great *kathak* dancer of Lucknow, stepped so lightly that he could dance on the edge of a sword without cutting his feet. Wajid Ali Shah must have been sufficiently accomplished for him to have been accredited, in another legend, with a similar feat.

The period of patronage under the *nawābs* of Awadh was a formative one in the history of Indian music. The courts offered patronage to a wide variety of musicians from different areas and backgrounds who specialised in a number of different forms and styles of music. Thus Lucknow was a melting pot for these many influences, from which emerged new instruments and styles of music catering to the predilection of the Kings and courtiers for the light and superficial. This trend has been continued right up to the present day. 'Lighter' vocal forms, such as *k͟hayāl*, *ṭhumrī* and *g͟hazal*, have increased in popularity at the expense of the more austere *dhrupad*. Additionally, their influence on the instrumental styles of the *sitār* and the *sarod* has promoted those instruments at the expense of the *bīn*, while bringing about the extinction of the Indian *rabāb* and *surshringār*.

Imam (1959) testifies to a large number of court musicians specialising in different genres of music ranging from classical *dhrupad* to semi-classical and light-classical forms such as *ṭhumrī* and *g͟hazal*, and instrumentally from the *bīn* and *rabāb* to the *sitār* and *sāraṅgī*. This led Solis (1970: 35–6) to make the point that there existed 'several ranks of musicians' between whom the 'social gulf . . . was quite marked'. His aim was evidently to separate the Seniyas, descendants of the great sixteenth-century court musician Miyan Tansen, from other musicians in order to highlight their considerable contribution to the development of Indian music during the *nawābī* period. Although they were in great demand as teachers, the social gulf, and a reluctance to teach their art and skills to all but their own descendants, forced the Seniyas to compromise with their other students. In public they sang *dhrupad* and played the *bīn*, the Indian *rabāb* and the *surshriṅgār*, while in private they taught *k͟hayāl*, the *surbahār* and the *sitār* (Solis 1970: 34–5). Solis thus speculates that the 'sarod may have been invented by Seniyas to circumvent the teaching of the rabāb'.

The origin of both the *sarod* and the *surshriṅgār* are contentious issues. It is known that two families of Afghan *rabābiyas*, who had previously migrated to Shahjahanpur and Bulandshahr (Solis 1970: 39), settled in Lucknow sometime during the first half of the nineteenth century in search of court patronage. Of these, Niamatullah Khan (1816–1911) is said to have been a disciple of Basit Khan (born 1787), to whom Imam (1959: 18), in the early nineteenth century, attributes the invention of the *surshriṅgār*. Miner (1981: 95) has put the *surshriṅgār*'s invention a little later, suggesting that it might even postdate the *sarod*, which she traces to Ghulam Ali during the first half of the nineteenth century. To make the *surshriṅgār*, the Indian *rabāb* was given a metal fingerboard and metal strings, and its wooden body was replaced with a gourd. Essentially the same modifications appear to have been made to the Afghan *rabāb* in order to develop the *sarod*, except that its wooden body was retained. Indeed, both Solis (1970: 23–6) and Miner (1981: 90–3) are at pains to show the organological similarity of the *sarod* to the Afghan *rabāb*. One possibility is that the Afghan *rabābiyas*, inspired by the alterations made to the Indian *rabāb*, made similar changes to their own instrument and themselves developed the *sarod*. This would then correspond with the claim of Omar Khan, a product of the intermarriage of the Shahjahanpur and Bulandshahr families of Afghan *rabābiyas*, that the *sarod* was invented by his ancestor Niamatullah Khan in the 1860s (Solis 1970: 26). That date, however, cannot be considered accurate as there is a reference to the *sarod* by Imam, who was writing at the end of the 1850s or early 1860s: 'Among the instrumentalists, Dahajudaulah Dhari of Lucknow, and Ghulam Ali Dome of Rampur, both Sarodiyas were masters of the time. But both are dead now' (Imam 1959: 24).

Apart from the above, there exists no other reference to the *sarod* in Imam, which seems curious if we are to wholly accept Solis's view that the *sarod* was popular during *nawābī* times. There appears to be little room for doubt that 'In all probability it was in Lucknow . . . that the *sarod* emerged both as an instrument and as a vehicle for "light classical" music' (Solis 1970: 36). However, setting a date to this instrument's 'emergence' is more problematic. I would suggest that the middle of the nineteenth century was still a period of transition for the *sarod* in its evolution from the Afghan *rabāb*. It may therefore not have been commonly heard in the Lucknow court. I would further propose that the Afghan *rabāb*, like the *sitār*, was ideally suited to the 'light-classical' music in vogue in the Lucknow court, and that this music was simple transferred to the *sarod* as the latter gained in popularity – it finally superseded the Afghan *rabāb* at a date sometime after the demise of the court, probably during the 1860s.

If this view is correct, then one of the lighter forms of music played by the Afghan *rabābiyas* would have been the *Raẓa K͟hānī gat*, an instrumental composition in *tīntāl* (sixteen beats), developed by the singer and sitarist Ghulam Raza Khan, whom it will be remembered was once appointed by Wajid Ali Shah as the Deputy Prime Minister of Awadh. This has now become the standard modern *gat* type in fast tempo which one may hear in every concert hall throughout North India. Imam's (1959: 23) comments are revealing:

> As for the style of Ghulam Raza I have not heard any other person playing it well except Ghulam Raza himself. This style follows no tradition and is unsystematic. Its gats in Titala are composed in the style of Thumri, Ragini and Dhun [and] are incomplete, hence I am not impressed. Undoubtedly Ghulam Raza had a sweet touch. The followers of this style are quite mad over it. But there is no room in this style for Thok and Jhala nor is there any scope for Raag, except for one or two. Ustads are averse to this style, and the connoisseurs are ashamed of it. Ghulam Raza developed this style only for the nobles of Lucknow.

Firstly, we can see how Ghulam Raza Khan was indebted to lighter forms to inspire this style and how, unlike the comprehensive compositions of classical *dhrupad*, the exposition of the *gat* was short and incomplete and, as such, was unable to express adequately the content of the *rāg* in which it was set. On the other hand the *Razā Khānī gat* was ideal for light and insubstantial *rāgs*, such as those created by Wajid Ali Shah, which he named, for example, 'jogi, juhi, jasmine, or Shah pasand, "favourite of the King"' (Sharar 1975: 138). Secondly, Imam's comments reveal the contrasting tastes of, on the one hand, the 'Ustads', here taken to mean the older, more knowledgeable musicians such as the Seniyas, for example, and, on the other, the nobility. As patrons, the latter's inclination towards the light and superficial in music shaped these developments and precipitated the decline of the more substantial and sophisticated classical forms, such as *dhrupad*.

Lucknow has been famous as a centre of *kathak* dance for over 200 years and many dancers were employed in the courts of the *nawābs* of Awadh, especially that of Wajid Ali Shah, whose passion for *kathak* is legendary. The distinctive Lucknow style of *kathak* dance is attributed by Sharar (1975: 142) to a fusion of the styles of, on the one hand, the courtesans who flocked to the court of Shuja-ud-daula in Faizabad and, on the other, the Hindu Kathaks of Ajodhya and Benares.

A vocal form closely linked with *kathak*, for it constitutes an important expressional and interpretive element of the dance, is the semi-classical *ṭhumrī*. While many popular myths attribute the invention of this form to Wajid Ali Shah, other opinions expressed by my informants, in particular the sitarist Ustad Ilyas Khan, suggested that *ṭhumrī* came to Lucknow from the Punjab. Wade's (1979: 178) view that *ṭhumrī* was 'cultivated' in mid-nineteenth-century Lucknow is shared by most writers, though both she (Wade 1971: 458) and Sharar (1975: 269 n.440) have remarked that the form was known long before in Benares. Thus *ṭhumrī* was most probably brought to Lucknow by the Kathaks of Benares as an integral part of their dance. As a form, *ṭhumrī* certainly flourished and developed in Lucknow, mainly due to the interest of Wajid Ali Shah, who himself wrote a large number of compositions under one of his many pen-names, Kadar Piya (Sharar 1975: 137). It was heavily influenced by other, more 'classical' forms such as *choṭā khayāl*, and indeed was distinguishable from it only by its greater reliance on the text of the *bandīsh* (composition) and the technique of *bol-bāṇṭ* (the dividing of words into syllables used for rhythmic manipulation). The Lucknow *ṭhumrī* thus became known as the *bandīsh ṭhumrī* or the *bol-bāṇṭ ṭhumrī* (Manuel 1986: 474).

The light-classical *g͟hazal* also flourished in Lucknow as a result of the local passion for poetry and the Urdu language. The *g͟hazal* was almost certainly introduced to Lucknow from Delhi by courtesans (Stewart 1974: 358).

The style of tabla-playing peculiar to members of the Lucknow *gharānā* arose mainly from the exigencies of providing accompaniment for the *ṭawā'ifs*, whose artistic medium of expression mainly comprised *kathak*, *ṭhumrī* and *g͟hazal*. Thus the style contains a large repertoire of *laggīs* used in accompaniment of these forms. Most characteristic, however, is the technical reliance on a wide variety of comparatively heavy resonating strokes, many in imitation of those used for the *pakhāwaj*, the instrument traditionally employed for *kathak* accompaniment. The most distinctive sections of the repertoire are therefore the *gats*, *ṭukṛās*, and to a certain extent *parans*, that were possibly borrowed from, or inspired by, *kathak*. This subject will of course be dealt with in greater detail in the chapters concerning the technique and repertoire of the Lucknow tabla *gharānā*.

Following the departure in 1856 of Wajid Ali Shah, and the Mutiny and Siege of 1857–8, musical activity came to a virtual standstill in Lucknow. For musicians still living in the city it became clear that the Nawab would never return, and the turmoil caused by the wholesale destruction of property forced many to leave in search of new sources of patronage. Some settled in nearby Kanpur, others in Patna and Calcutta. The British had taken firm control of the city and for a time there lingered an air of uncertainty while they reviewed their policy in India in order to avoid a recurrence of the events of 1857–8. The effect was such that the tabla player Haji Vilayat Ali Khan, a disciple of the family of Bakhshu Khan and founder of the Farukkhabad *gharānā*, on his return from Hajj, the pilgrimage to Mecca, 'found that the connoisseurs of Lucknow had ceased to hold music concerts because of fear of the new regime [the British]' (Imam 1959: 26).

Before long, however, music-making was resumed both under the patronage of the aristocracy still remaining in Lucknow as well as under a newly created nobility which had emerged with greater powers as a consequence of policy changes decided by the British. These were the local landowners and tax-collectors, the *zamīndārs* and *tāluqdārs*, who were seen as British allies and from whose ranks were created maharajas to administer the local regions. Thus, from about 1860, a new type of patron emerged to replace the old. This shift did not worry musicians unduly because the new nobles were to prove just as forthcoming in their patronage of music as the princes had been before them (Meer 1980: 120–1). Lucknow had been one of the great centres of the Indian music world in the early nineteenth century. Now, after the migration of so many musicians at the time of the disruption following the deposal of Wajid Ali Shah, it was rapidly regaining its position under the new system.

With abundant opportunities to perform, and the prospect of rich rewards for doing so, this was a golden era for the musician. The *kathak* dancer Vikram Singh indicated something of the extent of opportunity when he told me that musicians were to be found each evening in the residences of majarajas and *tāluqdārs*. The most eminent of India's performers were attracted by this abundance of patronage. Many came to settle, while others spent months at a time in the city entertaining in the houses of the rich, where they received large amounts of gold and jewellery in return for their services.

Vikram Singh also informed me that, as well as being patronised by the nobility, musicians were given support by prostitutes: 'Not those kinds of prostitutes . . . they were not prostitutes by . . . they belonged to prostitute families but they were . . . their delights were devoted to music: music and dance!' (The hesitation shown when mentioning anything to do with prostitutes or carnal pleasures, as seen here, is typical of virtually all who mustered the courage to even mention the subject of courtesans. This indicates the social stigma attached to *ṭawā'ifs* and to musicians connected with them.) The house of the courtesan Chaudhrayan Haider Jan was a famous meeting place where the best musicians could be heard accompanying *ṭhumrīs* and dance. I was told by Hirendra Kumar Ganguli that every few years a special assembly of *ṭawā'ifs* and musicians gathered there to honour Chaudhrayanbai (*bā'ī* is a term of respect appended to a *ṭawā'if*'s name), who was considered, as her title suggests (fem. of Chaudhri: head of caste or village) the head of the *ṭawā'ifs*. All *ṭawā'ifs* attending the assembly would perform their songs and dances.

From the *nawābī* era until the early twentieth century, musicians relied heavily on the *ṭawā'ifs* not only for direct patronage but also for introductions to the court or the houses of rich nobles. 'Musicians', explained Afaq Husain, would go to a *ṭawā'if* and tell her they wanted to get into court service . . . Now take someone like me or you. Today you go to Delhi, to some *ṭawā'if*'s house, and say that you are some *ustād* or some *gurū* or other. Now [the *ṭawā'ifs*] don't know if you are an *ustād* or not. So they get a programme set aside for you and then you play before them. In this way they examine you. Then they set you before kings and courtiers, saying: 'Listen to him! He is a very good artist, a good ustād who has come.' Now [the *ṭawā'ifs*] can really recognise whether you are an *ustād* or not . . . If they had never said anything, nobody would have ever recognised you.

The initiative for change came from the middle classes who had most actively responded to the British policy of Westernisation. They took advantage of a European education to unite with 'English as a common language and nationalism as a common ethos' (Meer 1980: 122), and their sphere of power and influence increased as that of the class they were gradually replacing, the landowners, decreased. For the puritanical middle classes, music was something associated with figures of the past, like Ghazi-ud-din Haider and Wajid Ali Shah, in whose decadent and debauched orgies of self-indulgence it became merely a means of arousing the senses. They realised, too, that music was available only to a select few. The public at large neither had an opportunity to listen to it, nor could they learn it, for musical expertise was confined to families of specialists (i.e. the *gharānās*) who, with the exception of their patrons, refused to share their knowledge with outsiders. Moreover, musicians were seen to associate with *ṭawā'ifs*, who were looked on with horror and were viewed simply as prostitutes. For the sake of one's moral reputation the *ṭawā'if* was to be eschewed, as were the musicians most closely connected with and dependent upon them, namely the tabla players and *sāraṅgī* players, who were branded as pariahs. Not surprisingly, therefore, the middle classes looked down on music, and it was only when their 'attention was drawn to the importance of the traditional arts as a binding force in the pride of the nation' (Meer 1980: 122) that attempts were made to make music available to a much wider audience.

The two figures most responsible for reviving Indian music and making it more easily accessible to the middle classes were Vishnu Digamber Paluskar (1872–1931) and Vishnu Narayan Bhatkhande (1860–1936). They were concerned that both the spiritual element of Indian music and the highly developed theoretical knowledge, which was traceable to the ancient treatises on music, were disappearing. Paluskar was a great performer and teacher who did much to activate interest among the middle classes. 'In the very teeth of opposition', he founded the first music school in Lahore in 1901, the Gandharva Mahavidyalaya (Misra 1981: 73). Another school followed in Bombay as he became more successful in reviving an interest in music. Bhatkhande was more of a scholar, a man who had travelled extensively to collect a huge storehouse of material from the country's experts and music libraries. He was a prolific writer whose aim was to provide source material for future generations of musicians and scholars. One of his most important contributions was the *Kramika Pustaka Malika*, published in six volumes between 1917 and 1936. This reference work, also widely used in institutionalised teaching, provides a large number of compositions in many *rāgs*. The *rāgs* are classified according to ten *ṭhāṭs*, or scales, and this system has become the most widely used in the study of North Indian music in India, although many Western scholars have questioned its viability (see Meer 1980 and 1984).

Bhatkhande organised a series of All India Music Conferences, the first held in Baroda in 1916, followed by others in Delhi (1917 and 1922), Benares (1918) and, in December 1924, in Lucknow (Misra 1977). Like Paluskar, he also began, with the support of wealthy enthusiasts, to open schools. Music schools were established in Baroda, Bombay, Gwalior and Nagpur, and in 1926, with the help of the Nawab of Rampur, Raja Nawab Ali, Rai Umanath Bali and Sri Rajeshwar Bali, in Lucknow. This, the Marris College of Music (named after the British governor at the time, who encouraged the idea), was later renamed the Bhatkhande Hindustani Sangeet Mahavidyalaya (or Bhatkhande Music College). It became the most celebrated of all India's music schools under the able directorship of Dr S. N. Ratanjankar, a disciple of Bhatkhande. During its early history many of India's top musicians were employed in the college, among them the sarodist Ustad Sakhawat Husain, the tabla player Khalifa Abid Husain and, in later years, the violinist V. G. Jog and the *dhrupad* singer Rahimuddin Dagar. By the 1940s there were 'hundreds of students with well over forty graduates' (Misra 1977a) at the college, and the public came to regard Bhatkhande as a saviour who had provided them with access to musical knowledge.

With the advent of radio and the opportunities it brought for musicians to broadcast, the State began to play its role as a patron of music. Lucknow was, in 1938, one of the first cities to have an All India Radio station. At first it was responsible for broadcasting over the whole of the United Provinces. Later, as other cities in the state were awarded their own stations and each was accorded its own zone, Lucknow's zone became smaller and more localised. In the beginning a host of great musicians broadcast regularly from the Lucknow station, including Ustad Faiyaz Khan, Ustad Amir Khan, Siddheshwari Devi, Bari Motibai, Ahmad Jan Thirakwa, Ali Akbar Khan and Ravi Shankar, to name but a few. Others, less well known, also came to Lucknow in search of jobs under the new State patronage, particularly from the large community of musicians in Benares.

State patronage could not, on its own, sustain many musicians because wages were low compared with the rewards they traditionally received from the *tāluqdārs* and maharajas. The music 'conferences' ('conference' denotes a music festival comprising several evenings of concerts at a specific locale) were better paid but, as one old *sārangī* player told me, 'not everyone got the chance to play in them!' Lucknow soon began to lose its famous musicians, who moved to big cities like Delhi, Calcutta and Bombay, where they could earn more money from the many conferences that were better funded in these rapidly growing, industrial, urban centres. My tabla teacher, Afaq Husain, visited Calcutta regularly from 1953 onwards and finally settled there in 1958. Before returning to his native Lucknow he spent a total of thirteen years in Calcutta. He explained that 'the field' was bigger, and one had plenty of opportunity to earn a living because music functions were as frequent there under public patronage as they had been in Lucknow in the last years of the nineteenth century under private patronage. He said:

> There used to by many artists here [in Lucknow] but some have died, some have gone to Calcutta, Delhi and Bombay because they saw that the field [here] was small and money was scarce, so they had financial worries and had to leave . . . There aren't as many businessmen here as there are in Calcutta or Delhi. There's more money there. We also gave it some thought and then went to Calcutta, where the field was bigger, there was more money, more connoisseurs. Those places get bigger every day in comparison to Lucknow.

Each of the three types of institution mentioned above is represented in present-day Lucknow: All India Radio, music colleges and public concerts. The All India Radio station is still relatively large but it is not as important as it once was. The Doordarshan Kendra, or television centre, as an employer of musicians, functions in a similar way to All India Radio and many consider it merely an adjunct to the radio station. The Bhatkhande Music College is the largest single employer offering full-time employment to musicians in the city, but in most people's eyes there are scarcely any musicians of repute in its ranks, in stark contrast to the early days. The public concert circuit is small, and few functions are held during the year. There is no private concert circuit as may be found, for example, in South Calcutta or in New Delhi's diplomatic circles.

All this adds up to the fact that Lucknow is now a musical backwater where musicians have little opportunity to make a name for themselves and where earning a good living wage is, to say the least, difficult. For anyone who has studied the development of Lucknow – its history, culture, and especially its music – the impression of its decline from the era of its prominence is inescapable.

2 *Musical life in present-day Lucknow*

The following sections set out the spectrum of music available in Lucknow and indicate the scope musicians have to earn a living in the city. Those who specialise in light or light-classical vocal music share few of the problems faced by classical musicians. There is a growing demand for light vocal forms in Lucknow and there are several performances throughout the year which are generally well attended and enthusiastically received. By contrast, classical music is not greatly in demand and audiences are small. No musician can therefore rely on public concerts as a viable source of income. In view of this situation, musicians are forced to seek permanent employment, the two main sources of which are All India Radio and the Bhatkhande Music College. The latter, in providing a cheap, socially acceptable, and easily available source of music education in the city, dries up another potential source of supplementary income for many who might otherwise earn from giving private tuition. A short section on *ṭawā'ifs* is added because these women have always been an important part of the culture and musical life of Lucknow and, although rapidly disappearing, a few still perform and thus provide work for a small number of musicians.

All India Radio and the Doordarshan Kendra

Organised broadcasting in India began in 1927 when the Indian Broadcasting Company inaugurated stations in Bombay and Calcutta. The government took control of broadcasting in 1930 and the name All India Radio (AIR), or Aakashvani, to give it its official Hindi title, was adopted in 1936 after the commissioning of a station in Delhi. Other stations followed soon afterwards in Madras, Tiruchirapalli, Dacca, Lahore and Lucknow, amongst others (Baruah 1983). All India Radio Lucknow came into being in 1938 and was responsible for broadcasting to much of the United Provinces (later Uttar Pradesh) and the surrounding areas. It is still one of the larger stations although its broadcasting zone has been gradually reduced in size as more local stations have appeared, such as Allahabad (1949), Benares (1962), Kanpur (1963), Rampur (1965) and Gorakhpur (1972), all of which were originally included under the umbrella of Lucknow.

Significantly, government patronage of music through AIR began at a time when the private patronage of the landowning nobility was disappearing. Both as a full-time and as a part-time employer of musicians, AIR is the most important patron of Indian music today, employing 'over 27,000 Hindustani and 30,000 Karnataka music artists' (Baruah 1983: 131).

Neuman (1980: 172–86) gives an excellent introduction to the organisation and workings of the Delhi station of AIR and my findings in the much smaller Lucknow station were very similar to his, especially concerning the social interaction of musicians. However, since Neuman's fieldwork (which was carried out between 1969 and 1971), television has become a much more widespread medium and many local stations have been set up all over the country.

Therefore, in addition to AIR I shall discuss the Lucknow Doordarshan Kendra, or television centre, which generally operates in much the same way as the radio station. The few differences are brought about by the medium of the televised broadcast itself.

I made two lists of musicians employed as staff members of AIR Lucknow, the first in 1981 and the second in 1984. The results, in terms of the number of posts, are given in Table 1. In addition to the posts listed, there were five musicians classified as composers or music directors. Their main function was to arrange pieces of light music, or accompaniments to *gīts* (songs) and *ghazals*, which were to be played by an orchestra comprising staff musicians. They also rehearsed and often directed the orchestra.

Table 1. *Staff artists of All Indian Radio Lucknow in 1981 and 1984*

Instrument	No. of posts		Posts filled		Posts vacant	
	1981	1984	1981	1984	1981	1984
Tabla	6	5	3	5	3	0
Tānpūrā	4	4	4	4	0	0
Sāraṅgī	3	3	3	3	0	0
Sitār	3	3	2	3	1	0
Violin	3	3	2	3	1	0
Clarinet	2	1	2	1	0	0
Sarod	1	1	1	1	0	0
Flute (*bāṅsrī*)	1	1	1	1	0	0
Dholak	1	1	0	1	1	0
Guitar	1	0	1	0	0	0
Dūtāra	1	1	1	1	0	0
Kiṅgrī	1	0	1	0	0	0
Total	27	23	21	23	6	0

Table 1 shows a clear trend towards retaining minimum numbers of staff musicians (minimum in terms of the requirements of the radio station). As Lucknow's broadcasting zone has been gradually diminishing in size, fewer staff artists have been engaged. The reduction in numbers is achieved through natural wastage: many musicians who have retired or died are not replaced. For example, had my initial survey been conducted about ten years previously the total number of posts for the tabla would have been eight, and for the *sāraṅgī* four. Between 1981 and 1984 the number of tabla posts was reduced to five. Whereas in 1981 there were two clarinet posts, by 1984 both clarinettists had retired and only one post had been readvertised and filled. Both the guitar post and the *kiṅgrī* (a folk fiddle) post were discontinued following the deaths of both musicians, and neither post was reallocated for a different kind of specialist.

There is normally no difficulty in getting musicians to fill any post that is advertised – any, that is, except for the *sāraṅgī*. Shortly after my survey of 1981 a *sāraṅgī* player retired. His post lay vacant for almost two years because very few musicians, and certainly none of the required standard, applied for it. This is a clear indication of the steady decline of the *sāraṅgī* despite the ban exercised on the harmonium as an accompanying instrument by AIR (see Neuman 1980: 184–6), which was partly intended to keep alive the *sāraṅgī* tradition. This is in stark contrast to the increased popularity of the tabla. A producer at AIR told me that any vacancy for the tabla is greeted with a flurry of activity and the radio station is inundated with applications.

In addition to the staff artists of AIR, many other musicians are contracted to broadcast. These are termed 'casual' artists, and they may be invited to perform several times each year. There are three categories of casual artist: 'classical', 'light' (i.e. singers of *ghazal*, *gīt*, *bhajan*, *qawwālī*, etc.) and 'folk'. Unfortunately, Baruah (1983) fails to differentiate between staff and casual artists at AIR, and instead lists the total number of musicians in each category for January 1982. Nevertheless, by subtracting 21 staff artists (as listed in Table 1 under 'posts filled' for 1981) from the 'classical' category, we arrive at the following figures for casual artists in Lucknow: classical, 92; light, 215; and folk, 244.

In order to be employed as a staff or casual artist at AIR or the Doordarshan Kendra a musician may at any time arrange for an audition at the local radio station, where he or she will be assessed by a panel of local experts. If a musician passes this initial test a subsequent audition is then arranged in Delhi. The Delhi panel of experts, comprising, in theory, unbiased and incorruptible musicians appointed by the directors of broadcasting, has the power to 'approve' an artist by awarding one of four grades: top-class, A, B-high and B. These grades are crucial as they, to some degree, indicate a musical status (though not one that is by any means recognised universally) and, most importantly, they regulate a musician's potential earnings from radio and television broadcasts.

The top-class grade is a category applicable only to classical and not to 'light' or 'folk' artists. It is reserved for the most distinguished musicians and, as a rule, is never conferred by the panel on the evidence of an audition. All grades are reviewable and therefore the panel usually awards the top-class grade after some years. No staff or casual artist was rated top-class in AIR Lucknow between the years 1981 and 1986.

In practice, grades are rarely changed as a result of a review. My teacher, Ustad Afaq Husain Khan, has for many years been widely recognised as worthy of the top-class grade, an honour many believe he will ultimately receive (perhaps when he reaches sixty or sixty-five years of age). He was initially awarded A grade status on 22 April 1950 at the age of nineteen, an indication of how long some musicians may wait for a change of status. Indeed, I know of one musician who has been playing professionally since 1974 but who has so far refrained from auditioning for AIR. His intention has been to gain experience and so improve his standard of performance and his reputation in order to be sure of a high grade when he does eventually audition. He is the exception. Most musicians look immediately to 'approval' by AIR in order to guarantee a certain number of broadcasting opportunities and thus a supplementary income.

Amateur musicians account for the majority of casual artists employed by AIR Lucknow: virtually all musicians in the light- and folk-music categories, and about half those in the classical-music category. I know several amateur musicians who are shopkeepers, scientists, and civil servants. There are also a few well-to-do housewives whose hobby it is to sing *ghazals* and *bhajans*. The remaining casual artists are professional musicians, the majority of whom are employed in the Bhatkhande Music College, the Uttar Pradesh Sangeet Natak Akademi and the Doordarshan Kendra. A few *ghazal* and *qawwālī* singers are the only musicians who are able to earn a living from giving public concerts.

Musicians see a permanent staff post in AIR as a desirable option and, quite often, an easy one. It guarantees a dependable source of income and, on the whole, is not very demanding in terms of the number of hours one is required to rehearse or perform. Several musicians are selected to form the orchestral group which plays daily in accompaniment to *gīt*, *ghazal* or *bhajan*. There is a rehearsal, usually on the day of the recording unless the piece or pieces are complex, in which case the group may be called to rehearse a few days beforehand. Should the orchestration require extra musicians or a specialist of a type not on the staff of AIR, for example a *santūr* player, contracts are sent out for casual artists to rehearse and play with the orchestra. Staff tabla players, *sāraṅgī* players and *tānpūrā* players may expect to be called upon three or four times a week to accompany singers and instrumentalists, that is those casual artists who have been contracted to broadcast. In addition to this, each staff artist may be required to give up to three solo performances a year, including *tānpūrā* players, who are primarily vocalists.

Much of the free time between rehearsals and broadcasts is therefore spent sitting around in the canteen chatting and relaxing, but not all musicians are entirely happy with the system in the radio station as it allows little or no opportunity for an individual to practise. There are no rooms reserved specifically for practice and the studios are in use virtually all day. When a musician is 'on duty' he may not officially leave the building, even in search of somewhere quiet to get on with his *riyāẓ*, or practice (see Neuman 1980: 178). Thus many object to the time wasted in being present while having little or nothing to do, as Akbar Husain, a staff tabla player for many years until his transfer to Bombay in 1985, explained to me:

> When I was about eighteen or nineteen years old [*c.* 1950] I did a couple of weeks in the radio station. It was written on the chart that my duty began at a certain hour and I was to accompany someone. I arrived an hour early and after finishing the item I was free to go. Then I might have had a couple of items in the evening and then again in the morning, but after that my duty was over. Then I could go back home. Now I have to attend for eight [actually seven] hours. So you see, even if we don't have a recording we sit there anyway. So where can we get the time to practise? They set the time [i.e. working hours on a shift] and we have to be there. In the old days people got so much more time and they could practise and think.

Staff musicians are divided into two groups, each of which is required to work a seven-hour shift. The first shift is from 07.00 to 14.00 and the second is from 11.00 to 18.00 though, despite Akbar Husain's claims, musicians rarely attend for the full seven hours, the times being quite flexibly interpreted. Staff learn of the times of their recordings or live broadcasts in advance, either from the office where they report for duty or from timetables attached to the notice board or issued by the office. Contracts for casual musicians are sent out approximately two weeks in advance of a recording or live broadcast. The date, time, nature of the item, and the payment, are all stipulated in the contract. If a musician is featured, he or she is often required to give two or three performances in a day, although the contract fee for three items is the same as for one. Sometimes items are recorded a few days in advance of the broadcast but they more frequently occur on the same day, the first item being live around 09.10. Other usual times for these items are lunchtime (approximately 13.10) and at night (approximately 22.30).

An average of three hours of broadcasting time out of a possible total of approximately twelve and a half hours is given over to music each day. The remaining time is occupied with news bulletins, weather forecasts, discussions, programmes for farmers and children, and plays. The station goes off the air from 09.30 until midday, and again from 14.45 to 17.00. No broadcasting occurs at night between 23.15 and 05.55.

A typical day's programme schedule of music items is as follows:

Wednesday 9 September 1981

07.05–07.15	*Manas gān* (spiritual song)
07.45–08.00	*Sāz-o-ghazal* (ghazals)
08.20–08.30	*Lok gīt* (folk song)
09.10–09.30	*Khayāl*: Ganesh Prasad Misra
12.00–12.10	Sanskrit *gān* (sanskrit song)
13.10–13.40	*Khayāl*: Ganesh Prasad Misra
17.00–17.05	Country song: Lakshmi Bai Rathaur
17.30–17.40	*Lok gīt*
17.45–18.00	*Gīt* and *bhajan*: Lakshmi Bai Rathaur
20.15–20.30	*Ghazals*: Lakshmi Bai Rathaur
20.30–20.45	*Ṭhumrī*: Sandhya Mukherjee
22.30–23.00	*Khayāl*: Ganesh Prasad Misra

Occasionally, old recordings of past masters, or new recordings of well-known present-day masters, are broadcast. Programmes are advertised in all the local daily newspapers, often printed with the musician's names alongside (from which the above timetable was compiled).

To estimate the size of the listening audience would be difficult in terms of actual numbers. My own guess is that, of the total number of radio listeners in Lucknow, up to 5 per cent listen to this station regularly. Most people choose the commercial station, which is also broadcast from AIR. Only the blaring advertisements for soap-powder and toothpaste break the monotony of an endless string of film song hits from past and present. As these songs ring out from the shops and houses into the bazaars and alleyways, everyone sings along, for all appear to know both the tune and the words by heart.

Being a staff musician in the Lucknow Doordarshan Kendra, or television centre, is very similar to being a staff musician in AIR. Staff must be 'approved' by AIR and the grading system determines the same levels of pay which apply to musicians employed in radio. There are further parallels with the radio station. For example, musicians have a great deal of free time but nowhere to practise at the television centre. They therefore spend much time idling in the staff canteen drinking tea and chatting to friends and colleagues.

There are five staff posts in the television centre: tabla, *sārangī*, *ḍholak*, *sarod* and clarinet. Their main function is to perform as an orchestral group for light music, though the tabla player, Ustad Afaq Husain Khan, is regularly engaged as an accompanist for classical-music programmes. If a large group is required for a special orchestration of light music, casual artists are brought in.

Unlike radio staff artists, the television staff members are strictly accompanists: they are never required to perform solo on television though they of course have that opportunity in their capacity as casual artists of AIR. The bulk of their work is orchestral because most of the broadcasts cater to the public demand for light music, especially *ghazal* and *bhajan*. The light-music soloists are casual artists, most of them local, and the standard of musicianship often leaves much to be desired. Programmes of classical music, however, are invariably of excellent quality, musically speaking. They feature many of India's top musicians, who are invited to broadcast especially if they are visiting or performing in or near Lucknow. Often, recordings are hastily arranged for an artist making an unexpected visit to the city. This gives rise to the impression that the Doordarshan Kendra is less well organised than AIR. Around the time of the annual Lucknow Festival, when many top-ranking artists are visiting the city, several recordings are made daily. These are broadcast at regular intervals later in the year. Dance recitals, impractical on radio, go to make up about half of all classical-music programmes on television. All casual artists are paid fees in accordance with their AIR grading plus an extra 50 per cent, which is termed the 'television fee'.

There is relatively little classical music to be heard on television: on average one or sometimes two programmes each week. Light music is more frequently broadcast and is to be heard three or four times each week. As is the case in AIR little rehearsal is needed, musically speaking, for broadcasts of classical music. Filming is rarely adventurous and therefore technical difficulties are minimal. Musicians have only to be positioned and the lighting adjusted before filming can commence. Main performers are usually daubed with orange-coloured make-up, but their accompanists, not being the main focus of attention for the cameras, rarely are. The filming generally displays a total ignorance of, and insensitivity to, the music. Most noticeable are the shots of accompanists doing nothing while the soloist is turning on a dazzling display of virtuosity, or alternatively shots of soloists doing nothing while their accompanists are improvising.

Broadcasts of performances of light music are, both musically and technically, much more elaborate. For example, a *ghazal* singer may have composed a melody for his or her lyric but it is normally left to a composer-cum-music-director to create the orchestral arrangements to accompany the song. As with the AIR orchestra, musicians learn their parts quickly by ear, memorising the whole piece. They then have to run through it several times altering details as they proceed until the director is satisfied with the product. Televisation is generally quite ostentatious, with angled shots, pans, zooms, fades, close-ups of the various instrumentalists as they play short solo lines, lighting changes, and richly decorated sets. In contrast to the filming of classical music, the producers appear to have a greater understanding of, and feeling for, light music, as their selection and timing of shots is much more sympathetic to the music. Because of the technical difficulties involved, extensive rehearsal is needed for the cameramen and lighting technicians, much to the chagrin of the patient musicians. I asked Afaq Husain how long it normally took to record a light-music programme of, say, thirty minutes' duration. He replied:

For a programme of half an hour, if there are three or four main artists, they'll have two or three days of rehearsal . . . two, four or six hours of rehearsal at a time. Light music requires all artists to attend rehearsals, including a ten-piece orchestra. You've got to tell them the pieces, and the singer has to remember the song. Where to do the cutting? Where to begin? Where to sit? Everything takes quite a lot of time.

This inevitably presents many problems for musicians, especially those with a training in classical music. Their main problem is boredom: they must play the same things repeatedly with no scope for variation. They must frequently also adjust to less well trained, amateur musicians who may take longer to learn a musical arrangement or may be limited by insufficient technique. Afaq Husain continued:

Classical musicians do get a bit bored playing a lot of light music, in the same way that light-classical musicians get a bit bored with classical music. For light musicians, classical music is rather difficult, and classical musicians are not used to being bound, which they find difficult [i.e. restricted by the precomposed piece]. I'm more involved in classical music, much less with light. We people have done so much more practice in classical music.

JK But even so you have to play a lot of light music.

AH Yes, things keep stopping in so many places; ten people have got to be together. Something is forgotten, then you stop. Somebody forgets the rehearsal, then one has to stay behind. But [despite this] you've still got to play with those people. We people find that a bit of a problem. Everybody has to be told what it is they have to do: the *ḍholak* and the tabla, and so on. We give a bit of *ṭhekā* [i.e. unelaborated accompaniment] and then stop, then start again and stop again. Classical musicians have the problem of gauging how much a light musician knows and how far he can go. [Light musicians] don't do much practice or hard work, so their hands [i.e. technique] aren't even half good. If you can only just manage to run two miles, then how can you possibly attempt to run ten?

The Lucknow Doordarshan Kendra broadcasts for approximately three and a half to four hours each evening, beginning around 18.00. Transmission time is increasing steadily, particularly at the weekends. As television is a relatively new medium, as well as being a luxury item, few people own television sets. Of those who do, few people showed much interest in classical-music broadcasts. Most preferred light music, especially programmes of *g͟hazals*, mainly because they could follow and appreciate the lyrics. However, by far the most popular weekly programmes broadcast on Lucknow television were *Chitrahaar*, the equivalent of Western pop-video shows but featuring Bombay film songs, and the feature film on Sundays, which is invariably a Bombay movie hit from the past.

Public teaching institutions

The rise of public institutions for the teaching of music has offered the prospect of permanent and secure employment to many musicians. In Lucknow, by far the most important institution is the Bhatkhande Hindustani Sangeet Mahavidyalaya, in which are enrolled approximately 1,300 students who take courses in all forms of Indian classical music and dance. In addition, the Uttar Pradesh branch of the Sangeet Natak Akademi offers courses in *kathak* dance. Employment is also to be found in some secondary schools where music education has become an important part of the school curriculum. In practice, posts in schools are rarely taken by performing musicians, instead being filled by graduates of the music colleges.

The Bhatkhande Hindustani Sangeet Mahavidyalaya (or Bhatkhande Music College) is the largest single employer offering full-time work to musicians in Lucknow. It was established in 1926 and has become one of the most important and respected institutions for the teaching of music in India. A staff list for 1981 numbers twenty-nine musicians holding teaching posts: three professors, ten assistant professors, four lecturers, and twelve junior lecturers. In addition, there are places for twenty-four musicians classed as accompanists, the majority of whom are tabla and *sāraṅgī* players. They are required to assist in the classes by providing an accompaniment to both teachers and students for practice and demonstration.

A post, whether it be for a lecturer or an accompanist, is advertised in the press, although musicians more often learn of a vacancy by hearsay. Applications are then received by the principal of the College and interviews and auditions are given in front of a panel. The panel usually comprises musicians and administrators who represent the Public Services Commission, an independent body created in order to select candidates for posts in governmental organisations. Apart from the obviously essential requirement that a musician should be competent, one must be a graduate holding a certificate of higher education in any subject in order to gain employment. Several lecturers are in fact graduates from the Bhatkhande Music College itself. It is widely believed that these educational requirements ensure the College gets a literate and socially respectable person who will behave properly with the students entrusted to him. Parents of students, especially female students, have told me how they would fear any situation which might allow an illiterate musician (illiteracy, to most, indicating a dubious moral character) to be in contact with their children, the risk of any impropriety in such circumstances being too great.

There are a number of objections to this system of appointing staff. Its critics complain that the Public Services Commission is open to abuse and that its members practise nepotism and are easily influenced by bribery. Common belief has it that, on the Commission, musicians are far outnumbered by administrators, who do not hold musical ability as a priority when appointing staff. In addition, critics claim that not all the best musicians have the necessary certificates to qualify for selection and that charges of illiteracy being an indicator of corrupt moral character are unjustified. One person was heard to joke that even if the great singer Miyan Tansen were to return to this world and apply for a post as a lecturer in a music college, he would be rejected on the grounds that he lacked formal qualifications. I put this to the principal of the Bhatkhande Music College, Dr S. S. Awasthi, who replied that this was not strictly the case. Should an exceptionally gifted, or highly respected, musician qualify on musical grounds alone and be considered a potentially successful teacher, then he would certainly be appointed and qualification requirements would be waived.

The academic year commences in January. Interviews for admission are held during the week prior to the beginning of courses. Candidates are overwhelmingly from middle-class, Hindu backgrounds, with females outnumbering males by approximately two to one. The vast majority of students are destined only to dabble in music, with perhaps just a handful, normally males, intending to make some sort of career out of music.

Students with some musical knowledge and ability are allowed to begin courses immediately in the first year proper, while those having no knowledge whatsoever are required to attend a preliminary course of six months' duration, beginning in July, designed to prepare them for the first year. Certificates are awarded to students on the successful completion of the various stages of the course: after the second year, the Prathma; after the third year, the Madhyma; after the fourth year, the Visharad Part I, and after the fifth year, the Visharad Part II. The Visharad Part II is unofficially recognised as the equivalent of a B.A. in music. A further three-year course, the Nipun Parts I, II and III, leads to a certificate which is equivalent to a Master's degree.

In the opinion of parents and musicians alike, fees are very moderate. Up to Madhyma the amount payable is ten rupees per month, while fees for the Visharad and Nipun courses are increased to twelve rupees and fourteen rupees per month respectively. However, parents whose income is less than 500 rupees per month are exempt from paying fees, as are handicapped students. This is termed a 'full freeship'. A 'half freeship', where only half the fees are payable, applies to parents with two or more children attending the College. There are scholarships to be won by the best student in each year for a given subject. The amounts range from a monthly award of ten rupees in the first year to twenty-five rupees in the second and third years, fifty rupees in the fourth and fifth years, and seventy-five rupees for students in the sixth, seventh and eighth years. Assessment of eligibility for these awards is made on examination results.

Examinations are held in December at the end of the academic year and are organised by the examining body of the College, the Bhatkhande Sangit Vidyapith. Students are required to sit theory papers, as well as practical tests which, in the presence of the tutor, are conducted by external examiners drawn from other colleges affiliated to, or recognised by, the Bhatkhande Sangit Vidyapith. In turn, many lecturers from the Bhatkhande Music College are required to be external examiners for other music institutions. In its prospectus for 1981 to 1983, the Bhatkhande Sangit Vidyapith listed no fewer than eighty-three affiliated institutions, though many more are officially recognised.

Classes in the Bhatkhande Music College are held from 15.00 to 20.00, Monday to Saturday, throughout approximately nine months of the year. The winter vacation lasts from the end of December to the end of January, while the summer vacation is longer, lasting from mid-May to the beginning of July. The College also closes on public holidays. In the five-hour teaching period, a lecturer may have up to four classes, elementary classes being of one hour's duration and the more advanced classes of ninety minutes. Depending on the demand for a particular subject, a teacher might find that his or her classes run consecutively, without a break, though other lecturers may have several free periods.

While in a few classes, *bharata natyam* (South Indian classical dance) and Manipuri and Bengali folk dances are taught, most students study Hindustani classical music. Classes are held in vocal music, *sitār*, *sarod*, violin, flute, tabla and *pakhāwaj*. Some subjects are more popular than others: vocal, *sitār*, and tabla are well subscribed, whereas flute and *pakhāwaj* are undersubscribed. Although one *sāraṅgī* player has a junior lectureship, no classes in *sāraṅgī* are held as there is simply no demand for tuition whatsoever.

As Neuman (1980: 199) has pointed out, and as nearly all musicians to whom I have spoken repeatedly claim, no student trained exclusively in a music college has yet become a recognised performer of Indian classical music. Bhatkhande's original idea was not to churn out professional musicians but rather to provide a basic education in music for all who desired it. A knowledge of the rudiments of the theory and practice of music would then be an invaluable aid for anyone wishing to become a professional musician. It was realised that, in order to attain the necessary performance skills to become a professional, a student would have to train further under a traditional, hereditary musician. At a time when it was accepted that few hereditary musicians were willing to part with their knowledge to outsiders, potential students had to be able to gauge whether or not they were receiving an appropriate training. Those who did not want to become musicians would at least form the basis of an intelligent and appreciative generation of listeners.

The Uttar Pradesh Sangeet Natak Akademi was established in 1963 and comprises two schools: the Kathak Kendra, in which *kathak* dance is taught, and the Bharatiya Natak Kendra, which is given over to the instruction of drama. There is also a library and an archive with listening facilities. In addition, the archive section comprises a survey unit for the state of Uttar Pradesh, whose main purpose is to make recordings of the many types of classical and folk music found in the state.

Although the Akademi and the Bhatkhande Music College are located side by side, they are not connected. The Akademi is autonomous, having its own governing body, the Executive Board, which selects and appoints staff. There are a small number of posts for musicians and dancers in the Kathak Kendra. There are two 'practical teachers', one of whom is also the director of the Kendra, and four accompanists: two tabla players, one *sāraṅgī* player and one singer-cum-harmonium-player.

Two classes are held in the Kathak Kendra: a preparatory class, in which there are fifteen students, and an advanced class, in which there are nine. Classes begin at 14.00 and go on until 19.00. The classes follow no fixed structure and students are free to remain for the full five hours. The preparatory course is of two years, after which students pass into the advanced class for training designed to take them up to professional performance standard. Fees of twenty-five rupees are payable monthly by all students not in possession of a scholarship. Those with scholarships are entitled to free training. There are five scholarships available, each amounting to one hundred rupees per month. Awards are also made available for research, or for the collection of material for the archives. Concerts are occasionally sponsored, and recordings are commissioned for the archives from a few of the top musicians of the state.

Since Independence, Indian music has become an important part of the school curriculum in most urban centres of the country. This is especially so in girls' schools and colleges, where it can be studied as an optional subject at high school and intermediate levels. However, the subject is rarely taught in boys' schools and colleges and, owing to religious prohibitions on music, is never taught in Muslim schools or colleges. Having passed examinations in music at intermediate level, a student is entitled to begin a course in the Bhatkhande Music College at an advanced level by joining the third-year class. However, final admission to this advanced stage is dependent upon an interview. Those who have passed high school examinations are entitled to join second-year classes. Music courses in schools are very basic, the standards and demands being generally very low.

A music education, for a Hindu girl, is seen as a positive asset when it comes to marriage, which is probably why female students far outnumber males in music colleges throughout India. Teaching posts in schools are rarely, if ever, filled by performing musicians; college graduates are considered by all to be much better suited to the work. Many girls graduating from music colleges go on to teach in girls' schools. Parents also tend to view this experience as a kind of insurance against any misfortune which might one day force their daughter to return to work in order to earn her own living.

Public concerts

Compared to the vast number of concerts for the public in Delhi, Calcutta and Bombay, there is little activity in Lucknow. No equivalent of the Tata Foundation in Bombay or the Indian Tobacco Company in Calcutta exists in Lucknow, and there is no longer a private concert circuit such as may be found in Delhi's diplomatic circles or among the richer communities of Bombay and Calcutta. The few opportunities that arise are scarcely enough to give more than a handful of musicians a small supplementary income.

A lack of sponsorship is not considered to be the only, nor even perhaps the main problem facing Lucknow's musicians. More important, in many people's eyes, is the general apathy of the modern audience. Lucknowis attend in relatively small numbers and are known for their tendency to drift away well before midnight, in contrast to audiences elsewhere that remain until the early hours of the morning. Musicians feel that the people of North-Central India differ greatly from, say, Bengalis or Maharashtrians, who show a far greater inclination towards the arts in general. As Afaq Husain put it, that 'hunger' for music is no longer a feature of the Lucknow public:

There was a time in Lucknow too when one would say: 'Today I'm hungry and thirsty but, instead of eating, I'll go to hear a music concert.' This is the state of things in Calcutta, even nowadays. And it's increasing too. There, there is that kind of music lover who, whether he's eaten or not, will buy a three-rupee or a ten-rupee ticket and go to listen to a concert. Just like some people are keen to go to see a film, whether they've eaten yet or not.

Lucknow audiences appear to reject the idea of paying money for the privilege of hearing classical music. I have frequently heard it said that whereas a concert with free admission might stand a chance of attracting an audience of Lucknowis, even a one-rupee charge would mean that few would bother to turn up. The system of issuing passes entitling government officials and other 'important' people to free admission serves only to make matters more difficult for the organisers, who must necessarily charge for tickets in order to finance musical events and pay the performers.

The main musical event in Lucknow's calendar is the Lucknow Festival. It was first organised in the mid-1970s to promote trade and tourism in the city and to give visitors a taste of Lucknow's heritage in culture, music, art and religion. It is held annually, usually occupying the last two weeks of February, and is run by the Uttar Pradesh State Department of Cultural Affairs. For the first three festivals I was able to attend, namely those of 1981, 1982 and 1983, a grant of around 700,000 rupees was made available, 200,000 rupees of which was spent on the music and drama festival alone. The festival of 1984, the fourth I attended, saw a major change in policy and a grant approximately ten times the previous amount was designated for the events. It had been decided to upgrade the Lucknow Festival to create an event of national and international importance. Several foreign ambassadors were invited to attend, so giving the occasion a mark of distinction. 1984 was also the year of the bi-centenary of Lucknow's most celebrated architectural achievements: the Bara Imambara and the Rumi Darwaza. Money was made available for the restoration of these buildings and for the creation of new riverside parks designed to beautify the city – symbols of a renaissance which would help to focus attention on it. Thus the general standard of the Lucknow Festival was raised in every respect, and all the events, especially the music and drama festival, caught the public's imagination and consequently met with unprecedented success in terms of the numbers of people who attended.

The programmes for the concerts in the music festivals were decided upon by a cultural committee, which was itself a subcommittee of the main Lucknow Festival committee. The subcommittee was headed by the Director of Cultural Affairs, or by the commissioner of the Lucknow division. The panel was said to comprise 'musicans and experts' drawn from the Bhatkhande Music College, All India Radio, and television. The selection of items and performers for the festival was guided firstly by the aim of presenting a wide range of music, ideally being a balance of vocal, instrumental and dance performances, both classical and light, and secondly, the availability and cost of engaging performing artists. A policy for introducing exciting new talent was counterbalanced with a tendency to invite back performers whom the committee believed to have been exceptionally successful in previous years. In this attempt to present, as one director put it, 'the topmost talent in the country', few musicians based in Lucknow had an opportunity to perform in the festival, especially in performances of classical music. Most people believed, with some justification, that there was little talent in Lucknow and therefore it was necessary to invite 'outsiders' to perform. But an additional factor must be taken into consideration, one which was colourfully explained to me as *Ghar kī murg͟hī dāl barābar* (The chicken cooked in one's own home tastes no better than lentils). Musicians who are based in other cities, especially Delhi, Calcutta and Bombay, carry a prestige value which a home-based musician can never have.

The attitude of the organisers towards Lucknow-based musicians was reflected in the fees they paid. One Lucknow-based tabla accompanist, who could comfortably earn 1,000 rupees in Calcutta, received 400 rupees for a solo item, while a Calcutta-based tabla player received 1,200 rupees for giving his accompaniment in the Lucknow Festival of 1983. Some of Lucknow's musicians, much to their great displeasure, were paid nothing for stage appearances. These were members of staff at the Bhatkhande Music College, who were sometimes called upon to perform at short notice, especially if a vacant slot arose owing to a last-minute cancellation. One such hapless musician told me how he was forced to cancel another engagement at the last minute in order to fill in for someone at the festival. He felt he could not refuse as, being a government-employed lecturer, he was at the mercy of his employers, who also happened to be the organisers of the festival. The promise of a small honorarium, to be added to his salary at the end of the year, could hardly be viewed as fitting compensation for having lost a chance to earn good money elsewhere.

Of the fourteen days of cultural events which featured in each of the festivals from 1981 to 1984, approximately four evenings were reserved for drama and folk theatre. The remaining evenings were given over to music and dance performances of various kinds. Classical music and dance were featured most, but what can only be described as 'disappointing' numbers of people attended the programmes in 1981, 1982 and 1983. An appearance by Ravi Shankar attracted large crowds in the past, and in 1981 I witnessed a half-full auditorium for another famous sitarist, the late Nikhil Banerjee. Apart from occasions such as these, an average of 150 to 200 people (and, on a rare evening perhaps a few more) were scattered amongst oceans of empty seats. The tent erected for the occasion was capable of housing an audience of around 2,000 to 2,500 when full. Tickets were sold at very reasonable sums, many at as little as one, two, or five rupees each. Still this did not attract the crowds.

As well as the occasional item of light-classical music inserted in a predominantly classical programme, one evening was given over entirely to performances, by several singers, of *g͟hazals*. In stark contrast to the concerts of classical music and dance, these were received by full houses. Another packed house witnessed an evening of *qawwālī* singing which, being a form of Muslim devotional music, attracted an almost exclusively Muslim audience. Few people attending these concerts would also be found attending a concert of classical music.

Much greater interest, however, was generated in the festival of 1984, financed as it was on a scale far greater than in previous years. General attendance for the exhibitions and amusements was greatly increased, and many more people wandered into the tent erected for the music and drama festival. The auditorium was packed to capacity, not only for the evenings of *g͟hazals* and *qawwālī*, but also for many of the concerts of classical music and dance. Even for potentially the least interesting of concerts there were well over a thousand people in attendance. Recent evidence, however, suggests that attendance figures for subsequent festivals have dropped slightly, a trend that bears out the views of the many people I spoke to who felt that 1984 was an exceptional year owing to the greatly increased publicity surrounding the event.

Music societies for the promotion of Indian music, such as the Jnanottejak Mandali in Bombay and the Sangit Samaj in Calcutta, had been created as early as the 1870s (Meer 1980: 123) and their number has grown steadily. The cities of India have a great number of societies, and through the winter season they regularly organise festivals and conferences. In Lucknow, with one exception, there are only a few small organisations, their functions are ill-advertised and ill-funded, and they frequently go unnoticed to all but their members. For South Indian music there is the Andhra Association and the Tamil Sangham, and for North Indian music, the Maharashtra Samaj, the Swar Vihar, and the Jhankar. The largest, most active, and most successful music society in Lucknow is UDCO (the Uttar Dakshin Cultural Organisation), created in 1974. UDCO has the distinction of being recognised by musicians all over India, it having invited most of the country's distinguished musicians and dancers in its relatively short history. Early in 1982 the society had about 200 members, a number that was steadily increasing. Subscriptions, payable annually, were 30 rupees per couple, which entitled members to a discount on tickets plus information about forthcoming events. In addition, a souvenir magazine was published annually, containing photographs and articles on music, sales of which helped the society to remain solvent.

To organise and run the society, there is a managing committee comprising a president, two vice-presidents, a secretary, a treasurer and ten other members. The committee decides on the programmes and selects and invites musicians to perform, acting mainly on the advice of the society's mastermind, Srimati Susheela Misra, the well-known broadcaster and writer on music. Committee meetings are held at least monthly, and sometimes weekly if the annual festival is approaching.

UDCO's annual festival, known as the Tansen–Tyagaraja Festival because it attempts to present both North and South Indian classical music, lasts about five days. In the first years of the society it lasted nine days, but owing to rising costs, mainly the increased fees demanded by performers, economies had to be made. Similarly, whereas the society used to stage an average of five or six concerts each month during the winter season, the number is now down to one or two. Although the society is committed to promoting classical music, calls for some light-music concerts have been made from within the membership. In future, therefore, UDCO may well have to branch out and accede to popular demand. Certainly, it has been losing money on its classical music programmes as a consequence of the same lack of interest which, until 1984, had plagued the Lucknow Festival.

The only musicians in Lucknow to benefit from the activities of the music societies are accompanists. They are booked by the committees on behalf of visiting solo performers who either have no regular accompanist or do not wish to travel with one. The main performers are all 'outsiders', a situation that is partly due to what is seen as a singular lack of talent in Lucknow, as well as *Ghar kī murg͟hī dāl barābar*. The only problem faced by the organisers is how to find talented musicians who also demand moderate fees. Susheela Misra told me that, in some cases, musicians who, only a few years ago were demanding 7,000 rupees, were now asking for 20,000 rupees or more per performance.

Apart from the activities of UDCO and the Lucknow Festival, there are few musical events in Lucknow, making it a frustrating city for musicians who, were they in Delhi, Calcutta or Bombay, might occasionally expect to earn some extra money from public concerts. The Department of Cultural Affairs, very infrequently, organises short concerts of music designed to entertain visiting committees, or groups of businessmen, gathered for a conference in the city. These are contrived affairs where musicians are given a set period in which to complete their items. I happened to overhear an organiser of one such function ask a musician if he would like a signal after eighteen minutes so that the performance would not exceed twenty. The musician declined, preferring to rely on his own watch. On another occasion, a well-known *ṭhumrī* singer was forced into curtailing her performance when the organisers chimed in in the middle of a song with loud applause, the allotted period having been completed.

The Bhatkhande Music College holds an annual festival in which staff, students, and sometimes guest performers, play to an audience largely consisting of other staff members, students and a few parents. The Sangeet Natak Akademi sponsors a number of small concerts in the year, but these are mostly for the benefit of up-and-coming young artists of the city.

A number of light-music concerts take place throughout the year in Lucknow and are invariably well-attended, being infinitely more popular than classical music concerts. This is reflected in the range of commercial recordings to be found at record shops in the city. Shelves of cassettes and records of film music and light-music albums far outnumber the few discs and tapes of classical music.

Private lessons

Private teaching offers to only a very few of Lucknow's musicians some kind of income, though to none does it guarantee a complete livelihood. The simple reason for this is that nearly all the demand for music education is absorbed by the Bhatkhande Music College, which offers approximately 1,300 places for students. Each year a large number of applicants to the College have to be rejected because there are not enough places for all who desire to learn. This surplus demand is not, however, to the advantage of musicians who offer the prospect of private tuition because most parents are only interested in sending their children to the College. The relatively low cost of College courses, the attraction of educational qualifications, and the respectability and security of a governmental institution are some of the reasons for this.

Musicians employed in the College do not, in most cases, have private students. Critics often accuse the College staff of earning a supplementary income by deliberately leaving incomplete the given syllabuses in order to inveigle worried members of their classes into becoming private students, particularly before the annual examinations in December. The staff members are quick to deny this, and I found little evidence to support these claims.

Whereas in Calcutta, Delhi, Bombay and Benares, many musicians can make private teaching their sole, or major, source of income, especially with the large numbers of Western students in those cities, this is quite obviously not possible in Lucknow. Only a small number of the better-known musicians have private students, Afaq Husain having by far the most with between eight and ten at any one time, and not all learn with the same intensity or regularity. Private students are, in nearly all cases, independent young men whose common aim is to become professional musicians. A few students of the Bhatkhande Music College also seek occasional private tuition because of their dissatisfaction with the standards of teaching there and the lack of personal attention.

Payment for lessons is a variable which depends on the financial status of the student, the number of lessons taken, and the needs of the teacher. Lucknow is not comparable to, say, Calcutta, where more demand, interest and money allowed one famous tabla teacher to display a notice on the wall of his music room stating unambiguously 'Fifty rupees per lesson' (in 1981). In Lucknow, payment for about ten lessons monthly, of between thirty minutes and an hour in length, ranges from between one hundred to two hundred rupees. Specific information is difficult to come by because the exact amounts are agreed upon between the teacher and the individual student, always with some degree of secrecy. As for my own payments, it is difficult to assess the exact amounts. Being a Westerner, I was a special case because my research grant constituted a relatively large income. Consequently, I paid according to my teacher's needs. If he required money for his daughter's dowry, for an installment on a motor scooter, for new instruments, or for domestic necessities, he would ask me for a certain amount. In return I had four or five lessons each week. These were of varying length depending on how much time was available: when Afaq Husain was busy I managed only a few minutes here and there, though on many occasions the entire evening would be spent at the tabla and sometimes we would continue deep into the night. In addition to making payments, students are required to offer their services freely: I was called upon to run errands, reserve and buy train tickets, pay for rickshaws or meals, and regularly provide *pān* (betel nut and leaf). I should add that teachers, being of a naturally generous and paternal disposition, very often do not allow their students to pay for everything, instead insisting that they themselves cover certain expenses.

One landmark in the life of a student is his *ganḍā bandhan* ceremony, which elevates him to the status of a close disciple of his teacher. Not all teachers still perform the ceremony, but Afaq Husain believed it remained a significant rite of passage and he therefore insisted on it for those students worthy of the honour. It is important to remember that a musician's sons are thought of firstly as disciples and secondly as sons and therefore, according to the son of Afaq Husain, they too must undergo a *ganḍā bandhan* ceremony. During the ceremony a thread is tied around the student's wrist, symbolising the bond between him and his teacher. The student then makes an offering of money and cloth to the teacher. Again, the amounts paid vary, depending on the financial resources of the student. Anything upwards of 500 rupees is generally offered. This payment is called a *nazrāna*, a term which implies the money is a gift, freely given with the greatest respect, and is not a payment for services rendered, which has a certain indignity about it. The *nazrāna* includes an extra one rupee over and above the rounded figure, be it 501 rupees or 1,001. This convention is believed to signify respect for the teacher. The new disciple must also play in front of those gathered for the ceremony, as must other disciples in order of ability, with the best performing last. The teacher himself is usually requested by his disciples to conclude the occasion with a performance. Having undergone this change of status the new disciple can expect to receive a more intensive training, including techniques and compositions not normally given to those students who have not had a *ganḍā bandhan* ceremony. Further details pertaining to the ceremony may be found in Silver (1984: 317–18) and Shepherd (1976: 54–8).

Those who have undergone the *ganḍā bandhan* ceremony are expected to offer a *nazrāna*, however small, at least once a year to pay homage to their teacher and reaffim their respect, dedication and love. This is usually given on the day of *gurū-pūrnamā*, an annual celebration in honour of all teachers. Afaq Husain visits Calcutta, where he lived for thirteen years, several times each year. On at least one of these occasions a student organises a small, private concert which is attended by a great many of Afaq Husain's students both past and present, and where *nazrānas* are placed at the feet of the *ustād* after he has performed. This represents a supplementary income for Afaq Husain and for many others like him in India who have had a great number of students. It should be stressed that in Lucknow few have the same opportunities as he does for this kind of earning.

Tawā'ifs

From the late eighteenth century onwards, Lucknow was a famous centre for *ṭawā'ifs*: the courtesans who entertained the social elite with their songs, graceful dances and sparkling company. From ancient times, courtesans played an important role in the life of the courts and cities of India (see Chandra 1973). They were accomplished, wealthy and highly respected women who symbolised the greatest artistic refinement. So significant has been their contribution throughout the history of North Indian music that Bor (1984: 1) has written: 'The music and dance of North India could not possibly have developed to such a height without the influence and inspiration of these female artists.'

I knew, when I first went to Lucknow, that *ṭawā'ifs* were largely a phenomenon of the past. Nevertheless, I had a suspicion that somewhere in the labyrinthine lanes and alleyways in the old city there were still a few *ṭawā'ifs* to be found performing, though naturally not in such large numbers as before. Initial enquiries proved my hunch to be correct. Unfortunately, those people from whom I had enquired refused to take me either to witness these performances or to meet the *ṭawā'ifs*. This made it very difficult for me to find out much about these women as people are, or in some cases just pretend to be, shocked at the mere mention of the topic and are therefore reticent. 'My reputation would be worth nothing if I were to be seen entering one of those places', said a friend, adding that I should not contemplate going alone owing to the undoubted presence of 'bad elements' who would no doubt rob me and possibly even knife me. I asked another friend if he had ever visited the house of *ṭawā'if*. He replied that he would never consider going to one in Lucknow in case he was recognised. However, he did admit to visiting *ṭawā'ifs* when away on business in Delhi, Calcutta and Bombay, where he was more anonymous.

As my relationship with Afaq Husain developed, I began to get a more positive response to my questions concerning *ṭawā'ifs* and the musicians who accompany them. He generally praised the *ṭawā'ifs*, saying that many had been excellent *k͟hayāl* and *ṭhumrī* singers in the past, as well as accomplished classical *kathak* dancers. At one time or another, most musicians spent time with them, both teaching them and accompanying their songs and dances. This is especially true of *sāraṅgī* players, who were traditionally responsible for giving the *ṭawā'ifs* their early training (Bor 1984: 3). As for his own family of tabla players, Afaq Husain confirmed that there had always been, until the present generation, a close tie with the families of *ṭawā'ifs* in old Lucknow. Nowadays, only a few *ṭawā'ifs* remain and a small number of musicians find employment with them, though members of Afaq Husain's family are no longer among them. Eventually it was arranged that I should go to meet some *ṭawā'ifs* in Chowk, the old city of Lucknow.

I was taken by Afaq Husain's sister's son (he plays the tabla reasonably well but is not a professional player – he earns a living from embroidering cloth) into the depths of Chowk. We finally arrived in a small alleyway and my guide suddenly disappeared through a tiny doorway. Owing to strict *parda* restrictions I could not follow him and so I remained outside, under the scrutiny of a thousand eyes that peered from behind curtains, through shutters and round doors. My companion returned within a few minutes saying he had asked about the whereabouts of a famous old *ṭawā'if* called Munirbai, and we were now to proceed to her house. On arrival we were viewed with suspicion until I mentioned the fact that we had been sent by Ustad Afaq Husain, at which point we were admitted and hospitably received.

I felt there was a degree of self-justification intended when the very first thing I was told was that *ṭawā'ifs* were different from prostitutes (who went by a number of different names, among them the most common being *peshawālī*, *raṅḍī* and *prās*) and that on no account were the two to be confused. As Bor (1984: 2) has noted, this confusion began as early as the late eighteenth century, when Europeans began to arrive in India in large numbers:

> The term 'dancing girl', as these women were usually referred to by Europeans, naturally included all kinds of professional entertainers, ranging from vulgar bazaar prostitutes to dedicated and talented songstresses ... Yet hardly any of the English or other Europeans appreciated the art of the so-called dancing girls and even less their cultural role in Indian society. In fact, most of them experienced Indian music as rather boring and put the girls on the same level as common prostitutes.

Ṭawā'ifs resent being associated with prostitutes because they operate in a very different way. They are faithful mistresses to anyone rich enough to keep them in relative luxury and wealth. This, however, does not prevent them from performing to others for financial gain. In an interview with Sethi (1983), Maya Devi, a famous *ṭawā'if* of Delhi, told of the official deflowering ceremonies involved in the lives of *ṭawā'ifs*, and is quoted as saying proudly: 'We are tawa'ifs, not peshewallis' (a *peshawālī* corresponds to our use of the word 'professional' as a synonym for prostitute). *Ṭawā'ifs* consider themselves to be artists who learned classical and light-classical vocal styles and were also the disciples of recognised dance masters. Many prostitutes also sing and dance but theirs are Bombay film songs and crude, arousing dances which the *ṭawā'ifs* refer to derogatorily as *nautaṅkī* (an unsophisticated dance, part of a drama with sung dialogue, usually performed at fairs) or *tamāshā* (non-serious entertainment, a spectacle). It is difficult to ascertain whether or not these prostitutes are accompanied by tabla and *sāraṅgī* players. In general, it appears that accompaniment is provided by non-specialist harmonium and *ḍholak* players attached to the brothels.

Ṭawā'ifs trained intensively to become performing singers and dancers of the highest calibre. Munirbai told me:

> We were called *gāyikās* [a respectable term for a female singer]. *Khayāl*, *ṭhumrī*, *dādrā*, *tarāna*, we sang them all. We learned ... from greats *ustāds*. In those days we were considered experts ... Shambu Maharaj taught me dance. Wajid Husain [father of Afaq Husain] played with me, because there was nobody else like him and he was the one who could play this music. Chunnu Khan Sahib taught me singing and so did Mumtaz Khan Sahib.

There are only a handful of *ṭawā'ifs* now left in Lucknow (it is virtually impossible to ascertain the exact figure), but the prostitutes who sing and dance are far more common, as is the case in all the major cities in India. Munirbai attributed the disappearance of the *ṭawā'ifs* to the loss of a knowledgeable clientele: the aristocracy and rich landowners. They not only demanded a high standard of performance in the classical forms of singing and dancing but also paid rich rewards for it. Munirbai told me that the listeners of former days

> were respectable people who were lovers of music ... They were big people, rich and important. The poorer classes weren't able to come here, neither did they have the courage to come ... Whenever [the *nawābs* and rajas] came [to Lucknow] they'd come here. We'd be called regularly to their residences or they'd come to our homes.

It is true that in place of those rich and knowledgeable patrons came the more puritanical middle classes who wished to see an end to *ṭawāʾifs*. But to apportion blame solely in that direction is misleading. Since the early days of colonial rule, the British had instigated repressive measures in a bid to improve general sanitation and to curb the rapid spread of venereal disease (see Oldenburg 1984: 133–44). Later, when classical music and dance began to move to the concert hall, the most musically accomplished *ṭawāʾifs* left their establishments and became celebrated and respected concert artists, notably in *khayāl* and *ṭhumrī*. Less talented women simply turned to prostitution. State repression continued well after Independence and culminated in the 'dramatic "night-raid" of December 1958 in Lucknow, when the police closed the salons and jailed many *ṭawāʾifs*' (Manuel 1986: 479). Consequently, all but a couple of establishments have disappeared, and musical soirées, known as *mujrās*, are held only by those *ṭawāʾifs* who have managed to retain a small and select clientele.

Since Independence, the rapid growth of the film industry and the influence of commercial Bombay movies has led to requests for lighter, more popular forms of music and dance. As another, younger *ṭawāʾif* explained to me:

> Now, of course, the influence of the films is everywhere. It's my fault too because compared to [Munirbai] I know nothing, I've learned nothing, so what can I possibly demonstrate to you? In the old days *khayāl*, *ṭhumrī*, *ghazal*, *dādrā*, that kind of singing was there. And now if one begins to sing a *ghazal* people say: 'What's this? Why don't you sing us a film song?'

Traditionally, musicians were also to be found in the same area of the city as the *ṭawāʾifs*, as were the prostitutes who used to tout for business from balconies overlooking the shops in the bazaar. A few musicians are still to be found there though many, like my *ustād*, have moved to other areas of the city. There is employment for a small number of musicians, mostly tabla players, *sāraṅgī* players and harmonium players, although I also met a young sitarist who was engaged as an accompanist at the house of a *ṭawāʾif*. I tried to ascertain whether or not these musicians had any other sources of income but it proved very difficult to get information. I know of a *sāraṅgī* player who is an accompanist in a teaching institution. I was told he also earns money by accompanying *ṭawāʾifs* in the evenings, but for him to admit so might cause an outcry of indignation and might possibly lose him his official job. The same would be true of a number of lecturers and accompanists in the Bhatkhande Music College who hail from Benares. It is said by other lecturers, in whispers of course, that on returning to their native city during the vacations, these musicians derive a supplementary income from accompanying the *ṭawāʾifs* and prostitutes of that city. (One never knows just how much these may be malicious rumours.)

The music of the *ṭawāʾifs* and dancing girls represents a very small part of the musical life of Lucknow. In Calcutta, I was able to observe that musicians gathered much more openly and freely in the Bow Bazaar area of the city renowned for its *ṭawāʾifs* and prostitutes. I noticed that, just before dark, dozens of musicians met in 'hotels' (more like tea-houses), the *sāraṅgī* players among them leaving their instruments propped-up in one corner. Here they were drinking tea and chatting to their friends before leaving for their evening's work. Most musicians were freelance and only rarely was one retained on a regular basis by a *ṭawāʾif*. A musician can earn money in two ways: firstly, from 'tuitions', where he may expect to earn 100 rupees by giving twelve to fifteen lessons each month to a *ṭawāʾif*, and secondly, from accompanying in the *mujrās*. Here tabla players, *sāraṅgī* players and harmonium players each take one-eighth part of that earned by a *ṭawā'if*. In most cases, a *ṭawā'if* will earn 200 rupees per hour for singing, and 300 rupees if she is also required to dance. On the rare occasions when a renowned musician is asked to accompany a *ṭawā'if* (it used to be very common) his share may be one-fifth or greater.

After dark, as I strolled around the Bow Bazaar, the air was full of melody and gave one a little taste of old Lucknow as portrayed by Ruswa in *Umrao Jan Ada*. The jingling of bells and the beating of drums came from all directions, testifying to the extent of this kind of musical activity in Calcutta. Before climbing the flights of stairs to large rooms scattered with comfortable cushions, those seeking admission had to pass a number of men who stood guard, ready to expel anyone who might be considered undesirable. Judging by the crowds of would-be listeners, there is enough work to sustain a relatively large community of musicians in Calcutta. One *sāraṅgī* player, giving a conservative estimate, claimed that about 150 musicians are able to earn a living wage from this occupation alone.

3 *The social relationships of musicians*

Living and meeting in Lucknow

Little information is available concerning the geographical organisation of musicians in Lucknow in the past. Edwardes (1960: 28) quotes an early nineteenth-century report which explains how a 'landlord may assign a piece of land to four or five prostitutes and their musicians on condition that they performed every year'. The majority of these 'prostitutes' (i.e. *ṭawā'ifs*) were centred in and around the Chowk Bazaar (see Map 2) and so a large and close-knit community of musicians, especially the tabla players and *sāraṅgī* players who coached and accompanied the *ṭawā'ifs*, developed in the area.

The earliest reference to the location of musicians' houses was given by members of the Lucknow tabla *gharānā*, who claim that their forefather and founder member, Miyan Bakhshu Khan, was rewarded with land, including a small village, in return for his services as a tabla player to the court of Nawab Asaf-ud-daula. The village was situated just south of the river Gomti on the western edge of the old city. Present *gharānā* members no longer recall its name ('It was a long time ago!'), although they assume the village was firstly absorbed into the city as Lucknow expanded in the early nineteenth century, and later confiscated and razed to the ground along with all the surrounding areas after 1858.

It was probably during those years of upheaval that the grandson of Miyan Bakhshu Khan, Mammad Khan, moved into the heart of the old city. He established his residence in Mehmood Nagar, an area just to the south of Akbari Gate, which marks the southern entrance to the Chowk Bazaar. Successive generations continued to live in the area and possessed property both in Mehmood Nagar and Hammam Wali Gali, a street adjacent to Akbari Gate. The latter property was retained until about 1970, at which time present family members moved to the Shish Mahal and Muftiganj areas to the north-west of Chowk.

Adjacent to Gol Darwaza, the gate standing at the northern entrance to the Chowk Bazaar, lived the other main family of tabla players in the city during the mid-nineteenth century. They had been rewarded for their services to the court with a large *koṭhī* (mansion) roughly where the Chowk police station is situated today. It is not clear who awarded the *koṭhī* to the musicians or when, but Akbar Husain, a descendant of this family, believes it may have been a gift from Nawab Wajid Ali Shah around 1850. The word Kothiwal (*wāl*: a suffix indicating possession) came to be used to distinguish these musicians from those of the other main family of tabla players in Lucknow. However it seems likely that the Kothiwal musicians abandoned their *koṭhī* and migrated from Lucknow after 1858 in search of fresh patronage.

Not all musicians lived in Chowk. It is recorded that the famous singer Haideri Khan lived in Golaganj about two kilometres to the east of Chowk (Sharar 1975: 135). The current head of the Lucknow *kathak gharānā*, Birju Maharaj, told me that further east still, also within the Aminabad area, property was given to his ancestors Bindadin and Kalka Prasad Maharaj.

This may suggest that there was something of a geographical division between accompanists and soloists, the former being concentrated largely within the Chowk area near the *ṭawā'ifs*, and the latter outside it, though conclusions are difficult to draw on such scant evidence.

The prospect of generous patronage from the aristocracy in the late nineteenth and early twentieth centuries and, to a lesser degree, the establishment of the Marris College of Music, in 1926 (later the Bhatkhande Music College), and the Lucknow branch of All India Radio, in 1938, attracted a great many musicians to Lucknow. Few immigrants had family ties with those musicians already living in Lucknow and the tendency was for the newcomers to settle in different areas of the city. However, the aristocratic patronage of music rapidly disappeared in the years leading up to Independence, causing an exodus of all kinds of musicians. Most fled to the big cities, whose musical 'fields' were expanding as rapidly as Lucknow's was shrinking. *Ṭawā'ifs* were being forced either to abandon their traditional profession or to settle elsewhere. This forced many tabla and *sāraṅgī* players from Chowk to move to Bombay and Calcutta, where, in the surviving communities of *ṭawā'ifs*, work could still be found. Those musicians who remained in Lucknow were scattered widely throughout the city. As a result, there is no longer a concentration of musicians in any one area.

Since Independence, Lucknow has witnessed both the rapid increase of its population and the expansion of its territory. New 'colonies', or housing estates, have sprung up to create a rambling, ugly suburbia, particularly to the north of the river Gomti. Inner-city development has been somewhat restricted in the crowded labyrinths of the city centre, although the government has sponsored the construction of large, modern flats for its employees, for instance in the Qaiserbagh area close to the Bhatkhande Music College. Several of these flats are allocated to staff members of the College. Those who have benefited from the scheme have been professors and assistant professors, who apparently have gained precedence over low-status employees in the College. The fact that they live in the inner city gives them a further boost to their social rank in the eyes of most observers. One not untypical junior lecturer living several kilometres from the city centre expressed his envy of colleagues who enjoyed comfortable, modern, centrally located and rent-controlled accommodation.

It is almost impossible to speculate on the nature of meetings between musicians in the past. However, I spent much of my time in Lucknow observing how modern social intercourse worked. Musicians related by blood, or sharing the same teacher or *gharānā* tradition, met frequently if they lived in close proximity. On the other hand, if they lived further apart meetings were restricted to a special occasion, such as a wedding, or a *ganḍā bandhan* ceremony for a student, or a *daʿwat* (feast) in someone's honour. However, during the years I spent in Lucknow, I was aware that only rarely did unrelated musicians visit each other to pursue a casual relationship. A junior lecturer at the Bhatkhande Music College was, I believe, as unconvinced by the reason he gave for this as I was:

> I try to meet people and find a place to sit and talk and so on, but I live so far away. I sometimes meet up with others in some music function or other. Then people say: 'Why haven't you been to visit me?', and you yourself ask them the same question. Anyway, everyone is immersed in his own work.

Inevitably musicians who appeared in the same concert met backstage. However, I was always struck by the fact that very few musicians attended concerts in Lucknow as listeners. Of those who did attend, only one or two were genuine enthusiasts, while the rest simply put in an appearance out of a sense of duty to their family, friends or colleagues. For instance, whenever the professor of tabla at the Bhatkhande Music College performed, all the lecturers and junior lecturers under him were present in the audience. My teacher only attended concerts in order to meet old friends he had not seen for years and invite them to a *da'wat* in their honour. But having carried out this duty, Afaq Husain rarely remained until the end of the concert.

The reason so few musicians attended concerts is simple, according to Susheela Misra. 'Musicians', she said, 'think it's their birthright to be invited free. You'll hardly find the professional artists in our UDCO programmes, because they say "You give us a pass!" We have no passes for anybody, no matter who they are.' This view certainly seems justified in the light of the tabla player Shital Prasad Misra's reason for attending so few of the concerts in the 1983 Lucknow Festival: 'I might have gone more if I'd been given a pass which allows you to come and go as you please . . . [However] I went to see my friends who were performing.'

I would suggest that the real underlying reasons why musicians rarely attend concerts and hardly ever visit each other are the same. I noticed in my informants an acute awareness of two factors which most affect the social relationships of musicians in India: hierarchy and politics. These two topics will be dealt with in greater detail in the ensuing sections of this chapter.

Social rank among musicians, Hindus and Muslims alike, is based on a complex combination of factors. But suffice it to say that most musicians are acutely aware that they are either equal to, higher than, or lower than, other musicians in the hierarchy, in the same way that Indians are aware of their relative position in the general social hierarchy. It is just 'not done' to visit a person of lower social rank as this would be deemed undignified and a possible compromise of one's position within the hierarchy. However, to visit a person of higher social rank may appear so deferential that it verges on the sycophantic. Thus the musician's strong sense of personal and professional pride prevents him from indulging in a wide range of friendly relationships.

Of course, it may be the intention of a person to cultivate a relationship because he has an ulterior motive in mind. By visiting another musician, being deferential, or demonstrating an allegiance, one may ultimately benefit in some way from the help or influence of that person. It may be expedient to form a network of allegiances with a view to motivating this group so that it may advance its members' interests. The group may already exist as a corporate group such as a *gharānā*. Alternatively, it may be an ephemeral group with an unspecified membership. Whatever its nature, musicians owe their allegiance to some kind of group. Such groups are restrictive and virtually rule out any possibility of friendly relations with other groups. For a musician to visit a member of another group or to attend his concert would be viewed with considerable suspicion. I have myself had some experience of this. Before the nature of my research was fully understood by Afaq Husain and other Lucknow tabla *gharānā* members, I found myself under suspicion for having visited and interviewed a tabla player of another *gharānā*. Their attitude was: 'What are you doing? He's not one of us!' It is therefore with these attitudes in mind that we should consider Shital Prasad Misra's statement: 'I went to see my friends who were performing.'

Naturally a musician can choose whether or not to visit another musician or attend his concert, but he is compelled to go to work in order to earn a living. Therefore the most common meeting ground for musicians is their place of work. At AIR or the television centre, small clusters of musicians gather in their spare time to chat and drink cups of tea in the canteens. One by one people drift away as they are scheduled to rehearse, broadcast or record, and the remaining artists are joined by others returning from the studios. An informative account of the interaction of musicians in AIR Delhi is given in Neuman (1980: 180–2). At the Bhatkhande Music College and its neighbour, the Uttar Pradesh Sangeet Natak Akademi, teachers and accompanists mill around, form small clusters, and wander across the road to one of the three tea-shops opposite, or take *pān* and cigarettes from a nearby vendor. Here, meetings are brief but frequent, with teachers taking any opportunity to break between classes. But as one lecturer, Krishna Kumar Kapoor, told me: 'When artists get together and talk, they don't discuss music.' Topics of conversation more commonly range from motor cycles to the latest situation in a cricket or hockey match. Ostensibly the relationships of musicians are amicable, though underneath the public mask of amity are concealed much deeper sentiments.

The variables that influence social rank

One of the all-pervading aspects of Indian culture is hierarchy (see Dumont 1972), and one's social rank within the hierarchy dictates, to a large degree, set patterns of social behaviour towards other people. Social rank may be based on many different criteria and can be extremely complex to determine. Two people may have different social ranks despite identical criteria applying to both individuals because, in the final account, much can be accredited to certain indefinable qualities of character which affect one person's standing in the eyes of another. This is important because, although we may be able to sketch the outline of a hierarchy, its details may give us problems. Hierarchy is relative, and therefore two people may have varying conceptions of its structure depending on their different perspectives. The 'modern common sense' example of hierarchy given by Dumont (1972: 104) – of '"Military hierarchy", the artificial construction of progressive subordination from commander-in-chief to private soldier' as an example of 'systematically graduated authority' – is therefore unworkable with reference to musicians. In the music world not all lieutenants will necessarily be considered subordinate to all captains.

Exactly how one individual of a relatively lower social rank acts towards someone higher than himself, or vice versa, varies considerably from person to person. Social etiquette dictates that the behaviour of a subordinate towards someone of higher rank should be deferential. Deference can be manifest in many ways: by the touching of feet; by speaking only when spoken to; by taking up a sitting or standing position slightly behind, or at a respectable distance from, one's superior; by small acts of courtesy such as the opening of doors or rising as a superior enters or wishes to leave a room, to mention but a very few. The behaviour of a person of higher rank to a subordinate is commonly marked by a distancing or aloofness, and can often be patronising or condescending.

In order to discover the structure of any hierarchy, one might take an etic approach and observe closely the ways in which individuals interact, noting carefully any instances of deferential or condescending behaviour. This might well prove more objective and accurate than an emic approach to the problem, because people's opinions of the hierarchy may be twisted as a result of prejudice of jealousy. I have often witnessed X venomously attacking his absent rival Y in private, only to show him the utmost respect and deference in an ensuing public meeting. But assuming we are able to establish relative social rank by observing who defers to whom, we are still left with the problem of determining the reasons for precedence.

These reasons may be analysed in terms of a number of variables, and these variables fall into two categories: those which, it could be argued, apply to Indian culture in general, and those specific to the state of being a musician.

General cultural variables

There are many factors that can be included in this category, of which religious affiliation, caste and employment are the most important. Secondary to these are the factors of age, living conditions, and education.

A person's religious affiliation provides him/her with a built-in bias towards his/her fellow members which may affect his/her judgement of rank. Muslims, for instance, are often guilty of vilifying Hindus, possibly out of a sense of insecurity in a society politically and culturally dominated by the latter. I heard many bitter complaints about how Hindus had 'taken over' the music world, and yet were such poor musicians. On the other hand, I have heard a Hindu tabla player assert (also not untypically) that 'Muslims can't play tabla!', thereby making the religious bias mutual.

Social rank determined by caste applies not only to the highly stratified Hindu society but also to the theoretically egalitarian Muslim society in India which, in practice, displays many similarities to the Hindu caste system. (For a very interesting summary of the arguments for and against caste in Muslim society, see Ahmad 1973.) In the same way that Brahmins are considered higher in social rank than Kshatriyas, so those Muslim 'castes' that trace their origin to outside India are considered higher than those of Indian origin, whose ancestors converted to Islam in India. At the top of the Muslim hierarchy are the Sayyids, who trace their ancestry to the prophet Muhammad. The Sayyids are followed by the Sheikhs, Mughals and Pathans, who trace their lineages to Arabia, Persia, Turkestan and Afghanistan. Further down the hierarchy are converts from high Hindu castes, 'clean occupational castes' and the 'untouchables' (Ansari 1960: 35–51). As will be seen later, this has added significance in a musical context owing to the fact that certain 'castes' continued their old occupational specialisations while others adopted new ones. This determined the musical role of an individual as well as his instrumental specialisation.

Rank entitles musicians employed in institutions, such as the Bhatkhande Music College, to a certain degree of official authority and responsibility. As such they are no different from any other government office or private company. At the College, the principal has under him professors and assistant professors, lecturers and junior lecturers, while accountable to all are the accompanists. For those employed by AIR or the Doordarshan Kendra, rank carries no similar official authority. There grades dictate pay scales for both 'staff' and 'casual' artists, and a grade is awarded following a critical appreciation of a musician's ability. Thus higher grades imply that superior rank is not only based on higher income but also on the prestige derived from being a 'better' musician.

Seniority according to age is an important factor in Indian culture, but it can be a misleading one. It is normally secondary to caste considerations, or to positions held in employment, although social etiquette demands that there will always be a measure of respect accorded by the young to the old. For example, a young Brahmin will be considered of higher social rank than an old Kshatriya, and an old lecturer will be subordinate to a younger professor. Age only becomes a determining factor of precedence when all else is equal: caste, rank in employment and musical specialisation.

The area of residence and the living conditions of individuals are, like age, used to determine social rank only when other conditions prove equal. It is evidently more prestigious to live in a smart comfortable, suburban bungalow surrounded by a lush garden, or alternatively in a spacious, modern, government flat in the city centre, than to live in a broken-down hovel in the dirty and crowded old city. These extremes are well reflected in the living conditions of musicians in Lucknow.

Although, in strictest confidence, a very small number of musicians have expressed a contempt for female artists because of the very fact that they are females, I have never found sex to be important as a basis for ranking individuals in the hierarchy of musicians. Although, in Indian society, opportunities for a woman to follow a vocation are severely limited by her expected domestic role, great respect is usually accorded any woman who actually achieves competence, especially in the arts. Women are highly regarded in the realms of music, poetry and literature and are not normally considered subordinate to men.

The final factor that is often cited as a reason for precedence in Indian culture in general is education. Highly prized in Indian society, education brings greater opportunity to the individual. This is undoubtedly to the detriment of the older generation of musicians, many of whom are illiterate or have the bare minimum of formal education. There is a tendency for the new patrons of music, the middle-class public, to respond more generously towards musicians who share their values and standards. For them, educational qualifications are clearly most desirable. Thus members of the younger generation of musicians are aiming to prove themselves educated and versatile as they realise how important a contributing factor this will be to their social rank. According to Susheela Misra, musicians of this generation are

> very polished people . . . well informed about various subjects . . . if you invite them to dinner they will talk about anything. Originally, musicians could talk about nothing but their own subject . . . Shiv Kumar Sharma is an M.A., and so are many others. They are all graduates, whether they make use of their degrees or not. For example, this Malika Sarabai, who's coming [to Lucknow soon], she's a dancer essentially, but she's got a degree in management. And she's a philosophy doctorate! All these are assets, don't you think?

Specific musical variables

The second category under discussion, that of variables specific to the state of being a musician, involves two factors which have an important bearing on the social rank of the individual. One is musical specialisation – what one plays; the other is musical expertise – how one plays.

Musicians are divided into two categories of specialisation which reflect their major functions in music-making. One category is 'soloists', musicians who create the melody, and the other is 'accompanists', who either provide an echoing secondary melodic line (traditionally *sāraṅgī* players but increasingly harmonium players) or provide the rhythmic element in the music (tabla players). The social identities of these two categories are quite separate: the identity of soloist carries prestige, while that of accompanist carries a stigma. Hence accompanists may well attempt to change their identity by becoming soloists but the reverse is never true (see Neuman 1974, 1980). Of course an accompanist may perform a solo musical item, a *sāraṅgī* or tabla solo for instance, but although in these cases the musical role has changed, the social identity of the musicians has not.

The soloist has a musically high status: he is responsible for all the major musical decisions made during a performance, such as regulating the tuning of the accompanist, deciding the metric cycle in which a composition is to be played, establishing the tempo, allocating slots for the accompanist's solo sections, and determining the beginning and end of the performance (Neuman 1980: 138–9). The accompanist is subservient to the soloist and has a musically low status. The soloist also has a socially high status: traditionally, soloists were hereditary musicians from high-caste backgrounds who had no kinship ties with the families of accompanists. Accompanists were recruited from low castes and were, in former days, closely associated with *ṭawā'ifs* and prostitutes, a fact responsible for the stigma that still lingers on today.

There are, of course, exceptions to the rule. Neuman (1980: 141) has noted that a 'famous accompanist and "novice" soloist performing together will normally exhibit the structured status relationship, although the potential for conflict is easily manifest'. In practice, I have often witnessed a situation where the roles have been reversed. For instance, when a famous tabla accompanist deigns to play with a 'novice' he almost certainly assumes a number of the musicial decisions in the performance: he regulates the tuning of his own instrument and accepts no advice; he makes gestures to regulate the tuning of the soloist; he allows himself as much time as he wishes for his own solo sections; and he impatiently interrupts the solo sections of the soloist if he so desires.

Many accompanists, especially *sāraṅgī* players, have become soloists by simply switching from their instrument to vocal performance. This change is traceable to the early twentieth century. Furthermore, the recruitment of musicians nowadays is from a much wider base, particularly the non-hereditary middle classes. Although such changes mean that soloists can no longer, in all cases, boast of their high-caste ancestry unpolluted by the blood of accompanists, the associations of social superiority remain. Musical authority has, of course, been kept firmly in the hands of the soloists by the very nature of the musical performance structure itself.

Turning now to musical expertise, the immediate problem we face is how to obtain objective judgements of a musician's ability which rank him above or below his fellow musicians. One often hears 'He is the best', or 'She is better than him', but these statements exhibit little more than a personal preference which may be based on a whole complex of prejudices. It is agreed among musicians, scholars and listeners alike that, in general, grades awarded to musicians by AIR represent a broadly accurate appreciation of musical ability. But few individuals are content with their own grade and every musician has at least one complaint concerning some injustice in the system. Therefore, remembering that any hierarchy of musicians is subjective, we should not attempt to fix social rank just as we would not, I think, attempt to rank performers of Western classical music. Music competitions are common in India, as they are in the West, but rarely does the result satisfy everyone. Any subsequent ranking should be seen as one of many possible views of a hierarchy based on musical expertise.

Musicians are always polite in public about a fellow musician's performance and are ready and willing to give praise, even when they obviously do not mean what they say. In private, however, they give vent to their likes and dislikes by placing others into one of three main categories: good (*acchā*), bad (*bekār* – lit. useless) or indifferent (*ṭhīk* – lit. fine, OK). A musician will also often pass comments which refer to specific aspects of a performer's ability. I shall give here a few of the most typical comments.

Clear articulation in an instrumentalist has provoked the response *Un kā hath bahut ṣāf hai* (His hand is very clear); rapidity of articulation has been referred to as *Voh bahut ṭaiyār hai* (He is very fast); and a person who sings or plays a melodic instrument and makes a pleasant sound would be called a *bahut surīlā ādmī* (a very melodious person), though if he were a drummer, the comment might be *Un kā hāth bahut mīṭhā hai* (His hand is very sweet). But these remarks do not necessarily imply that one likes a performer who is *surīlā*, or would rank one musician whose hand was *ṣāf* above another whose hand was *ṣāf nahīṅ* (not clear). It may happen that one person, though conscious of clear articulation, attaches less significance to it than he does to, say, melodiousness or sweetness. Another musician with a different perspective may hold the opposite opinion.

More helpful than subjective statements of ability are observations of certain conditions which provide substitute criteria for the assessment of musical expertise and therefore social rank. To refer to these substitute criteria when judging a musician is to assume a level of competence on the part of the performer, not necessarily apparent in reality. The most important of these criteria is the degree to which an individual is connected with a *gharānā*: a group of hereditary musical specialists with a body of knowledge and a distinct musical style. The highest social rank is accorded the head of the *gharānā*, known as the *khalīfa*, who will normally be the oldest performing authority on the *gharānā*'s repertoire and style. Other members of the *khāndān* (family), the musical inheritors, will also carry this pedigree, as will eminent students (i.e. non-related members) of the *gharānā*, as they have greatest access to this specialised knowledge. Approval or acknowledgement of an artist such as 'Ah yes, he is a *khāndānī* artist' or 'he is a *gharānedār* [lit. having the *gharānā*] artist' is common. The terms *khāndānī* and *gharānedār* are often used interchangeably, but *gharānedār* is applicable to eminent students of the *gharānā* as well as blood relatives, whereas *khāndānī* only applies to the latter.

The remaining substitute criteria are connected with where and with whom one has played. If one is a tabla player or *sāraṅgī* player, then to have accompanied one of the great masters of the past or present has a definite prestige value. Soloists 'collect' famous tabla players, and are ready to reel off a list of those who have accompanied them. The greater the accompanist (and it is important to remember that a musician's greatness invariably increases after his death) the more prestige for the soloist. Many musicians are admired when they relate stories of how they have been accompanied on the tabla by Ahmadjan Thirakwa, who died in 1976, one of the legendary figures of the past. Some musicians tell of having been billed in the same concert as a famous artist, and all refer to their performances or tours which have taken place outside Lucknow or even, in a few cases, abroad.

From an exploration of the variables that influence social rank it may be seen how complex the structures of hierarchy can be among musicians. On the one hand the difference in social rank between individuals can act as a barrier to social relationships of a friendly nature. This can lead to, or reinforce, the isolation of individuals or groups and can help to foster sentiments of mistrust, jealousy, animosity and disdain. On the other hand we may look at hierarchy as a vertical structure of authority and note how it may prove beneficial to cultivate relationships in order to exploit the power and influence wielded by members of high social rank.

'Politics': competition and conflict among musicians

The English world 'politics' is a term widely used in the world of Indian music to refer to contests among musicians to gain power, power which may be realised in terms of fame, money and the wider propagation of a musical style. In the eyes of most, these are the constituents of success. From discussions with many musicians, and from careful observations of how they used the word, I have defined 'politics' in the following way. It describes any act aimed at influencing the beliefs or decisions of other people unfairly with a view to advancing one party's interests to the detriment of another party or parties. It can be an act by one person or by a group of people with common interests. With the group in mind, my informants sometimes referred to politics as *grūp-bāzī*, which literally means 'group-play'. It is recognised that by aligning himself with a group an individual may, in certain circumstances, more effectively achieve his ends. He may benefit from the help and support of other group members, for example in securing jobs or opportunities to perform using the network of contacts already established by the group. He may also be less vulnerable to personal victimisation by other individuals or groups seeking to destroy the reputations and careers of their rivals.

Politics as such is nothing new, though as far as the Indian music world is concerned the word appears to have gained currency within the past two generations. Man's ambition for success and power means that, to some degree or other, individual and inter-group rivalry is intrinsic to any population. What is interesting in the Indian context is that the emphasis of this rivalry has shifted from competition of a purely musical nature in the past to competition largely of a non-musical nature in the present, or so we are led to believe. Accompanying this shift, allegations of corruption, manoeuvring and intrigue have become increasingly common, particularly since Independence. Thus politics has come to mean a certain kind of competition which involves stratagems, conspiracies and foul play; where the rules of the game are unknown, unfair or are conveniently replaced by new ones. In contrast, a straightforward musical duel between musicians, as was apparently common in the past, would not be considered as politics because all concerned, musicians and audience alike, understood that the purpose of the musical event was to compete. In other words, everyone knew the rules of the game. The words for a competition of this kind were *muqābala* (lit. competition) or *dangal* (lit. arena, especially one for wrestling matches).

There are numerous examples of competition between musicians in former times, the majority taking the form of a staged contest where those concerned would battle for supremacy like the elephants, tigers and quails of the *nawābs*. This was often seen as an amusement as much as anything, with musicians attempting to defeat one another by performing longer, faster and technically more brilliantly, and by displaying a more profound knowledge of the music. The following account concerning the legendary *kathak* dancer Bindadin Maharaj as a child, is just one such example. Here the story is set in the Lucknow court around the mid-1850s, but, in common with a great many stories, it is merely another version of a tale that has cropped up throughout history in different guises, the earliest reference being the *Guttila-Jataka* from the Pali Jatakas of the fourth century BC (see Cowell 1895: 172–8), in which events from the Buddha's former births are described:

The head of the Lucknow *kathak gharānā*, Durga Prasadji, was in the service of the King, from whom he received a pension for each of his male offspring. Also employed in the court was a great *pakhāwaj* player who was jealous because, unlike the dancer, he received no pension from the King. Thus he complained. The King decided there should be a contest between Durga Prasadji and the *pakhāwajī*. If the *pakhāwajī* were to win he would be rewarded with Durga Prasadji's pension, but were he to lose he would forfeit his hands.

When Durga Prasadji heard about this he became very worried. He feared that he might lose the contest as he was no longer as young and agile as he used to be. The ignominy of defeat and the loss of his pension would surely bring about the end of the Lucknow *kathak gharānā*.

Durga Prasadji's gifted seven-year-old son Bindadin Maharaj also heard about the contest, and he pleaded with his father to allow him to compete against the *pakhāwajī* instead. Durga Prasadji finally agreed, and Bindadin prepared for the contest by practising only one element of *kathak* dance, *tatkār* (footwork), for one month.

The day of the contest arrived and everyone gathered in the court in an atmosphere of tremendous excitement. Bindadin immediately began to dance at a fast speed and the *pakhāwajī* accompanied him accordingly. After twenty hours of continuous dancing and playing throughout the day and night neither had the upper hand. The King had by this time become rather restless and hungry. Noticing this, Bindadin suddenly doubled his speed and continued to increase it for the next four hours. He ultimately danced at so great a speed that it appeared he was floating a few inches off the ground. At this point the *pakhāwajī*, exhausted and confused, lost track of the *tāl* and everyone realised Bindadin had won the contest and had saved his *gharānā*.

The King summoned Durga Prasadji and told him to name his reward. Durga Prasadji said: 'I want nothing but that you spare the hands of the *pakhāwajī*.' Much to everyone's relief the wish was granted and the embarrassed and defeated *pakhāwajī* disappeared from public view for some considerable time.

Such accounts of past events, if taken literally, tell us very little about what music was like in former times and reveal nothing of the social relationships of musicians and other kinds of rivalry that may possibly have gone on behind the scenes. It does not take a musically sophisticated audience to recognise that one musician has triumphed over another by sustaining a greater speed for a longer period of time. But we should not understand this example in these terms alone. Rather, we should see it as an allegory, an immediate and tangible symbol of more complex and subtle musical elements used in competition, such as intricate techniques, the ability to memorise and reproduce compositions, and the ability to improvise on a given theme, to name but a few features that appear in such stories. However, these stories do tell us more about the present-day musicians who relate them and of their perception of competition as it was in the past as compared to competition now. The primary purpose of relating such stories may well be one of self-promotion: by praising the greatness of one's forefathers one is indirectly claiming high artistic pedigree for oneself. This, of course, can be used as a kind of politics in itself. Another purpose is to draw our attention to the sharp contrast between musical competition and the now more prevalent non-musical competition, in other words the politics, that characterises relationships between musicians.

I collected a large amount of data on politics during my time in Lucknow, a fact which, I believe, reflects the importance of the subject in the minds of musicians. Musicians tend to view the cities in which they live as being rife with politics, and the musicians of Lucknow are no exception. As a reason for so much politics in the musical life of the city, people point to the fact that there is relatively little opportunity to earn a living. Competition is therefore fierce for any opportunities that do arise in Lucknow.

There were many problems encountered in collecting this data which arose out of the sensitive nature of the topic itself. Naturally, no musician would ever have admitted to acting either alone, or in coalition with others, in an underhand manner. Yet everyone I spoke to could relate stories of foul play which had affected them or their acquaintances. The information, however, was not easily obtained: there was a genuine fear on the part of all but the most outspoken of my informants as they wanted to be sure in their own minds that I would not use the information they gave me in a way that would bring retribution on them at a future date from those about whom they spoke. The more I became trusted, the more data I was able to collect, but few informants were willing to allow themselves to be recorded for fear that tapes might fall into the wrong hands. Before narrating one story, an informant stopped and said: 'It is difficult to put it on record because it may land me in a ditch. It may start legal cases for defamation of names [i.e. character] . . . I don't want to mention names.' More often than not, I was ordered to switch off the tape recorder altogether.

Thus the problem of ethics arises in the reporting of instances of politics. Should data of a sensitive nature be reported at all and, if so, then in what way? I fail to see any advantage in raking up stories that are potentially damaging to individuals. After all, they may not be true. Thus my intention here is simply to discuss some of the stratagems that are resorted to in the Indian music world and to offer an explanation for the apparent shift in the emphasis of competition from *muqābala* to politics. For illustration, I have chosen examples of which some are common knowledge in Indian music circles while others are typical of stories one can hear in any city in India. As nearly all the information was given to me in the strictest confidence my first duty is to protect the identities of my informants. I also realise that to expose the identities of those involved in the following examples would not only be ruinous to my relationship with musicians in India but would also create considerable ill-feeling within the musicians' community.

Acts seen to be 'political' in nature can be divided into two categories: those within the context of the musical performance, and those outside it. I shall begin by dealing with acts outside the context of the musical performance.

Politics outside musical performance

Those wielding power within the music world, whether they be government officers, concert organisers or famous musicians, have constantly to contend with attempts to influence their decisions. In most cases they are approached by sycophants ruthlessly chasing favours. An agent may be offered favours in return for assisting a musician. A musician may ingratiate himself with a famous artist or concert organiser, flatter him, perform small tasks, bribe him, even offer his musical services free in order to establish himself firmly in the music world. I have also heard of musicians playing gratis for government ministers and officials at their residences, or offering free music coaching for their children, all in return for recommendations for jobs or inclusion in government-sponsored cultural delegations to be sent abroad. Many musicians condemn acts such as these (while realising their efficacy) saying those who do these things have 'sold their *'izzat* (honour, pride)'.

Other methods rely essentially on the spoken word to convey a message of either promotion or derogation. I follow Paine's view (1970) that the messages of promotion and derogation are both types of gossip or rumour: both may be factually true or untrue, and both may be sent out concerning oneself as well as others. It is recognised that there is a great deal of overlap between the terms gossip and rumour. However, Paine distinguishes gossip as information passed on through a 'signed chain', in other words the identity of the originator of the message is known, while rumour is passed on through an 'unsigned chain' in order to reduce the risk of the identity of the originator of the information being discovered. In some of the following examples, situations are complex and involve both gossip and rumour.

The Public Services Commission comes in for much criticism in Lucknow. The Commission is seen by many to misuse its powers, especially in connection with the selection of performers at the annual Lucknow Festival. There are many allegations, some appearing in local newspapers, of members inviting their friends to perform each year, whether or not they are in public demand. The following case is one that was talked of a good deal in Lucknow:

> The wife of an influential member of the subcommittee of the Public Services Commission, being a singer of light music, desired to enter into the world of the Bombay films as a 'playback singer', a singer of film songs. The film music industry, though highly competitive and difficult to enter, offers considerable opportunities to accumulate wealth and to become famous. Being responsible for choosing artists to perform in the Lucknow Festival, the subcommittee was influenced into inviting certain musicians who could in turn help this singer by recommending her to their known contacts in the film world.

The Public Services Commission is also implicated in the following example. It is a case which shows the important part a group can play in politics. This group was alleged to comprise staff members of a teaching institution who came originally from another city in North India. The group is widely believed to be the most 'politically' active in the city:

> A post fell vacant at a music institution in Lucknow. There were several applicants for the job, including one from another city who was known to be related to at least one lecturer teaching in the institution at the time. The auditions and interviews for the job were suddenly and unexpectedly postponed for one month, the reason being, it was widely alleged, that the candidate in question was unable to attend the auditions on the set date. Suspicion centred around activities by a group in the institution whose members hailed from the same city. Their intention was to obtain a postponement so that their candidate could attend a future audition and ultimately be selected for the job. A disgusted informant, also connected with the institution, said: 'It's quite obvious who's going to get that post eventually!'

But groups such as the one mentioned here present us with a problem in that my informants never seemed to agree on their precise membership. Unless a particular group is also identified as a *gharānā*, we are not dealing with corporate groups as such, for they lack a defined structure and do not appear to be permanent. Groups are usually no more than expedient allegiances formed between people with a common interest. The allegiances may change according to circumstances. A group may comprise a few friends, or a teacher and his disciples, or kinsmen, or even musicians from the same city or area, and it may take on an imagined formal structure in the minds of observers, particularly those musicians affected by the actions of the group whose main aim is to promote its members. The literature concerning groups of musicians has to date dealt only with permanent, corporate groups such as the *gharānā*. I would argue that the evidence here suggests the existence of factions. Most of these factions are ephemeral groups: their memberships are determined by circumstances and the group is activated on specific occasions. (For a full discussion of the characteristics of factions, see Pettigrew 1975: 63–6.) The *gharānā*, too, can in certain circumstances be termed a faction if and when some or all of its members are mobilised and its 'raison d'etre is political competition' (Bailey 1969: 52).

Gossip can be very straightforward and as simple as saying: 'He's no good! He plays really badly. Why on earth do you want to hear him?' To this may be added a little promotion: 'Why don't you listen to my friend instead? Now he's really good!' Comments such as these prey on the gullibility of others who perhaps know very little about music and will easily be persuaded by an experienced musician or connoisseur. Suggestions in turn become beliefs which can then affect one's judgement. A rumour, however, is passed on more deviously, as by nature it is talk or report of a hearsay kind and not original expression (Firth 1967: 141); in other words it is an 'unsigned' message. But when the intention of the gossip or rumour is to damage an individual or group I follow Paine's (1970: 186) use of the term 'scandal', which he defines as 'communication in the form of gossip or rumour whose purpose is to denigrate or maliciously raise misgivings about a person'.

Scandal may be circulated concerning a musician's unreliability in performance. This could make the difference between his being engaged by organisers for a concert and his being disregarded. It may be suggested that he rarely turns up on time, if at all, or that he is likely to walk off the stage if his mood is not right. It may be insinuated that a musician is unsuitable for a job because his moral conduct is in question. It may also be hinted that a musician is quite simply mad. An appropriate example of this sort of unsigned message was given to me when a famous sitarist said: 'Had I known before that X was available I would never have suggested any other accompanist . . . Actually, I didn't know, but somebody told me X had got some mental disbalance.'

The following two cases are more sophisticated examples of scandal. In the first, there is both the actual and the implied criticism of a musician's musical and moral unsuitablity for a job as a music teacher:

Some years ago a musician was being considered for an important teaching post in a music institution. The decision to appoint came from the government itself, which was advised by the Public Services Commission. It is widely thought that a certain group used its contacts with influential ministers in the government to spread the scandalous rumour that the musician was rhythmically suspect owing to his habit of regularly accompanying the *ghazals* of the *ṭawā'ifs*. [A musical device often employed in this light-classical vocal form is the speeding-up and slowing-down of the tempo.] Government ministers, knowing little or nothing of music, believed this information indicated the musician's musical deficiency, and were alarmed at these claims of moral degradation. They refused to entertain any longer the idea of appointing that musician, instead choosing another candidate who had been vigorously promoted by the group.

The specific criticism levelled here was double-edged, for it pointed not only to musical deficiency but also to moral deficiency. To be associated with *ṭawā'ifs* is a slur on one's character, and the implication here was that there would be a high risk of an impropriety should such a musician be appointed to a respectable public institution where a large proportion of the students were young females.

The other case shows quite clearly how information management, or more accurately misinformation management, was designed to discourage a musician from partitipating in a seminar:

A seminar was organised, the central topic of which concerned the tabla. Many Indian musicologists were scheduled to deliver papers, and several tabla players were invited to give short demonstrations of some of the stylistic features of their different musical heritages. The exact fee to be paid to the musicians was shrouded in secrecy, there being in circulation several different rumours as to the correct amount. One musician received an offer of 150 rupees, which, though considered inadequate, did not force him to decline the offer until the rumour reached him that other performers were each to get 250 rupees for their identical contributions to the seminar. This rumour was purported to have been circulated by one of the organisers of the seminar who was a well-known antagonist of the musician involved, as well as being a student of a different tabla *gharānā*. [However, that in itself may have been just another attempt at a slur.] The rumour had its desired effect because the indignant tabla player refused to participate in the seminar. It was then suggested that the real reason the tabla player did not wish to take part in the seminar was that he was secretive, selfish and too proud to part with his knowledge.

This scandal was designed to blacken a musician's name, for not only was he hailed as secretive and selfish but he also appeared greedy because he had not accepted a fee which others had already agreed to. Incidentally, I heard much later that the actual fee had indeed been fixed at 150 rupees for each artist to perform at the seminar.

Politics within musical performance

Turning to the second category, that of politics in the context of the musical performance, we find many examples of acts designed to discredit musicians. The aims of acts which occur in performance are either to produce a direct effect on a musician's mood so that he plays poorly, or to actually force him into making mistakes and so appear inadequate, foolish or substandard. The following case is quite well known in India and is often quoted as an example of how one musician can make another lose face and appear a complete fool:

A famous instrumentalist was to perform in a concert. However, the organiser of the concert disliked the musician and wanted to teach him a lesson. He paid a well-known accompanist handsomely and instructed him to play something complex in order to force the soloist into making an error. Word eventually reached the latter's ear. And so, fully prepared, he began the concert with a short unaccompanied exposition of the *rāg* (*ālāp*) and then proceeded immediately to the accompanied section (*gat*). The accompanist began playing *tīntāl* [a metric cycle of sixteen beats]. The soloist turned to the accompanist and simply shook his head. A different *tāl* was tried, and then another, and yet another, but each time the instrumentalist shook his head, all the while playing the seemingly confusing composition. Eventually, he put his instrument down and said to the concert organiser, who was seated in the front row of the packed auditorium: 'Can you not find an accompanist who can provide me with straightforward *ṭhekā* [the basic articulation of a *tāl* using drum strokes]?'

The accompanist, looking perplexed and abashed, apologised both to the instrumentalist and the audience. The instrumentalist then sang the composition and clapped the *tāl*. It was simple *tīntāl* after all, the most commonly used *tāl*, although the accents of the *gat* melody were irregular and mostly fell on off-beats, thereby creating considerable confusion. Needless to say, the accompanist no longer entertained ideas of outwitting the instrumentalist, and the organiser's plot had been foiled.

Many similar stories deal with musical tricks which force another musician into making an error in *tāl*. Examples are not only confined to soloists fooling accompanists. They sometimes show how accompanists are able to confuse a soloist merely with an elaborated and embellished form of his *ṭhekā*.

An accompanist can deliberately play too loudly, knowing that this will annoy the soloist and affect his mood. He may also attain the desired effect by injecting small flourishes between, or even in the middle of, melodic phrases, with the intention of breaking the flow of melodic development the soloist has in mind. However, if the soloist feels confident and in control of the situation he can, and often does, reassert his authority by glowering at, or even repremanding, the accompanist in full view of the public. He may also choose to reduce speed marginally, pedantically indicating the new tempo until the accompanist has readjusted to it. Such an action indicates that the accompanist was entirely to blame for an increase in speed, a musical decision which should only be taken by the soloist. In this way the audience is made to recognise the impetuosity of the accompanist.

Informants sometimes referred to two other methods used to affect the mood of a musician. In both cases a third party is involved. Firstly, people have been known to bribe a sound technician to distort the amplification of a musician's voice or instrument. A technician may reduce the volume to a level at which the musician cannot be heard, or alternatively increase it so that the levels distort the sound. Each time the musician's train of thought is disturbed and the chances of him giving a convincing performance are lessened.

Secondly, a performer may place his students, family, or members of his group, in the audience to clap and cheer, so inducing the rest of the audience to applaud also, whether the applause is warranted or not. In this way, a whole audience can be made to believe they are listening to an exceptional performance, even when the standard is far from being so. This technique can also be used to ruin a musician's reputation, especially if it is the accompanist who has organised partisan supporters in the audience. An informant explained:

Suppose a tabla player and a *sitār* player are on stage. When the tabla player gets an opportunity to give a little solo in reply to the sitarist, he'll get some clapping from the audience. This is a kind of politics today, that a tabla player will get his students to sit in the audience, who bring along their friends and clap when he plays something. When the *sitār* player plays, they will not clap. When you next go to the Ravindralaya [a concert hall in Lucknow], listen carefully. Then you'll realise where the clapping begins because the whole audience will not clap. With [Indians] it's a peculiarity that if four people start clapping, the whole hall will erupt into applause without thinking whether or not the performance is good . . . That causes the other artist to lose heart if he's receiving no applause, because he thinks the audience doesn't like what he's doing.

The final case is a particularly interesting example of a musician scheming to stultify his accompanist by musical means. I was present at both the first meeting of the musicians involved as well as the second, which took place at the Lucknow Festival. I was therefore aware of, and able to monitor, the events as they took place:

An instrumentalist was encouraged by friends to exact revenge on his accompanist for an earlier encounter in which the tabla player had apparently taken control of the performance by playing too many long solos in a style far too imposing for the instrumentalist to match. Having come off second best in the previous meeting, the instrumentalist was determined it should not happen again.

Behind the stage in the dressing rooms, the instrumentalist and the tabla player had finished tuning together and the tabla player had parted to take a relaxing stroll before the performance. At that moment, a disciple of the tabla player went to the dressing room to look for his teacher only to hear, as he stood outside the door, the hushed voices of the instrumentalist and a friend plotting to play a composition in a difficult *tāl* with the aim of restricting the tabla player to giving simply the *ṭhekā* of the *tāl*. The friend, a musician known to dislike the tabla player, was inciting the instrumentalist to perform a composition in eight and a half beats. He was overheard saying that this tabla player never performed in any *tāls* other than *tīntāl* and other common *tāls*. Therefore, choosing a difficult *tāl* would demonstrate this limitation to the public and the tabla player's reputation would be damaged. [Eight and a half beats is a *tāl* in which a tabla player would not normally have any set compositions and in which he would find it very difficult to improvise.]

The disciple immediately reported what he had heard to his teacher, who was both upset and annoyed at this attempt to undermine his musical integrity. Nevertheless, he sat down in a corner and in the ten minutes remaining before the performance he could be seen deep in thought, counting away on his fingers and muttering drumming patterns to himself. Thus he prepared a variety of pieces and had familiarised himself with the structure of the *tāl*.

The performance began with a composition set in the most commonly played *tāl*, *tīntāl*, and the tabla player helped himself to his customarily long solo passages. The instrumentalist became visibly more nervous and nonplussed,the result being a rather undistinguished performance. The friend of the instrumentalist, who had by this time become quite excited, was in the audience surrounded by a handful of others also known to be antagonists of the tabla player. They had been encouraging the instrumentalist with bursts of applause after some of his solo passages, and there was now an air of expectancy about them as they awaited the next composition in eight and a half beats. But they were visibly disappointed to find that this, the final piece of the evening in *rāg Bhairavī*, was set in nothing more complex than common *jhaptāl* [ten beats]. The instrumentalist had evidently decided not to take the risk of playing in such a difficult *tāl*, and may also have surmised that his accompanist was confidently prepared. The tabla player, once again, played his customarily long solo passages but it was another nervous and undistinguished performance by the instrumentalist.

Several days later the tabla player in his capacity as a 'casual' artist of All India Radio, was scheduled to record a tabla solo of twenty minutes' duration due to be broadcast later that week. He chose to play in a *tāl* of eight and a half beats. I questioned him regarding the chain of events I had witnessed:

INFORMANT Yes , it was to test me. People like Ravi Shankar and Ali Akbar, they play six and a half beats, seven and a half etc. It's all about *mātrās* [beats, i.e. counting], nothing special. But these things are used in fighting. People are not accustomed to these *tāls*.
JK Even so, a couple of weeks after that you played a tabla solo of eight and a half beats.
INFORMANT I thought I was being tested. I wouldn't want people to think I can't play any uncommon *tāls*. So I did it to show them and to test [i.e. challenge] them in turn . . . This *tāl* of eight and a half beats has no meaning at all.

What observations can be made from a study of these kinds of politics in the Indian music world? It can be seen that stories of competition from the past are almost always restricted to musical contests the rules of which, we may assume, were known to musicians and listeners alike. In contrast, competition in the present day is markedly different. Both inside and outside the context of the musical performance, musicians are using a variety of stratagems in order to succeed at all costs. This supports musicians' beliefs that the nature of competition has changed and is now dominated by politics. These beliefs, I feel, have a strong basis in fact, although it is wise to be cautious here. Obviously we are forced to judge relationships between musicians in the past on the evidence of stories that have been handed down as part of the oral tradition. But it does not necessarily follow that, owing to the lack of stories describing non-musical competition, politics did not exist before, say, 1900. Furthermore, in many of the modern performances I have witnessed, it is frequently difficult to draw the line between politics and healthy, enthusiastic interplay between performers without a certain knowledge of background information, in particular that of how the musicians themselves assess these events.

Certainly it can be seen that there are few rules governing the use of politics. It appears that anything can be done by anyone to anyone with no regard for rank or authority, whether based on age, ability, heredity, instrumental specialisation or musical role. Naturally one tends to avoid competing with those in a position to help one, for example other members of one's *gharānā* or group. The tendency is also for musicians not to compete with those who have become highly successful and influential, though in some cases it does of course happen. In general, however, it would be considered far more politic to curry favour with those who have 'made it' in order to benefit, if possible, from their help or patronage. Thus it is not those who are necessarily the best musicians, but rather those who can manage politics most expertly to their advantage who are best equipped to succeed in the Indian music world. The inevitability of that fact has led many to express their fear that ultimately it is the music itself that will suffer.

4 *Tabla* gharānās *in Lucknow*

Tabla *gharānās*

The concept of *gharānā* is a subject to which nearly all writers on Hindustani music address themselves at some stage in their work. Whereas most restrict themselves to a definition of the term and an outline of the characteristics of *gharānā*, some writers have dealt with the concept in considerable detail (see Deshpande 1973; Neuman 1974, 1978, 1980; Silver 1976; and Meer 1980). A detailed discussion of *gharānā* is beyond the scope of the present work. However, I feel compelled to deal with one vital aspect of *gharānā* which has a direct bearing on this study, namely the applicability of the term *gharānā* as a unit of social organisation among tabla players.

For a working definition of the word *gharānā*, I have drawn on that offered by Silver (1976: 27), who claimed that his was an 'idealised definition among musicians': 'A *gharānā* is a musical lineage – paralleling a literal or symbolic blood lineage – through which not only musical techniques, compositions, and theories, but other cultural data as well, are transmitted orally from one generation of practitioners to the next.' The word derives from *ghar* meaning 'house' and literally means 'family' or 'household'. Its secondary meanings are 'family, race, lineage' (Platts 1977: 932), and one might suppose, therefore, that the word enjoys wide currency in North India. However, I have never heard *gharānā* used outside a musical context.

The most detailed anthropological study of *gharānā* to date has come from Neuman (1974, 1980), who puts forward the thesis that *gharānā* as a unit of social organisation should not apply to groups of tabla players. Rather, he believes it applies only to groups of soloists (i.e. vocalists and other instrumentalists excluding *sāraṅgī* and tabla players). In the following list, I have summarised what Neuman believes to be the essential ingredients of *gharānā*:

1. The *gharānā* must have, at its core, a family (*k͟hāndān*) of musicians passing on a musical tradition from generation to generation through their disciples and students.
2. The *gharānā* must have a founder member with a charismatic personality.
3. The *gharānā* must be represented by a living member of the original *k͟hāndān*.
4. The *gharānā* must have a famous personality who is living.
5. There must have been at least three generations of distinguished musicians representing the musical tradition.
6. The *gharānā* must have a distinct and unique musical style.

To this list must be added the important qualification that 'Gharanas as stylistic schools are represented only by soloists, not accompanists' (Neuman 1974: 200–1). Additionally, Neuman states that even a soloist's claim to *gharānā* membership would be automatically invalidated were it shown that accompanists were present anywhere in his lineage.

Neuman admits that the word *gharānā* is indeed commonly used by tabla players to describe their own unit of social organisation, and he gives three examples in which the term is used, or, in his opinion, misused. In order to understand his argument, the meanings of two other terms need to be clarified. Firstly, *khāndān*, which encompasses all individuals believed to be consanguineally related through known ancestral links. Secondly, *birādarī*, the literal meaning of which is 'brotherhood'. It is derived from *birādar*, the Persian word for 'brother', and is defined by Neuman (1974: 147) as encompassing all individuals sharing a common ancestral place of origin and between whom there are potential or existing affinal connections.

The first example of what Neuman purports to be the misuse of the term *gharānā* is when it is named after the ancestral home of the *khāndān*. This is usually a town, but can be a village or a state. If a *birādarī* is recognised and associated with the same ancestral home as the *khāndān*, Neuman claims that *gharānā* has been used synonymously with *birādarī*. He explains (Neuman 1974: 207): 'In another program [the musician] is described as a "well-known tabla player of Delhi. He belongs to the Delhi Gharana of musicians. . . ." The term [*gharānā*] clearly refers in this context to the Delhi *birādarī*, i.e. a social group.' However, Neuman goes on to add that in circumstances where a *birādarī* does not correspond to the ancestral home of the *khāndān*, the term *gharānā* is nevertheless still used as an identity by many musicians.

In the second example, Neuman (1974: 207) dismisses a musician's claim to membership of the Farukkhabad tabla *gharānā*, saying that 'this is the name of a well-known baj . . . there is no *gharānā* of this name'. In other words, the musician concerned has mistakenly used *gharānā* for 'style of playing', for which the word *bāj* exists.

A third example shows how musicians sometimes use *gharānā* when they mean both *birādarī* and *bāj* together. This is when the geographical centre of a recognised playing style, or *bāj*, corresponds directly to the ancestral home of the *birādarī*.

Essentially, then, Neuman acknowledges that *gharānā* is widely used among tabla players. Yet instead of attempting to formulate this as a valid folk concept, he chooses to treat *gharānā* as an analytical concept in order to show that when tabla players use the word they really mean *birādarī* when speaking of a social group, and *bāj* when speaking of a 'style of playing'. This, I fear, indicates that Neuman's ideas are more a consequence of his own concern for clarity than of an attempt to understand the ways in which musicians themselves perceive *gharānā*. His conclusions may conceivably reflect the views of his informants, but they certainly do not reflect the views of those people with whom I worked. I feel, therefore, that Neuman was mistaken in not accepting situational variation in actors' self-ascription. In contrast, my own research methodology involved the detailed monitoring of the ways in which tabla players and other kinds of musician used the word *gharānā*, and I also took notice of other concepts such as *bāj* and *birādarī*. As a result, my findings proved to be very different from Neuman's.

Returning, firstly, to Neuman's qualification that 'Gharanas as stylistic schools are represented only by soloists, not accompanists', all tabla players with whom I worked in Lucknow, Delhi and Calcutta rejected this distinction outright. It was even stated quite categorically by soloists that certain groups of tabla palyers constituted *gharānās*. Furthermore, even if we were to accept Neuman's own ingredients of *gharānā* as summarised in the six main points above, we would find that many groups of tabla players who call their unit of social organisation a *gharānā* easily fulfil all these requirements. These may not only include groups with whom I worked in Lucknow, as will be seen later on in this chapter, but also groups with whom Neuman formerly worked in Delhi. I found that Neuman's six points, unlike his qualification that *gharānā* applies only to soloists, were generally represented in the views of tabla players and other musicians, and I therefore endorse them as essential elements in the definition of a *gharānā*.

Next we come to the concept of *birādarī*, upon which Neuman has laid great emphasis. From conversations with members of the Delhi tabla *gharānā* in 1984, I can corroborate Neuman's findings that the *birādarī* was indeed recognised. In fact, its members had last met in 1983 in order to discuss arrangements for a marriage. But it is important to note that the existence of the Delhi *birādarī* by no means detracted from musicians' claims that certain (though by no means all) of its members also belonged to the Delhi *gharānā*.

Apart from Delhi, however, I found no other group of musicians ready to acknowledge the existence of *birādarīs*. Throughout my period of close contact with musicians of the Lucknow *gharānā*, as well as with musicians of other *gharānās*, I never once heard the word *birādarī* used unless I myself prompted it by introducing the concept into the conversation. Having read Neuman's work prior to fieldwork, I was therefore particularly surprised to find my informants uncomprehending, and dismissive of the idea that *birādarī* should constitute a unit of social organisation among them. One informant, who dismissed the idea of *birādarī* out of hand was the venerable *sāraṅgī* player Ustad Habib Raza Khan of Calcutta, who had once arranged for the marriage of his daughter to Munnu Khan of the Delhi *gharānā*. If Neuman's point regarding potential or existing affinal connections is accepted, then Habib Raza should have been a member of the Delhi *birādarī*. He certainly traced the origin of his family ultimately to Delhi, which satisfies Neuman's other requirement. Yet Habib Raza Khan did not recognise the *birādarī*.

Musicians did agree that *birādarī* was an abstract term covering people who called each other *bhā'ī* (brother). However, this was shorn of any socio-musical associations. It should be realised here that 'brother' can mean anyone ranging from one's real brother, to one's cousin, either closely or distantly related, to one's friends and acquaintances, in fact to anyone of roughly the same age group. Consequently, what I think Neuman's conclusion concerning the *birādarī* indicates is an attempt by the analyst to apply a model derived from a limited amount of data to the wider context of the social organisation of all tabla players in India. What I believe my findings show is that such a model is by no means recognised or accepted by all groups of tabla players.

Turning to the question of *bāj*, it appears that Neuman has failed to recognise the significance of the point that *gharānā* has, in addition to its technical sense of implying a social group, a colloquial sense which is synonymous with *bāj*, or 'style of playing'. 'He plays Delhi *gharānā*' and 'He plays Punjab *gharānā*' are phrases I heard very frequently from a wide range of musicians during my research. But this is not to say that musicians fail to distinguish between the terms *bāj* and *gharānā*, or that they cannot use them analytically. For example, when Afaq Husain said *Hamāre yahāṅ gharāne kā bāj alag hai* (lit. Here with us, the playing style of the *gharānā* is different), he is clearly separating and differentiating between the two concepts. Each *gharānā*, therefore specialises in its own particular *bāj*. So Neuman is right when he says that Farukkhabad 'is the name of a well-known *bāj*', but he is wrong to say that 'there is no *gharānā* of this name'. The musicians of the Farukkhabad *gharānā* certainly believe they constitute a *gharānā*, and one that is widely recognised by soloists and accompanists alike throughout North India.

Gharānā, then, is polysemic, and it is important to emphasise that it is used both as a technical and as a colloquial term. In striving for clarity in his analytical definition, Neuman has failed to take into account an extremely important folk evaluation: that the term *gharānā* as representative of a unit of social organisation is justifiably applicable to certain groups of tabla players.

Origins of the Lucknow *gharānā*

Much controversy and confusion exist concerning the origins of the Lucknow tabla *gharānā*. I do not intend to impose on the data presented here my own analytical interpretation aimed at a definitive version, but rather hope to show what the musicians concerned believe to have been the true story of their origins, confused and incomplete as it may be. The majority of data to be presented are drawn from written documents in the possession of Ustad Afaq Husain Khan, as well as from the verbal statements of many musicians, most prominent among whom was the late Ustad Habib Raza Khan. The documents are notebooks in which the genealogy of the lineage, a little commentary and several rare compositions have been recorded in Urdu by Afaq Husain's father, grandfather and other unspecified members of the *gharānā*.

Ustad Habib Raza Khan, who died in May 1983 in his nineties, was affinally related to both the Lucknow and Delhi *k̲h̲āndāns*. He was a straightforward man with an extensive and crystal-clear memory. He never speculated and was not ashamed to reply to a question that he did not know the answer. He was therefore regarded by all members of the Lucknow *gharānā* as an authority on Lucknow genealogy and history. Habib Raza generously shared with me, in a series of interviews, his version of the facts with a view to correcting the misconceptions generally held about the *gharānā*'s origins, membership and history. These misconceptions, he believed, had arisen because scholars had failed to consult Lucknow *gharānā* members before publishing genealogies and stories concerning *gharānā* history. Even a short time before his death, Habib Raza had offered his account to the writer Susheela Misra in the hope that she might report the true picture as he saw it. She told me later that she had dismissed this information as unreliable, and had continued to endorse the history of the *gharānā* as presented in the literature (see, for example, Misra 1984). Not surprisingly, the version I have been given by Habib Raẓa and Afaq Husain is greatly at variance with all previously published material.

Perhaps the only undisputed claim in the genealogy and history of the Lucknow tabla *gharānā* is that its founder member was Miyan Bakhshu Khan, who travelled to Lucknow from Delhi in search of court patronage. Whose son he was, when he arrived in Lucknow, and, indeed, whether or not he was the sole founder member are questions all open to debate. Habib Raza assured me that Miyan Bakhshu Khan arrived soon after the accession of Nawab Asaf-ud-daula in 1775. On the other hand, Afaq Husain put the date a little earlier:

> Bakhshuji came [to Lucknow] in Shuja-ud-daula's period [i.e. 1754–75]. That was also Allauddin Khalji's era. There were many musicians in Delhi at that time, including Bakhshuji and Makkhuji. They were there just after Allauddin Khalji's era . . . In Akbar's court were the Nauratan, among whom Amir Khusrau was prominent. In this group were a number of musicians, including Bakhshuji, Amir Khusrau, and also Shitab Khan.

This apparently bizarre statement is typical of the many anomalies in historical data given by musicians. Here, Bakhshu Khan is seen to have flourished 'just after' the reign of Allauddin

Khalji (Sultan of Delhi from 1296 to 1316), during the reigns of the Emperor Akbar (1556–1605) and Nawab Shuja-ud-daula of Lucknow (1754–75). The elasticity of the time scale also allows for him to have been a contemporary of Amir Khusrau (1253–1325). But perhaps this statement is only bizarre if we choose to see it purely as historical data. It seems to me that it is exceedingly difficult to draw the line between fact and fiction in anything musicians say about the past, and that it would be far more useful to treat such statements as a reflection of contemporary ideas. If we do this, we can see the value of linking one's ancestors with such legendary figures as Amir Khusrau and the Nauratan (the 'nine jewels' or nine great men of Akbar's court) in terms of the prestige and historical depth this brings to the lineage.

Mention of the Shitab Khan in the above statement, whom Afaq Husain described as 'a relative, perhaps a forefather of Bakhshu Khan', provides a link between the *gharānās* of Delhi and Lucknow. Shitab Khan features prominently in the *shijrā*, or genealogy, of the Delhi *gharānā*. However, there is no mention of Bakhshu Khan, as I saw for myself when invited to examine documents in the possession of the *khalīfa* of the Delhi *gharānā*, Ustad Inam Ali Khan, and his paternal uncle, Ustad Munnu Khan. How, therefore, was Bakhshu Khan related to the musicians of the Delhi *gharānā*? It can be seen in Chart 2 that Husain Khan (son of Sudhar Khan) had four sons, of which only the name of one, Chajju Khan, survives. Inam Ali believed that Bakhshu Khan was another of the sons of Husain Khan. This ties in well with an account given both by Inam Ali Khan and Afaq Husain that Miyan Bakhshu Khan was one of four brothers, two of whom remained in Delhi while two left to seek court patronage in Lucknow. The present-day members of the Lucknow and Delhi *gharānās* firmly believe they represent lineages of the same clan, and support this by pointing out that they are both members of the minority sect of Shiite Muslims.

The identity of the other brother who apparently left for Lucknow along with Bakhshu Khan remains a mystery. Two possible solutions arise from the fact that Bakhshu Khan is often mentioned by many musicians in the same breath as either Makkhu Khan (as may be seen, for example, in Afaq Husain's statement above) or Modhu Khan. Shepherd (1976: 8) has even suggested that Bakhshu Khan moved to Lucknow with his two brothers, Modhu and Makkhu. However, my key informants totally rejected all these suggestions.

Makkhu Khan appears in Imam (1959: 25) as 'Makku of Delhi . . . an able exponent of the old baj of tabla', though the writer does not indicate any relationship between Makkhu Khan and Bakhshu Khan, whereas he clearly indicates relationships between other musicians. What appears to be the clearest indication of Makkhu Khan's identity came from Inam Ali, who claimed he was the disciple of Bugara Khan of the Delhi *gharānā* for twenty-five years, during which time he also became his teacher's son-in-law. Inam Ali claims descent from Makkhu Khan through his *nanihāl* (mother's family), which is also indicated in Chart 2. It seems likely, therefore, that Bakhshu Khan and Makkhu Khan were roughly contemporary, that they were both employed as court musicians in Lucknow in the late eighteenth and early nineteenth centuries, and that they were not real brothers although each may have loosely referred to the other as *bhā'ī*.

By far the most commonly held belief among scholars and writers on tabla is that Modhu Khan was the brother of Bakhshu Khan (see, for example, Gottlieb 1977; Srivastav 1982; Vashishtha 1982; and Misra 1984). This is also the account widely propagated in music schools and colleges throughout India. In rejecting this claim, my informants told me that Modhu

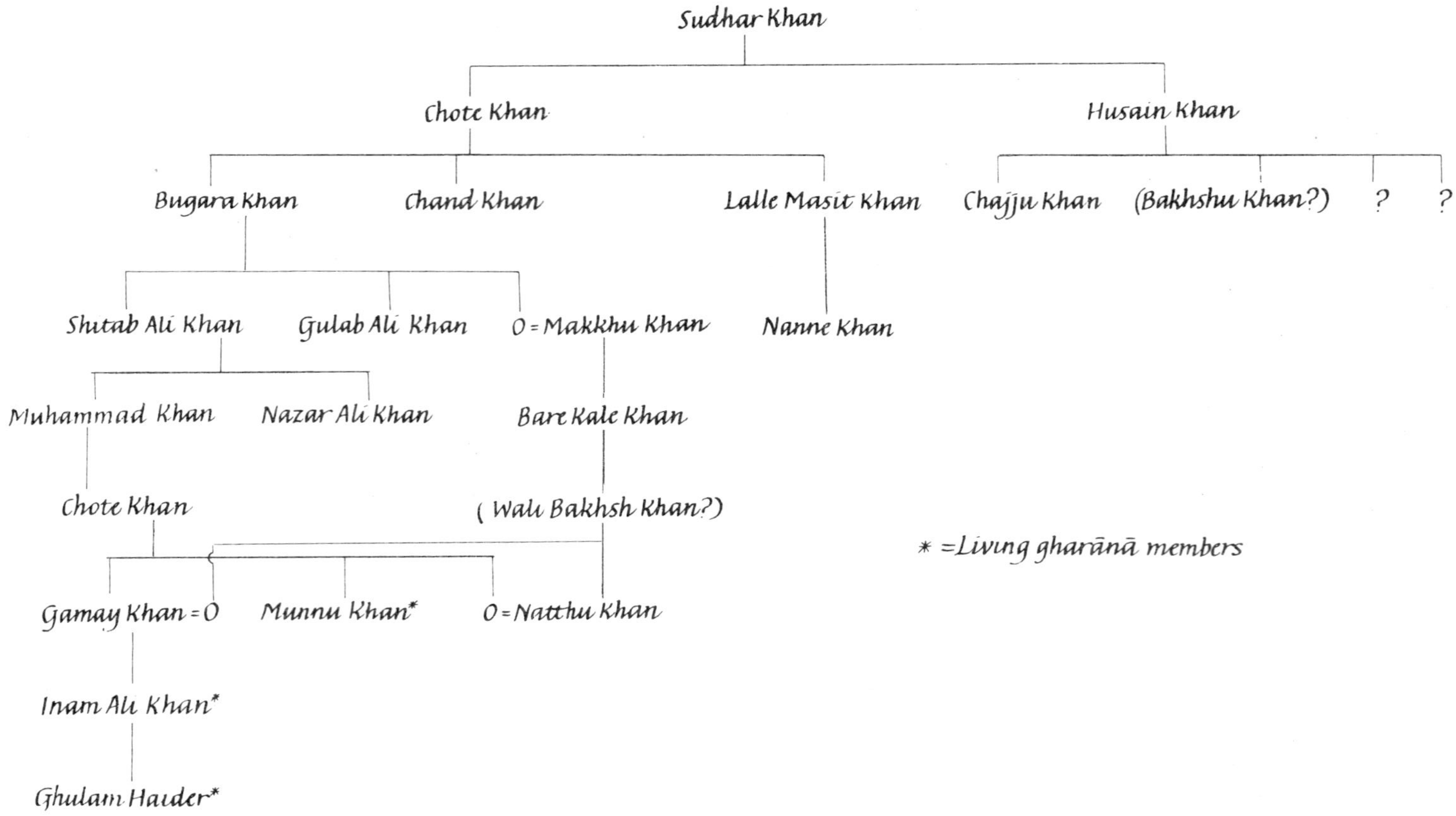

Chart 2. Genealogy of the Delhi *gharānā*

Khan first arrived in Lucknow with his brother, Zahid Khan, during the reign of Nawab Nasir-ud-din Haider some fifty years after the arrival of Bakhshu Khan. The brothers came from the small state of Jhajjar in the Punjab, some forty miles to the west of Delhi. As the state possessed a court with a *nawāb* who employed musicians (Miner 1981: 195a), it may be assumed that members of this family were formerly in that *nawāb*'s service. Although Modhu Khan and Zahid Khan were members of the same Islamic sect as members of the Delhi and Lucknow *gharānās*, their's was apparently a quite distinct and unrelated lineage. It will be remembered that possibly around 1850 the family of Modhu and Zahid Khan was rewarded with a large *koṭhī*, or mansion, by Wajid Ali Shah, by association with which they later came to be identified as the Kothiwal *gharānā*.

The Kothiwal *gharānā* has failed to gain recognition by outsiders as a separate *gharānā* from Lucknow primarily because of popular stories identifying Modhu Khan as the brother of Bakhshu Khan and hence as co-founder of the Lucknow *gharānā*. Modhu Khan is also popularly noted for having been the teacher of the founder of the Benares tabla *gharānā*, Ram Sahai (see, amongst others, Shepherd 1976). Roach (1972: 29–33), basing his account on information given by Kanthe Maharaj, gives this story in its most widely accepted form, though there are some major inconsistencies in chronology in his account. For example, Ram Sahai is said to have been born in 1798, to have travelled to Lucknow at the age of seven (i.e. 1805) in order 'to attend a musical gathering at the court of the Nawab of Oudh, Shujatud-dhaula', and, at the age of twenty, to have played on the day of Wajid Ali Shah's coronation. If Ram Sahai had been born in 1798, he would have been forty-nine years of age when Wajid Ali Shah was crowned in 1847. In addition, Saadat Ali Khan was the ruling *nawāb* in 1805, not 'Shujatuddhaula' (presumably Shuja-ud-daula), who had died some thirty years earlier. Details given in Shepherd (1976: 22–33), also based on statements given by Kanthe Maharaj, differ slightly, though the general gist remains the same. Here, Ram Sahai is said to have been born in 1780, and he played not for Wajid Ali Shah's coronation but for a total of seven nights as entertainment for Wazir Ali, in 1797.

Some information about Modhu Khan himself appears in both Shepherd's and Roach's accounts, the validity of which was totally rejected by my informants, who included descendants of Modhu Khan. It is stated that 'Modhu Khan had neither a son nor a disciple', and that 'He had taken a vow never to initiate anyone from Lucknow into his musical tradition because of [other musicians'] inimicable [*sic*] attitude towards him' (Roach 1972: 30; see also Shepherd 1976: 25). As Chart 3 clearly indicates, Modhu Khan actually had two sons, to whom, his descendants assured me, he taught everything. That is not to say that Ram Sahai was not a great musician. However, once again it is important to remember that we should try to understand claims made about Modhu Khan by Benares *gharānā* musicians not as historical data but as a reflection of contemporary ideas. Clearly, it would be of considerable advantage to Benares musicians to suggest that – owing to Modhu Khan's 'vow never to initiate anyone from Lucknow into his musical tradition'– only they received the musical heritage of Lucknow

The genealogy and history of the Lucknow *gharānā*

In this section, I shall trace the genealogy of the Lucknow tabla *gharānā*, and relate something of its history using illustrations of events in the lives of *gharānā* members. Although most of

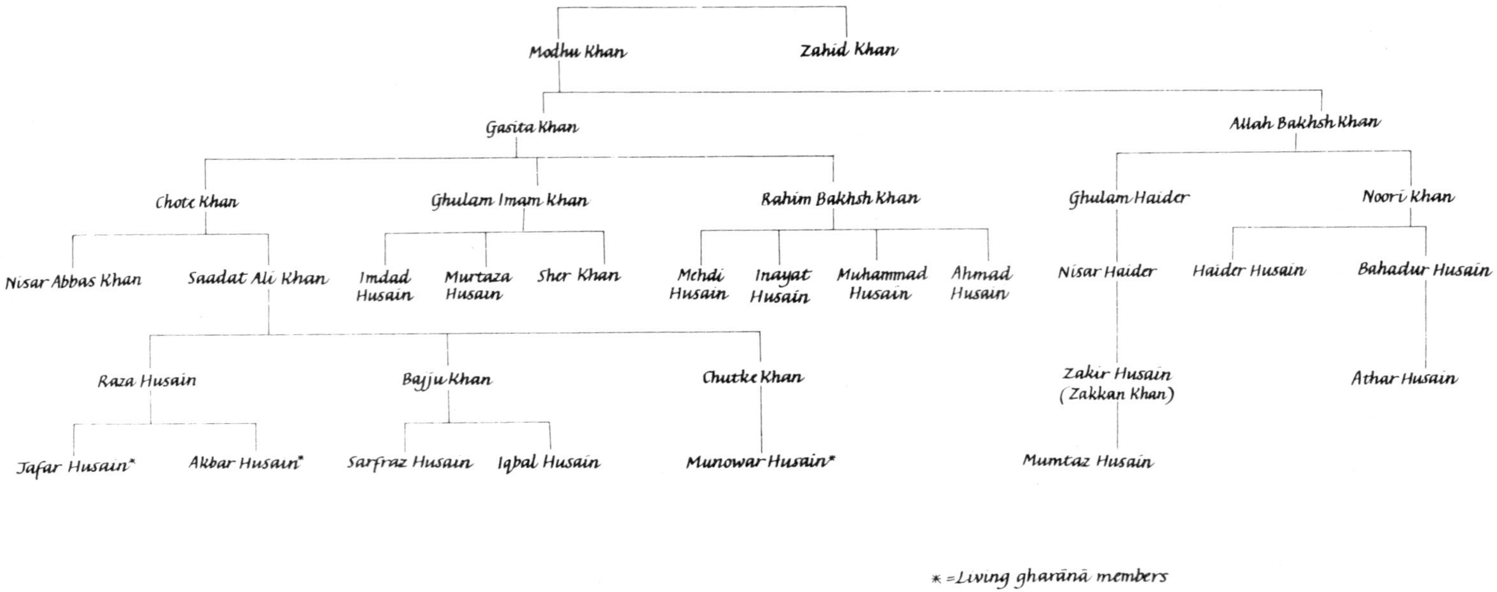

Chart 3. Genealogy of the Kothiwal *gharānā*

the accounts relate to members of the *khāndān*, or lineage, some refer to their famous disciples who apparently were not consanguineally related to them.

When Nawab Asaf-ud-daula took up residence in Lucknow in 1775, musicians who had found patronage in Faizabad under his predecessor, Shuja-ud-daula, as well as musicians from the crumbling imperial capital of Delhi, arrived in Lucknow to take advantage of the new *nawāb*'s reputation as a liberal and generous patron of the arts. Among those coming either from Delhi or in the King's entourage from Faizabad was Miyan Bakhshu Khan, who was employed as a court musician. He was later rewarded for his services as a tabla player to the court of Asaf-ud-daula with land which included a small village situated on the western edge of the city. Little else is known about Bakhshu Khan or, indeed, about any of his descendants until we come to Abid Husain Khan, his great-grandson. Several compositions survive from the period before Abid Husain, a few of which are attributed to Bakhshu Khan. However, I was informed that the majority of compositions from the early period had been lost or forgotten.

Bakhshu Khan is mentioned in Imam (1959: 25) along with other members of the Lucknow *gharānā*: 'In Tabla playing Bakshu Dhari was a veteran of repute. While his son Mammu is a specialist in playing Gat and his other son Salari Khan is very good at Gat-paran. Both of them are masters of their style.' We should therefore assume that Bakhshu Khan, described here as 'a veteran of repute', was a good tabla player. Imam (1959: 25–6) twice used him as a yardstick to indicate the quality of other musicians: 'Ghuran Khan stands supreme in playing the Nakkara and Tabla. His disciples had defeated even the great Ustad Mian Bakshu . . . Aghawan Naqqarchi of Unnao was an adept in playing Tabla and Naqqara. In fact Bakshu of Lucknow could not excel him in this art'.

As can be seen from Chart 4, Bakhshu Khan is indeed said by informants to have had two sons: Mammu Khan and Kesri Khan. Yet according to Imam, the sons of Bakhshu Khan are Mammu Khan and Salari Khan. Are we to suppose that Salari Khan and Kesri Khan were one and the same person? My informants thought not. Afaq Husain explained that he believed Salari Khan to have been a disciple of Bakhshu Khan, and told me the following story involving Salari Khan and another disciple, Haji Vilayat Ali Khan:

Both Miyan Salari Khan and Haji Vilayat Ali Khan were disciples of the same *ustād* [i.e. Bakhshu Khan]. Haji Vilayat Ali Khan was a specialist in the playing of *gat* and there were very few musicians of his calibre around at that time. Salari Khan, on the other hand, was famous for playing *rang*, a composition similar to *relā*, which utilises only open *bols* such as *dheneghene*.

Salari Khan's father was a keen wrestler and, in his youth, Salari Khan shared his father's passion for the sport and would often miss his tabla *riyāẓ* in order to exercise and train. But his father was not pleased because he wanted Salari Khan to become a great tabla player. On Salari Khan's teacher's advice, he locked his son in one part of the house and forbade him to come out until he had developed into a worthy musician. Salari Khan's mother was told to take trays of food and hand them through a small hatchway in the door. Here, Salari Khan was to stay for twelve years.

In the beginning, Salari Khan was intensely unhappy. He refused to touch his tabla and, in fact, threw the drums away. But after some time he was forced to realise that tabla really was the most important thing in his life. He began to practise again and, as he had thrown away his tabla, he played on the edge of his *takht*, or wooden bed. This was ideal for the light, bouncing strokes employed in playing *rang*, and he practised so much that he eroded the wood leaving dents where his fingers struck the surface of the *takht*.

When his father learned of this renewal of interest, he rewarded Salari Khan with a new set of tabla.

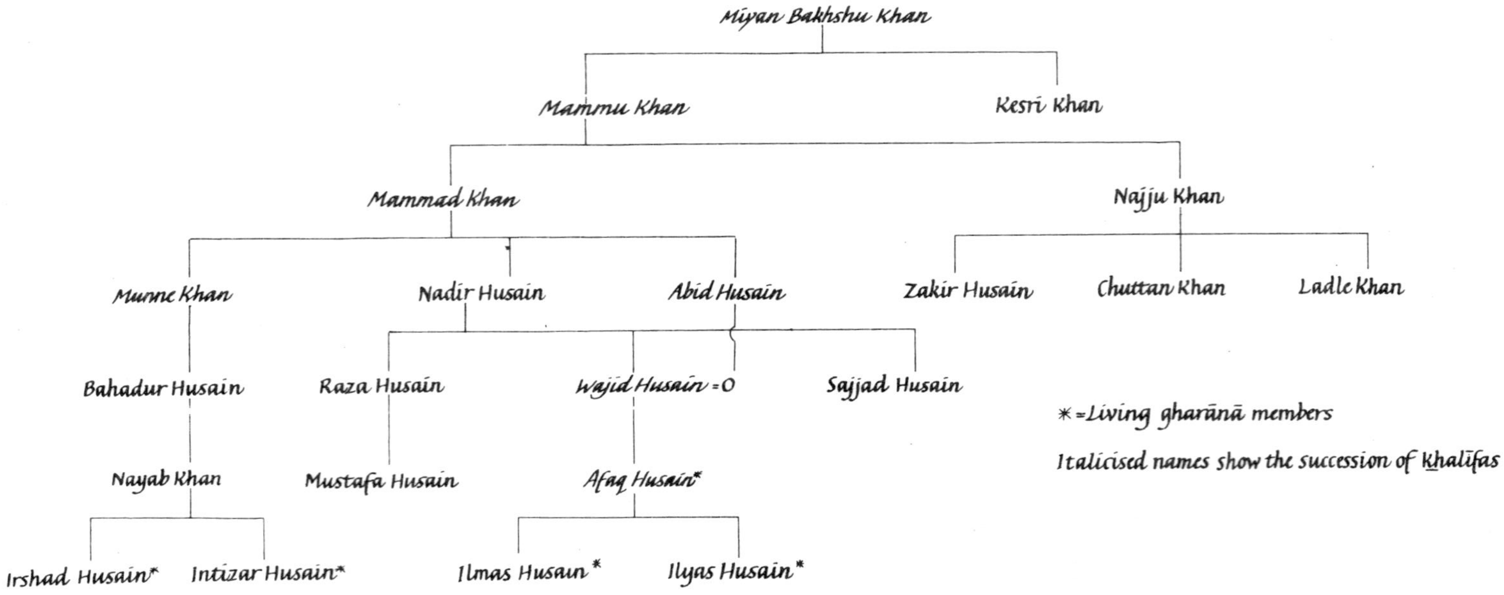

Chart 4. Genealogy of the Lucknow *gharānā*

Salari Khan's teacher also began visiting and continued to give his pupil lessons through the hatchway of the door. And when Salari Khan emerged from his apartment after twelve years, he had received a complete education in tabla and had remembered and practised to perfection everything he had been taught.

It so happened that, soon after, a *mahfil* was arranged and Salari Khan and Haji Vilayat Ali Khan were both invited to play. Many great *ustāds* of the day were gathered together for the event. This kind of event was known as a *dangal*, where musicians came together to compete, like wrestlers, in order to claim superiority over one another. The would play, sometimes for many days at a stretch, stopping only to take midday and evening meals. By playing alternately, they would test the strengths and weaknesses of each other's knowledge and skill, and assess how much practise each had done.

The competition between Haji Vilayat Ali Khan and Salari Khan had already lasted three days, and neither had shown any signs of weakness. Each answered the other's compositions with appropriate *joṛē*, or pairs, because they had both recieved the same *ta'līm* [instruction] from the same *ustād* and knew each other's repertoire by heart. But suddenly, Haji Vilayat Ali Khan caught his opponent unwares with one of his own *gat* compositions, of which Salari Khan had never before heard the like. Salari Khan was baffled and needed time to think. He quickly hit upon a plan, and proceeded to take out a few *gaṭṭē* [wooden blocks for tuning the tabla], tighten the *baddhī* [straps], replace the *gaṭṭē*, and retune the drum. In the time it had taken him to do this he had composed a perfect *joṛā* for Haji Vilayat Ali Khan's *gat*. He played it, and Haji Vilayat Ali Khan was utterly stunned and amazed that his opponent could have matched his composition. The assembly, in appreciation, burst into a chorus of *Wah, wah, wah*! and the two 'wrestlers' emerged from the *dangal* with honours shared.

Salari Khan also appears in the stories of Ram Sahai as recounted by Shepherd (1976: 28) and Roach: 'One tabla player, Salar Khan, immediately offered Ram Sahai his entire repertoire' (Roach 1972: 31).

The other musician concerned in the above story is Haji Vilayat Ali Khan, so named because he completed no less than seven pilgrimages (Hajj) to Mecca. It is said that each time he reached his destination he prayed that he be given the grace of God to develop his talents to the extent where no other musician could match him. He was the founder of the Farukkhabad tabla *gharānā* (Farukkhabad presumably being Haji Vilayat Ali Khan's ancestral home), recognised by all musicians as an offshoot of the Lucknow *gharānā*. It appears that both he and Salari Khan were disciples of Bakhshu Khan as well as of his son Mammu Khan in later years. Gottlieb (1977 vol.2: 39) in fact suggests that Salari Khan was the disciple of Haji Vilayat Ali Khan, but this was refuted by Afaq Husain in his story of the competition between the two musicians.

More is known of Salari Khan and Haji Vilayat Ali Khan than of their other teacher, Mammu Khan. We know that Iman (1959: 25) thought of him as 'a speciali t in playing Gat' and we come across his name in a further reference which concerns another disciple of Bakhshu Khan:

Najju Deredar is a tabla player and disciple of Bakhshu. But for him the singers would have had an upper hand over the accompanists. He trained his son also with the aim of accompanying singers. I have listened to his sons playing and can vouchsafe that they were better than the son of Mammu Khan and grandson of Bakshu.

Chart 4 shows that Mammu Khan had two sons: Muhammad Khan (known more commonly by his alias, Mammad Khan) and Najju Khan (not to be confused with Najju Deredar; incidentally, Neuman (1980: 100) correctly notes that the title *deredār* refers to the son of a *ṭawā'if*, a definition somewhat more elegant than the one given by my informants: 'a whore's brother'). To which of these sons Imam is referring in the above quotation cannot be ascertained, but we may assume that Mammad Khan was the greater of the two if it is accepted that the 'Muhammad Ji' mentioned by Sharar (1975: 139) is, in fact, Mammad Khan. Sharar praised him as 'the most expert tabla player . . . who was renowned throughout India'. He goes on to recall an incident of about 1870 (Mammad Khan died in 1879) where a 'Maratha gentleman', not content with being entertained by the finest singers of the day, disclosed the real reason for his visit to Lucknow:

> 'The real reason for my coming here is to sing a *tarana*, with Muhammad Ji accompanying me on tabla.' Muhammad Ji was immediately sent for and the Maratha's singing and Muhammad Ji's playing were much appreciated and applauded by all present. Finally the Maratha admitted, 'I have been everywhere but I have never heard a more accomplished tabla player'.

Like his father and grandfather before him, Mammad Khan was a renowned teacher. Among his students were Amman Khan and Anis-ud-daula, who were engaged in the service of the exiled court of Nawab Wajid Ali Shah in Matiya Burj, Calcutta.

Mammad Khan and Najju Khan each had three sons. All played tabla but not all reached the same level of musical achievement. Of Mammad Khan's three sons, Munne Khan, Nadir Husain and Abid Husain, the greatest was the eldest, Munne Khan. As Harendra Kishore Roy Chowdhury (1929: 12) stated quite categorically: 'Mammoo Khan, Mahammad Khan and Moonneh Khan were the best Tabla players of their time, a fact which is still admitted beyond contradiction by every school of Tabla in Hindustan.'

Munne Khan was closely associated with Bindadin and Kalka Prasad Maharaj, the legendary *kathak* dancers of Lucknow. His fame, unlike that of Abid Husain in later years, was more or less restricted to Lucknow mainly because he did not travel widely in India – travel was more difficult until the railway network was completed around 1900. An indication of Munne Khan's greatness can be taken from the following recollection of a prominent disciple of the Lucknow tabla *gharānā*, Bhupal Ray Choudhuri:

> One old man here [i.e. in Calcutta], who was an amateur tabla player . . . said he had been to Lucknow and had heard Munne Khan play. Apparently Munne Khan went to other provinces but he didn't come to Calcutta. The old man said: 'You are interested in Khalifa Abid Husain Khan, I know, but if you had heard Munne Khalifa you would have said that Abid Khalifa is nothing before his elder brother.' He was so superb, Munne Khalifa, the eldest brother. He was much better than Abid Khalifa.

Munne Khan's death, in 1890, left the Lucknow *gharānā* in serious difficulties, for it no longer had a figurehead, the authoritative *khalīfa* and there was no successor within the family deserving of the *khalīfa*'s mantle. Nadir Husain, though a professional tabla player, did not have the authoritative knowledge which would have enabled him to assume leadership of the *gharānā*. Afaq Husain said of him: 'He played, but much less. Only a little. He was a professional, and he supported the other brothers [after Munne Khan's death]. It's not necessarily the case that each brother is equally good.' Abid Husain, Bahadur Husain (the son of Munne Khan), and the three sons of Najju Khan were all too young and inexperienced to be authorities. There was, at the time, a crisis during which it was by no means clear what the future held in store for the *gharānā*. This was emphasised by remarks said to have been made by the dancers Bindadin and Kalka Prasad Maharaj to the effect that they had lost their great accompanist, Munne Khan, and now the Lucknow *gharānā* was no more. However, it was out of this critical situation that Abid Husain rose eventually to become the new *khalīfa*. To

Plate 8. Khalifa (Ustad) Abid Husain Khan

successive generations, therefore, Abid Husain gained the reputation of being something of a saviour. With a supreme effort, he practised his way to a level of ability where, it is said (Roy Chowdhury 1929: 12), he was unparalleled throughout India:

Abid began practising Tabla under the instruction of his father when he was only seven years of age; but he lost his father at the age of twelve. On the death of his father he received lessons under the direction of his brother Moonneh Khan for eleven years, when the latter died. The death of his brother made Abid so earnest in preserving his family reputation that he began practising Tabla daily for about thirteen hours. Practising thus consecutively for twelve years he came out of home and travelled throughout India, acquiring exceptional fame and fortune.

There are differing versions of the length of time Abid Husain actually practised. Hirendra Kumar Ganguli, a disciple of Abid Husain from 1919 to 1936, claims his *ustād* practised eighteen to twenty hours daily for sixteen to eighteen years. Habib Raza and Afaq Husain agreed that Abid Husain undertook to do a rigorous *cillā* which involved daily practice for a minimum of twelve hours over a period of twelve years. Evidently Abid Husain, who practised throughout the night, and as legend would have it, did not leave his house during the twelve-year period, achieved his goal and earned a formidable reputation as a knowledgeable and well-practised tabla player.

Stories concerning the exploits of Abid Husain are plentiful and, more often than not, describe him as the guardian of the honour of his *gharānā*, his city, and of lesser tabla players who had suffered at the hands of malicious soloists. The following account from Hirendra Kumar Ganguli is just such an example:

HKG In 1920, December, Abid Husain left for Mecca on Hajj, and then came back after two months or so. According to Muslims tabla playing is a *gunah*, or sin. So when they go to Mecca and come back they usually give up the tabla saying that it is a sin.
JK Yes, but he didn't stop playing, did he?
HKG No [he means yes], but I tell you he stopped it. He stopped it for about six to eight months. Then a great *ustād* from somewhere outside [i.e. outside Lucknow], I don't remember where, went on a tour throughout India. And wherever he went, he was such a *laydār* [good at rhythm, especially rhythmic complexities] artist that nobody could follow him rightly. He was such a giant of an artist. So he went to Lucknow, and he sang one day. Nobody could follow him. He didn't get a good accompanist. Then he said: 'Oh, this is Lucknow! The seat of music! Is there no accompanist who can follow me rightly?' On that day there were lots of *nawābs* present who were patrons of music: Thakur Nawab Ali and others. The approached my *gurū*, Khalifa Abid Husain, and said: 'Ustadji, what is this? You see this big musician has come to Lucknow and he doesn't find anybody competent enough to accompany him! It is an insult to us.' Then Ustadji thought it would be a disgrace for Lucknow if no competent accompanist could be found to follow the soloist. He said: 'I will do it.' He had not touched the tabla for eight months. Then there was a big soirée arranged and Ustad played. And he played so marvellously well that the soloist, after two minutes, fell on Abid Husain's feet and said: 'Nawab, you are a *k̲h̲alīfa*.'

It was said of Abid Husain that he was so knowledgeable, fast and well-practised that no other tabla player ever knowingly challenged him. The following story, related by Afaq Husain, indicates the way in which he earned his reputation:

The greatest player at that time in Benares, a player whom my grandfather [i.e. Abid Husain] appreciated and praised a lot, was Biru Misra. He was also well practised and had a God-gifted hand. There was a festival once where Abid Husain and Biru Misra met for the first time. It was in a royal state, Nepal or Indore, I can't remember, I was told by my elders. In those days the tabla used to be tied around the waist and one stood up to play it. When the music started there were eight or ten tabla players who began together. Among them were Abid Khalifa and Biru Misra. Well, after a couple of hours, eight or so tabla players stopped playing and left, leaving these two great players together. Neither of them knew who the other was at the time. Biru Misra asked some people who the other player was but they pretended they didn't know and said: 'How do we know who he is? Who can tell?'

They went on playing for three or four hours. The speed increased and began to reach a great height. Neither player was getting tired; they were both well-practised players. After four or five hours Biru

Misra thought: 'I have got this far but I can go no further!' He stopped, took off his tabla and went to hail Abid Khalifa as a *gurū*. 'Khan Sahib, I didn't know who you were, and these people wouldn't tell me. I'd like the opportunity of hearing you play solo.'

So the time came, and at midday all the *ustāds* and *gurūs* and *k͟hān sāḥibs* gathered for a *maḥfil*, 150 or 200 of them. Abid Husain played for six or eight hours. Then Biru Misra said: 'Yes, you are a true *gurū*, a *k͟halīfa*.' He had a *gaṇḍā bandhan* ceremony and gave Abid Husain a shawl and presents. But Abid Husain was himself very honest and praised Biru saying: 'Come to me and I'll give you what I can, but your hand is so God-gifted that God himself must have given it to you.'

An amusing insight into the character of Abid Husain, and the nature of his relationship with the *kathak* dancers Bindadin and Kalka Prasad Maharaj, was provided by Birju Maharaj. The three used to practise together a great deal at Bindadin and Kalka Prasad's house, where Abid Husain was welcomed like a member of the family. They loved to play jokes on each other. For example, Bindadin Maharaj, a Brahmin, often prepared an exquisite dish of lentils which he served to Abid Husain with a large wooden spoon. Abid Husain, a Muslim, would purposely lift his bowl so that it touched the spoon and thus 'polluted' the lentils. Consequently, Bindadin and his brother could not themselves partake of the food and were forced to give it all to Abid Husain, who needless to say eagerly accepted the extra helping.

Abid Husain emerged as one of the wealthiest tabla players of the day, abundantly rewarded with gifts of money and jewellery from his patrons, who had invited him to perform all over India. He owned a total of four properties in the Mehmood Nagar area, and travelled within the city in his own phaeton. He spent a large proportion of his time in Calcutta, where he married. Habib Raza informed me that this constituted the first marriage contract between the two families of the Lucknow and Kothiwal *gharānās*. Until that point in time, the two families had remained rivals and had strictly avoided intermarriage. Now, Abid Husain had paved the way for a close new relationship between the two families. So, from the early 1900s onwards, members of the two lineages intermarried to the extent that some observers now fail to distinguish between the two, conceiving the whole as a single lineage in the Lucknow *gharānā*.

Abid Husain was appointed as the first professor of tabla at the Marris Music College (inaugurated in 1926 and later renamed the Bhatkhande Music College), where he taught for the last years of his life. An interesting impression of Abid Husain is obtained from a recollection of a certain Dr Chaubey, one of the first graduates of the College, which is quoted by Misra (1977b):

In our younger days we were fortunate that we knew Lucknow's great Tabla-player, Abid Husain, who was respected and feared by his contemporaries. He played wonderfully with an effortless ease and charm of his own. I can conjure up a slim, graceful figure bending over his incomparable Tabla with the gallantry of a lover and a courtier, producing sounds that turned into music the moment they were born.

Most probably as a direct result of the way in which he had practised in order to gain his pre-eminent position among tabla players in India, Abid Husain suffered from ailments in the last years of his life. He suffered from a knee complaint which had been aggravated by the kneeling posture he habitually took to play the tabla. This was the posture adopted in the courts of the *nawābs*, for tabla players, when not standing to play the tabla (in which case it would be tied around the waist in a cloth called a *bastanī*), would kneel to avoid the misdemeanour of pointing their feet at the kings and nobles. Abid Husain is said to have replied stoically to his doctors' advice: 'I may become ill but the name of my *gharānā* will live on.' During the twelve years of his *cillā* he was constantly being warned not to stay awake practising all night as it was beginning to induce in him a state of insomnia. He also suffered frequently from headaches. He eventually suffered a brain haemorrhage and died in June 1936 aged seventy.

Of the sons on Najju Khan, 'Haji' Zakir Husain is said to have had 'a good hand', one of the usual epithets for a good player. Chuttan Khan achieved fame, not as a result of his playing, but because he was a knowledgeable musician and a respected teacher. Amongst others, he taught Nayab Khan of the Lucknow *gharānā* and Akbar Husain of the Kothiwal *gharānā*. Chuttan Khan is said to have had a profound respect for the playing of Haider Husain of the Kothiwal *gharānā* (see Chart 3), and it is also likely that for a while he learned the tabla from the latter, for he was acclaimed as the only tabla player of the Lucknow *gharānā* who had knowledge of Kothiwal compositions. Chuttan Khan is also said to have been a regular visitor to Patna, where Haider Husain's father, Noori Khan, had settled after 1858. The youngest son of Najju Khan, Ladle Khan, remains an obscure figure. None of the three sons of Najju Khan themselves had any sons.

The succession of the *k̲h̲alīfa* had passed from Munne Khan to Abid Husain. Had Munne Khan lived longer, his son Bahadur Husain would have followed him as the next *k̲h̲alīfa*, provided he had been an accomplished performer and had possessed an authoritative knowledge of the *gharānā*'s style and compositions. Abid Husain himself had no son, but he did have a daughter, Kazmi Begum, whom he married to his nephew and foremost disciple, Wajid Husain. Thus, after the death of Abid Husain, Wajid Husain became the next *k̲h̲alīfa* of the Lucknow *gharānā*.

Of the three sons of Nadir Husain, Wajid Husain was outstanding: a musician who, throughout his life, remained devoted to intensive practice. His brothers, Raza Husain (more commonly known by his alias Rajju Khan) and Sajjad Husain, as well as his nephew Mustafa Husain, were all professional tabla players, though none showed the same ability as either Wajid Husain or his son, Afaq Husain. Wajid Husain delighted in speed of articulation, and was capable of playing the most difficult combinations of strokes with a rapidity and an effortless ease none could match. Like his contemporaries, among them Ahmadjan Thirakwa and Habibuddin Khan, he was essentially a tabla soloist, but he flourished at a time which proved to be an important socio-musical crossroads in Indian music.

Born in 1900, Wajid Husain was raised in an atmosphere of court audiences and elite soirées, and was thus led to expect rich rewards for his artistic services. However, on reaching maturity, he found he could no longer rely on this source of support, and he, like many of his contemporaries, was ill-equipped to adapt to the changes that took place in the patronage system. Only Ahmadjan Thirakwa managed the transition successfully, as much on the grounds of his personality as on the brilliance of his playing. The new world was markedly different from the old. Competition became stiffer for the diminishing sources of private patronage, and although the State became a major patron of music with All India Radio, this work was comparatively poorly rewarded. The new recruitment of musicians, notably from non-hereditary backgrounds, added to the numbers competing for work. The new middle-class audience identified strongly with the new recruits, and began to demand a different and more spectacular music. In addition, Indian music was beginning to be opened up to the

Plate 9. Khalifa (Ustad) Wajid Husain Khan

West, a change which heralded a rush of opportunity for those best equipped to cope with the challenge of the modern world.

The wealth created by Abid Husain began to dwindle away. In accordance with his supposed affluence, Wajid Husain was morally obliged to give sizeable dowries to the families of his two sons-in-law. The wealth was raised principally by selling off family property. At one critical stage just after Independence, when the money raised from further property sales had been spent and little work could be found, he and Afaq Husain were forced to open a small shop selling a few groceries, *pān* and cigarettes in order to make a living. However, this did not last long, and as post-Independence India sorted itself out after the carnage of the Hindu–Muslim riots and Partition, enough work was found to support the family. For a short time, Wajid Husain was engaged as a staff artist at AIR Lucknow.

The present *k͟halīfa* of the Lucknow *gharānā*, and the product of a patrilateral parallel-cousin marriage, is Afaq Husain Khan, who succeeded Wajid Husain on the latter's death on 24 May 1978. Born in November 1930, Afaq Husain began learning tabla from Abid Husain

Plate 10. Khalifa (Ustad) Afaq Husain Khan

at the age of four, and had learned twenty-five or so basic compositions by the time his grandfather died in 1936. Abid Husain's daughter, Kazmi Begum, was an intelligent and literate woman who had received a good education and could read and write Persian and Arabic as well as Urdu. She is said to have noted down many of Abid Husain's compositions, retaining a good many of them in her memory. Thus Afaq Husain's *taʿlīm* from his father was occasionally supplemented by compositions from his mother.

Afaq Husain was more successful than his father in that he did not have to adapt to a new artistic climate following Independence. He often travelled to Calcutta, where there was a good market for his playing, something he found increasingly difficult to come by in Lucknow. In 1958 he moved to Calcutta, leaving his family in Lucknow. He swiftly rose to fame by accompanying all the top artists of the era. He was the preferred accompanist firstly of Bade Ghulam Ali Khan and then Amir Khan, the greatest singers of the 1950s and 1960s. He recorded many discs, including several with Amir Khan.

Success, however, had one severe drawback: it incited jealousy in other tabla players in Calcutta, which resulted in a secret campaign to discredit Afaq Husain. He was subjected to *grūp-bāzī* and suffered a steady decline in his popularity, which in turn induced in him a state of depression. Finally, he left Calcutta, in 1971, and returned to Lucknow, where he worked in the Sangeet Natak Akademi before joining the Lucknow television centre, where he is currently a staff artist.

Afaq Husain's son, Ilmas Husain (born *c.* 1957), is also a professional tabla player and is on the staff of the Sangeet Natak Akademi of Lucknow as an accompanist. Both Afaq Husain and Ilmas Husain, like Wajid Husain before them, broadcast regularly from AIR. They also make several trips each year away from Lucknow to perform in music festivals and conferences. Afaq Husain has one other son, Ilyas Husain (born 1978), who began casual training in the tabla in 1986. While admitting that Ilyas would eventually learn the tabla, Afaq Husain was undecided about the future of his second son. He felt that, unless Ilyas showed a particular gift for, or interest in, tabla, he would not train him to be a professional musician. Afaq Husain is, at present, investing in a good education for his son, something which, he believes, will offer more security than a career as a tabla player.

There remain but two members of the Lucknow *gharānā* yet to be mentioned: Irshad Husain and Intizar Husain, the sons of Nayab Khan. I could discover little about them except that they 'give programmes' to earn a living, a phrase used to disguise the fact that they probably do most of their playing for *ṭawāʾifs*. I was told they were not accomplished musicians, and they appeared not to be in regular contact with other members of the *gharānā*.

Kothiwal: a separate *gharānā*?

Data already provided concerning the origins of the Kothiwal *gharānā* can be briefly summarised in the following way. Modhu Khan and his brother Zahid Khan, the founder members of the *gharānā*, arrived in Lucknow from a village called Jhajjar in the Punjab, during the reign of Nawab Nasir-ud-din Haider (1827–37). Modhu Khan was the teacher of Ram Sahai, who was later recognised as the founder of the Benares tabla *gharānā*. The family of Modhu Khan was given a *koṭhī* or mansion, as a reward for services as tabla players in the court of Nawab Wajid Ali Shah around 1850, and the family was henceforward referred to as the Kothiwal *gharānā*. Apart from this, no anecdotal information apparently remains, and we know virtually nothing about individual members of the *gharānā*. However, a limited amount of information is available regarding two major events in the history of the *gharānā* which affected nearly all members in the group. Firstly, family members migrated from Lucknow to other cities in India after 1858. Secondly, around the turn of the twentieth century nearly all members abandoned playing the tabla and instead took up the *sāraṅgī*.

With the departure of the court and the upheaval caused by the reorganisation of Lucknow by the British, there was a temporary loss of the demand needed to sustain a large community of musicians. Some left as members of the entourage of the King, while others parted in search of new sources of patronage. Of the five grandsons of Modhu Khan, two, Chote Khan and Rahim Bakhsh Khan, left for Kanpur, while three, Ghulam Imam Khan, Ghulam Haider Khan and Noori Khan, went to Patna. Some of Chote Khan's descendants returned to Lucknow from Kanpur in later years, but it is not known exactly when, nor how many. The descendants of Noori Khan remained in Patna while many of the descendants of Rahim Bakhsh, Ghulam Imam and Ghulam Haider left for Calcutta towards the end of the nineteenth century.

Around the turn of the twentieth century, all the great-grandsons of Modhu Khan, with two exceptions, abandoned the tabla for the *sāraṅgī*. The exceptions were Nisar Haider and Haider Husain, who, it was implied by my informants, were somewhat older than others of their generation. Haider Husain had no sons, but the son of Nisar Haider, Zakir Husain (alias Zakkan Khan), learned the *sāraṅgī*. So, also, did Bahadur Husain, who was considerably younger than his brother, Haider Husain. My two main informants on the genealogy and history of the Kothiwal *gharānā*, Habib Raza (whose paternal grandfather was a disciple of Allah Bakhsh Khan and Noori Khan, and whose family intermarried with the Kothiwal lineage) and Akbar Husain, both stressed the fact that all those who took up the *sāraṅgī* retained their tabla *taʿlīm*. For example Habib Raza said: 'They all had tabla *taʿlīm*, but gave up playing the drums in order to take up the *sāraṅgī*. Nevertheless, they still remembered a lot of tabla technique and compositions. For instance, Imdad Khan remembered how to play the tabla, and Bahadur Khan played the *sāraṅgī* well but still knew a great deal about the drumming of his *gharānā*.' And Akbar Husain said: 'My father's father [i.e. Saadat Ali Khan] played the tabla as well as the *sāraṅgī*, but he gave up the tabla at an advanced stage and concentrated fully on the *sāraṅgī*. In later years he taught the *sāraṅgī* to his children.'

There were conflicting opinions as to the reasons for this sudden change. Akbar Husain's argument was that the tabla was a less respected instrument than the *sāraṅgī* in the late nineteenth and early twentieth centuries, owing to its association with *ṭawāʾifs*. The reason, according to him, that the *sāraṅgī* had fallen in popularity during the course of the twentieth century was that it, too, had had its reputation smeared by the same association. This explanation appears unlikely because both the tabla and the *sāraṅgī* have always been associated with *ṭawāʾifs*, a fact Akbar Husain seemingly ignores. More probable, perhaps, is the explanation given by Habib Raza. He claimed that around eighty to one hundred years ago a *sāraṅgī* player could earn a higher income than a tabla player because of the much greater demand for *sāraṅgī* players as music teachers to the *ṭawāʾifs*, particularly in the larger and rapidly expanding cities such as Calcutta and Bombay.

At present, two members of the lineage play the tabla professionally: Akbar Husain, who for most of his life has lived in Lucknow, working as a staff artist of AIR until his transfer to the radio station in Bombay in 1985, and Munowar Husain, who lives in Bombay. Munowar Husain is not considered to be an accomplished performer, and from whom he learned the tabla is unknown. Munowar Husain 'gives programmes' to earn a living.

That there originally was a Kothiwal tabla *gharānā* quite distinct from the Lucknow *gharānā* is, I think, beyond dispute. Whether or not it still exists today, or whether or not it has been subsumed by the Lucknow tabla *gharānā*, is more difficult to determine. There is even considerable disagreement between the musicians concerned. Akbar Husain tended to refer to the past when supporting his claim that Kothiwal was still a separate *gharānā*: 'In Lucknow, it was accepted that there were two *gharānās*: one was Lucknow, the *gharānā* of the Khalifa Munne Khan Sahib and Khalifa Abid Husain Sahib, and the other was of Modhu–Zahid.' Afaq Husain, however, pointed to what he believed to be the present-day situation, and stressed that 'Kothiwal are our people . . . Kothiwal is respected as part of Lucknow . . . In the Lucknow *gharānā*, there are really only two players: Akbar Husain and me.' He certainly acknowledged that there were two lineages involved, but owing to the degree of intermarriage between them, he emphasises that 'the family is all one'. Akbar Husain, he said, was a disciple of Chuttan Khan, a Lucknow *gharānā* tabla player. He had consequently learned the Lucknow style of playing. Additionally there was a lack of continuity of tabla playing in the Kothiwal lineage, and little (if any) of the specialist knowledge of that *gharānā* survived.

Akbar Husain acknowledged that there had been a musical discontinuity in his lineage owing to the fact that his forefathers had chosen to take up the *sāraṅgī* instead of the tabla. His justification for the continued existence of the Kothiwal *gharānā*, however, was twofold. Firstly, it will be remembered that those musicians who gave up the tabla nevertheless retained their *taʿlīm*, and so it is implied that the specific body of specialised knowledge, including techniques and compositions, was never totally lost. Secondly, Akbar Husain's teacher, Chuttan Khan, is said to have learned the Kothiwal style and many of the *gharānā*'s compositions from Haider Husain, a style which he in turn taught to Akbar Husain. Chuttan Khan apparently told his pupil: 'Son, I took things from your home (*ghar*), and so I'm now giving back to you the things of your own home.'

As analysts, we should not try to judge the right and wrong of what these musicians believe. Instead, we should examine their possible motives in order to understand why and in what situations they hold these beliefs. There are quite obvious reasons why Akbar Husain should claim to be the only remaining tabla player representing the Kothiwal *gharānā*: it gives him the distinguished status of being a unique musical authority, a rarity because he is the last of a dying tradition and, hence, a musician of considerable importance. Most of all, perhaps, it gives him a separate identity. There are obvious reasons, too, why Afaq Husain should claim that only the Lucknow *gharānā* now remains: it reinforces his authority as the *k͟halīfa*, and asserts the musical dominance of his own lineage.

In summary, then, Akbar Husain believes he has retained the distinct style and knowledge of his forefathers of the Kothiwal tabla *gharānā*, while Afaq Husain believes that there is now only one style played by members of two closely allied lineages. If we must therefore reply to the question of whether or not Kothiwal constitutes a separate *gharānā* today, the answer must simply be that it depends on who one asks.

Assessing genealogical and historical data

The genealogical data presented in this chapter contains a certain amount of confusing and contradictory information concerning the membership of the *gharānās* under discussion. In addition, some members of the genealogies are far more conspicuous personalities than others owing to the greatly varying amounts of anecdotal information available to us concerning different individuals. For example, whereas we know a great deal about Abid Husain of the Lucknow *gharānā*, we know virtually nothing about his brother Nadir Husain. Consequently, important questions need to be asked: do genealogies ever represent true records of descent? (A prominent feature of many patrilineal societies, for example the Nuer (see Evans-Pritchard 1978: 192–248) is their use of genealogy as charter.) Furthermore, is anecdotal information a reliable record of the history of a *gharānā*? If not, then what exactly is it?

That genealogical and historical accounts are incomplete is quite obvious. This is a common experience in social anthropological research. However, it should perhaps be established whether or not their incompleteness is due to forgetfulness or lack of knowledge on behalf of successive generations of members, or, indeed, whether members have been deliberately selective with the information they wished to be passed on (sometimes known as structural amnesia). Both seem probable. Yet in the latter case, there may well be important reasons why certain information was selected in this way. Inevitably, I feel, the process reflects a strong tendency to omit the inglorious while perpetuating information which is necessary to explain the present and which glorifies the *gharānā*. This happens even in the present day. For instance, I was never told directly of the existence of the brothers Irshad Husain and Intizar Husain (see Chart 4) until one day I overheard a conversation in which their names were mentioned. This may be accounted for firstly by the fact that they most probably play the tabla in some of the country's less salubrious establishments, which is considered ignominious, and secondly that they have little or no Lucknow *taʿlīm* and therefore do not represent the *gharānā* musically. Likewise, I have never been fully informed about several members of the Kothiwal genealogy who were 'not worthy of mention' (and who therefore still do not appear in the genealogy given in Chart 3). The point is clear. If this selectivity occurs nowadays, then why should it not have been practised in the past?

An analysis of historical data reveals a strong tendency to idealise the past. Thus many statements may be found which refer to the abundant patronage offered by kings and nobles, to knowledgeable and musically sophisticated audiences, to glorified competitions between musicians, and to the seemingly unlimited time available for learning and practice. In contrast, contemporary affairs tend to be dominated by the necessity for musicians to find full-time employment, which leaves comparatively little time for practice. Prevalent also is competition of a 'political' rather than musical nature between musicians, as explained in Chapter 3. Thus the present compares poorly with the past. Perhaps this indicates a decline in the *gharānā* system in general as perceived by present-day *gharānedār* musicians. If so, then it is possible that this decline is also reflected in the three genealogies presented during the course of this chapter: namely, those of the Delhi, Kothiwal and Lucknow *gharānās*. Each appears to demonstrate, in very different ways, deterioration of the tabla *gharānā*. In the Kothiwal genealogy, tabla-playing was phased out and now only confusion remains as to whether or not it still constitutes a separate *gharānā*. In the Lucknow genealogy, it appears that the number of *gharānā* members has diminished owing to a lack of male offspring. As for Delhi, it is by no means clear why so little genealogical information now remains unless it has been selectively pruned by successive generations, for one reason or another.

Our conclusion must be that genealogical and historical data should not be taken literally as true accounts of the descent and history of musical families, though they no doubt provide us with a strong guideline. Most writers, I feel, have failed to recognise this, with the result that their interpretations may be weakened (see Owens's (1983) treatment of statements by, amongst others, the Dagars). Instead, we should treat such data as symbolic of contemporary ideas concerning both the past and present states of being a musician in India, and also as 'texts' available for manipulation in specific situations.

5 *Musical change as a result of perceptions and attitudes*

In this chapter, I shall draw on several examples to show how tabla players and the general listening public feel towards, and think about, each other. They demonstrate that attitudes are often influenced by general images of the tabla player as a lower-class, hereditary musician of moral ill-repute, and of the listening public as middle-class enthusiasts with little or no knowledge of the subtleties of tabla music. I feel justified in dealing with these general viewpoints in the knowledge that the ideas expressed here by both musicians and listeners alike recurred with almost predictable regularity. What is more, the attitudes of tabla players towards the listening public were frequently echoed by all kinds of non-tabla-playing musicians.

My aim is to show the profound effect such concepts have had on the development of Indian music with reference to two particular, and essential, aspects. The first is the kind of music and the type of musician audiences have chosen to patronise in recent times. It is important to remember here that the general listening public has become the ultimate patron of music, for it has decided who or what is to be popular and worthy of its patronage. Musicians, in turn, have aspired to popularity, which they believe will serve to propagate their systems of knowledge and styles of playing, and to recruit new and interested students who will continue the traditions and proclaim the names of their teachers for posterity. Many musicians have therefore capitulated to public taste while others, more usually (but by no means always) the older, hereditary musicians, have not only found this artistic compromise difficult to achieve but also undesirable. Members of the new generation of tabla players have been attempting both to break the musical mould and to free themselves from the ignominy associated with their social category by presenting the public with a new, clean-cut image. Socially and culturally, younger players identify more closely with the public they serve and, though they may well appreciate and admire musicians of the older generation for their musical abilities, they have openly joined in public condemnation of, and have thereby distanced themselves from, the lax moral behaviour that was associated with previous generations of tabla players. Indeed, to analyse the stereotypical tabla player in detail is to understand that public response is not primarily to the musician as an artist, but to the musician as a social being. In other words, public opinion has been swayed very little by musical factors and very largely by extra-musical ones. Naturally, this has fuelled musicians' arguments that audiences have little knowledge of music. They back up their claims by pointing to the fact that what little public response there has been to music is more often directed towards the trivial rather than to factors of great import.

The second aspect which these concepts have had a profound effect on is that of music education, more particularly the kind of music education the general middle-class public has demanded for its children, most of whom will form future generations of music listeners but some of whom are themselves potential professional musicians. The two systems under examination are, on the one hand, the *gharānā* system as embodied in the *gurū–shishya* (or *ustād–shāgird*) relationship, which until the twentieth century was the sole medium for transferring knowledge from generation to generation, and, on the other hand, the system used in the majority of music colleges. It will be seen once again that for a number of social, and not musical, reasons the public has chosen overwhelmingly the college system of music education.

Perceptions of, and attitudes towards, tabla players

Tabla players owe their low status to their socio-musical identity as second-class citizens of the music world. Musically, their occupational specialisation was the subservient role of accompanying the soloists: singers, dancers and instrumentalists. Socially, tabla players were traditionally recruited from low castes, in particular the *mīrāṣī* caste comprising communities of *doms* and *ḍhāṛīs*. Solvyns, writing in 1810, claimed that tabla was 'played only by *Loutchias*, people of dissolute manners, and by public prostitutes, who have it played in their houses by those who frequent them and share in their debaucheries'. '*Loutchia*' (i.e. *luccā*) was probably the most disparaging term Solvyns could have used, for its meaning implies a base, corrupt, vicious vagabond addicted to gambling, brawling and rioting (Platts 1977: 953).

The attitude taken by Solvyns is by no means defunct, for during my stay in India I frequently heard talk of music having been 'debased' by its connection with *ṭawā'ifs*, and I continually came across references to the 'moral corruption' or 'moral degradation' involved in the 'disreputable occupation' of tabla-playing. This historical association with *ṭawā'ifs* has branded tabla players with a stigma which still attaches today, although few actually perform, or are even in contact, with the small number of women still practising that profession. Nevertheless, a reputation for deviant behaviour, drunkenness and debauchery is reinforced by tabla players' supposed illiteracy – a historical fact for many members of the older generation, though rare in the present-day, younger generation. This reputation earned them the name *ṭabalci*, a pejorative term which, though still surprisingly common, has given way to the politer *ṭabliya* or tabla *bajānewālā* (lit. tabla player).

The close association of tabla players with *ṭawā'ifs* is a highly emotive issue. When raised, the subject was guaranteed to strike deep chords of horror in most 'decent' people I talked to, who found the matter embarrassing and inappropriate for discussion. It is true to say that, in the past, dancers and soloists also kept close company with *ṭawā'ifs*, both in their capacity as teachers and as admirers. Interestingly, most were then regarded with the same suspicion and mistrust that accompanists are still viewed with today. Consequently, rather than send their children to the *ustāds* to learn to sing or dance, the preferred option was for middle-class parents to choose a college of music. Nevertheless it was the accompanists, the tabla players and *sāraṅgī* players, who were closest to the *ṭawā'ifs*, because they relied on them for much, or in some cases all, of their work. Many tabla players and *sāraṅgī* players lived in or near the houses of the *ṭawā'ifs* and, like servants, formed an essential part of courtesans' entourages. As a result, they have retained the stigma of the association whereas the soloists, who were considerably more independent of *ṭawā'ifs* and who were traditionally drawn from higher-caste backgrounds, have not. Indeed, the prejudice against tabla players is as deep-rooted as ever with many people, as I found out for myself when I was looking for accomodation in the predominantly Muslim Firangi Mahal quarter of the old city of Lucknow. I had found a flat and had agreed on terms with its owner. He knew very well that I was interested in music and was involved in some kind of music-related research. Having viewed the flat, we went for a cup of tea and a chat, during which my potential landlord was curious to learn some further details of my research. I told him that I played the tabla and was researching into various social and cultural aspects of tabla playing in Lucknow. 'Oh dear!', he said worriedly, 'Does that mean you will also be visited regularly by other tabla players?' I replied that I expected my teacher to visit me both socially as well as to give lessons and that, in addition, a few of my fellow disciples would drop by from time to time. After a long, silent deliberation, the owner seemed somewhat embarrassed as he told me I could not rent that flat after all. He believed a great many people would raise objections on hearing the sounds of the tabla and on seeing recognised tabla players going to and from a house in the area. The local residents were bound to assume there were '*ṭawā'ifs*, dancing girls and prostitutes' in the area, which would not only reflect poorly on the local community, but very badly indeed on the owner of the property himself. I knew that Firangi Mahal was famous for its school of Islamic studies and so I asked if it was on the grounds of a religious prohibition on music that people would object. Apparently not, came the reply. Local residents would not have minded singing perhaps, but the sounds of the tabla and visits by recognised tabla players 'conjures up a particular vocation'.

People often pointed to the illiteracy of tabla players as an explanation for the deviant behaviour they assumed them to be either guilty, or capable, of. The sitarist, Ilyas Husain Khan, indicated the problem when he said of tabla players: 'Mostly they're illiterate, so they can't get on in the modern world because they know no etiquette: how they should speak to others.' Shankar Ghosh, a prominent member of the new generation of non-hereditary tabla players, gave the following reasons: '*Gharānā* players had no education because, in any case, it would have detracted from their work and practice. What use was an education to them? It was all a waste of time.' All this is certainly true. Afaq Husain admitted that he spent most of his childhood practising and little of it at school, for he knew that sustained *riyāẓ* was the single qualification required of him for his hereditary profession and not schoolwork. But like many of his contemporaries, he has had to change many of his attitudes to adapt to the modern world and has insisted on an education for his sons.

Education is an essential factor in elevating one's social rank, and many people considered degrees and other qualifications a positive asset to musicians, and that those with them might in consequence expect to progress further in their careers. Afaq Husain fully realised that the older generation had been 'left behind', as he put it, and that education would lead to an ability to incorporate new ideas, so allowing his sons to compete in a music world increasingly dominated by socially more sophisticated and worldly performers. However, it is important to remember that, although Afaq Husain changed his attitudes about education to adapt to the modern world, he never advocated the kind of musical compromise he believed many musicians of the new generation were making. His view that they played an assortment of unorthodox material, and his attribution of this to their worldliness, is supported by the opinion of the popular young tabla player Kumar Bose:

> I belong to the Benares *gharānā* but I take material from all sources. One shouldn't be limited or narrow-minded. We are a new generation of musicians. We are more educated and sophisticated than our forefathers. Therefore we should show that we have knowledge of [the old masters of the various *gharānās*] and can incorporate everything in our playing.

There has remained a genuine respect for the traditional knowledge possessed by *gharāne-dār* tabla players, but this has been far outweighed by the fear of what it might take to obtain it. Just such a fear was expressed by the father of a female student of tabla at the Bhatkhande Music College:

Ustāds have, first and foremost, the need or desire for service. The more a student serves the needs of his teacher and pays him well, the more he will get. If the student can't keep up with the expectations of him, then the teacher will just keep him going along in the dark. [The teacher] will go on wasting [the student's] time.

Of course, everyone understood that in order for a *gurū–shishya* or *ustād–shāgird* relationship to flourish, obedience and devotion on the part of the student were essential ingredients. But behind this understanding lay the realisation that an *ustād*'s 'need or desire for service' may lead to more than just paying him well. The student may be called upon to perform all kinds of services – from fetching *pān*, to doing household chores, or even washing clothes. If the student were female, she would be seen to be acting the totally unacceptable role of a mistress. The historical association of tabla players with *ṭawā'ifs* has led people to believe that students might well come into contact with, and be influenced by, a whole company of bad characters. Essentially, therefore, the fear was of moral corruption and, especially in the case of female students, of sexual impropriety. It is hardly surprising, then, that parents, considering their opinion of tabla players, have preferred the safer option of sending their children to music colleges.

The parent's remarks given above indicate a typical suspicion and mistrust of the *ustāds*, implying they are money-minded, secretive and insincere. Naturally, tabla players admitted to none of these charges. They defended themselves against accusations of being money-minded by pointing out that they too needed to earn a living wage and that students should never expect to get something for nothing. They totally rejected the notion that they were insincere, but acknowledged that because they were artists they were more prone to moods, which tended to make them appear erratic. Importantly, they claimed they were willing to put as much effort into teaching students as students themselves were willing to put into learning.

That tabla players are secretive and do not 'bring out their treasures', as one person put it, was a very common accusation. (Indeed, this was an accusation levelled at all kinds of musicians.) 'If one learns privately,' said a student of a music college, 'the teacher will keep certain private things from you. He won't give everything to all his students. A student won't get any more from the teacher than the teacher himself allows.' Most musicians, of course, asserted that they never hid things from anybody, especially their students. However, in practice I believe accusations may have been justified under certain circumstances, for I observed that musicians could be intensely proud of their knowledge. Afaq Husain certainly admitted to having compositions that he had never given to anyone, not even to his own son. Bhupal Ray Choudhuri suggested that there were two reasons for this kind of secrecy. Firstly, the student may not have proved himself worthy of learning certain techniques and compositions. With reference to my own playing, Afaq Husain told me: 'I keep something from you because I know it won't suit your hand, and if I give it I know you'll get bored trying to get it right and it may eventually spoil your hand.' Secondly, the teacher may judge the student to be untrustworthy. Sometimes knowledge was kept secret because, Afaq Husain went on, 'the student might go to someone else and give him that knowledge. That person doesn't already have that knowledge and he'll spoil the material because he has little *taʿlīm* and has done no hard work and *riyāẓ*. He has learned little and he'll destroy that knowledge.' In other words, knowledge was not given to a student regardless of his character and ability. So much depended on the student, as I found out for myself. As I progressed and improved, I was given increasingly difficult pieces along with the techniques needed to play them. At the same time I was warned not to give certain compositions to some of my fellow disciples, nor even to play these pieces to them. It was considered that they were not yet sufficiently advanced for such developments and they might try to imitate me, an attempt which might result in damage to their techniques. We each had material appropriate to our standards and, in much the same way, I could not expect to learn pieces from those more advanced than me. Still, it is easy to see how critics can misinterpret this behaviour, believing instead that material is withheld in order to exact a higher price for it, or that the dissemination of knowledge among disciples is forbidden so that each student in turn is forced to pay the price. With certain teachers, I was told, this is in fact what happened, but in my experience secrecy was generally employed as a method of safeguarding the integrity of the music.

A further example of secrecy designed to protect material from falling into the wrong hands occurred when I accompanied Afaq Husain to a concert in Benares. I saw how he first covered the skins of his tabla with a cloth before sitting to practise in our hotel room. This had the effect, rather like a silencer, of stifling the drum sounds. The reason for this action rested on the fact that the room was adjacent to those occupied by other tabla players who had converged on Benares to perform in the same music conference. Afaq Husain did not want his rivals to hear compositions that he wished to practise or perform for fear they might remember and perform them without acknowledging their true origin.

Gharānedār tabla players have also been seen as secretive for reasons which Meer (1980: 129) explains. *Gharānās* were traditionally closed groups contained largely within families, and music was considered a commodity which needed to be jealously guarded. This led to competition between the *gharānās*, and the only way to prevent competitors from getting to know techniques and compositions from one's own *gharānā* repertoire was to deny this knowledge to all but one's own sons. This, of course, is no longer the case. A son may well find himself in a better position than most to receive a fuller training than other students because he is constantly in contact with his father. But, as Bhupal Ray Choudhuri pointed out, a son had still to prove himself a worthy disciple before he could expect to learn everything. It may be that an unrelated disciple will prove himself more capable than the son of an *ustād*, and will consequently learn more. It is interesting to note, in this respect, that Ilmas Husain regarded himself primarily as the disciple of Afaq Husain, and secondly as his son.

Perceptions of, and attitudes towards, the listeners

In common with most North Indian musicians in general, tabla players regarded their audiences as being composed largely of unknowledgeable and unsophisticated listeners unable to appreciate the subtleties of the music being presented to them. Musicians displayed a wide range of emotions when referring to the listeners: some were cruel and contemptuous, while others were exasperated and despairing. With reference to the sheer stupidity of some listeners, one tabla player recalled an occasion when people sitting beside him in a concert asked when the *sitār* player was going to finish tuning his instrument. The sitarist, of course, had already begun to play. Nevertheless, considering their views they still took a great deal of notice of audience reactions.

More frequently, musicians referred to their audiences by comparing them with audiences of the past: either from personal experience or from what they had been told of past generations of listeners by older musicians. Sentences, therefore, often began with 'Nowadays . . .', or 'In the past . . .', and the word 'change' was liberally used. The content of these references may best be illustrated by the comments of one informant who said: 'Listeners have changed. Those discriminating people are not found in the galleries'; and by another who indicated that the change had been one 'from knowledgeable connoisseurs to ignorant laymen'.

When did this change occur? Most informants suggested that this had been a gradual process which began before Independence and was effected by the late 1950s or early 1960s. The renowned tabla teacher of Calcutta, Jnan Prakash Ghosh, told me that 'even thirty years back, a performer . . . would have occasion to play before an audience where he would find knowledgeable people who could understand what music was [and] who understood music better than the masses'. Significantly, throughout my research, I never once heard anyone say they considered the quality of audiences to have improved over the last two generations.

The general view of the modern audience was that it was one not only of ignorance and unsophistication but also one of unruliness and ill-discipline. Combined with this was the strong feeling that the interest of the audience lay not in the performance as a musical event, but rather as a social one. This opinion has been best illustrated by Ravi Shankar (1966: 45–6), who wrote: 'Audiences . . . who assemble for Indian music in our country have not as yet learned any discipline. They come and go as they please, talk loudly during the performance, greet their neighbours and circulate through the hall for a very sociable evening, much to the discouragement of the artists.' This view was reinforced by the former director of All India Radio Lucknow, A. A. Hanfee, who went on to explain that music had become 'a status symbol for the neo-rich class . . . They don't understand it, they're bored, but they will keep on sitting and listening to, or giving the impression that they are listening to, a musical performance.' This in turn was echoed by Shital Prasad Misra, who claimed that it had become fashionable merely to say 'I've heard Ravi Shankar' or some other notable musician.

But what is 'the audience'? To whom were tabla players, and indeed musicians generally, referring when they mentioned 'the audience', or 'listeners'? There is some considerable difficulty in defining the audience, as is acknowledged by Neuman (1980: 69), for it is a variable dependent upon the nature of the social or musical occasion. I agree with Neuman that musicians have tended to make black-and-white distinctions between connoisseurs and ignorant laymen, with little room for any intermediate category. In truth, each type of audience is composed of varying quantities of one or the other.

There are, broadly speaking, three types of audience. The first type comprises almost exclusively connoisseurs and is the smallest group in terms of numbers. Such an audience gathers mainly for private occasions like the birthday of an *ustād* or *gurū*, a disciple's *gaṇḍā bandhan* ceremony, or for *gurū-pūrnamā* in honour of a teacher. This audience mostly comprises other musicians, members of the musician's family, close friends, and students (see Neuman 1980: 69–70).

The second type of audience generally includes a large proportion of connoisseurs. In size it may number anything from twenty to fifty listeners or perhaps a few more. The nature of the musical event is in general not entirely as private as is the case with the first type of audience, but neither is it exactly open to the general public. Such functions are usually organised by small-scale music societies or affluent music-lovers with the facilities to hold a concert in their homes. This type of gathering is known as a *maḥfil*.

The third type of audience, while no doubt also containing a small number of both musicians and connoisseurs, is made up largely of unknowledgeable and unsophisticated listeners: the 'ignorant laymen'. In size, numbers can range from a hundred to several thousand, depending on the scale of the musical event envisaged. This has been taken to extremes in recent years by Ravi Shankar and Ali Akbar Khan, who have performed to vast gatherings of over 20,000 in sports arenas. It is precisely to this, the third type of audience, that musicians referred when speaking of 'the audience', for which they also used other English words, such as 'the public', 'the gallery', 'the mass audience', or simply 'the masses'. (It is noteworthy that most of my informants used English terms to describe this kind of gathering, even when speaking in Hindi or Urdu. The only Hindi/Urdu expression commonly employed was *ʿām log* – lit. the common people.) Whereas musicians often received gifts and small amounts of money from the first type of audience, and generally earned larger sums from the second type, it was from the third type of audience that they stood to gain most in terms of financial reward and general publicity. As stated earlier, the simple reason for this is that the general listening public has become the ultimate patron of music in the modern age.

Far from perceiving the audience to be a uniform block of people, as implied by their sweeping generalisations, musicians were able to distinguish between different kinds of audience, particularly between good and bad ones. Good audiences were to be found in Calcutta and Bombay, with pride of place going to the former in the eyes of most musicians. Audiences in Delhi and the cities of Uttar Pradesh and Bihar states were widely recognised as comparatively poor, both in terms of size and discipline. Lucknow fell into this second category.

Having cleared the ground by, firstly, noting that musicians believed audiences to be unknowledgeable and unsophisticated and, secondly, by identifying what is meant by 'the audience', we must now examine what the musicians perceived to be audiences' responses to music and the musical performance, for there clearly was a response, even if it was not to the musical intricacies and subtleties of the performance. The Calcutta-based sarodist Buddhadev Das Gupta suggested that audiences responded positively to music 'which is not really so substantial, but which pleases your ears and appeals to your lighter instincts instantly'. He also believed that many musicians today realised what they had to do in order to elicit such a response, and this resulted in 'a general tendency to cater to those particular tastes which will make you much more popular'. Some musicians, usually the older artists, have refused to make this compromise and have instead aimed to present their art as they thought it should be, whether or not this gained the audience's approval. (However, this is not to say that their music did not undergo changes.) Other musicians, more usually those of the younger generation, have attempted to be 'popular'. This implies a capitulation to public taste which in turn has precipitated changes in the music.

Musicians believed that the audience responded to things which, for analytical purposes, I have broadly divided into two types. The first type includes extra-musical factors, things unconnected with the music itself. The second type is very much part of the music and may best be described as 'musical trivia' or, as Buddhadev Das Gupta put it, music 'which is not really so substantial'.

Extra-musical factors consist, primarily, of the appearance and demeanour of an artist both within and outside the musical performance. Neuman (1980: 77–8) has drawn our attention to the importance of stage appearance, especially for members of the younger generation, who have become acutely sensitive to the powers of persuasion possible through visual communication with the modern audience. This is hardly surprising as it is a generation that has been raised under the strong influence of Bombay films. Since about 1960, not only films but also the advertising and literature surrounding the film industry have become far more widely available to the consumer. As part of the inexorable pursuit of the cult of the film star, films and magazines have become merely vehicles for promoting fashions in clothes, hair styles and, to a certain extent, behaviour. Great attention has therefore been given by many musicians to dressing elegantly, or even spectacularly, and to preening their good looks, as they have become aware that this could well have a positive effect on the audience. Neuman (1980: 77–8) has mentioned how one musician practised in front of a mirror in order to rid himself of grimaces and funny expressions and, instead, trained himself to smile and 'look nice' for the audience. The Lucknow-based sarodist Narendra Nath Dhar admitted that he himself tried to avoid bad facial expressions in performance and added the perceptive comment that audiences today were spectators, not listeners. He implied that bad looks or untidy dress could easily have an adverse effect and create considerable disaffection in the audience.

A practical example of the interest taken in appearance comes, paradoxically, from Calcutta, where audiences have tended to be musically more sophisticated. In 1981, I witnessed a concert given by the *santūr* player Shiv Kumar Sharma and the tabla player Zakir Husain. Vijay Kichloo of the Sangeet Research Academy, himself a musician, introduced the artists with the words: 'Firstly, I must say what a great pleasure it is to see two such handsome young men on stage tonight.' This precipitated a warm 'Ah!' of approval from the audience, which was followed by an enthusiastic burst of applause.

Susheela Misra agreed that this view of the audience as spectators and not listeners was quite justified, though she claimed it was essentially a phenomenon pertinent to North and not South India. Interestingly, she showed that she, as a connoisseur, also found appearance to be an important factor:

> Today musicians are very smart and very well dressed. Many of them are so good-looking. These are very important points. You can't ignore that. Good looks are definitely an asset. Same as actors . . . if an actor is good and if he is also good-looking, isn't it a plus point? . . . But, you know, in the South [of India] it's entirely different. I must tell you that in Karnatak music there are some extremely ugly musicians but they get such a big audience. There audiences are only concerned with the art . . . Actually they make fun of people in the North [who are] more concerned about looks.

The message is clear: if relatively sophisticated connoisseurs are impressed by looks, then one may imagine the effect appearances have on less sophisticated listeners.

Many musicians believed that an awareness of the importance of appearance to the audience had led some to take extreme measures to communicate visually with the public. Some complained that musicians appeared on stage dressed more appropriately for 'a fashion parade' than a concert, and others joked about artists who changed their costumes after each musical item. I have myself witnessed the bizarre spectacle of a young tabla player who wore a gleaming, shiny, purple and yellow shirt studded all over with sparkling sequins.

The second category of things to which the audience has responded, as perceived by musicians, is 'musical trivia'. Into this category fall elements of light, folk and film music which were often incorporated into a 'serious' performance. Also included are musical gimmicks or special effects which, according to many older musicians, had no meaning in the context of the traditional repertoire. Speed for speed's sake, or excessive noise, or overcomplex rhythmic devices and mathematical calculations, were all criticised for being trivial and insubstantial although it was recognised that their use has provoked a positive audience response.

That musical subtleties were lost on most people who formed the audience was supported by statements from two informants whose opinions broadly represented those of the man in the street. One indicated a preference for lighter forms of music and said: 'The man in the street prefers *g͟hazals*. The words are more easy to follow.' This was echoed by another, who further suggested that 'an ordinary person like me gets bored by classical music. If it were to be presented in a more modern way, I'd like it better.' Musicians were aware of these kinds of preference and often adapted to cater to these lighter tastes. Krishna Kumar Kapoor, in a vocal recital before a gathering of about 200 music students from the Bhatkhande Music College in Lucknow where he lectured, was disconcerted by the lack of response in the audience to his singing and so slipped deftly from a classical composition (a *choṭā k͟hayāl*) into a Hindu devotional song (*bhajan*). This had a startling and immediate effect. A sudden wave of interest swept through the hall and audible appreciation increased tremendously. In similar fashion, some of the most vociferous and enthusiastic approval of tabla music I have witnessed followed an item by a drum ensemble comprising tabla, *ḍholak*, *naqqāra* and *nāl*. The tabla player began to incorporate folk rhythms into his playing in imitation of the other drums. This obviously created great interest among the general public and was a popular topic of conversation for many days.

Susheela Misra sensed a problem in offering the audience a type of music to which it would be able to respond. The result, she claimed, was that the audience had begun to request, or even demand, that its tastes be met. She had frequently heard people impatiently calling out for a *ṭhumrī* after, and even during, the first item in a performance of a *k͟hayāl*. Another consequence was highlighted by Vikram Singh, who claimed that the concert atmosphere was no longer conducive to performances of 'serious' music:

> In the old days, the music conferences . . . were genuine conferences. Only genuine classical artists were invited. Today, that stage has been captured by light musicians, pop musicians and film musicians. And the real, genuine artists . . . can't come to the stage, even for five minutes, because they would be booted out! . . . Big sitarists today come here and they start playing *ṭhumrīs* and *g͟hazals* on the *sitār*. That is playing to the gallery because this is not *sitār bāj*. And vocalists come here . . . and when people say, 'Kindly sing that *g͟hazal*', [they] will stop everything and sing it.

Gimmicks and special effects are frequently employed in catering to the lighter tastes of the audience and in attracting applause. There are many kinds of gimmick, but I shall limit the discussion to one example often heard in tabla-playing. This is the excessive use of portamenti in the playing of the *bāyāṅ*, the bass drum in the set, most frequently referred to by the English word 'modulation'. Naturally, modulation has always been used in tabla-playing to add inflection to the 'voice' of the drums and to introduce colour and variety to the sound. It is when modulation becomes a device used in isolation, in other words as the main voice of the tabla, that it has been termed a gimmick by its critics. Susheela Misra believed that the use of *bāyāṅ* modulations always attracted audience response and said: 'Kanthe Maharaj was the first person who began this *bāyāṅ* modulation business, as far as I know. Now of course everybody does it, because the audience wants it.' But we are dealing with two very different contexts here. Kanthe Maharaj, according to his disciple Shital Prasad Misra, used modulation as a kind of deliberate musical joke: imitating the roaring of lions. Younger tabla players, however, nowadays often employ endless whoop-whooping sounds on the *bāyāṅ* as an integral part of a serious performance.

In all fairness, it was recognised that *bāyāṅ* modulations could be tastefully employed too. Afaq Husain Khan was quite approving of Zakir Husain's use of the *bāyāṅ* to produce the special effect of playing the pitches of the *lahrā* composition in unison with the accompanying *sāraṅgī* player. He may not have sanctioned this so readily had the effect been used in total isolation, but, in fact, he admired the way Zakir Husain had threaded the strokes of the *bāyāṅ* into a *relā* in combination with rapidly articulated strokes in the other hand.

A gimmick or special effect provided an unsophisticated audience with something palpable and easy to understand in a music that often proved rather abstract and difficult to grasp. Something else which may be considered equally tangible is speed, both in terms of actual tempi as well as the rapid physical articulation of notes or strokes. An example of the use of sheer speed to gain audience applause came from Narendra Nath Dhar. As part of a presentation designed to entertain a delegation of businessmen attending a conference, this sarodist was allocated twenty minutes in which to perform. Of the twenty minutes, the final five were devoted solely to the rendition of superfast *jhālā*, a technique which utilises rapid articulation of the *cikārī* (drone) strings of the instrument. The audience broke into loud applause several times in appreciation of this display of virtuosity. Following the performance, Narendra Nath Dhar asked me if I had enjoyed his playing. I said I had, but asked him why he had decided to play so fast in the *jhālā* section. He replied that the kind of audience which he was playing for responded most favourably to this device. He later explained to me his reasoning, which was based on a differentiation between two types of listener and his perception of their differing tastes. On the one hand, there were the *jānkārs* (lit. one who knows), who understood the music, thought deeply about it, and felt it in their hearts: 'They will appreciate the tempo, the colour, the actual [sound] production and the tone.' On the other hand, the 'ordinary listeners will appreciate the gimmicks. If you play very fast they will start to clap.'

The same was true of tabla-playing. Any rendition involving rapid finger movement, often verging on the purely acrobatic, was more than likely to be greeted with applause. Thus many players used combinations of strokes which allowed for the maximum audio-visual effect, an increase in visible articulation being accompanied by a corresponding increase in noise, which was channelled through invariably poor-quality amplification systems to produce a truly deafening and visceral noise. The effect has often been jokingly referred to as 'machine-gun fire', especially when endless strings of high-speed *tirakiṭatakatirakiṭataka* rip through the listeners' ears. Jnan Prakash Ghosh, in a comment referring both to audiences and to the younger generations of tabla players, said: 'People have taken a fancy to speed today. Just as in vehicles and transport, so in music. Go fast and people will like it. Go as fast as you can! Doesn't matter if you are not clear!'

Something which was often mentioned in the same breath as excessive speed and noise was the use of complex arithmetical calculations and difficult cross-rhythms. Many people felt that this aspect of music had been overemphasised in modern playing, often to the extent that musical qualities had been sacrificed. The majority of tabla players asserted that one of the main reasons for the popularity of Allah Rakha Khan, Zakir Husain and Kishan Maharaj with the general public was their undoubtedly amazing ability to play cross-rhythms and produce complex calculations, particularly in *tihā'ī* patterns, an ability which tended to impress an audience greatly.

It must be said, however, that nothing was held to be entirely bad. There was broad agreement that the trend towards rhythmic complexity in music was a good thing, and also that speed of articulation was welcome provided other technical features were not lost, such as the clarity of the strokes or the general design of the composition. Many times I heard musicians say: 'Zakir [Husain] is good: his hand is very fast and clear, and he has a good brain for arithmetical calculations.' Our conclusion must be that an awareness of what interests and excites the audience, and what mobilises its responses in a person's favour, has had a profound effect on what tabla players (as well as musicians in general) have chosen to present to their listeners in performance.

Changes in performance

The tendency to rely upon musical gimmicks may be said to constitute musical change in the sense that such devices were most probably avoided in the past except, as could be seen in the case of Kanthe Maharaj, in deliberate jest or play. While being critical of gimmicks, many older musicians, like my teacher, tolerated them as nothing more than minor and relatively unimportant changes affecting only the surface structure of Indian music. What did give real cause for concern to traditionalists like him were more important changes which hit at the deeper structures of the music. In this section, I shall discuss some of these fundamental changes in Indian music with particular reference to tabla-playing. Included are changes to the structure of the musical performance, the gradual disappearance of many compositional types and playing techniques, and the decrease in importance of the tabla solo as a performance genre.

Many critics believed that fundamental changes were affecting all forms of classical music in the present day. Taking the example of vocal music, though implying that his statement was relevant to a much wider field, the Calcutta-based sitarist, lecturer and music critic, Subroto Roy Chowdhury, said:

> In the last fifty years, I could say that vocal music has gone towards lighter forms . . . In vocal music you fail to get a definite structure . . . this you would never find in any vocalist fifty years ago like Faiyaz Khan Sahib, or even Bare Ghulam Ali Khan Sahib . . . There is a tendency among so-called modern vocalists of trying to mix a few purple patches which are linked by the audience into a performance. So at most we find brilliance, brilliance in patches.

Implicit in this statement is the general public's ignorance of the structure of a vocal performance. Subroto Roy Chowdhury believed, like so many others, that this ignorance had ultimately been responsible for changes in the music. In conversation, he frequently referred to the audience as 'the gallery', as a group of spectators who above all demanded entertainment from a concert as if it were a circus show. This was an idea shared by the sitarist Nishat

Khan, son of Ustad Imrat Khan. Not only did the audience expect circus-like entertainment, but modern musicians gave the listeners exactly what they wanted:

Nowadays it's bang! bang! bang! bang! bang! bang! bang! It's like a circus show, it's like an entertainment. This aspect of bang! bang! is a musical subject which should appear maybe for five minutes in a three-hour performance . . . or it could come for two or three minutes. But to make a whole concert like that is exactly like a circus show with people laughing, clapping and clowning. Now, one common tendency is to begin playing slowly, then making it double the speed, then [doubling it] again, then taking it to a climax, and then playing a *tihā'ī* as if a helicopter is landing.

From this it may be seen that Nishat Khan did not object to gimmicks and special effects if used in moderation, a view shared by some traditionalists, though others argued forcefully that there should be no room for them at all in a serious performance. What was strongly objected to was a performance which comprised nothing but gimmicks, special effects, elements of light or popular music, and speed for speed's sake. The structure of this type of performance has proved to be radically different from traditional performance structure: gone is the development of *rāg*, and gone is the logical progression from one compositional type to another. All that is left is 'brilliance in patches', a series of gimmicks which the audience perceives and accepts as a performance. It was Subroto Roy Chowdhury's belief that, as a result, the modern performer could survive by relying on only a handful of tricks that he could demonstrate to the audience regardless of the particular requirements of any musical situation. He gave examples of young tabla players who had built up small repertoires of a dozen or so gimmicks which they played whenever the opportunity arose, regardless of whether they were accompanying vocal, instrumental or dance music, or indeed performing tabla solo. To compare the traditional structure and content of performance to these new developments was, according to Nishat Khan, like trying to compare a film by Satyajit Ray to a commercial Bombay movie, or Beethoven to pop music. Audiences today were more intent on enjoying the entertainment of the latter, he felt, rather than appreciating the art of the former. His verdict that art had suffered with the increase of playing to the gallery was one shared by many.

That art has suffered as a consequence of the audience's lack of interest in traditional performances is illustrated in the following extract from a critique of a tabla solo recital given by Afaq Husain (Anon 1981):

Tabla solo in all its detail was presented by this gharanadar khandani artiste to the delight of the young maestros of tabla present. Kaida, Gatha, Paran, Rela, Tukra and Chakradhar flowed with a pleasant awareness of the aesthetic purpose and one admired the way Afaque Husain avoided the conventional stereotyped phrases which most tabla players use to get audience applause. A brilliant balance between the right and the left hand enhanced the effect of the bols and one marvelled at the way the bayan was used at half pace even with superfast bols, demonstrating the height of technical mastery.

This unassuming tabla player, a doyen of the Lucknow *gharānā* and a musician's delight, has all the good qualities of classical tabla playing. His inability to cater to the gallery has been largely responsible for the few opportunities we have of listening to him.

This last sentence is the really important one. It shows that, although Afaq Husain may well have been able to delight the young maestros of tabla with superb technique and 'all the good qualities of classical tabla playing', he could not attract the interest of the general public and was therefore consigned to relative obscurity. The point is that the 'young maestros' will avoid making this mistake and will aim to give audiences the 'conventional stereotyped phrases' they prefer. Hand in hand with the relative obscurity of musicians who adhered to the traditional structure and content of performance was the relative obscurity of their traditional music, a music that has not been widely propagated because it has failed to capture the imagination of unsophisticated listeners. Its place has been taken by a type of tabla-playing that has not adhered to traditional values but instead has adopted new values, the most essential of which is catering to the gallery.

There is no such thing as a 'correct' structure or order for a tabla performance. Tabla players held different opinions as to what the order of compositional types should be, as has been clearly demonstrated in the six solo tabla performances transcribed by Gottlieb (1977). Differences of opinion were not only held by musicians of different *gharānās* but also by musicians of the same *gharānā*. Furthermore, an individual played structurally different tabla solos depending on the circumstances of the performance, the time available and, above all, his mood. However, there appeared to be a general consensus of opinion that, following an introductory composition (e.g. *peshkār*, *mohrā* or *uṭhān*), pieces which may be generally termed 'theme and variations' (e.g. *qāʿida*, *calan* or *relā*) were to be followed by 'set compositions' (e.g. *gat*, *ṭukṛā*, *cakkardār* or *paran*). Latif Ahmed Khan likened this progression to that found in instrumental music of *ālāp* followed by *gat*, the *ālāp* and 'theme and variations' being given over to the development of ideas through the expansion of basic material, and the *gat* and 'set compositions' being devoted to the treatment of precomposed pieces. (Though an interesting and credible parallel, not dissimilar to that made by tabla players of the Benares *gharānā* between *ṭhekā-qāʿida-relā* and *ālāp-jor-jhālā* (Shepherd 1976: 177), I have heard little support from other musicians for this idea.) But in catering to the tastes of the modern audience, some young tabla players I heard perform ignored even this most fundamental of progressions from 'theme and variations' to 'set compositions'. Indeed, many of the individual compositional types were mixed together to form larger, hybrid units. Afaq Husain often said that the tendency in young tabla players today was to begin with a *qāʿida*, turn it into a *relā*, and then to round it off with a *ṭukṛā* or *cakkardār*. This formula was then repeated a number of times with a few gimmicks thrown in for good measure. Care should be taken to distinguish between the kind of haphazard construction implied by Afaq Husain and the highly structured performances of Benares musicians as described in Shepherd (1976), and demonstrated in Kishan Maharaj's performance as documented in Gottlieb (1977).

The above observation highlights the fact that few modern musicians have chosen to explore the full range of traditional compositional types available to them and have often broken the rules of those in which development or improvisation is possible and desirable. Subroto Roy Chowdhury perceived that many forms had been simplified and that *qāʿida* in particular was frequently subject to incorrect development, something I was continually being told by my teacher. Inam Ali Khan, the *khalīfa* of the Delhi tabla *gharānā*, whose speciality is the *qāʿida* form, went as far as to say that *qāʿida* is performed incorrectly by everyone in India but himself, an accusation supported with a great deal of expert knowledge, analysis and demonstration in the discussions I had with him.

The techniques of improvisation used in playing *qāʿida* are basic to all theme-and-variations compositional types. I have shown elsewhere (Kippen and Bel 1984: 28) that these techniques rely on rules which, if violated, result in the incorrect rendition of the form. It was pointed out to me time and time again, by both Afaq Husain and Inam Ali Khan, that nowadays even the most elementary rule was frequently broken, namely that the player had to limit himself to the range of *bols* stipulated in the *qāʿida*. To give a simple example, when a *qāʿida* is constructed from a strictly limited vocabulary of *bols*, as in the famous Delhi composition of Natthu Khan,

dhāti ṭedhā	tiṭe dhādhā	tiṭe dhāge	tīna kīna
tāti ṭetā	tiṭe dhādhā	tiṭe dhāge	dhīna ghīna

then the *bols tirakiṭa* or *dhirakiṭa* should not be used in the ensuing development. Of course, in practice they frequently are by players who ignore the rules.

Many traditionalists, like my teacher, lamented the lack of certain types of set composition in the performances of the new generation of tabla players. He observed with dismay the decrease in importance of compositional types such as the *gat*, of which there are many varieties. I believe this may be for three reasons. Firstly, *gats* have always been widely considered as the most technically difficult of all pieces. Secondly, they are traditionally the most highly prized of compositions and have been guarded in the past by *gharānedār* musicians for special occasions, such as a musical competition or as part of a dowry. Thirdly, whereas a few *gats* end with simple *tihā'īs*, the majority have no *tihā'ī* at all. Afaq Husain, however, had noticed that *ṭukṛās* had, in fact, become more common and that they often concluded with much longer and more complex *tihā'īs* than in the past. It seems, therefore, that the modern tendency has been towards the increased size and complexity of the *tihā'ī*, probably for the musical tension it creates and the corresponding relaxation it brings in resolution, an effect easily enhanced by some spectacular histrionics from performers.

This leads us to another criticism frequently made by older musicians of tabla players of the younger generation. It rested on the belief that, in terms of actual playing technique, tabla-playing was now much easier than it had once been. Habib Raza Khan remembered what tabla-playing was like at the beginning of the twentieth century and observed that much more difficult combinations of strokes were commonly used then than were generally found today. Jnan Prakash Ghosh, also with a memory stretching back to many of the great tabla masters of the early twentieth century and in possession of an extensive private library of tapes and records of old masters, suggested, with some authority, that the material played was 'technically much more difficult'.

Many explanations were given as to the reasons for this change. One such explanation related to the size of the *dāhinā* used in the past as opposed to that widely used now. Hirendra Kumar Ganguli showed me an old *kāṭ* whose head measured seven inches in diameter. He told me that heads with a diameter of between six and seven inches were standard in the past and were commonly tuned to the *pancam*, *madhyam*, and even the lower *shaḍj*, of the scale. In comparison with the size of head in use today, which measures between five and five and a half inches in diameter, thus allowing it to be tuned to the upper *shaḍj*, combinations of strokes then required far greater finger and hand movement and were in that sense more difficult.

Another explanation given was that in the past, when knowledge was retained within families of occupational specialists, and disciples often lived with their teachers, there was a great deal more time not only to observe and learn but also to practise difficult motor skills. Now, few disciples live with their teachers and many are forced to work in order to support themselves, or are studying in schools or universities.

Whatever the reason, and it is likely to be a combination of many factors, most critics believed that many technical skills had been lost in the pursuit of a kind of playing in popular demand with the modern audience, in particular the demand for speed of articulation. The old masters, such as Ahmadjan Thirakwa, restricted themselves to much more moderate speeds while paying greater attention to the beauty and clarity of individual strokes and the shape of each phrase. In doing so they applied themselves to the finer details of finger placement in the articulation of complex stroke combinations in order to fully develop technical dexterity. According to Bhupal Ray Choudhuri, many modern players had retained in their repertoires only those combinations of strokes that facilitated the greatest speed of articulation. Most of these are closed, non-resonating strokes such as *tira kiṭa taka* and *dhira dhira kiṭa taka*. When taken to high speeds these *bols* are spectacular and have a tremendous audio-visual impact on the audience. What is more, when used in combination with crisp, open *kinār* strokes, they are particularly effective with the poor-quality amplification systems so common in India. However, there are many other stroke combinations that, owing to their relative technical difficulty, do not allow for such high speeds, as I found out for myself in my own practice. Thus, *bols* such as *ghiṛa naga dhiṅga naga* and *dhā ghiṛa naga dhene ghene* are rarely heard in tabla-playing nowadays. It will also be noticed that these are open, sonorous strokes whose resonances overlap and become garbled if played at high speed. The jumbled effect is further exaggerated by the poor amplification and all subtlety is lost.

As an example of a limited repertoire of stroke combinations, Bhupal Ray Choudhuri often cited the playing of Allah Rakha and Zakir Husain. He made it clear that his was neither a value judgement of their ability nor an attack on their integrity as musicians. His was purely an observation resulting from an analysis of their techniques and compositions. Bhupal Ray Choudhuri referred specifically to the very high incidence of the *bols dhā tira kiṭa, tira kiṭa taka*, *dhātiṭe dhitiṭe* and *tiṭe katā gadī gina*, an observation which Gottlieb's transcription of a performance by Allah Rakha (1977 vol. 2: 185–223) has gone a long way towards substantiating.

Another, and in my view extremely important, reason given for the undermining of the structure, compositions and techniques of tabla performance is the gradual demise of the tabla solo itself. By this I mean not only that there have been apparently fewer opportunities for musicians to perform tabla solos, but also that the social circumstances, and therefore the environment, most conducive to its performance are rarely, if at all, found nowadays in any but the most private musical gatherings.

Neuman (1980: 70) has quoted Ahmadjan Thirakwa as saying that tabla solos were, in fact, less common in the past and were heard only in *maḥfils* by an audience of 'brother musicians'. The evidence I collected in fact points to the opposite being the case. Tabla solo was, I was frequently told, more commonly heard in the past and was a feature not only of *maḥfils* but also of the courts and the houses of the aristocracy, as well as being a popular item in the early music conferences. Latif Ahmed Khan (Anon 1984: 5) has said:

> In the old days, I think the tabla was more important – in the festivals, and in the courts of the rajahs and maharajahs. At that time, the accompaniment was very different. You could not show yourself very much in tabla. So that's why they used to have many tabla solos, in both the festivals and the courts. But now since the style has changed, you can hear a great deal of tabla with sitar, and very much with dance. So tabla solo performances have become less frequent in the festivals.

Subroto Roy Chowdhury expressed much the same opinion that tabla solos were now a rarity, and that tabla players 'are earning their bread by playing with instrumentalists'. Because of this, many structurally complex compositional types found in the traditional solo performance, such as *qāʿida* and *gat*, have not been propagated, and this has resulted in their incorrect rendition or even their exclusion from the modern repertoire. When opportunities have arisen for a tabla solo performance, many traditional musicians who have relied on forms such as *qāʿida* and *gat* have found they are rarely appreciated or understood. According to Jnan Prakash Ghosh, these opportunities are usually better exploited by younger musicians:

> Young people . . . don't have any occasion to give a performance of solo tabla. And if they have any chance, it is in front of people who don't understand what tabla is . . . Naturally the whole point is economics. You see, every tabla performer wants to earn, and he can by playing for people who don't understand. Therefore the performer plays things which [listeners] can understand and that means the much lighter things, rhythmic things, and rhythms.

Apart from there now being fewer opportunities to perform tabla solos, changes in tabla-playing have come about, according to Bhupal Ray Choudhuri, because of the absence of an essential element that was common in the past: the *farmāʾish*. The *farmāʾish* (request) involved the active participation of connoisseurs and fellow musicians, in other words a gathering of knowledgeable listeners who thus created the most conducive environment in which the player could develop all the skills necessary to exploit the tabla solo fully. Any member of the audience was at liberty to make a *farmāʾish* in order to test the knowledge and technical ability of the tabla player. Requests were made for rare examples of certain types of composition, or conditions and limitations were imposed upon the musician within which he had to play. If the tabla player was unable to draw on material from his repertoire, he was forced to compose spontaneously. For instance, a few simple examples of *farmāʾish* might be:

1. Compose a *tihāʾī* in *tīntāl* beginning half way through the fourth *mātrā*.
2. Play a *cakkardār* in three cycles.
3. Within one cycle, beginning and ending on *sam*, play the same phrase five times in five different speeds.
4. Play a particular *qāʿida*, but instead of utilising the *kinār* for the strokes *dhā*, *tā*, or *nā*, use the *sūr* (centre of the drumhead).

Quite clearly, then, without a knowledgeable audience to question and test the musician, and without the intimacy of the small gathering, such as the *mahfil*, which allows for a greater two-way 'conversation' between artist and audience, the *farmāʾish* has become obsolete. The 'inhospitable and impersonal environment of large concert halls' (Higgins 1976: 23) has obviously not proved conducive to the *farmāʾish*, nor has the general public shown itself to be sufficiently educated, musically speaking, to know how best to test players' skills and knowledge. The dilemma for those musicians who have received a more traditional training, and who have inherited repertoires of *farmāʾishī* pieces, is that they now have little scope to perform these compositions because they are confronted with audiences that neither understand nor appreciate the particularity of their knowledge and skills.

At this point, I would like to return to the statement made by Latif Ahmed Khan that 'since the style has changed, you can hear a great deal of tabla with sitar, and very much with dance. So tabla solo performances have become less frequent in the festivals.' What is implied here is that the new style of accompaniment used in instrumental and dance performances has more or less supplanted the tabla solo by incorporating several of its features into the structure of the accompaniment. In order to investigate this I intend to discuss briefly the differences between the old and the new styles of tabla accompaniment in performance.

I received conflicting statements outlining the nature of the style of accompaniment prevalent in the past for classical vocal and instrumental genres. On the one hand there were those who referred to the tabla player as a subordinate who played nothing but a 'straight (*sīdhā*) *ṭhekā*', in other words a plain, unembellished form of the *ṭhekā*. Take, for instance, the comment by A. A. Hanfee: 'In earlier days, [tabla] performers were given a subordinate role. The best praise which a tabla player could get when accompanying a great artist was that he was keeping the *ṭhekā* alright.' But, on the other hand, many informants referred to a *laṛant* (fighting) style of accompaniment being prevalent in the past. This style was also known as *sāth saṅgat* (lit. together accompaniment). Here the tabla player would respond to the *tāns* (rapid melismatic passages) of the instrumentalist by playing set compositions, or improvising, simultaneously. He aimed to 'shadow' the soloist by following the same rhythmic patterns and by attempting to create strings of *bols* which he felt matched the melodic contours of the *tāns*. The essence of this kind of accompaniment may still be heard in much *pakhāwaj* accompaniment to *dhrupad* singing, notably in the playing styles of Rama Shish Pathak and Ramji Upadhyaya. The latter informed me that, by 'shadowing' the soloist, the accompanist was reinforcing and enhancing the effect of the soloist's music.

The late Nikhil Banerjee related to me the story of his encounter with the tabla player Kanthe Maharaj of Benares. Before their concert together, Kanthe Maharaj said: 'Look son, in our day we used to go along together. Come on brother! Let's go together!' In the concert, every *tān* that Nikhil Banerjee played received a spontaneous and simultaneous response from Kanthe Maharaj. Thus they enjoyed a friendly but competitive relationship on stage. Evidently, as is implied by the word *laṛant*, relationships between soloist and accompanist were not always so friendly, and many stories tell of how musicians attempted to outplay each other in performance.

It seems obvious to me that neither of these conflicting statements about the nature of the style of accompaniment in the past is mutually exclusive. I would suggest that some soloists may have preferred one or other of these styles or may, under certain circumstances, have called for both simple and *laṛant* accompaniment within the same performance with different effects in mind. The comparative status of soloist and accompanist may also have been a factor, with senior, more experienced and competent tabla players preferring to indulge in the *laṛant* style.

Nowadays styles of accompaniment are very different, particularly that used in what has become the most widespread of classical music genres: instrumental music. It is this style that has incorporated solo tabla-playing as an essential structural feature and which has therefore done most to supplant the tabla solo as a form. This is only partly true of the style of accompaniment for *kathak* dance, where solo tabla-playing is not normally an integral part of the dance performance. The dancer may of course opt to take a rest for a few minutes between items, allotting this period to the tabla player, who might then fill the gap, as it were, with a short solo. The style of accompaniment for most vocal genres allows little or no scope for solo tabla-playing. Here the 'straight *ṭhekā*' has predominated. Hence it is the style of accompaniment for instrumental music which I shall now discuss in some detail.

Following the *ālāp*, in which the soloist plays alone, the metered *gat* section is accompanied. Whenever the soloist is improvising, the tabla player is required to maintain a 'straight *ṭhekā*'. The soloist compartmentalises his improvisations by interspersing the actual *gat*, or composition, with them. With the soloist maintaining the *gat*, the tabla player is himself free to improvise and thus the two players alternate, although proportionately less time is given to the accompanist. Many soloists and tabla players have agreed that the aim of the accompanist should be to maintain the shape of the performance as dictated by the soloist's improvisations. This was very frequently described to me as 'keeping the mood'. The resulting continuity represents a very different conception of participation in performance as compared with the *laṛant* style of former days. Taking Zakir Husain as an example of a player who excelled at the modern style of accompaniment, Jnan Prakash Ghosh said: 'he very seldom will play anything which can be called a traditional form.' Nowadays, this was no longer thought to be of great importance. He went on:

> The trend in accompaniment is changing a lot nowadays. Today, performers think about the totality of the music in which they are participating. In the old days, tabla masters used to be themselves when they accompanied and therefore they did whatever they felt like regardless of the wider context of the whole performance.

Some examples of the ways in which a tabla player might 'keep the mood' of a performance are as follows:

1. The soloist improvises a section in *tīgun* (triplet) rhythm. The tabla player follows with a short solo section also in *tīgun*.
2. The soloist plays quietly, slowly and lyrically. The tabla player follows with a slow and lyrical solo in which he concentrates on open, sonorous strokes.
3. The soloist begins slowly and quietly but gradually doubles and redoubles the speed of articulation, intensifying the sound all the while. The climax comes with a spectacular and complex *tihā'ī*. The tabla player follows by beginning slowly and quietly, and gradually builds up in similar fashion to the climax, where he attempts to imitate the *tihā'ī* formula given by the soloist.
4. The soloist plays a *chand* (rhythm) in, say, *sātgun* (septolets – also known as *viāṛ*). For instance, he may play:

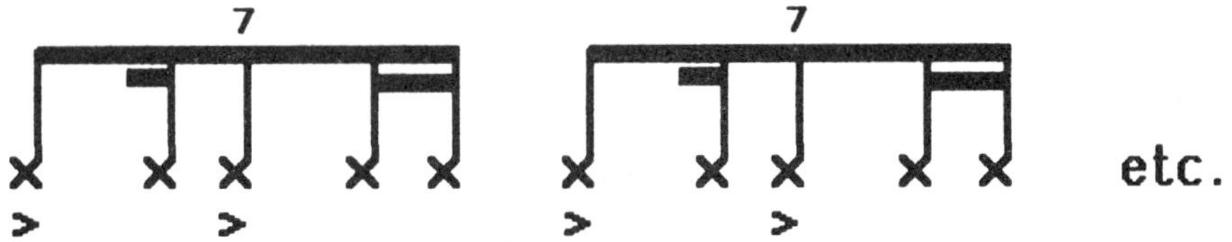

Not only does the tabla player follow with a solo section in the same *chand*, for instance:

dhā-nadhā-tiṭe dhā-nadhā-tiṭe

but he also interpolates the *chand* whenever the soloist breaks off between phrases, so helping to maintain the continuity of the *chand* in the soloist's section.

With the emphasis firmly on 'keeping the mood', and the limited amount of time available to the accompanist to play solo tabla passages, the tendency has been for tabla players to avoid the traditional compositional types of the tabla repertoire, whose structural confines often prove too limiting. A *qā'ida*, or any other theme-and-variations-type composition, requires more time to develop fully and successfully. Most set compositions, however, are too short and may well not fit with the 'mood' created by the soloist. The tabla player therefore improvises something that will fit, drawing on and mixing together segments of various compositional types. The result may be something similar to that criticised by Afaq Husain above, namely a piece which begins as a *qāʿida*, develops as a *relā*, and ends as a *ṭukṛā* or *cakkardār*.

The individual most responsible for changes in style of accompaniment is Ravi Shankar. Indeed, I feel he has been most influential in changing the overall course of Indian music since Independence, and has done more to change tabla-playing than has any single tabla player. Kamal Krishna, a disciple of the Lucknow *gharānā*, explained that 'Ravi Shankar was the first instrumentalist to give the tabla accompanist ample, even equal, opportunity for solo playing in performance'. Subroto Roy Chowdhury put Ravi Shankar's contribution to Indian music in perspective:

> Formerly . . . the solo performer was a jealous person. He wouldn't like the tabla player to be applauded. He would reduce him to the minimum [i.e. allow him no scope for solo playing and make him play *ṭhekā* only]. And if he met a tabla player with a good [i.e. strong] personality who would not be sort of cowed down by his instructions or his eyes then they just fought on stage. Ravi Shankar was perhaps the first person to take a tabla player with him, rehearse him, and then present a complete picture with tabla playing an active role and yet not fighting. Allauddin Khan was the person who started it, but Ravi Shankar remained in this style.

I feel that this element of rehearsal is of crucial importance here. Ravi Shankar patronised a number of young tabla players, including Kanai Dutt and Chatur Lal, and trained them in the 'alternating' style of accompaniment. Essentially this involved non-interference with the soloist's improvisations, thus allowing for the potentially unhindered development of the *rāg*, and the full exploitation of the many opportunities given for short, interposed tabla solos. Thus Ravi Shankar controlled the entire performance and, because of their relatively low status and inexperience, his accompanists were malleable enough to be shaped to fit in with the new style.

Ravi Shankar was at the forefront of the competition for the new patrons of music of the 1950s and 1960s: the 'mass audience'. Not only was he a good musician; he was also intelligent, charming, good-looking, a natural diplomat and ambassador for his art, and, dare one say, a high-caste Hindu in a strongly nationalist, post-Independence India. He was able to perceive the level of the audience's understanding, and by developing the 'alternating' style he provided variety through the shift of emphasis from one player to the other. This also allowed the audience to concentrate on each instrument separately, unlike the *laṛant* style where often both musicians were playing at the same time. Ravi Shankar's innovation is epitomised by the *sawāl–jawāb* (lit. question–answer), a climactic element of his performances in which the accompanist literally 'answers' by imitation the rhythmic patterns of the soloist. Question and answer alternate in ever shorter phrases until the two players merge for the final cadential *tihā'īs* played in unison.

This new trend in instrumental peformance was quick to catch on. Not only were soloists in greater control of their performances, but also the allocation of time to their accompanists seemed fair recognition of the latters' important supporting role. Indeed so dominant is this style that it has become exceedingly unusual to hear the *laṛant* style in modern instrumental performances of North Indian music.

Trends in education as precipitants of musical change

In the eyes of most educated Indians, particularly middle-class Hindus, a music education is seen as a great asset (for reasons which will become apparent), and is thus highly desirable.

During the twentieth century, music has been raised as a symbol of the revival of Indian culture, and has been especially important in the struggle for Independence and a new national identity. It is now seen as a refinement in much the same way that a musical education was regarded as such by middle- and upper-class nineteenth-century Europeans. Literally hundreds of music schools and colleges now exist throughout India. Agarwala (1966: 75) made the amusing observation that 'To-day there are as many music schools and music colleges as there are Goshalas [lit. cow sheds] in the country.' Meer (1980: 125–6) has noted that every neighbourhood in Delhi 'has its own little music school', and that 'Many women of the middle class have taken up the study of Indian music.'

In the most general sense, there are two systems of music education in India: the *gharānā* system, and the college, or institutionalised, system. Both '*gharānā* system' and 'college system' are my own gloss terms. For example, with reference to the latter, I fully realise that there are many kinds of teaching institution in India, each operating in a slightly different way. Firstly, there are universities that offer degree courses in music where considerable emphasis is laid upon academic studies, particularly for B.A. courses, though perhaps less so for B.Mus. courses. Secondly, there are colleges themselves, whose degrees are officially recognised as equivalent to those of the universities. Academic studies are still important, but a practical training in music is given precedence. Both universities and colleges are run, and largely funded, by the government. Thirdly, there are music schools, where students receive a mainly practical training in preparation for a diploma. Schools are government-approved institutions, not affiliated to universities or colleges, that receive a certain amount of private funding, but which survive largely on the fees paid by students for the course. All these types of educational institution share a great many common features in the way they organise practical music training. The main body of my data comes from close observations of the system operated by the Bhatkhande Music College in Lucknow. Therefore not only does my term 'college system' refer specifically to this type of institution, but it also refers, at a more general level, to institutional training as a whole.

The *gharānā* system has been in operation for many hundreds of years and is the traditional Indian system for the transmission of knowledge and skills. It revolves around the relationship between a master (*ustād* or *gurū*) and his disciple (*shāgird* or *shishya*). In essence, the disciple undergoes a process akin to an apprenticeship. As my term suggests, the *gharānā* system operates mainly among those musicians who belong to *gharānās*, but importantly it also extends to others who do not claim *gharānā* membership but who nevertheless practise these traditional methods of instruction. In contrast, the college system grew up in the early twentieth century as part of the general trend to institutionalise and systematise music education, so making it a respectable subject easily available to all interested parties. One of the pioneers of this movement, Pandit V. N. Bhatkhande (often referred to as the 'saviour' of Indian music by those who have supported the college system of music education), stated his vision for the future in a speech of 1916 (quoted in Neuman 1980: 200): 'I cannot but hope that in a few years more there will be an easy system for the instruction of our music which will lend itself to mass education.' The specific ways in which each system operates will be explained fully in the next chapter. In this section, there will follow a general discussion of the main features which distinguish the *gharānā* system from the college system of music education, and of the ways in which the latter is precipitating musical change.

Nearly all present-day performing musicians are, to a greater or lesser extent, trained under the *gharānā* system. Despite such rapid growth, therefore, institutional training is not replacing *gharānā* training as such. However, it is true to say that increasing numbers of potential musicians are enrolling for college courses before going on to train privately under the *gharānā* system. In some cases, college students simultaneously combine a college training with a *gharānā* training. Others who have studied under the *gharānā* system since early childhood attend merely to obtain a degree or diploma of some sort. What effect this actually has on the student is difficult to say. The majority of musicans to whom I spoke, both inside and outside the music colleges, detected that the 'conditioning' of students to accept 'college values' was indeed having a subtle effect on music as a whole.

It has already been suggested that it is for a number of social, and not musical, reasons that the vast majority of parents prefer their children to study music in a government-run or government-approved institution. (Here, I speak mainly for North-Central India. There is reason to believe that the situation in Calcutta, and possibly Bombay, is different, in that greater numbers of students learn privately.) Dr S. S. Awasthi, the principal of the Bhatkhande Music College, explained:

> Most of these traditional musicians have a very peculiar way of living [which is] looked down upon by the so-called persons of status. So, in general, such persons would not relish the idea of sending their daughters particularly, and also their sons, to such traditional musicians [for fear they may be] demoralised [i.e. corrupted in morals].

Far preferable were:

> institutions where all sorts of persons are studying and are being taught, and [there exists] some strict discipline . . . [and] supervision is there. A supervisor is expected to maintain harmony and discipline, and the government is there in case some mishap arises.

It will also be remembered that *ustāds* were often perceived to be secretive, and were thought to withold knowledge from the student in order to exact a higher price for it. Naturally, the music colleges are viewed very differently. Their structured courses and syllabuses guarantee that a certain amount of knowledge will be given to each student in a fixed number of years. Thus, knowledge is seen to be easily accessible. The fees for courses are very low compared to what an *ustād* might demand for private lessons, and therefore the colleges are perceived to be offering something of a bargain: easily accessible knowledge for comparatively low fees.

Another very important reason why the college system is widely preferred to the *gharānā* system is the tangible reward for completing a course: the degree. This constitutes a major incentive as this qualification helps those who wish to obtain work in the field of music education. The degree as proof of a completed music education is a particularly important factor for girls. It was often referred to by my informants as a 'marriage certificate'. It was thought that girls who obtained degrees in music increased their chances of being married into a good family. Indeed, I have evidence to suggest that in certain marriage arrangements the degree has been regarded as such an asset that the burden of the dowry on the girl's parents has considerably lessened. Even Dr Awasthi agreed that 'Girls come here to the college for fashion, and to get a certificate which will help them to get married.' The exact way in which the degree helps in this process was explained to me by K. K. Kapoor:

> I know people who ask if a girl knows singing, or some other musical genre, when they meet to discuss marriage. And it's a great plus-point if the girl has been to Bhatkhande College and has passed her exam [i.e. obtained a degree]. It speeds up the process and people agree to take such girls more readily.

Partly as a consequence of the special power of the degree to influence marriage contracts, female students are in the majority in music colleges throughout India. Admission to a college is a must, even if it means studying a subject not of one's first choice. The most befitting subject for a girl is thought to be vocal music, though classes are largely oversubscribed. Consequently a substantial number of girls now study the tabla, not an instrument traditionally played by women.

Musicians raised exclusively under the *gharānā* system view music education in a very different way. They tend to look beyond social reasons or the advantages degrees bring and see the processes of learning music in more purely musical terms. Their concern is for the effectiveness of the education, though they realise that the aims of *gharānā* and college teaching are very different. All my informants reinforced Mattoo's statement (quoted in Neuman 1980: 200) to the effect that no music institution in India had ever produced a really great performing musician. Yet they agreed that the aim of music colleges was not primarily to produce performers but, as Keskar (1967: 43) suggested, 'to create good judges and listeners'. Citing his own experience in this respect, the amateur tabla player and advocate of institutional education, Dr D. P. Johari, distinguished the aims of the college and *gharānā* systems as follows:

> The colleges prepare postgraduate students in a much shorter time [and] with a much broader understanding of the art, as well as the technology of the instrument. I feel that when a student is under the teaching of an organised system, he can very well complete the task [i.e. of becoming a performing musician] by becoming the disciple of an *ustād*.

For producing musicians, then, the suitability of the *gharānā* system and the inadequacy of the college system is not in doubt. The majority of my informants expressed the same opinion as the former principal of the Bhatkhande Music College, Professor S. N. Ratanjankar (1961: 212–13):

> Nobody can challenge the superiority of individual coaching [i.e. the *gharānā* system] . . . over class and mass training [i.e. the college system], with regard to qualitative merit . . . In the present times . . . in the place of half a dozen talented personal pupils, each receiving his own special training from the Guru according to the convenience of time, the pupil's capacity to learn, his talent, application and devotion, and moments of inspiration of the Guru himself, the modern trainer in music has to teach a class of students of varying talents, tastes, qualities of voice, and temperaments.

The merits and demerits of both the *gharānā* and college systems of music education is a broad subject worthy of detailed discussion. However, I have chosen here to condense the main arguments into five points.

The relationship between the teacher and the taught

When Keskar (1967: 20) wrote condemning *gharānās* for having claimed for themselves 'the same sanctity and rigidity as for a religious sect', he was, I feel, both underestimating and rejecting the spiritual power that has distinguished the *gurū–shishya*, or *ustād–shāgird*, relationship, and which has made it so successful. This spiritual power arises from what Maitra (1977: 22) has called 'a direct communion', and 'an intimate rapport between the master and the pupil'. There is a fundamental difference between a relationship of this kind, which may aptly be termed a master–disciple relationship, and the teacher–pupil relationship found in an institution. With the former goes a sense of dedication and commitment only rarely encountered in the latter, where duty is the guiding force. What is more, the fact that a student may be taught by several different teachers implies that the teacher–pupil relationship is frequently strained by divided loyalties. The master–disciple relationship is an intimate one, based on love, devotion and loyalty, similar to that found, ideally, between father and son. The implications for music education are thus obvious: the commitment involved in the master–disciple relationship ensures that knowledge will be passed on with great care and attention to detail.

Total reliance upon the master–disciple relationship for the transmission of a musical tradition does, of course, have its negative aspects. Most importantly, when knowledge is maintained in the hands of a small number of people, the tradition is vulnerable to the premature demise of its principle bearers. With reference to the history of the Lucknow tabla *gharānā*, it will be remembered that the untimely death of Munne Khan, in 1890, left Abid Husain unprepared to assume the mantle of *khalīfa*. Only by means of a supreme effort was he able to salvage something of the *gharānā*'s knowledge and so propagate the musical tradition. The same may be said of the sitarist Vilayat Khan, who was about eleven years of age when his father Inayat Khan died, and possibly, too, of the Dagar family of *dhrupad* singers.

The transmission of a style

The word 'style' encompasses a number of factors, the most important of which is a general conception of the music that governs aesthetic preferences, and thereby dictates the form and content of two other vital components of style: technique and repertoire. Technique may be further broken down into the production and control of the voice, posture, fingering, strokes, and hand positions. Repertoire may include not only the types of composition specialised in, but also the techniques of composition and improvisation which form an integral part of any musical performance.

Under the *gharānā* system of tuition, a disciple undergoes an apprenticeship with one master. His knowledge may be supplemented by lessons and advice from other *gharānā* members, particularly the master's son. Therefore there is a coherence and continuity in the teaching which allows for a particular style to be grasped in its entirety. In other words, the disciple becomes fluent in that style. Under the college system of tuition, there is no comparable coherence. A pupil may find that he or she has a different teacher for each stage of the course. One critic explained the problem with reference to institutionalised tabla-teaching:

> The teachers all play different styles of tabla. One will tell you something and you'll go to another person and he'll tell you it differently. Benares, Lucknow, they'll tell you how to place your hands differently. This is the thing. You go to one class and get something from a Benares person, then the following day the Lucknow person says it's wrong!

The result is that students trained under the college system may well find that they know a little of many styles, but are far from being fluent in any one of them. They may have no clear conception of the music, and may have hybridised techniques which are not suited to certain types of playing. They may also have a distorted conception of composition and improvisation techniques, which differ greatly from style to style. Maitra (1977: 25) recognised this danger, and expressed it in terms of the absence of any coherent style of exposition. This is primarily due to the fact that [students] are taught to imitate the best points, which the different Gharanas have in their delineations of a Raga or Ragas, and then to incorporate them in their own performances. But this cannot be done unless one is initiated in a particular style of a Gharana in a very strict and disciplined way. The most unhealthy effect of such a slipshod manner of training is that the students virtually become what may be termed as a 'conglomeration of musical curios'.

The teacher–pupil ratio

Professor Ratanjankar's statement that 'Nobody can challenge the superiority of individual coaching . . . over class and mass training' highlights another important difference between the systems under examination. In the *gharānā* system, teaching is on an individual basis. Other disciples may of course be present, but the master nevertheless concentrates on one disciple at a time. Indeed, I was always being told by my teacher that one could learn just as much from observing closely the lessons of fellow disciples as from one's own. The advantages of this system are obvious: the master can focus his undivided attention on one person, and can impart a personalised training for the particular needs of the individual.

Under the college system, 'there is no personal teaching, only mass teaching . . . the teacher must attend to the masses, not the single student' said the professor of tabla at the Bhatkhande Music College, Ranganath Misra. This creates problems; for example, not all students in a class are of equal ability, as K. K. Kapoor explained:

If there is a talented student, I can't devote all my time to him. Suppose there are fifteen or twenty students in a class, and the class lasts one hour, or ninety minutes. I have to look after the weaker members of the class in that time in order to keep the standard relatively equal. I cannot devote the same amount of time to an intelligent student and a weak student. I have to spend more time on the weak.

The implication here is that the college system does not cater to the needs of a talented student, who must perpetually wait while others catch up with the lessons. Furthermore, the teacher's attention is never focused on one student for very long and, much of the time, he is unable to hear individuals because many students are singing or playing together.

The emphasis of the teaching

Although each master may have his own individual approach to teaching, the emphasis of a *gharānā* training, especially in the early stages, is firmly placed upon establishing a solid foundation for correct technique. In general, this is effected with the help of only a very limited amount of musical material. The disciple is often encouraged to practise simple, basic exercises, sometimes for several years. Two *rāgs* at the very most are taught, in which compositions and exercises are given. For example, the *dhrupad* singer R. Fahimuddin Dagar (with whom I also studied briefly) would teach in *rāg Bhairav* in the mornings, and in *rāg Yaman* in the evenings, in accordance with the stipulated performance times of these *rāgs*. Disciples were expected to do their morning and evening *riyāẓ* in these rāgs. No other *rāg* was taught for many years. Likewise, my early tabla lessons with Afaq Husain revolved around a limited number of *qāʿidas* and peshkārs, all in one *tāl*: *tīntāl*. The *qāʿida* is itself a form of exercise, and I was encouraged to practise the same basic material over and over again, each day for several months. The reasoning behind this kind of approach to training is that once the fundamental principles of technique have been firmly grasped, and the disciple has gained a basic understanding of *rāg* structure and delineation, or *tāl* structure and improvisation, a greater variety of musical material may be introduced into the lessons.

In stark contrast, the college system of training recommends that a large repertoire of material be taught for each year of the course, as dictated by a syllabus. The following is an extract from the practical course for first-year vocal students at the Bhatkhande Music College (Bhatkhande Sangit Vidyapith n.d.: 21):

The following Ragas with songs:

(1) Yaman, (2) Bilawal, (3) Khamaj, (4) Bhairava, (5) Bhoopali, (6) Desh, (7) Kaphi, (8) Asawari, (9) Bhairavi.

One Sargam, one lakshan geet and one Khayal in each of the above named Ragas. One Madhya or Drut Khyal with five Tanas in each of the Nine Ragas, and two Dhrupads in any two Ragas.

This constitutes a considerable repertoire of musical material. The danger of this scheme is that, though the teacher may intend to teach the basic principles of technique and the structure and delineation of *rāg*, he will most probably find that his time is consumed in teaching students the notes of compositions, in preparation for end-of-year examinations. The result is that students develop an essentially superficial understanding of many *rāgs* and compositions without having a deep knowledge of basic technique and the structure and delineation of any one *rāg*.

Time limits

One of the most frequently expressed, and widely held, opinions is that it takes a great deal of time to become a musician. Not only must students undergo a lengthy and rigorous training, but they must also devote themselves to long and hard practice. In the *gharānā* system of training, great emphasis is laid upon perfecting the basic elements of technique and form before progressing to a more advanced level. Consequently no time limit is imposed on the disciple: he or she will move on only when considered by the master to be sufficiently prepared for the next stage of training. The master adjusts the amount of time spent on each individual to suit the requirements of the situation.

As was evident from the discussion of the emphasis of the training under the college system, a syllabus has to be covered for each year of a given course. Therefore, regardless of whether or not individuals have understood and perfected a particular technique or composition, the teacher is forced to press on with the next topic. In other words, he has a limited amount of time to spend on each stage of the course, and to spend too much time on one feature is to run the risk of having to omit something else. But perhaps the time limit teachers dislike most, and this emerged frequently in discussions I had with many of them, is that which dictates the length of each class, the termination of which is marked by a bell. This sometimes proved a rude interruption to a teacher who had just begun to make headway with a group, and who had generated a mood of interest and responsiveness.

An ever-increasing number of musicians are being trained, at some stage in their careers, under the college system. But I have tried to show that because of the nature of the courses, which are not designed primarily for aspiring musicians, students acquire a broad but shallow knowledge, inadequate basic technique, and a distorted conception of musical structure and style. Whether or not they go on to train under the *gharānā* system in order to become performers or just become 'good judges and listeners', a college education and the musical values it propagates is subtly affecting the nature of North Indian classical music.

There has been a gradual realisation of the many defects of the college system of training, and steps are being taken to create a more efficient system that will cater for those students who wish to develop into performing musicians. Dr S. S. Awasthi revealed to me his scheme for reorganising the courses at the Bhatkhande Music College. The major difference concerns the serious student, who would enrol for a course of full-time studies, similar to that offered at a university. The implication is that there would be a smaller number of more serious students, who would have increased contact hours with their tutors. The syllabus would be altered to cover a smaller number of *rāgs*, and increased emphasis would be given to elements of style in the lessons. 'Hobby classes' for those less intent on attaining high standards of musicianship, but keen to become more knowledgeable listeners, would be held separately, perhaps in the evenings. Whether or not this scheme can be implemented remains to be seen.

6 *Learning the tabla*

I have already indicated, in very general terms, the major differences between what I have called the '*gharānā* system' of music education and the 'college system'. So far, observations have not been specific to any one instrument. In this chapter, I shall explain the processes of training in much greater detail, with reference to the instrument at the centre of this study: the tabla.

In comparison with information on drum strokes and repertoire, surprisingly little has been written on the specific nature of the transmission of music in either *gharānā* or college contexts. The main aim here is therefore to redress this balance, for it may be argued that training is interesting not so much because of what is given, as for the ways in which it is given. Most of the information pertaining to the *gharānā* system is inevitably based on my own and my fellow disciples' training as tabla players under Afaq Husain. Some corroborative material was obtained from other teachers and their disciples, but I am aware that our experiences may not have been shared by all those who have learned the tabla on a personal basis through methods traditionally employed by *gharānedār* musicians. Data concerning the college system derives mainly from my observation of classes held in the Bhatkhande Music College between 1981 and 1986, with further information provided by teachers employed there and friends and acquaintances who have studied there.

The *gharānā* system of training

The initial stages

Once a student has decided from whom he wishes to learn the tabla, introductions to the teacher are normally arranged through the latter's sons or established disciples. I was myself asked to introduce aspiring students to my *ustād* when it had become known that I was a close disciple of Afaq Husain.

A common courtesy on first meeting one's *ustād* is to touch his feet in a gesture of respect, a gesture which should be repeated whenever a student or disciple meets or takes leave of his *ustād*. It signifies humility and, at the same time, requests the responding gesture of the *ustād*'s blessing. Another common courtesy is to offer a small gift of sweets. In point of fact, sweets are generally presented by visitors to their hosts in India, and are invariably offered during celebrations of any kind. The *ustād* takes this opportunity to ask a number of questions in order to find out something about the background of the candidate. Has he learned the tabla before? From whom? For how long? Where does he live? What do his parents do? What are his general interests? And so on. He may also request the candidate to give a short practical demonstration of some pieces from his repertoire, limited as that may be. Thus a general impression of the candidate's character and musical ability is gained, so helping the *ustād* to decide whether or not to take him on. It must be said that rarely is a student refused. Teaching is an economic necessity, and any supplementary income is considered most welcome.

Once the *ustād* has made it clear that he will teach the student, he arranges regular times for lessons, taking into account restrictions imposed upon him by other commitments, such as full-time work and concert engagements. If the *ustād* is committed to a full-time job, for example as a staff artist at the radio station or television centre, the best times for lessons are usually early mornings and evenings, before and after work. The new student is usually given three lessons per week, each of about one hour. He is normally taught alone, in isolation. Great stress is laid upon the unbroken regularity of the initial six-month period of training. It is a test period in which the *ustād* assesses the student as a possible candidate for discipleship, and he must therefore observe how the student responds to regular and disciplined training. Lessons will only be missed if the *ustād* has to travel far afield to give concerts, or on special religious occasions where the playing of music is prohibited, for example during the first ten days of Muharram if the *ustād* is a Shiite Muslim. Owing to *parda* restrictions on women in the homes of many Muslims, lessons are normally held in the student's home, or at the home of another disciple of the *ustād*. Lessons may only be held at the *ustād*'s home if there is a spare room which can be partitioned off from the rest of the house.

In the early stages, a student has no obligations to the *ustād* save paying him money and showing him the greatest respect. Similarly, the *ustād* displays no commitment to the student. It is a purely pecuniary arrangement. From the *ustād*'s point of view, he is testing the student and making a complete assessment of his musical ability and character. It should be noted that this is not an assessment of ability and potential alone, but is equally a test of the student's sincerity and trustworthiness, as Afaq Husain himself indicated:

> I certainly have to assess how worthy the student is: how much love he will show, how much practice he will do, how well he will develop. All men do not have exactly the same kind of mind. They're all different. Some people are fraudulent, some are cunning, some are loving, some are sympathetic, some are ready to follow their *ustāds* faithfully. The *ustād* would give his material away if he found good students. On the other hand, if they're cunning I've got to think twice about taking them on.

Inherent in this statement is the apprehension of giving musical material to a student who will either waste it, or in turn give it to some unauthorised person. I have already shown how *ustāds* were generally considered to be secretive by those who failed to realise the motives behind the very selective distribution of their knowledge to chosen disciples.

There is no fixed time limit for the student's initial period of examination. As Bhupal Ray Choudhuri said: 'Maybe the student passes in one month, but maybe in ten years he doesn't pass because the *ustād* doesn't believe in him.' However, if the *ustād* considers the student to be worthy enough, he will offer him the opportunity to enter into an *ustād–shāgird*, or master–disciple, relationship by undergoing an initiation ceremony: the *gaṇḍā bandhan*. Though essentially a Hindu concept (see Shepherd 1976; and Silver 1984), Muslims have traditionally practised the *gaṇḍā bandhan* initiation, though many *ustāds* no longer perform the ceremony. My *ustād* still believed it to be a significant rite of passage to his inner circle of disciples. Indeed, he insisted on it even for his own son. Those disciples close to the *ustād* are then in a position to receive a considerably more intensive training, where the only restrictive factor is the disciple's own technical limitations. My own *gaṇḍā bandhan* ceremony was performed after an initial period of six and a half months. I considered myself lucky, as Afaq

Husain had not offered the initiation ceremony to certain other students who had learned with him for over six years. These were students studying at the Bhatkhande Music College who came to Afaq Husain for extra-curricula lessons, but who displayed an inability or unwillingness to understand and adapt to the basic forms and techniques of the Lucknow tabla *gharānā*.

Following the *gaṇḍā bandhan* ceremony, a distinct and palpable change of attitude towards the new disciple is evident. He is admitted to the *ustād*'s family circle and *parda* restrictions within his household no longer apply. Fellow disciples, known as *gurū-bhā'īs*, or 'brothers under one *gurū*', behave fraternally towards the initiate and there is a strong feeling that one is part of a group whose members are fully committed to one another. The commitment of the *ustād* to his new disciple becomes evident too because he begins to act much more like a father than a teacher. The intimacy of the relationship increases steadily: the disciple frequently eats with his *ustād*, and, on occasion, may even stay at his house.

The format of music lessons changes markedly following the *gaṇḍā bandhan*. Having established closer contact with his *ustād*'s family, the disciple thereafter spends a great deal of time in the *ustād*'s home. Lessons may be taken daily if time and opportunity permit, or one may witness the lessons of one's *gurū-bhā'īs*. The actual timing of the lessons becomes less fixed and they may last anything from a few minutes to several hours. On occasions when my *ustād* was in a particularly favourable mood my own lessons lasted well into the night, though there was another side to the coin where I occasionally received short lessons. Generally, though, one lived more in the musical atmosphere of the *ustād*'s home. For example, I noticed that the more advanced disciples, including Afaq Husain's son Ilmas, received very few direct, formal lessons but rather relied on observing and listening to Afaq Husain's own playing and the advice he gave to other disciples. Thus much of the music and the style of Lucknow tabla-playing was absorbed through this kind of close contact within the home. Afaq Husain's other son, Ilyas, was often present while lessons were taking place. From as early as four years of age he could be heard reciting quite accurately long strings of tabla *bols* while playing with his toys, just as a European child might sing nursery rhymes. As Afaq Husain explained, a disciple becomes 'full time, just like my children. He stays in my house twenty-four hours a day. I can always listen to him, and I can always check-up on him. After supper I can check up on him a little, and when I feel like it, I can say "Now look, understand this".' Afaq Husain often illustrated the importance of living in the musical atmosphere of the home by saying that, although women were not traditionally taught to play the tabla, even his mother and sisters had absorbed, and could competently recite, many of the compositions of the Lucknow *gharānā*. This, he felt, was not unusual. He cited the fact that young girls and boys nowadays could remember the words and tunes of a whole host of film songs by listening to them repeatedly on the radio.

The disciple's obligations to his *ustād* increase under the master–disciple relationship. The *gaṇḍā bandhan* signifies a tie or allegiance: 'the tying of the thread that binds the pupil symbolically to the teacher' (Silver 1984: 317). It implies complete surrender, in which the disciple puts his faith and trust in the advice and control of the *ustād*. Once this has happened, the spiritual communion and intimate rapport between master and disciple is established and should not be broken. As Afaq Husain put it: 'If there is love between the *ustād* and the *shāgird*, this makes for very good things.' The disciple demonstrates this allegiance by performing all kinds of tasks, such as carrying, fetching and generally helping out whenever necessary. A task frequently assigned to me was the administering of a body massage to my *ustād*, which helped him to relax in the evenings.

I have distinguished here between two distinct phases in the life of a tabla student: pre-*gaṇḍā bandhan* and post-*gaṇḍā bandhan*. Once a *gaṇḍā bandhan* ceremony has been performed, it is the *ustād*'s primary aim to prepare a disciple for a career in music, no matter how long it takes. Some will progress quickly and will enjoy successful careers as performing musicians. Others may progress less quickly and may not become professional performing musicians; rather, they will be teachers, or perhaps amateur musicians with full-time jobs outside the music world. Whatever their circumstances, they must each be a credit to the *ustād*, propagating both his name and his musical tradition for future generations. As Bhupal Ray Choudhuri said: 'The *gurū* wants to leave his mark after his death, and the only way to leave it is through his disciples. If he leaves behind good disciples, he will be immortal.'

Taʿlīm

Taʿlīm is the 'instruction' or 'education' a student or disciple receives from his teacher. It is important to clarify the concept of *taʿlīm* because its meanings are multiplex. Neuman (1980: 50–1) distinguishes between, on the one hand, the 'substantive training or instruction in technique' which he calls the *taʿlīm* and, on the other hand, the body of knowledge, including compositions and special techniques, to which he does not give a name. That is a rather limited view, for *taʿlīm* is all this and more. It is also the giving of a musical intelligence to the disciple, an intelligence that will help him to think creatively and to make his own musical decisions in, to quote the phrase commonly used by many musicians, 'the light of the *taʿlīm*' (*taʿlīm kī roshnī meṅ*). Bhupal Ray Choudhuri explained the concept of *taʿlīm* by saying that it was not merely the giving away of pieces and techniques:

> That is like a student who gets help from books, but when he has to rely on himself, he's a failure. If I have learned by heart, say, five essays for the exam but none of those five come up, I am lost. I am gone. But if I am taught how to compose, what to start with and how to end, *that* is *taʿlīm*. Every part of the compositional process must be learned.

Taʿlīm is never static, like a fixed body of knowledge comprising numerous compositions particular to one person or tradition. Repertoires may extend to hundreds, or even thousands, of compositions and it is difficult to imagine how they may all be handed down completely intact because, as Afaq Husain said, 'you can't give everything . . . some things will get left out'. Thus an instruction in creative thinking is crucial, as it allows for the repertoire to develop and change, and to incorporate new ideas with each succeeding generation. It is an unending process, as Afaq Husain explained:

> Actually, you can never run out of *taʿlīm* in your life. The elders keep on teaching you, and you keep on learning. I do calculations, my mind continues to work, and then I compose and add to the repertoire in the light of, or under the guidance of, the *taʿlīm*. That's the way it goes on.

Like most other *ustāds*, Afaq Husain's policy was always to treat students and disciples as individuals with different strengths and weaknesses. Some were able to learn quickly, others less so; he assessed the particular needs of the individual accordingly and adjusted the intensity of the training: 'Should I give the disciple a year's teaching in five or six months, or should I give four or five month's worth of tuition over one or two years?'

The training does not differ in respect of repertoire during the early stages. Each student receives the same basic compositions to work on, although an *ustād* may choose to emphasise different aspects of technique depending on the particular limitations of the individual. It is very much a period of assessment in which the *ustād* judges the student's general capabilities and potential, as Afaq Husain explained:

Of course there are things [e.g. compositions, techniques] that all my students get, and many of the lessons are given to several students in the same way. But I look first to see how best he'll understand the lessons and how his mind is. I'll find out how quickly he'll develop, and how best he'll understand the lessons. If he can only lift a total of two *mann* [about 160lb.] and I give him five *mann* to begin with, it'll be useless.

I mentioned earlier that, whereas before the *gaṇḍā bandhan* ceremony lessons are given to students in isolation, those following initiation are often conducted in the presence of one or more *gurū-bhā'īs*. With several disciples in attendance, the *ustād* tends to make general statements which have a wider relevance, in addition to personalised advice designed for the

Plate 11. Afaq Husain teaching his disciple Pankaj Chowdhury with the author looking on

individual whose lesson it is. It is therefore considered an important element of one's *taʿlīm* to witness the lessons of other disciples, as one may learn a great deal from them. Group participation inspires an atmosphere of enthusiasm and enjoyment from which the individual may derive considerable motivation.

The format of the lessons may change depending on a number of factors including the time available, the mood of the *ustād* and the particular needs of the individual. In general, though, a lesson is usually divided into three parts: firstly, one plays the material given in the previous lesson; secondly, one plays pieces picked at random from the repertoire given to date; thirdly, one receives new material. Of course, sometimes these areas become mixed together, and new material is not necessarily given in each lesson. Moreover, the *ustād* may himself feel like playing, and therefore much of the lesson is taken up with listening to a demonstration of a tabla solo. This often happens when a ready-made audience of several disciples is present.

Musical instruction falls into four categories: sound production, technique, repertoire, and musical ability and creative thinking. Segregating these areas in this way may well give a false impression of *taʿlīm*. In reality, all four are inextricably intertwined and ever-present. For example, sound production is impossible without the correct technique needed to articulate the strokes; correct technique is learned through the playing of the repertoire; composition and improvisation are possible only by means of a thorough knowledge of the processes at work in examples from the repertoire. However, for the sake of convenience I intend to discuss each aspect of tabla-training separately.

Sound production

It is especially difficult to divorce sound production from technique, but in doing so a certain purpose is served in that an indication may be given of the enormous emphasis placed on the 'correct sound' of strokes and phrases by Afaq Husain. This is, of course, a very subjective notion and each *gharānā*, indeed each individual musician, will no doubt hold different opinions as to what may be called 'correct sound'. Yet I believe that certain generalisations can be made about the 'correct' Lucknow sound, because recognising it is as much a part of the learned behaviour of Lucknow *gharānā* musicians as is Lucknow technique and repertoire, for one has one's attention drawn to it from the very beginning of one's lessons. In fact, Afaq Husain frequently used to say that the most important element in tabla-playing was a 'good sound' and the technique needed to produce it. He claimed that he would far rather listen to a player who had 'good sound' but a small and simple repertoire than to another player who made a 'bad sound' but who could perform from a wide and varied repertoire.

The word 'sound' as used here is a translation of *sūr*. *Sūr* has very positive and good connotations rather than negative ones. For example, when someone says of a tabla player *Un ke hāth meṅ sūr hai* (lit. There is sound in his hand) it is implied that 'He is able to produce a good sound'. The significance of *sūr* was forcefully stressed by Afaq Husain by means of a comparison with *sūr* as produced by the human voice and its supposed effect on the listener. His explanation is a particularly interesting example of the expression of difficult concepts by analogy:

> In the olden days, when Tansen sang, the rain fell and fires lit by themselves. These things will happen with this kind of *sūr* . . . So *sūr* comes from God. True *sūr* is rare: you can't find it nowadays, you understand? He sends it. *Sūr* makes one cry.

Afaq Husain explained that tabla was *ek sūr kā sāz* (lit. an instrument of one sound, pitch or note), but emphasised that 'It shouldn't be thought that whichever way it is played is acceptable.' The disciple, guided by his *ustād*, must search for the true *sūr*, and must fully exploit the limited 'voice' of the tabla. I was constantly told to 'keep on searching and good things will eventually come'. It is therefore implied that *sūr* in tabla applies specifically to two strokes: *tā* (also known as *nā* and other names depending on context) as played on both the *kinār* and the *sūr*. However, in its wider application, good *sūr* refers to the balance of these two strokes with all other strokes, a balance which gives the 'voice' of the tabla an evenness and beauty of phrasing.

During the early period of training, great emphasis is laid upon the correct production of the *bol tā* as played on the *kinār*. It features prominently in *qāʿidas*, the first pieces given to the student. Once the student has reached a more advanced stage, he may be required to move on to more technically difficult compositional types such as *ṭukṛā* and *gat*, in which *tā* as played on the *sūr* predominates. Only then will a similar emphasis be placed on the correct sound production of this stroke. Such an emphasis is designed to sensitise the student to the desired sound, getting him to reproduce it precisely by instilling the physical technique of the stroke through constant repetition. Thus an aural training is as important as a technical training in that, without one, the other may not be achieved. For the first three months of my training under Afaq Husain, 80 per cent of lesson time was devoted to this one stroke *tā* (*kinār*) alone. He would demonstrate the correct stroke and point out the sound. I copied him and he manipulated my fingers and hand, minutely adjusting the position and readjusting the balance and the weight of the stroke. Each time I produced the correct *sūr* he smiled and pointed it out to me. I repeated the stroke literally thousands of times during the lesson, sometimes for as much as two hours. And thus I began to be able to differentiate between good *sūr* and bad *sūr*. It took a great deal of effort and concentration to recognise the delicacy and refinement of the sound, but I realised it was worth it when I began to hear the difference with my own ears. This delicacy and refinement could only be achieved when a musician played with 'love', as Afaq Husain put it. I used often to notice that a particular *gurū-bhāʾī* found he could not produce good *sūr*, and would impatiently strike the drumhead with considerable force in attempting to achieve the correct result. Afaq Husain often said to him: 'You must play with love, not hatred.'

Although extremely difficult to express in words, the ideal Lucknow *sūr* has a characteristic resonance, an openness and clarity of tone which derives from the technique of lifting the fingers from the skin of the drum after striking. In most other styles of playing, the third finger is left in contact with the drumhead following the stroke, a factor which, Lucknow musicians believe, prevents the skin achieving maximum resonance. Generally speaking, this technique of raising the fingers after striking is referred to as *khulā bāj*, or 'open style'. When teaching, Afaq Husain likens this resonance to the steady, unwavering flame of a candle. Each stroke should produce the precise *sūr*: open, ringing, and constant like the flame. If the *sūr* is inaccurate, the resonance is lost and the flame flickers: the constancy has gone.

The word commonly used for the general sound produced by Lucknow musicians in this way is *miṭhās*, or 'sweetness'. *Miṭhās* is recognised by other musicians as a trait of the Lucknow tabla *gharānā*, and is usually expressed in the phrases *Un kā hāth bahut mīṭhā hai* (lit. His hand is very sweet) or *Un ke hāth meṅ miṭhās hai* (lit. There is sweetness in his hand). With the emphasis on correct *sūr* from the very beginning of the training, the foremost aim of the student or disciple is therefore to achieve *miṭhās*. 'For what good is a vast knowledge of compositions without a beautiful sound?', I was told in all my early lessons.

The importance of *sūr* and *miṭhās* to Lucknow tabla-playing, then, should not be underestimated. Musicians of other tabla *gharānās* stress different aspects of playing as their priorities in training. However, few of them lay as much emphasis on sound production. I was told by Bhupal Ray Choudhuri that some teachers advocated practice on solid wooden tabla in the initial stages of training. I have also heard that others forced their students to wear heavy bangles on their wrists. All these devices may have been designed to increase the strength of the fingers, hands and arms. Yet when Bhupal Ray Choudhuri told this story to Afaq Husain, the latter's response was: 'They will never have *sūr* in their hands.'

Technique

The word commonly used for technique is *nikās*, which literally means 'out-going', 'exit' or 'outlet', and thus refers to the way in which one makes an 'outlet for the sound'.

Whether or not the student has learned the tabla before, Ustad Afaq Husain spends a great deal of time, particularly in the initial stages, concentrating on establishing a firm foundation for correct technique. Essentially this implies posture, arm and hand positions, and finger placements. An underlying theory is that tension in the musician's body will result in tension in the sound produced, and therefore early training is geared towards alleviating tension from the student's entire body. One lesson passed where I did not play a single stroke on the tabla, but instead practised sitting in front of the instrument and placing my hands on the skins in the manner advised. Sometimes I would play only one stroke, or one combination of several strokes, over and over again. Interestingly, little, if any, verbal communication was needed to describe whatever Afaq Husain advocated. He would manipulate my arms and wrists, or poke my elbow from time to time, causing me to think about what I was doing with it. Afaq Husain usually sat opposite me demonstrating complex combinations of motor movements by imitating my mistakes and then showing the correct technique. Non-verbal it may have been, but explicit it certainly was.

Although individual strokes are taught and practised in isolation, combinations of two or more strokes are rarely taken out of context. No special repertoire of exercises exists in Lucknow tabla-playing because the repertoire is itself used as a means of exercise. The compositional type that is treated as an exercise *par excellence* is *qāʿida*, for its structure allows ample scope for repetition of the basic phrase. Variations on *qāʿida* are derived from the permutation, substitution and repetition of elements of the original phrase. Thus each variation based on *qāʿida* is a reconstitution of the piece, like a view of the same object from a slightly different angle.

Qāʿidas given in the first lessons are short and simple, comprising a small number of *bols* which represent basic technical features of the tabla. For example, the basic phrases of three such *qāʿidas* might be:

o 2	o 2	o o	▼ o
dhā tit	**dhā tit**	**dhā dhā**	**dhī na...**
1	23	1 23	1

o o	2 1		
dhā dhā	**ti ṭe**	**dhā dhā**	**dhī na...**
1 23			

o o	2 1 V		
dhā dhā	**tira kiṭa**	**dhā dhā**	**dhī na...**
1 23	×		

where a distinct progression from *tit* to *tiṭe* to *tirakiṭa* is evident. Afaq Husain believed that a command over the *bol tit* facilitated command over *tiṭe*, which in turn gave rise to *tirakiṭa*. Thus each stage is a technical extension of a previous stage. Other basic *qāʿidas* also used to develop technique in the early stages are:

o o o	o o o	o o	▼ o o
dhāge nadhā	**gena dhādhā**	**genadhāge**	**dhīna ghīna...**
1 23 1	23 1 23	1 1 23	1 23

which is particularly important in the Lucknow *gharānā* as it concentrates both on the repeated articulation of the *kinār* stroke *tā* and the *bāyāṅ* stroke *ghe* (which together form *dhā*); and the famous Delhi *qāʿidas*:

dhāti ṭedhā	tiṭe dhādhā	tiṭe dhāge	tīna kīna . . .
dhāti dhāge	nadhā tirakiṭa	dhāti dhāge	tīna kīna . . .

the second of which includes a considerable variety of strokes from the earlier *qāʿidas* and is the springboard for more complex compositions at a later stage in the training.

The speed at which one articulates the strokes is crucial in the beginning. Afaq Husain constantly gave the advice that one should never play faster than one's technique allowed for. Indeed, the slower and more correctly one played initially, the faster and more clearly one would be able to articulate ultimately.

As I progressed, more complex *qāʿidas*, comprising new *bols* and a greater variety of stroke combinations, were introduced. Any technical deficiency occurring at this level was treated by the prescription of another simple *qāʿida* that featured the difficult phrase. If no simple *qāʿida* existed for a particular combination, Afaq Husain composed one, so catering to the individual needs of the student.

Following *qāʿida*, other compositional types related to the *qāʿida*'s theme-and-variations structure are introduced to the student, such as *calan*, *chand*, and *peshkār*. The steady progression from simple to complex is maintained and the student is introduced to new strokes and techniques only gradually, so as not to extend him too far beyond his capacity. However, once the student or disciple is firmly in control of basic techniques, he is encouraged, firstly, to develop his speed of articulation in preparation for *relā* and, secondly, to expand into 'set compositions' such as *ṭukṛā*, *gat*, *cakkardār* and *paran*. As a transition from *qāʿida* to *relā*, a number of compositions are given which are known as *qāʿida-relā*, though structurally they are *qāʿidas* and are sometimes referred to as such. They feature strings of *bols* which are articulated at great speed, such as *tirakiṭataka*, *tiṭegiṛanaga* and *dhiradhira*, and which appear in the following three basic phrases taken from three well-known compositions:

dhā tiṭe giṛa naga	dhā tiṭe giṛa naga	dhā tiṭe giṛa naga	dhī nā giṛa naga . . .
dhā tiṭe giṛa naga	dhira dhira giṛa naga	dhā tiṭe giṛa naga	dhī nā giṛa naga . . .
dhā tira kiṭa dhā	tira kiṭa dhā tira	kiṭa taka dhā tira	kiṭa dhā tira kiṭa . . .

Essentially the same method of instruction is employed here as for *qāʿida*, namely that the teacher demonstrates the strokes, manipulates the hands of the student, indicates correct renditions, and mimics the mistakes of the student. But in order to attain maximum speed it is necessary to make some fine adjustments to the hand positions to facilitate the quickest movements. Just how minute such an adjustment can be may be demonstrated by an example given to me by a former disciple of Wajid Husain. He once practised the first of the three *qāʿida-relās* given above daily for six hours over a period of about three months. He was greatly frustrated because, no matter how hard he tried, he could not surpass a certain speed of articulation, whereas his *ustād* was able to play it twice or three times as quickly. Eventually, the disciple spoke of his problem to his teacher, who analysed his technique and made one small and simple adjustment to his finger placement. Almost immediately the disciple was able to double his speed.

The techniques encountered in *qāʿidas*, *qāʿida-relās* and other theme-and-variations compositions are quite different from the techniques needed to play set compositions such as *ṭukṛā*, *gat* and *cakkardār*. A far greater variety of strokes and stroke combinations are used in the latter, with heavier strokes generally predominating. As before, there is a progression from simple pieces containing few *bols* to complex, extensive pieces, and new strokes and combinations are introduced gradually. I found the transition to set compositions a shock to the system as it was just like starting to play all over again. However, this scheme is designed so that a student or disciple does not confuse the two distinct techniques, referred to loosely as '*qāʿida* style' and '*ṭukṛā* style'; he is allowed plenty of time to master one before progressing to the other.

Repertoire

It is evident from the foregoing discussion of technique that a disciple's repertoire is built up gradually. As he develops, new pieces that emphasise particular technical features are given. The more competent the disciple becomes, the greater the number of pieces he receives.

The basic repertoire of each disciple is drawn from a general body of musical material which contains many well-known Lucknow pieces, as well as compositions that are common to other *gharānās*. Individual disciples' repertoires therefore overlap to a large extent. But there exists another repertoire which is not necessarily accessible to all and sundry. It includes many compositions from the *gharānā* stock, some of which can be traced back approximately 200 years to the founder of the *gharānā*, Miyan Bakhshu Khan. This material constitutes an important and substantial body of knowledge without which the Lucknow tabla *gharānā* would not exist, for it is widely acknowledged that one of the qualifying features of any *gharānā* is that it should possess its own particular and distinct repertoire of compositions. These compositions are not generally played in public, but may sometimes be heard during a private sitting in the presence of connoisseurs who are able to appreciate their uniqueness and value. Each *gharānā* has its speciality, and the Lucknow *gharānā* is celebrated above all for its *gats*, which appear in a variety of forms.

But how does a disciple gain access to this repertoire of special compositions? Afaq Husain believed it was necessary not only to develop an adequate technique to cope with these rare and often difficult pieces, but also to prove oneself to be entirely worthy of them by means of one's conduct. He explained:

> When a disciple comes into some form, and becomes reasonably good, he is given good material. If he's not up to it, he could easily ruin the material and would definitely not enjoy playing those things which are very difficult . . . But, of course, it all depends on the mind, love, the manners and the general behaviour of the disciple. A disciple can get more than a son if he is a good person.

It is unclear what the exact extent of this special repertoire of *gharānā* compositions is, precisely because the vast majority of pieces are retained in the memories of only two or three musicians. Some tabla players and *pakhāwaj* players boast of being in possession of 3,000 *gats*, or 5,000 *parans*, figures which perhaps stretch the imagination a little too far. As a player's status may be assessed partly on the extent of his knowledge, these figures are easily exaggerated. Afaq Husain certainly has several hundred, perhaps even a thousand or more pieces which are kept in reserve in this manner. These include many of the compositions of all his forefathers and their prominent disciples. However, Afaq Husain recognised that not every composition in a repertoire is necessarily passed on, and that much is forgotten or omitted as the material is passed from generation to generation. I was fortunate enough to receive a number of these special compositions. Some were given to me alone, in complete confidence, while others were given to a select group of advanced disciples. Afaq Husain indicated clearly that these compositions were not to be played to outsiders without his express permission, and could not even be practised if others were listening. As a result just a few appear in this book, for the publication of too many special pieces would be tantamount to their loss in Afaq Husain's eyes.

Whenever Afaq Husain gave new compositions during a lesson, we were generally encouraged firstly to practise speaking the *bols* fluently, and secondly to translate this into actual strokes. We wrote down the *bols* of the composition either before moving on to another piece, or at the end of the lesson. There were also a few occasions, however, when we were told firstly to write down a piece from dictation, then to speak it, and lastly to play it. It is interesting to note that Afaq Husain stressed the need for one to remember one's repertoire, while also insisting that everything should be written down.

In the past it appears that the majority of tabla players remembered everything and notated nothing. This was partly due to the fact that many were illiterate, and also partly due to their fear that, once notated, a piece could then be stolen by a rival (see Shepherd's (1976: 32) account of the theft of books belonging to Ram Sahai). As far as the Lucknow *gharānā* was concerned, the shift in emphasis from memory to notation began with Abid Husain. Afaq Husain told me that his grandfather 'said a very special thing: "What's the use of writing all this [material] down? My mind is the book in which this is written. How much would you write?"' However, in later years, Abid Husain evidently changed his mind because either he or his daughter, Kazmi Begum, wrote down in Urdu a great many compositions, mostly *gats*, 200 pages of which are still extant. Exactly why he changed his mind is unclear. I would suggest that he fully realised up-and-coming generations were becoming more educated, and that this detracted from their ability to memorise such vast repertoires of compositions. This is what I believe was implied when Afaq Husain said that musicians in the past 'had the capacity, without being educated, to remember all their knowledge. They composed thousands and thousands of things. They knew them all by heart. Now we're more educated and can read and write. I can write things down so I don't forget them.'

As I stated earlier, the vast majority of Afaq Husain's repertoire is memorised. He has the facility to memorise on one hearing long and complex compositions played either by other tabla players, or by his disciples who compose new pieces for him to correct during lessons. Yet he does possess a few small exercise books in which are kept a number of special compositions by his forefathers, as well as some of his own making. These represent pieces of particular value to him that he especially wishes to preserve for posterity.

Musical ability and creative thinking

A number of factors come under the general rubric of musical ability. It may be argued that the capacity to recognise and produce a good sound, as discussed above, is one of the most important. There is, however, one crucial factor considered necessary for good musicianship and that is the ability to think creatively. Creative thinking implies composing new pieces to add to one's own, or to the *gharānā*'s, repertoire, as well as improvising (which, after all, is spontaneous composition) on given patterns of *bols*.

In order to compose or improvise in tabla-playing, it is obvious that a facility in rhythm is vital. Not only must a musician cope with complex cross-rhythms, but he must also know instinctively where he is within a metric cycle and, particularly, where he must begin and end his composition or improvisation. Consequently many exercises aimed at developing the pupil's sense of general rhythm (*lay*) and his knowledge of the structure of specific *tāls* are given in the initial stages of the training. In my own lessons, several exercises were given, from which the following three are extracted:

1. This exercise derives from the recitation of the *bols* for *tīntāl* (sixteen beats) in a number of different speeds relative to a steady beat. The student begins in *barābar lay*, or 'equal rhythm', which denotes one *bol* per beat. He must then recite the same *bols* in *ḍe'oṛhī*, *dūgun*, *tīgun* and *caugun lays*, thus increasing the speed proportionally to one and a half, two, three and four times that of the original metric cycle, whose structure is maintained throughout by clapping on the first (x), fifth (2) and thirteenth (3) beats, waving on the ninth (o), and indicating beats in between on the fingers.

Barābar

nā	dhin	dhin	nā
(x)	2	3	4
nā	dhin	dhin	nā
(2)	6	7	8
nā	tin	tin	nā
(o)	10	11	12
nā	dhin	dhin	nā
(3)	14	15	16

De'orhī

nā – dhin	– dhin –	nā – nā	– dhin –
dhin – nā	– nā –	tin – tin	– nā –
nā – dhin	– dhin –	nā – nā	– dhin –
dhin – nā	– nā –	dhin – dhin	– nā –
nā – tin	– tin –	nā – nā	– dhin –
dhin – nā	– nā –	dhin – dhin	– nā –
nā – dhin	– dhin –	nā – nā	– tin –
tin – nā	– nā –	dhin – dhin	– nā –

Dūgun

nā dhin	dhin nā	nā dhin	dhin nā
nā tin	tin nā	nā dhin	dhin nā
nā dhin	dhin nā	nā dhin	dhin nā
nā tin	tin nā	nā dhin	dhin nā

Tīgun

nā dhin dhin	nā nā dhin	dhin nā nā	tin tin nā
nā dhin dhin	nā nā dhin	dhin nā nā	dhin dhin nā
nā tin tin	nā nā dhin	dhin nā nā	dhin dhin nā
nā dhin dhin	nā nā tin	tin nā nā	dhin dhin nā

Caugun

nādhin dhinnā	nādhin dhinnā	nātin tinnā	nādhin dhinnā
nādhin dhinnā	nādhin dhinnā	nātin tinnā	nādhin dhinnā
nādhin dhinnā	nādhin dhinnā	nātin tinnā	nādhin dhinnā
nādhin dhinnā	nādhin dhinnā	nātin tinnā	nādhin dhinnā

2. This again involves maintaining the metric cycle of *tīntāl* by clapping and counting throughout. Here the speed is increased proportionally to *sawā'ī*, *ḍe'oṛhī*, *paune-dūgun*, and *dūgun lays*, or one and a quarter, one and a half, one and three quarters and two times that of the original speed. However, instead of repeating the *bols* of *tīntāl*, the student recites the *bols* of *jhaptāl* (ten beats) in *sawā'ī lay*, *ektāl* (twelve beats) in *ḍe'oṛhī lay*, *rūpak* (seven beats) in *paune-dūgun lay*, before returning to *tīntāl* in *dūgun lay*. This facilitates complex subdivisions of the beat while forcing the pupil to maintain the basic cycle of *tīntāl* at any cost.

Barābar

nā	dhin	dhin	nā
nā	dhin	dhin	nā
nā	tin	tin	nā
nā	dhin	dhin	nā

Sawā'ī

dhī – – – nā	– – – dhī –	– – dhī – –	– nā – – –
tī – – – nā	– – – dhī –	– – dhī – –	– nā – – –
dhī – – – nā	– – – dhī –	– – dhī – –	– nā – – –
tī – – – nā	– – – dhī –	– – dhī – –	– nā – – –

Ḍe'oṛhī

dhin – dhin	– dhā ge	tira kiṭa tī	– nā –
kat – tā	– dhā ge	tira kiṭa dhī	– nā –
dhin – dhin	– dhā ge	tira kiṭa tī	– nā –
kat – tā	– dhā ge	tira kiṭa dhī	– nā –

Paune-dūgun

tī – – – tī – –	– nā – – – dhī –	– – nā – – – dhī	– – – nā – – –
tī – – – tī – –	– nā – – – dhī –	– – nā – – – dhī	– – – nā – – –
tī – – – tī – –	– nā – – – dhī –	– – nā – – – dhī	– – – nā – – –
tī – – – tī – –	– nā – – – dhī –	– – nā – – – dhī	– – – nā – – –

Dūgun

nā dhin	dhin nā	nā dhin	dhin nā
nā tin	tin nā	nā dhin	dhin nā
nā dhin	dhin nā	nā dhin	dhin nā
nā tin	tin nā	nā dhin	dhin nā

3. An exercise devoid of the need for recitation but aimed at strengthening the student's ability to subdivide the beat. A steady, fixed beat is maintained with one hand while the other is used to tap cross-rhythms. Initially only one in every four beats is indicated. The student must then double, treble, quadruple and quintuple the ratio, continuing until he arrives at the point where he is tapping sixteen times in the space of four beats.

Fixed	1	2	3	4
1.	1			
2.	1	–	2	–
3.	1 – –	– 2 –	– – 3	– – –
4.	1	2	3	4
5.	1 – – – 2	– – – 3 –	– – 4 – –	– 5 – – –
6.	1 – 2	– 3 –	4 – 5	– 6 –
7.	1 – – – 2 – –	– 3 – – – 4 –	– – 5 – – – 6	– – – 7 – – –
8.	1 2	3 4	5 6	7 8
9.	1 – – – 2 – – – 3	– – – 4 – – – 5 –	– – 6 – – – 7 – –	– 8 – – – 9 – – –
10.	1 – – – 2 – – – 3 –	– – 4 – – – 5 – – –	6 – – – 7 – – – 8 –	– – 9 – – – 10 – – –

etc. up to sixteen divisions of the beat.

Although competence in *tāl* is considered essential from the very beginning of one's training, it is interesting that there is no attempt to teach the playing of *ṭhekā* until much later on in training. Vikram Singh regarded this as a general principle of *gharānā* training, and criticised the method of teaching in many music colleges where the *ṭhekā* of a *tāl* is treated as a beginner's priority. For *ṭhekā* is a very complex and difficult feature of tabla-playing that must be developed over a long period of time. For instance, the *ṭhekā* of *tīntāl* consists of much more than the *bols nā dhin dhin nā*, which are used to articulate the *tāl*. It incorporates small, personalised touches in the form of embellishments which make each musician's *ṭhekā* slightly different and individual. It is possible, in many cases, to identify a musician by his rendering of *ṭhekā* alone. It is therefore important for the disciple to have reached a relatively advanced stage of technical and musical development before he concentrates on *ṭhekā*.

Afaq Husain believed that in order to gain confidence and ability in *lay* and *tāl* generally, it was essential firstly to develop a mastery over one *tāl*. Consequently, early training was given exclusively in the most commonly played *tāl*: *tīntāl*. This, again, is radically different from college-teaching, where students must deal with several different *tāls* from the outset. Afaq Husain believed this approach merely obfuscated the students' feel for, and understanding of, *tāl* by introducing to them too wide a variety of metric cycles at too early a stage in their training. Many college students who had approached him for lessons had displayed a fundamental insecurity in *tāl* which he attributed, in part, to this particular feature of the college system of training.

With a thorough knowledge of the musical material given to me during the first months of my training, I had already imbibed many of the unspoken rules of composition. I had also observed my teacher in the act of composing and improvising on numerous occasions. From this I drew the inspiration to attempt composition myself, afterwards exposing my efforts to close scrutiny. Some of the rules of composition and improvisation are in fact conceptualised and verbalised, though a great many more are only intuitively felt. For example, I received some precise comments in which rules were clearly formalised, such as: 'No, you can't have that because it is not in the original "vocabulary" of the piece!' On the other hand, it was necessary to surmise other rules in response to comments like: 'Well, that doesn't feel right somehow.'

My first compositions were simple variations based on given *qāʿidas*, or other theme-and-variations pieces. Although, initially, I wrote down the variations and practised them before showing them to Afaq Husain, who made corrections, I later found that new variations were coming to mind during my lessons. I began to perform them spontaneously and received a great deal of encouragement, as it indicated to Afaq Husain that I was showing signs of grasping the *taʿlīm*. He said:

> Improvisations [*ūpaj*] are very excellent things. Another word for *ūpaj* is *damāgh* [mind]. New formulas ought to come to mind, and they do eventually come in the light of the *taʿlīm*. As the *taʿlīm* increases, the disciple finds the strength of mind to create new things if his mind is good. *Ūpaj* means the exertion of the mind.

Following elementary variations, I then attempted to compose simple *ṭukṛās* and *gats*. Although some were new, most were rearrangements of old pieces designed to fit different *tāls*, or with different cadential formulae appended. Each composition was checked by my teacher and corrected if necessary to show me how it ought to have been constructed.

Another way in which Afaq Husain managed to get his disciples interested in composition and improvisation was by introducing games, or setting puzzles. This was done both during lessons, as well as to pass the time on long train journeys. For example, he would often recite a composition in a given *tāl* and ask his disciples to set the same composition in a number of different *tāls*. Counting-games, in which numbers were used instead of tabla *bols*, were also very popular. A simple example involves the creation of *tihāʾīs* in *tīntāl* using numbers from one to seven. Dozens of solutions are possible, but the following two will demonstrate the point adequately:

1 2	3 4	5 6	7 –
– –	– –	– 1	2 3
4 5	6 7	– –	– –
– –	1 2	3 4	5 6
7			

1 –2	– 3	–4 –	5 –6
– 7	– –1	– 2	–3 –
4 –5	– 6	–7 –	– 1
–2 –	3 –4	– 5	–6 –
7			

Although we have only been dealing with numbers here, the value of such a process may be comprehended when tabla *bols* are superimposed on the numerical formulae. However, sometimes a string of *bols* is given as the basis for a particular compositional type. For instance, a special kind of *tihā'ī* known either as *nau kī tihā'ī* (a *tihā'ī* of nine sections) or *tihā'ī kī tihā'ī* (the *tihā'ī* of a *tihā'ī*), in which a given phrase must appear not three times, as with the *tihā'ī*, but three times three. The *bōls* here may be, say, *dhī nā tit dhā*. Again, many solutions are possible, but the following two will suffice:

– –	– –	– –	–dhī nātit
dhā dhīnā	titdhā –dhī	nātit dhā	– –
dhīnā titdhā	–dhī nātit	dhā dhīnā	titdhā –
– –dhī	nātit dhā	dhīnā titdhā	–dhī nātit
dhā			

–dhī nātit	dhā –	–dhī nātit	dhā –
–dhī nātit	dhā –dhī	nātit dhā	– –dhī
nātit dhā	– –dhī	nātit dhā	–dhī nātit
dhā –	–dhī nātit	dhā –	–dhī nātit
dhā			

Games and puzzles are thus designed by the *ustād* to activate the minds of his disciples. They are especially effective when a group is present as a great deal of enthusiasm is generated by the competition to create interesting and viable solutions to the set problems. Furthermore, whenever I met with a group of *gurū-bhā'īs*, similar games formed a substantial part of our social interaction outside the context of our tabla lessons.

Riyāẓ

Riyāẓ is the most commonly used word for practice, although very occasionally the word *mashq* is also used in the Lucknow *gharānā*. *Riyāẓ* is where one puts into practice all one has learned, and where the highly technical skills needed for the performance of North Indian classical music are developed. Sorrell and Narayan (1980: 67) have drawn attention to parallels between the Western and Indian systems, both of which 'lay considerable stress on virtuosity and solo performance'. That practice is essential to every musician in India is beyond dispute. Habib Raza Khan said: 'Making music is the action to beat all actions, and without proper practice it is impossible.' Akbar Husain stressed the role of *riyāẓ* in the technical and musical development of the student or disciple: 'If you keep on practising, you create a path that begins to show you the way.'

Riyāẓ is a very prominent concept among Indian musicians. It forms one of the most popular and perennial topics of conversation: *gurū-bhā'īs*, particularly, are constantly asking one another how much practice they have done and whether or not they have mastered a certain technique, and *ustāds* are constantly urging their disciples and students to increase the amount of time they spend doing their *riyāẓ*. Conversations nearly always include references to the great feats of prolonged and sustained *riyāẓ* performed by famous musicians of both previous and present generations. No doubt Neuman (1980: 31) is correct when he writes of the 'moral function' of such stories in encouraging the student. They are designed to instil in the pupil a certain sobriety and an awe of the massive task which lies ahead of him. Thus one frequently hears how Ahmadjan Thirakwa sat 'where bugs and insects and scorpions used to bite . . . so he wouldn't feel sleepy', and how he used to tie his hair to the ceiling in order to stay awake during extended periods of practice (Neuman 1980: 33). In the Lucknow *gharānā*, the achievement of Abid Husain, who is said to have practised twelve hours daily for twelve years, is regularly cited.

Undoubtedly, such feats of discipline and perseverance in practice lead to greater social status in the eyes of other musicians. As Sorrell and Narayan (1980: 67) have pointed out, 'such musicians clearly believe that one's status and credibility as a musician are in direct proportion to the number of hours spent practising'. The danger with this is that musicians, like anyone else, are apt to inflate their claims in order to achieve greater status. It is not only very tempting but also extremely easy to exaggerate one's actual achievement of maybe six or eight hours daily to one's ideal achievement of perhaps twelve to sixteen hours.

All musicians claim to do a considerable amount of daily *riyāẓ*, claims which have received support in most of the literature on music and musicians in North India. I was therefore rather surprised to find that very little empirical evidence emerged to support this. Indeed, I rarely came across a musician who could be said to be displaying anything even remotely resembling discipline and perseverance in practice. Of course, the majority of musicians I encountered in India were forced to take on full-time employment, and this disposed of a considerable amount of their time. Very few earned sufficiently from concerts alone, and none had endless free time to devote to *riyāẓ*; likewise, none were financially supported on anything akin to a *nawāb*'s stipend, as was apparently common in the nineteenth century. Nevertheless these claims concerning *riyāẓ* were frequently made, a fact that served to highlight the significant discrepancy between what musicians do, and what they say they do.

The ideal maximum amount of time to be spent in practice was rarely dictated, though the minimum was frequently stated. Afaq Husain knew that I was also engaged in fieldwork, which meant reading, interviewing, transcribing, typing and many other time-consuming activities. Nevertheless, he insisted that I devote at least four to five hours daily to *riyāẓ*: two to three hours in the early morning, and two to three hours late in the evening. For those disciples aiming to become professional musicians, he advised at least eight hours per day. However, this may be misleading because primary emphasis was laid not upon the exact quantity of time spent practising, but rather on the need for two things: the regularity of the *riyāẓ*, and full mental and physical concentration during it. In other words, a little good *riyāẓ* each day is considered preferable to a lot of bad *riyāẓ* done at irregular intervals. Students are therefore advised never to skip a day's practice because, as Afaq Husain said: 'The hand is like a wrestler who trains daily with his weights. Should he miss a day's training, he'll get aches and pains on resuming.' His advice was always to reduce the amount of *riyāẓ* if absolutely necessary, for example during school or college examinations or illness, but never to compromise on regularity.

Regularity is vital in building up the ability to concentrate the mind on the task in hand. Afaq Husain often likened *riyāẓ* to the study of a book. By reading with full concentration one misses nothing, but by allowing one's concentration to lapse even for a few seconds one may miss a very important or beautiful sentence in which the essence or meaning of the book is contained and without which the whole remains incomprehensible. The idea of a combination of regularity and concentration in practice was once conveyed to Bhupal Ray Choudhuri by Afaq Husain, who suggested that he should treat his *riyāẓ* as he treated his daily worship. Bhupal Ray Choudhuri, in his devotions, concentrated his best efforts on preparing fruits, flowers and other offerings, with a tremendous attention to detail. Afaq Husain told him to consider God to be his audience, and to meditate on his practice in the same way that he meditated on God.

Musicians had differing opinions as to the best time of day for *riyāẓ*. Many chose the early morning, beginning at or before sunrise. However, as far as members of the Lucknow *gharānā* were concerned, the ideal time was always the night, when distractions were fewer and extraneous noise was minimal. It is said that for twelve years Abid Husain began his *riyāẓ* after the call to prayer had sounded at sunset, and put his drums away on hearing the first call to prayer just before dawn the following morning. Afaq Husain also did the majority of his *riyāẓ* at night during his youth, lighting candles and practising until they had burnt out. Interestingly, however, during the time I spent in Lucknow I rarely saw him practise, which was perhaps surprising in view of his advice to students. Occasionally, he was apt to perform an intensive period of *riyāẓ*, perhaps before a particularly important concert, in which he played each night for a fixed period of ten, fifteen or twenty days. When questioned about this discrepancy, Afaq Husain simply said that he had done the bulk of his hard work in his youth and that now he did not need to practise diligently in order to achieve maximum efficiency in performance.

An important method of organising one's *riyāẓ* is the *cillā*. Neuman (1980: 41) describes a *cillā* as literally 'a discipline which is undertaken for 40 days without a break . . . a vow that one assumes, to concentrate on whatever one is desirous of achieving.' Specifically, *cillā* refers to a spiritual discipline in which a person recites the same prayers each day at the same time and in the same place. On completion of the *cillā*, God grants whatever the person has wished for. Interestingly, I heard numerous accounts of how *cillās* had failed on the thirty-ninth day owing to some unavoidable mishap. They are widely acknowledged to be difficult to complete successfully.

Cillā as a religious discipline is clear, but as a musical discipline it was interpreted more loosely by Afaq Husain and his family:

> The meaning of *cillā* is that daily, and there mustn't be a gap of one single day, you do five to eight hours of *riyāẓ* from nine in the evening. I fixed a time, and whether there was a storm or typhoon, whether it was snowing, raining, or whatever happened, I played from eight or nine in the evening.

Here the stress is clearly on the regularity of *riyāẓ* not on the exact place where it should be done, nor on its duration or content. The only qualifying feature of *cillā* is that it cannot be achieved in anything less than forty days. Afaq Husain's own *cillā* lasted for approximately two years, a period which he recognised to be insufficient in comparison with the great feat of his grandfather, Abid Husain. Once I asked Afaq Husain if I should myself consider undertaking a *cillā*. He dissuaded me, saying that my lifestyle was not suited to this particular kind of discipline and that no doubt something or other would crop up, so preventing me from completing the allotted period. His message was clear: that one should never take on a *cillā* unless there is a reasonable chance of it being successful.

Having established that it is not the length of the *riyāẓ* that is important but the way in which it is performed, I shall now discuss how good *riyāẓ* should be structured to attain the best results, as practised by members of the Lucknow tabla *gharānā*. For if one is to be 'a master over one's fingers', as Bhupal Ray Choudhuri put it, then 'it has to be regular and ordered *riyāẓ*: good *riyāẓ* according to the rules'.

It is essential to build up to good *riyāẓ* gradually, because it is considered impossible to achieve overnight. Afaq Husain often likened the process to weightlifting. Nobody, he said, could be expected to lift five *mann* immediately. One must start with one *mann* and gradually increase the load to one and a quarter, and so on upwards to one's goal. Of course, there are different kinds of *riyāẓ* for different people. Beginners will doubtless spend more time practising basic strokes and playing simple *qā'idas* for exercise, whereas advanced disciples will treat their *riyāẓ* more like a private performance, though they may still stop to repeat pieces if necessary. My own *riyāẓ*, as performed while I was living in Lucknow, reflected something of both these approaches: it included elements of basic technique as well as a number of the more advanced pieces. It is therefore a description of my ideal *riyāẓ* which will follow here. (The fact that I did not always achieve this ideal should not detract from its description, for it was a model to which one could aspire.)

My ideal daily *riyāẓ* was divided into two periods, as suggested by Afaq Husain. I practised for three hours early each morning, and for about two hours late in the evening or at night, depending on the time I was working or taking lessons. Each morning began with a twenty-minute period during which I merely sat at my drums and consciously relaxed my muscles and adjusted my posture. I set the basic arm and hand positions for both right and left hands and played *tā* (*kinār*) several hundred times with the right hand, and *ghe* several hundred times with the left. This completed, I embarked on the main section of the *riyāẓ*: the practice of *qā'ida*. Fully two hours were spent practising four basic *qā'idas* designed to develop my technique. As Afaq Husain explained, *qā'idas* are essential 'to build up the hand bit by bit, by concentrating on small aspects of playing. Practise them hard and understand them, and slowly you'll get the right weight. You'll get into good habits.' Thirty minutes were allotted to each basic *qā'ida*, the original composition of which was repeated without variation throughout. I began very slowly indeed, fixing my attention on every detail of hand and finger positions, arm movement and body posture. Afaq Husain frequently said that accurate playing in very slow speeds facilitated far greater accuracy in fast speeds in later years. It was meaningless, he said, to be able to play at lightning speeds when one could not manage to play correctly in a slow speed. Indeed, he believed that a person required a far better overall technique to play slowly than to play quickly.

I increased the speed of articulation gradually, though not by means of an accelerando as I was told this encouraged the bad habit of unconscious speeding during performance. Instead, each change of speed was immediate and proportional, without any intervening acceleration. The transition from slow to fast was therefore effected in a series of step-like motions. Once a new speed had been established it was necessary to maintain it for about five minutes before moving up a stage. This continued to the point where I had difficulty in sustaining a speed without allowing tension to creep into my hands, arms and body. Whenever this occurred, my orders were to drop back to the fastest speed I could manage to maintain without physical tension. On no account was I to stop as this would have defeated the object of the *riyāẓ*. *Riyāẓ* is not like a physical exercise that involves sweating and straining, for straining implies tension and the slightest tension in one's body affects both one's technical facility and the sound produced.

Needless to say, full concentration had to be maintained constantly during *riyāẓ*. I was always told to focus my ears, eyes and mind on my playing. Firstly, I had to listen carefully to make sure that I always produced the desired sound: good *sūr*. Secondly, I had to watch for precise finger placements and hand positions to control my technique and produce the right sounds. Thirdly, I had to think in order to control my body and rid it of tension and to remember the music. Only when these three factors were focused together could full concentration be maintained.

The remaining forty minutes of the morning session were occupied with playing the basic *qāʿidas*, but this time with sets of variations added. Ten minutes were spent on each *qāʿida* during which each variation was repeated between six and a dozen times. Essentially, if one has achieved complete control over the basic *qāʿida* composition, the variations should present no technical problems whatsoever, because they represent the reworking of the material.

For the first hour of the two-hour evening session I repeated detailed work on two basic *qāʿidas*. The other hour was devoted to other types of composition, particularly those given by Afaq Husain during lessons. These included *ṭukṛās* and *gats*, which I repeated many times, beginning at a slow speed and gradually increasing the tempo in stages, as was the case with *qāʿida*.

In order to help the disciple relate his practice to performance, Afaq Husain advocated that at least one hour each week be devoted to performing to the accompaniment of a *sāraṅgī* or harmonium player. At one stage I hired a *sāraṅgī* player on a weekly basis to assist me, but generally disciples helped each other in this respect by accompanying their *gurū-bhāʾīs* on the harmonium. Each disciple used this period to practice a sequence of compositions in preparation for a hypothetical solo performance, beginning with *qāʿidas* and ending with difficult *gats*, *ṭukṛās* and *cakkardārs*.

Finally, mention must be made of one vital, even indispensable, aspect of practice which was still referred to as *riyāẓ* by musicians, but which might more conveniently be termed 'silent practice', or '*riyāẓ* of the mind'. Sorrell and Narayan (1980: 69) claimed that 'Ram Narayan distinguishes between physical practice and mental practice, the latter being virtually synonymous with composition'. Although composition certainly does figure here, as could be seen with the examples of the musical games and puzzles that Afaq Husain set for his disciples, much of this mental practice is dedicated to the silent rehearsal of the actual *riyāẓ* that one physically performs. It may therefore be considered more accurately as a supplement to physical *riyāẓ* where, as Afaq Husain said, one 'thinks about how the *riyāẓ* should be'. 'There isn't just one way to practise', Afaq Husain continued, 'there's one way where you understand your *riyāẓ* and another where you do it.' Silent *riyāẓ* essentially involves the verbalisation of one's musical material (which may be performed vocally or mute) in order to help one memorise and study the structure and divisions of individual compositions in relation to the *tāl*. 'With *riyāẓ*', affirmed Afaq Husain, 'you have to keep thinking and doing your own research in order to get the most out of it.'

Character-training

Afaq Husain believed that a person could not become a good musician unless he was also basically a good human being. The point here is not to define one particular view of what makes a musician or person good, but instead to acknowledge that Afaq Husain linked the ideas of musicianship and personality and, in consequence, spent some of his time giving moral advice to his disciples with a view to guiding the development of their characters. Hence this kind of training should not be seen as a feature totally separate from practical advice concerning tabla-playing technique, or the giving of compositions from the repertoire. It is all *taʿlīm*; it is all part of the same process of learning.

Afaq Husain is a Shiite Muslim. Despite rarely saying his prayers or attending the mosque, he displayed a strong belief in God and an unequivocal acceptance of His powers. Afaq Husain did not expect or want his disciples to become Muslims, but he did imply that they should, like him, aquiesce in the authority of God and so be religious in the general sense of the word. Religion was manifest in Afaq Husain's disciples' training in two ways. Firstly, they had to obey certain religious observances by avoiding playing at certain sensitive times of the day or year. Afaq Husain recommended that his disciples suspend their *riyāẓ* during the first ten days of Muharram and for three days late in Ramadan, periods of deep mourning for the martyrdom of Imam Husain and Hazrat Ali respectively. They were also advised to refrain from playing whenever they heard the call to prayer (*aẕān*) issuing from a mosque, or whenever they heard people performing *mātam*. However, it appears that actions such as these had less to do with respect for the religion itself (which theoretically prohibits music) than with respect for the beliefs and sensibilites of other Muslims who might object to music being played at these specific times. For example, Afaq Husain accepted professional engagements during Muharram and Ramadan, and did not object if disciples who lived in non-Shiite areas of the city continued to practise at these times. Moreover, whereas he advised disciples to desist from physical *riyāẓ* on hearing *aẕān* or *mātam*, he strongly encouraged mental *riyāẓ* in its place.

The second way in which religion was manifest in the disciple's training was when Afaq Husain chose to talk directly about God. He rarely used the name Allah, selecting instead words that have a more general relevance to Muslims, Hindus and Christians, such as *k͟hudā*, *bhagwān*, *ishwar*, and the English term 'God'. Most of his disciples were non-Muslims and he was evidently attempting to broaden the concept of God and to make accessible his ideas concerning the importance of a belief in His omnipotence. Afaq Husain was concerned to teach his disciples that all are subject to the Will of God and that man can succeed at nothing unless He so desires. One must therefore accept the authority of God and trust that He will regard us as His true devotees and consequently reward us with success.

These ideas appeared prominently in each of two interesting acronyms that Afaq Husain used to elucidate the three essential prerequisites for the success of a musician. The first was the word *ʿilm*, meaning 'knowledge'. *ʿIlm* is constructed of three letters: *ʿain*, *lām* and *mīm*. *ʿAin* stands for *ʿināyat-e-illāhī*: the Gift of God; *lām* stands for *luṭf-e-ustād*: the pleasure of the *ustād*; *mīm* stands for *miḥnat-e-shāgird*: the sheer hard work of the disciple. Only when *ʿain*, *lām* and *mīm* are taken together do they constitute true knowledge. The second acronym is the word *hunar*, meaning 'skill'. *Hunar* is also constructed of three letters: *he*, *nūn* and *re*. *He* stands for *hāẓma*: disgestion – the full disgestion, and hence understanding, of the knowledge one has been given; *nūn* stands for *nafāsat-e-ustādī-o-shāgirdī*: the exquisiteness and refinement of the *ustād–shāgird* relationship; *re* stands for *raẓāʾe illāhī*: the Will of God. Only when *he*, *nūn* and *re* are taken together do they constitute real skill.

Both acronyms incorporate the idea that success is built upon the involvement of three agents: God, the *ustād* and the student. Of these three prerequisites, the role of the *ustād* or *gurū* in the development of the disciple was given greatest emphasis by those with whom I spoke, greater even than hard work or God's gift, which I think we may take to be a metaphor for 'talent'. Bhupal Ray Choudhuri went as far as to suggest that ultimate success depended 'eight annas on the *gurū*, four annas on *riyāẓ*, and the rest on God' (using the old system of sixteen annas to the rupee). It was therefore deemed vital that the disciple lay his complete trust and faith in his *ustād*, who would guide him on the path to knowledge and so expand his mind and his understanding of his art. The disciple had to take care to cultivate the 'most exquisite and refined' of relationships based on the utmost respect possible for a human being. Indeed, Bhupal Ray Choudhuri often said that one should love one's *ustād* or *gurū* even more than one's own father.

On the importance of the role of the *ustād*, Afaq Husain more than once quoted the following couplet by Jamil Mazhari during my tabla lessons:

بقدرِ پیمانۂ تخیّل سرور ہر دل میں ہے خودی کا

اگر نہ یہ ہو فریبِ پیہم تو دم نکل جائے آدمی کا

Baqadr-e-paimāna-e-takhayyul sarūr har dil meṅ hai khūdī kā, agar na ye ho fareb-e-paiham to dam nikal jā'e ādmī kā.

The delight of sense-of-self is in every heart proportionate to its capacity for imagination. If there were not this continuous self-deception then a man's breath would expire.

What this means is that the delight a man takes in contemplating himself is proportionate to the scale of his powers of imagination. The more vivid his imagination, the more joy he feels in his (imagined) unique powers. This self-contemplation is really self-deception, but without it man could not survive. Although this may all sound rather esoteric on first hearing, it must be taken in the context of the message Afaq Husain was attempting to convey at the time. Here the point is that in order to succeed in any sphere, particularly music, one must have *shauq*, which may be translated as 'enthusiasm' or 'passion'. A bad tutor will only stifle the pupil's *shauq*, or channel it in the wrong direction. Alternatively, a good tutor will expand the capacity of the pupil's mind, thus increasing his powers of imagination and understanding. A good tutor therefore encourages the pupil's *shauq*, which, in turn, leads to greater fulfilment.

From this example it may be seen that Afaq Husain shared the most typical of cultural pastimes among Lucknowis, an interest in Urdu poetry. He frequently used poetic extracts in this way in order to emphasise a particular point he wished to argue. This was especially true with regard to moral issues, and so poetic illustrations constituted an important component in the character-training of Afaq Husain's disciples. The following are three examples of the advice given to me during my own training.

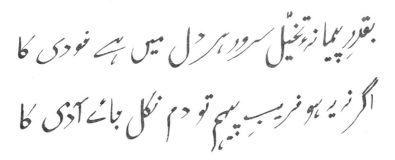

Firstly, one must always be honest both with oneself and with other people. In the same way that truth will always come to light, so lies will always be exposed. As a musician, it is especially important to be honest with one's art. As Akbar Husain so meaningfully said to me once: 'If your heart is true, then your fingers will tell the truth. If your heart is false, then your fingers will always lie.' Afaq Husain's own method of illustrating this point was by quoting the following couplet:

صداقت چھپ نہیں سکتی بناوٹ کے اصولوں سے

کہ خوشبو آ نہیں سکتی کبھی کاغذ کے پھولوں سے

Ṣadāqat chup nahīn saktī banāwaṭ ke uṣūlon se, ki khushbū ā nahīn saktī kabhī kāghaz ke phūlon se.

Genuineness cannot be hidden by the principles of artificiality. For fragrance cannot ever come from paper flowers.

Secondly, one must always contrive both to practise humility and to show the greatest respect for one's fellow human beings. A man should never try to deceive himself into believing he is better than his neighbour. He should firstly know himself and know his own limitations, for this is the true mark of wisdom. Afaq Husain drew on the following *rubā'ī* (four-lined verse) by Mir Anis to illustrate this point:

کر عجز اگر عاقل و فرزانہ ہے

دانائی پہ بھولا ہے تو دیوانہ ہے

تسبیح کے دانوں پر نظر کر ناداں

گردش میں گرفتار ہے جو دانا ہے

Kar 'ijz agar 'āqil-o-farzāna hai, dānā'ī pe bhūlā hai to dīwāna hai, taṣbīḥ ke dānon par naẓr kar nādān, gardish men gariftār hai jo dānā hai.

Practice humility if you are intelligent and wise. Once you deceive yourself about your wisdom you are mad. Foolish one, turn you gaze upon the beads of the rosary. If you are *dānā* [this is a pun, because it means both 'wise' and 'a bead'] then you are imprisoned in moving round.

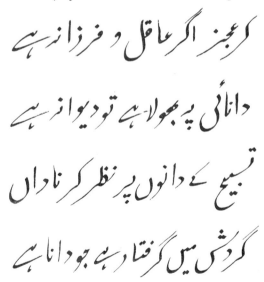

In other words, once you deceive yourself that you are wise, that is the equivalent of becoming insane. The wise man is content to move within the limits laid down for him, just as the bead can only move along the string of the rosary.

Thirdly, and finally, Afaq Husain used frequently to say that, in this life, a man could only cultivate real friendship with a small and select number of people. He often warned against those who were ostensibly friendly but who had in mind some ulterior motive, such as money or gain. Consequently one should be careful in life and not overindulge in a wide range of friendships. On the other hand, it was also important to avoid enmity, for God did not forgive those who created enemies. There was no limit, however, to the amount of friendship and love one could enjoy with one's real friends. In other words, one should be equable of temperament, a quality expressed in the following couplet by Kabir Das:

کبیر کھڑا بیچ بازار سب کی مانگے خیر

نا کہو سے دوستی نا کہو سے بیر

Kabīr kharạ̄ bīc bāzār sab kī mānge khair, nā kahū se dostī na kahū se bair.

Standing in the middle of the bazaar, Kabir [the poet's pen-name] prays for everybody's good. He has neither friendship with anyone nor enmity for anyone.

Preparation for a career

A practical training in the tabla prepares the disciple in what is essentially a solo instrumental tradition. Yet on becoming professional, a tabla player must necessarily earn his living mainly as an accompanist and, as all tabla players admit, solo and accompanimental playing styles differ greatly one from the other. Therefore, an *ustād* must somehow shape the training in such a way as to cater for this eventuality. His responsibility to his disciples does not stop at teaching them how to play the tabla. It in fact extends to preparing them for, and advising them about, a career in the competitive world of music in North India.

Disciples are trained to be soloists from a relatively early stage in the learning process. Afaq Husain used to set aside specific times at which his disciples would play to him short solos comprising pieces from their lessons. Either he would himself accompany the tabla on the harmonium, or else this role would be performed by another disciple. Occasionally, one would be required to perform short solos of, say, ten to fifteen minutes' duration in the context of a *gaṇḍā bandhan* ceremony, where the audience would extend to a number of family musicians and close friends. Thus one had always to think in terms of structuring short solo performances designed not for oneself, but for other people to listen to. From time to time, a certain mood would come over Afaq Husain and he would take the tabla during a lesson and embark upon a long tabla solo, accompanied by a disciple on the harmonium. He thus provided us with a model of solo tabla-playing from which we could derive inspiration and to which we could aspire.

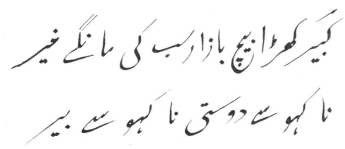

A similar process whereby disciples learned by listening and observing occurred in the context of public performances. I and other fellow disciples often travelled with Afaq Husain to hear him perform at concerts, whether in Lucknow or in another city. Listening to one's *ustād* in actual performance was seen as an essential part of one's training, as K. K. Kapoor explained to me:

> Gharānā musicians are performing musicians too, and they teach their students, their sons, or whoever, on the stage as well . . . One sees the stage and gets a feel for it, and understands that the audience appreciates the art . . . In the relationship created between audience and artist, there are certain [musical] things that come out by themselves as a result of the atmosphere and rapport, and these don't necessarily come out in lesson time.

First-hand experience, therefore, taught disciples the different approaches to the various styles of accompaniment that are used for dance, vocal and instrumental musics. No specific training existed for these different styles other than the live context of the concert itself, for only in actual performance could the disciple learn what it was feasible to play in a certain musical context and when it was feasible to play it. However, Afaq Husain did occasionally invite young soloists to play with his disciples in private. This provided him with the opportunity both to assess the accompanimental skills of his pupils and to give them practical advice on how to improve.

Finally, Afaq Husain always kept in mind the fact that some of his disciples would one day become professional musicians. He therefore did his best to prepare them for the transition from being amateurs to being professionals in what I have already indicated is a highly competitive music world. For example, he introduced and recommended his disciples to other well-known musicians in the hope that this might lead to them being engaged at some future date. In addition, on occasions when Afaq Husain was invited to perform for a private gathering of fellow musicians and connoisseurs, he sometimes allowed a disciple to precede him with a short solo performance of ten to fifteen minutes' duration, thus effecting yet another kind of introduction to those who might one day wish to employ the disciple.

Introductions were not the only kind of help given. Whenever jobs became available, Afaq Husain made sure that his disciples were fully prepared for the auditions and could fulfil the basic requirements of the job. For instance, a post for a tabla accompanist became vacant in 1983 at the Sangeet Natak Akademi of Lucknow, an institution specialising in the teaching of *kathak* dance. Afaq Husain gave one of his disciples, who intended to apply for the post, an intensive training in dance accompaniment beforehand, and furnished him with a considerable repertoire of dance compositions.

A *gharānā* training, then, comprises a highly individualised instruction in tabla-playing which caters to the specific technical and musical needs of each pupil. In its ideal form it is a total and integrated system of training, the social and musical aspects of which are not separable. Becoming a musician is just as much a question of developing one's character as it is of learning the music. The disciple is thus guided by his *ustād*, with whom he shares an intimate rapport, from his initiation to the point where he is ready to enter into the professional world of Indian music.

The college system of training

Having described a *gharānā* training, I wish now to concentrate briefly on the format of classes and the methods employed in the teaching of the tabla under the 'college system'. I do not claim that all teachers, colleges, music schools or universities operate the same system, but I do believe they share a number of important basic features.

In the classes I observed, each student, on entering a classroom, performed a gesture of respect by touching the teacher's feet and greeting him with hands joined in a *namaskār*, thus simulating the signs used by disciples to show respect to their *gurūs* or *ustāds* under the *gharānā* system of training. However, similarities between the two systems stop there, for arguably the most important difference is that a teacher in an institution cannot get to know his students on a personal basis but must instead respond to the members of his class as a group. The students have no obligation to the teacher, and the teacher's sole obligation to the students ends when he has completed the course and they leave his class for another at the end of the college year. It is certainly not seen to be his job to give moral advice and character-training, as is the case in the relationship between *ustād* and *shāgird*. So a rapport does not exist in the teacher–pupil relationship that is comparable with that found in the master–disciple relationship. The teacher–pupil relationship is typically characterised by a remoteness and lack of commitment from both teachers and pupils.

Students selected their instruments from cupboards at the back of the class. The drums were owned by the college and were for the use of members of all classes. They were invariably in appalling condition, some with broken skins that had been taped to prevent them from splitting further, others with broken *siyāhīs*, and even a few that displayed large, open cracks in the wood of the *dāhinā*. Everyone acknowledged that it was almost impossible to get any kind of presentable sound out of these drums.

Having selected their instruments, students sat on a large *takht* (raised platform) measuring about fifteen feet square which was covered with a white cotton cloth. They formed a semicircle around the teacher, who occasionally sat on the *takht* in order to demonstrate on the tabla, but at other times sat at a desk just to one side of the room. The size of the classes ranged from about six students to fifteen, though the average number was about ten, of which half were females. Finally, before each class began, a register of those present was formally taken.

The syllabus for each stage of the course was published in a prospectus published by the Bhatkhande Sangit Vidyapith of Lucknow. The course was designed to prepare students for examinations at the end of each academic year (i.e. December), success in which enabled them to progress to the next stage of the course and onwards finally to a degree. Failure in an examination forced a student to repeat that particular stage of the course, though in practice very few actually failed. Essentially, then, the teaching had to be geared primarily towards getting students through examinations.

The syllabus provided a framework for the course in that it stipulated that a certain number of *tāls* and compositional types had to be covered. However, the choice of actual pieces was left up to the individual teacher, as long as they were within the guidelines set out by the syllabus. The following example is taken from the Madhyama (third-year) course as specified in the Bhatkhande Sangit Vidyapith's *Prospectus and Syllabus for 1981 to 1983*:

1. Trital: Two advanced Quidas with eight Paltas in each. Three advanced Gats, Two Mukdas and Relas, Three Tukdas and simple Tihais and the playing of Trital in Adilaya.
2. Barabar, Dugun, Tigun and Chaugun of the Thekas of the following Talas: Sawari, Roopak, Sool.
3. Sawari and Roopak [*tāls*]: Two Quidas, Two Gats, Two Relas, Two Mukhdas, Two Tukdas and advanced Tihais in each Tal.

4. Chautal and Sool[-*tāl*]: Four Tukdas and Two Parans (Sada and Chakradar) in each Tal and advanced Tihais.
5. Thekas of the following Talas in Barabar and Dugun Layas with simple Tihais: Matth, Gajajhampa, Teora, Jhampa.
6. Tuning of the Instrument.
7. Padhant [recitation] of all the Tals and Bols prescribed.

This demonstrates quite clearly that a considerable repertoire must be learned at what is still a relatively elementary stage of the training. The repertoire includes a knowledge of many different *tāls*, some of which (e.g. *gajajhampā*) I have to this day never personally heard played publicly or privately by any tabla soloist or accompanist. This perhaps illustrates that the syllabus bears little relation to the reality of tabla-playing. It also shows that the emphasis of the training lies more with the quantity of music to be learned rather than the quality of the students' technique and musicianship. And in prescribing the repertoire in this manner, syllabuses are not structured to cater for the individual technical and musical needs of each student.

By the end of the fifth year of the course (Visharad Part II – equivalent in value to a B.A. degree), an extraordinary number of *tāls* and compositions had to be learned:

1. Trital – Advance[d] Peshkars, Gats, Quidas, Relas, Tukdas, Mukhdas and Parans.
2. The following Talas: Basant, Brahma, Laxmi, Vishnu, Ganesh and Mani with the ability to perform on them, Four sada Tukdas, Two Chakradar Tukdas – Four Sada Parans – Two Chakradar Parans – Two Mukdas and Two Relas in each Tal.
3. Ability to play the Theka of Trital in Barabar, Dugun, Tigun, Chaugun, Chehgun and Atgun Layas.
4. Perfect tuning of the instrument.
5. Ability to play the Thekas of all prevalent Talas in Vilambit Laya and those Talas that are Simple [and which are] played with String instrument[s] and Drut Khyal and Tarana as well[, in] Drut Laya.
6. Perfect Padhant of all the Talas and Bols learnt in any given Laya.

The *tāls* mentioned under point 2 above are usually only heard in the repertoires of a limited number of *pakhāwaj* players, notably Raja Chatrapati Singh of Bijna, who delights in such rare and complex cycles. Furthermore, they are *tāls* that have considerable significance for Hindus: many bear the names of gods and carry stories relating them to events in Hindu mythology. They are totally unrelated to the tabla repertoire and represent part of an attempt to root the instrument in a largely alien historical and musical context. In the same way that modern Hindi is becoming more and more Sanskritised to rid it of all Persian and Arabic influences, so the tabla is becoming more and more Hinduised and *pakhāwaj*-oriented in order to demonstrate that it is essentially an indigenous instrument and not, as Stewart (1974) concluded, a hybrid formed from a complex interweaving of alien and indigenous influences, such as the *naqqāra*, *ḍholak* and *pakhāwaj*.

Examinations, involving both a written theory paper and a practical test, were held each December. The theory paper lasted three hours and consisted of a choice of several questions from a total of roughly six to eight. For example, candidates for the Visharad Part II were set a range of questions that asked for life sketches of famous tabla players, tested students' knowledge of the different notational systems for the tabla, required descriptions of the musical and technical differences between the various tabla *gharānās*, and sought definitions of a number of musical terms. Some of this theoretical knowledge was taught in class time but the onus was on the student to make full use of the library facilities provided by the Bhatkhande Music College when preparing for this part of the examination.

In the practical test, the student was effectively examined on his or her completion of the course. He/she began by playing a tabla solo of fifteen to twenty minutes' duration, which was followed by detailed questioning by the examiner about his or her repertoire. The student was then requested to play a range of compositions in a number of different *tāls* chosen by the examiners. With a pass mark of around 33 per cent, few students actually failed the examination. In addition to a general 'pass', which was attained by most, categories like 'merit' and 'distinction' were awarded to those with higher marks.

The format of most classes I observed followed a similar pattern, a fact which pointed to a certain inflexibility in the teaching methods displayed by college tutors. Lessons usually began with everyone playing the *ṭhekā* of a given *tāl* in *barābar* (also known as *ṭhā*) *lay*. After several cycles of the *tāl*, the teacher called at intervals for proportional increases in *lay* to *dūgun*, *tīgun*, *caugun* and so on. Following this, the teacher asked each student in turn to recite the *bols* of the *tāl* and to count the beats by indicating the structure of the *tāl* with claps and waves of the hands. Once again, they were asked to double, treble and quadruple the speed of their recitations while maintaining the original speed with their hands. Then they played on the tabla everything they had previously recited. The exercise concluded with everyone playing the *tāl* once more in unison.

Next, students played in unison a composition learned in a previous lesson and set in the *tāl* practised as the initial exercise. As with the first exercise, speeds were increased proportionally, and then individuals each played the composition separately before joining together again in unison. Lastly, a new piece (or a new variation on a piece) was written on the blackboard in Hindi for the students to note down. The notational system employed was generally that created by Pandit Bhatkhande himself, as described by Shepherd (1976). Interestingly, each lecturer interpreted the system slightly differently, and this resulted in a number of varying notations. The teacher demonstrated the new piece several times very slowly before asking each student in turn to recite and play it. The class ended with a unison rendition of the new piece.

One or two weeks were spent on a particular *qā'ida* along with about eight variations and a *tihā'ī* derived from it, or several days were devoted to learning a set composition such as *ṭukṛā* or *gat*. In this way, the course was learned by heart, piece by piece. During the last few weeks of the academic year, teachers spent time revising the repertoire in preparation for the examination, making sure nothing had been forgotten. Thus teachers satisfied the priority of completing the course and fulfilling the quantitative aspects of the training. However, many expressed the opinion that they faced a dilemma in that they were not free to concentrate on other qualitative aspects of the training owing to the constraints imposed by having to complete syllabuses in the limited time allowed for each class and each term. For example, the system denied them the opportunity to encourage good technique and good sound, qualities that required a training honed to individual needs. Of course, personalised training was virtually impossible during classes despite the fact that the situation demanded it in view of the hugely varying levels of ability displayed by students.

Owing both to the truly appalling conditions of the instruments used, as well as to the need for so much playing in unison in order to save time, it was virtually impossible for teachers to concentrate on the sound production of individual members of the class. Whereas sound production was of crucial importance to Afaq Husain in the *gharānā* system of training, it had a very low priority in the college system. But this seemed not to worry the professor of tabla, Ranganath Misra, who insisted that the condition of the drums did not matter during the initial stages of training, where it was more important to 'set' the hands. He naturally agreed that a good instrument became more important in the later stages of students' training, once the hand had been 'set'. Nevertheless, a lecturer in tabla, Shital Prasad Misra, expressed amazement that one should be expected to teach students on drums from which no adequate sound could emerge, while another lecturer, Ram Kumar Sharma, expressed his annoyance at the poor results he achieved when trying merely to tune some of the drums for students in his class.

The varying musical and technical abilities of the members of each class presented teachers with a special problem in that they were forced to pick a level of teaching that catered for stronger as well as weaker students. They were unable to make things too difficult or to progress too rapidly for the less able, nor could they go too slowly, so creating boredom and stagnation in the talented. The problem of varying ability among class members was created, in part, by the rules of admission practised by the Bhatkhande Music College. It will be remembered that many students gained admission to the College on the strength of having previously passed high-school and intermediate examinations, passes which made them eligible to enter second- and third-year classes respectively. In theory, potential students were also screened by means of practical auditions before final admission to a class, but in practice this appears to have been, in many cases, less than successful, as Shital Prasad Misra pointed out:

> Many students come into my intermediate [i.e. third-year] class straight from school. But only God knows why they have such bad hands! I get a headache from continually trying to make them understand. I've toiled and sweated blood over other students throughout the first and second years, and I've brought them to the stage where if I tell them to play a certain *bol*, they can. And [the new students] can't even get *nā dhin dhin nā* right. Instead of *tin* they'll play *tūn*!

Individual attention, although sometimes used to bring weaker members of a class up to standard, could not be given to more able students because class and term time was strictly limited and the course had to be covered fully. As Professor Ranganath Misra said: 'Suppose there are ten students, and the period is of ninety minutes. How is it possible to give personalised attention?' Thus for well over 50 per cent of lesson time students played in unison. Shital Prasad Misra told me he watched each student in turn for one cycle of the *tāl*, but he admitted that mistakes were extremely difficult to detect because his attention was diluted and his mind had to be 'in all directions at once'.

My detailed notes on tabla classes included observations of students' abilities to remember or recite pieces, play the set strokes, and demonstrate compositions given during lessons. Results consistently indicated that approximately one-third of all students were competent and could play and recite over 90 per cent of all exercises and pieces; one-third managed to play about 50 per cent of the material given; and one-third were unable to play or recite well over 80 per cent of the pieces, and generally responded very poorly to the teacher's efforts to train them. In such cases, the teacher was forced to spend a disproportionate amount of time coaching these weaker members of the class, a course of action which often led to great frustration on the part of both teacher and other members of the class. An outburst from one lecturer (whom it is prudent to allow to remain anonymous) who had finally lost all patience went as follows:

TEACHER You're hopeless! Don't you ever do any practice? You won't get anywhere without it. Who do you get to do your practice for you? Your father? Does he do it for you?
GIRL I don't have a father. [Starts crying. Teacher mellows.]
TEACHER Oh, sorry! But, you see, if I have to spend this much time on you, the others will suffer. This is after all a third-year class. How did you get into it? Perhaps you should go to the first-year class.

As a consequence of the inadequate attention paid to the finer details of technique, a great deal of insecurity was evident on the part of the students, many of whom did not know the correct fingering for a particular stroke. I observed classes in which nearly all students used markedly different fingerings for the same *bol* combinations, and displayed a variety of postures, arm and hand movements, and finger placements. This situation was aggravated by two factors. Firstly, college students were usually taught by a different teacher for each stage of the course. Therefore there was no uniformity of technique because what was considered by one teacher to be a correct fingering may have been incorrect in the eyes of another. Secondly, the syllabus recommended the teaching of the different styles (i.e. the techniques and compositions) of tabla as found in the six major *gharānās*. There was therefore no continuity of style, a situation which tended to confuse students.

Quite often, particular features of style were taught incorrectly because teachers were not experts in any style other than their own and knew neither the correct versions of other *gharānās*' compositions nor the specific techniques used. In other words, a player of the Benares *gharānā* was in most cases unable to teach compositions and techniques of the Delhi *gharānā*, and vice versa. This point may be illustrated by two examples: firstly, an examiner for the Bhatkhande Music College told me that Lucknow *gharānā* compositions and techniques were represented in the course, in spite of there being no teacher specialising in that particular style. He proceeded to give an example of what he said was a famous Lucknow *qāʿida*, the basic phrase of which he recited and demonstrated as follows:

```
o  ⁽²³⁾1 23  1      23 1     o       o  2     o      ▼ o     o
dhātra kadhe        teṭe genā        dhāti genā      tunā katā
23          1           23           23   1                 ×
```

There are several versions of this *qāʿida* in the Lucknow repertoire, but none corresponds to the above. The following is the version most widely used in performance by Lucknow *gharānā* tabla players:

```
o  1 23  1     23 ●      V     o  2       V     ▼ o       V
dhāti ṭedhi    ṭetā ghena      dhāti ghena      dhīna ghena
1     23  1      23  1         1     23         1     23
```

This clearly indicates the differences between the two versions, both in the *bols* recited as well as in the strokes employed. The examiner's version is a complete misrepresentation of the Lucknow composition, though it appears to correspond to a Farukkhabad version of the *qāʿida*. Perhaps this is not surprising as the examiner himself learned from a musician of that *gharānā*.

The second example was provided by two of my *gurū-bhā'īs* who had previously studied at the Bhatkhande Music College. They displayed techniques which comprised a mixture of elements of different styles. The strokes they used were often inaccurate and quite inefficient for producing the required *bols* of certain compositions. Both had been trained by teachers of the Benares *gharānā* to play the famous Delhi *qā'ida*:

dhāti dhāge nadhā tirakiṭa dhāti dhāge tīna kīna

However, they were not taught to produce *tirakiṭa* using Delhi technique. Rather, they employed Benares technique, which effectively precluded the consecutive use of *tirakiṭas* because the rearticulation of the *bols ti* and *ṭa* (both fingered 23) at high speeds is a difficult and clumsy motor movement:

23	1		23	23	1		23
ti	ra	ki	ṭa	ti	ra	ki	ṭa
		X				X	

On the other hand, the Delhi technique for *tirakiṭa* (which is also used in the Ajrara *gharānā* and by Lucknow and Farukkhabad musicians when playing *qā'ida* and *qā'ida*-related pieces) allows for the rearticulation of *ti* or *ṭa* in fast speeds, and is often employed in variations:

2	1		V	2	1		V
ti	ra	ki	ṭa	ti	ra	ki	ṭa
		X				X	

Of those who eventually pass Visharad and Nipun examinations, few continue to become professional musicians. However, those whose intentions do lie in a career in music normally ally themselves to another teacher who can complete the instruction necessary to prepare them for the stage. Indeed, even before completing their courses, most have also taken lessons outside the college context. Afaq Husain received the majority of these students from the Bhatkhande Music College, though usually with a degree of caution. He realised that most would leave Lucknow and would not continue learning from him once they had completed their official studies, and he knew, too, that they used him to supplement their repertoires with genres of compositions not given during their courses. It was indeed interesting to note that these students visited Afaq Husain far more regularly in the weeks leading up to examinations, a clear indication, perhaps, of the inadequacies of tabla courses at the College.

7 *Lucknow tabla technique*

It is not my intention that the final two chapters of this book be seen as an attempt to teach the tabla by providing a concise description of Lucknow techniques and repertoire. Even if time and space allowed, it would not be an easy task to construct a manual that could in any way replace aspects of the kind of teaching offered by experts. My aim, therefore, is to establish those technical characteristics that are hallmarks of Lucknow tabla-playing, and to map out the kinds of composition that figure in the Lucknow repertoire, so that I may convey something of the particularity of this tradition.

In common with many other studies of the tabla, this chapter deals with a description of individual strokes and stroke combinations (see Kaufmann 1967; Baily 1974; Stewart 1974; Shepherd 1976; Sharma 1981). However, I intend to take the analysis a stage further by also discussing aspects of technique in which motor movements are modifed in particular contexts in order to facilitate speed and ease of articulation. Descriptions are necessarily brief, and examples are limited to a number of features central to an understanding of Lucknow technique.

The placement of instruments and playing posture

Anyone who has had the opportunity to see a variety of tabla players perform will not have failed to notice that different players favour placing their drums in different ways. The *dāhinā* may be positioned at any angle from upright to almost horizontal, with the drumhead facing directly away from the player. The *bāyāṅ* may also be placed so that its *siyāhī* is farthest from, or nearest to, the player, or else is somewhere in between. Differences occur simply because musicians choose to position their drums to suit the techniques they use. For example, members of the Delhi *gharānā* point the eccentric *siyāhī* towards twelve o'clock (from the player's angle), whereas Pandit Shanta Prasad and his pupils (who represent one of the branches of the Benares *gharānā*) rotate the *bāyāṅ* so that the *siyāhī* faces six o'clock. Members of the Lucknow *gharānā* favour pointing the *siyāhī* to somewhere between two and three o'clock, as this is the most effective position for the techniques they use to play the *bāyāṅ*.

Similarly, a variety of different postures are adopted by tabla players when playing their instruments. No one posture is intrinsically better than another, except that certain positions may facilitate the particular quality of sound production that an individual requires. Several members of the Benares *gharānā* advocate kneeling with one's feet together and knees spread wide apart. The extra height and the slightly inclined posture that result allow for greater vertical leverage and for weight to be exerted from the shoulders, especially when playing the *bāyāṅ*. This is ideal for the powerful strokes which predominate in that style. I have seen some members of the Delhi *gharānā* adopt a semi-kneeling, semi-squatting position in which one

Plate 12. **Afaq Husain demonstrating the basic posture and hand positions for the tabla**

knee is raised between the player's outstretched arms. Other players sit in lotus, or half-lotus positions, but by far the majority simply sit cross-legged on the floor.

The cross-legged and half-lotus positions are the ones used and taught by Afaq Husain, though his forefathers evidently stood or knelt to play as a courtesy to their princely patrons. According to him, a good posture is one in which the whole body is balanced and totally relaxed: the spine must be vertical and the shoulders, arms and wrists must be loose (see Plate

12). We were advised to avoid excess movement of the head, and were told to eradicate the tensing of all facial muscles, especially those in and around the mouth, a surprisingly difficult thing to achieve! Afaq Husain was himself expressionless during playing. He further suggested that one's breathing should be normal and regular: it did not have to be deep, nor did it need to be in time with the music. The adoption of a relaxed posture allowed motor movements to become quicker and more energy-effective. Afaq Husain's theory was that tension only served to block a movement by creating resistance in the muscles being used. Physical tension, therefore, was seen as the enemy of efficient technique. In addition, relaxation facilitated concentration. Although he himself did not make the connection, Afaq Husain's ideas were very similar to those found in yoga. In the West, concentration is often achieved through effort and tension. In yoga, the opposite is true.

Strokes

Resonating strokes on the *dāhinā*

Either by themselves, or in combination with the *bāyāṅ* resonating stroke *ghe* (thus forming the compound *bol dhā*), *tā* on the *kinār* and its counterpart on the *sūr* are the most frequently played strokes in the repertoire. These are arguably the most important of all tabla *bols*, for they represent the most common points of departure both for individual compositions as well as for many of the smaller building blocks of drumming phrases, such as *dhātiṭe*, *dhāgena*, *dhā tira kiṭa*, *dhā – na*, and so on. They are also the most common point of return, for the cyclical nature of the music dictates that pieces or phrases come full circle and end where they began: on *dhā*. Furthermore, their pitch is directly related to that of the drone and melody instruments used in conjunction with the tabla (whether the tabla is accompanying or is itself being accompanied); *tā* is usually tuned to the tonic (*shaḍj*) of the scale in use, though it is not unusual for it to reinforce the fourth (*madhyam*) or fifth (*pancam*) when appropriate.

Both versions of *tā* do occasionally appear within the same composition, but in most styles each predominates in specific domains of the repertoire. *Kinār tā* is commonly found in pieces whose form may loosely be described as 'theme and variations', including *qā'ida*, *qā'ida-relā*, *relā*, *calan*, *chand*, *peshkār* and *laggī*. The *sūr* form of *tā* figures predominantly in fixed compositions such as *gat*, *ṭukṛā*, *cakkardār* and *paran*, although it is also found in *rang*, a *relā*-related form peculiar to Lucknow, and certain other theme-and-variations pieces of Lucknow origin. Indeed, so important is the *sūr tā* to the Lucknow style that the term *sūr kā bāj* (*sūr* style) has often been used to distinguish this from *kinār kā bāj*, as prevalent in the Delhi style of playing.

Hand positions for these two strokes are considered to be the basic starting points for nearly all *dāhinā bols*. Motor movements used to articulate them are relatively complex and require detailed description, and so I have also used photographs for added clarity.

Tā as played on the *kinār* (see Figure 5) requires the wrist to be loose; ideally it should sag below the level of the *puṛī*. The palm of the hand, at the point where the head-line cuts across almost horizontally, rests lightly against the *gajrā*. As the first finger is raised and lowered, a point on the palm just beneath the fourth finger becomes a pivot for the stroke and thus should remain in contact with the *gajrā* throughout articulation. In preparation for striking (see Plate 13a), the first finger is raised high as the hand rotates from the wrist at an angle of

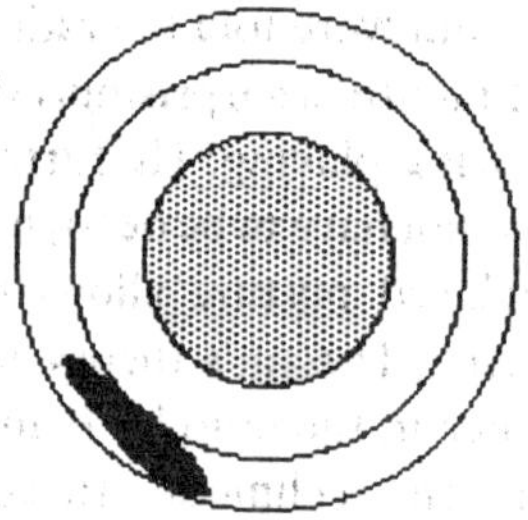

Name	Symbol	Alternative syllables
tā	○	ta nā na

Figure 5

roughly forty-five degrees. It is very slightly curved, as is the second finger, which is held a little lower but which does not strike the *puṛī*. The third finger is bent into the shape of a hook and is held rigid. Afaq Husain was at pains to distinguish between rigidity and stiffness or tension. Here the finger is locked in position and is firm without being tense. Likewise the top joint of the thumb is bent and remains in line with, and in contact with, the first finger. The fourth finger is relaxed, but care must be taken that it does not curl under the third finger. The actual contact of fingers on the *puṛī* (see Plate 13b) is caused by the rapid rotation of the hand from the wrist, with the forearm and elbow remaining still. Initially, the third finger hits the *puṛī* at the point where the *siyāhī* and *maidān* meet; its point of contact is not the fingertip but the very outer edge of the fingernail. Secondly, the first finger strokes the *kinār* and simultaneously the thumb just touches the *gajrā*. The pad and the second segment as far as the second joint of the first finger are involved in the stroke, yet the contact is light. All the weight of the stroke is concentrated on the third finger, which makes a tiny 'click' just before the first finger produces the sound of *tā* proper. After contact (see Plate 13c), the first finger ricochets from the *kinār*, followed by the raising of the third finger as the hand once again rotates back towards its pre-contact position. The note produced is the first harmonic of the fundamental, which is reinforced by the 'nutty' resonance of the *kāṭ* that lies underneath the *kinār*.

Those who know even a little tabla will quickly realise the uniqueness of this motor movement. Unlike all other playing styles, no finger remains in contact with the *puṛī* following the articulation of this or any other resonating stroke. Here, the third finger only gives transitory support to the main striking finger, and so the *puṛī* is left 'open' in order to achieve maximum resonance. The resulting tone quality is widely recognised by musicians to be a hallmark of the Lucknow tabla *gharānā*.

Tā as played on the *sūr* (see Figure 6) shares few similarities with its *kinār* counterpart. To begin with (see Plate 14a), no part of the hand is in contact with the drum. Instead, the hand

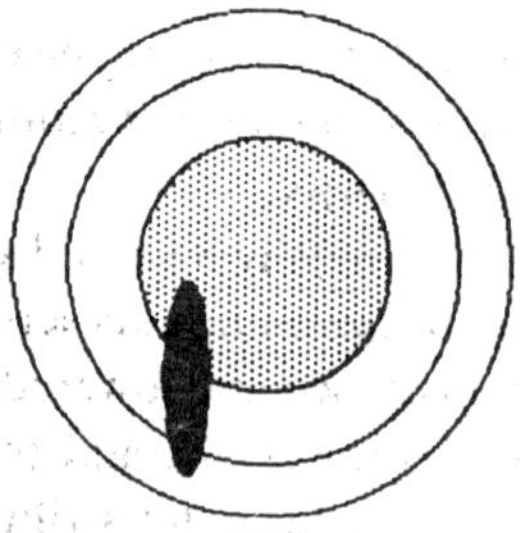

Name	Symbol	Alternative syllables
tā	●	ta nā na tin

Figure 6

Plate 13a. *Tā* (*kinār*) before contact

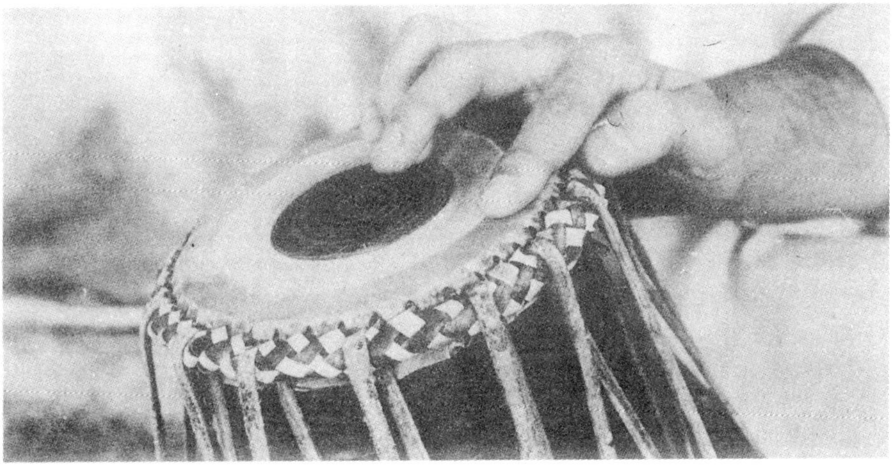

Plate 13b. *Tā* (*kinār*) on contact

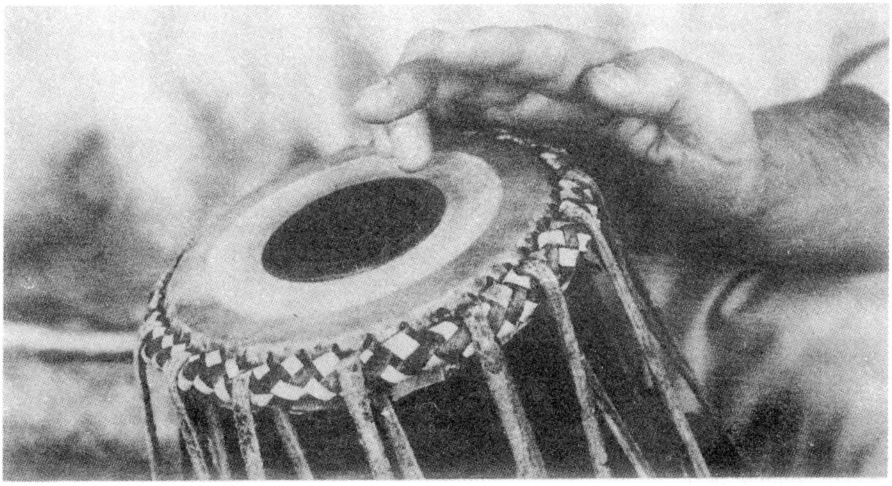

Plate 13c. *Tā* (*kinār*) after contact

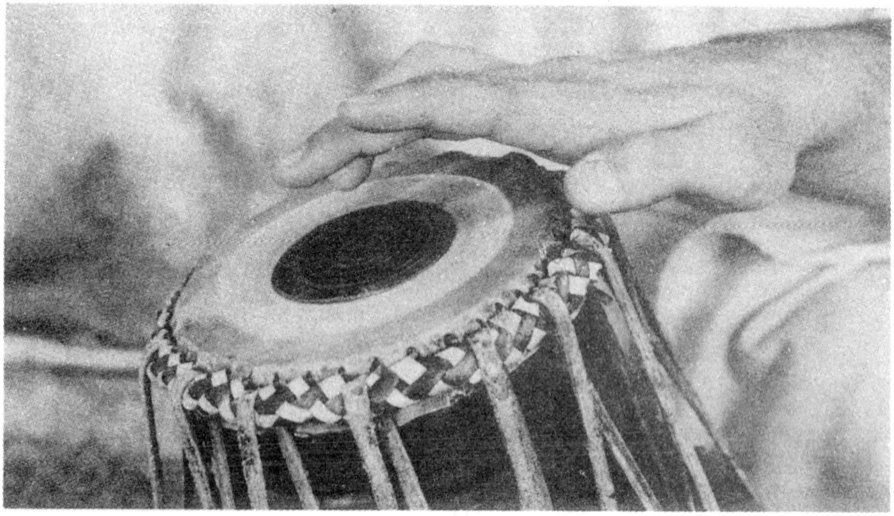

Plate 14a. *Tā* (*sūr*) before contact

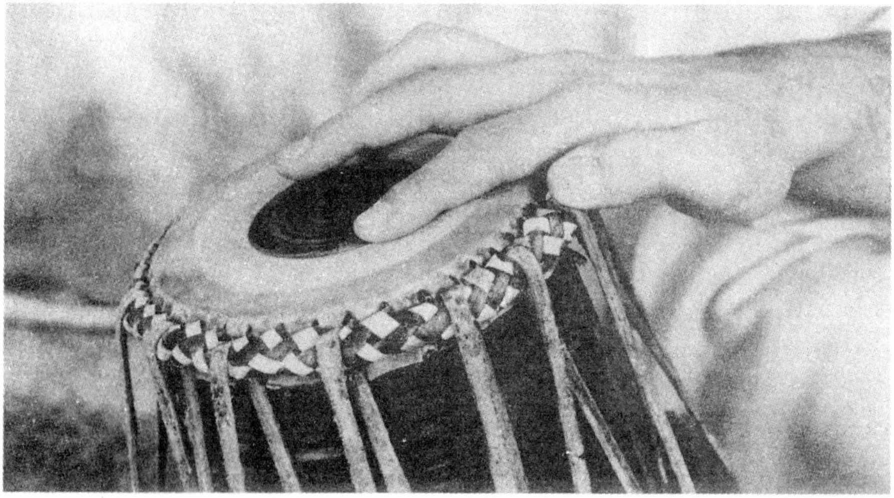

Plate 14b. *Tā* (*sūr*) on contact

Plate 14c. *Tā* (*sūr*) after contact

hovers approximately two inches above the *puṛī*, and the wrist is raised so that the hand and forearm form a straight line. The first finger is kept straight, and is held slightly higher than the rest. The second finger is slightly curved, the third is bent, and the fourth is relaxed. Contact (see Plate 14b) is made by a combination of a very small rotation of the hand from the wrist, the dropping of the hand onto the *puṛī*, and the downward striking motion of the first finger itself. The entire length of the first finger and the tip of the third finger strike the *puṛī* simultaneously, while the underside of the knuckles and the tip of the bent thumb touch the *gajrā*. After striking (see Plate 14c), the hand springs back almost to its pre-contact position. Whenever rapidly articulated *sūr bols* predominate in a piece, the visual effect is such that the player's hand appears to hover above the *puṛī*. The pitch of the note produced from this *tā* is a mixture of the first and third harmonics, and it represents a 'purer' quality of tone than that of *kinār tā*. Afaq Husain used this stroke when tuning the *dāhinā*.

Ṛā and *ta* (see Figure 7) are unsupported ricochet strokes using just the pads of the fingers

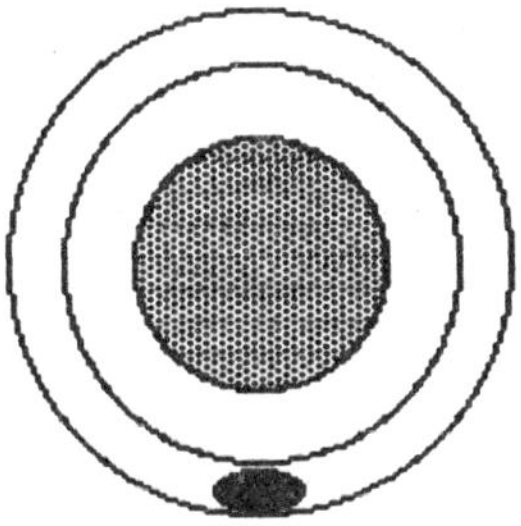

Name	Symbol	Alternative syllables
ṛā	▽	nā na ti te nan
ta	△	na ne

Figure 7

on the *kinār*. The action comes predominantly from the downward striking motion of the fingers themselves, though some leverage is added from the hand, which moves vertically up and down from the wrist. The sound produced resembles that of *kinār tā*. Although *ṛā* is occasionally played in isolation, these strokes usually combine in phrases common to fixed compositions such as:

△ ▽ ∧
ta ṛā – na

▽ △ ▽ ∧
nāgina nāgina
× ×

and in the *rang* phrases:

▽ △ ▽ △
dhene dhene
1 23

▽ △ △
dinagina
1 23

When these strokes feature in the rapid sequences typical of *rang*, the hand must swing from side to side so that each stroke hits the same spot on the *kinār*. Additionally, both strokes may be played on the *dāhinā* by the *bāyān* hand. However, such instances are rare.

The motor movements involved in playing *tī* and *ne* (see Figure 8) are similar to those of *ta*

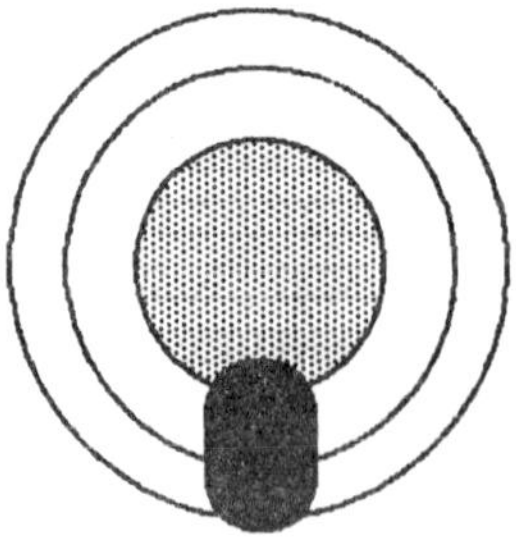

Name	Symbol	Alternative syllables
tī	▼	tī tin tū te
ne	▲	na

Figure 8

and *ṛā*. Only their position on the drumhead and the resulting pitch are different: striking the *sūr* on the edge of the *siyāhī* and *maidān* produces a note a minor seventh below that of *tā* on the *kinār*. Whereas *tī* alone is a common stroke, *ne* is rare. Sometimes called 'the reverse *tī*', it appears predominantly in Lucknow *gats*, none of which I have received permission to notate in full here. However, one phrase is as follows:

▼ ▲ ▲ ▼ ▲ ▲ 123 123
dhene ghene dhene ghene taka taka
1 23 1 23 × ×

Dī (see Figure 9) is a ricochet stroke which is the heavier, fuller, *pakhāwaj* version of *tī*. It is

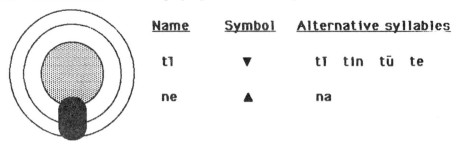

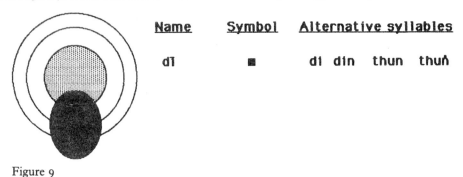

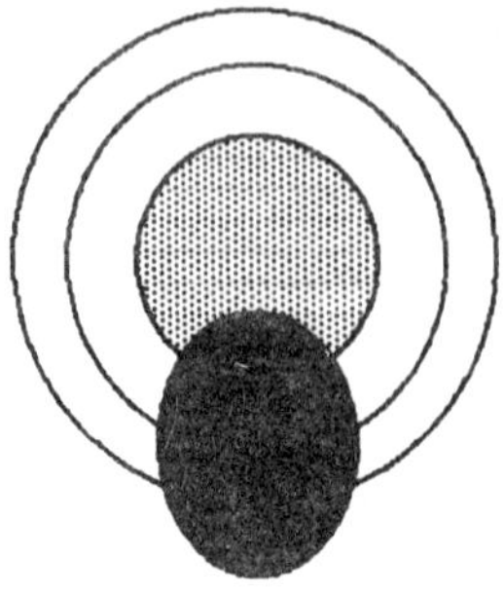

Name	Symbol	Alternative syllables
dī	■	di din thun thuṅ

Figure 9

used in stroke combinations that are derived directly from the *pakhāwaj* repertoire, such as:

∧ 1 ● ■ ∧
ti te ka tā ga dī gi na
× 1 23

It involves the striking of all four fingers, from the pads to the underside of the knuckles, on the *puṛī*. The top of the palm hits the *gajrā*. The whole hand is involved in a downward motion from the wrist.

Ma (see Figure 10) is a *pakhāwaj* stroke which features in the combination *dhumakiṭa*. It

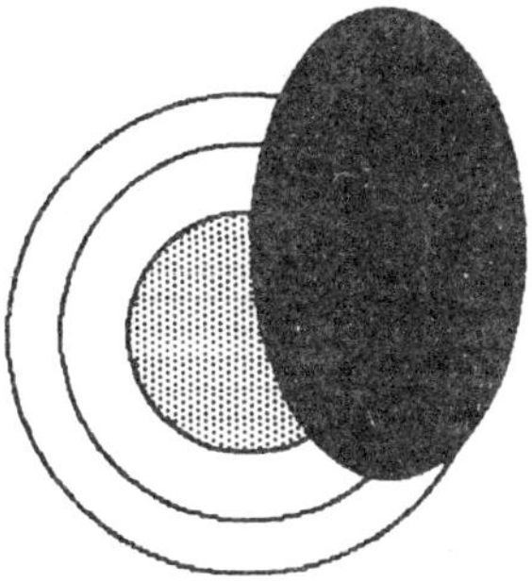

Name	Symbol
ma	⊗

Figure 10

has many different 'translations' in tabla technique, the most common of which is *tī*, but the one favoured by Lucknow musicians involves the striking of the *siyāhī* and *maidān* with the ball of the thumb and the ball of the first finger simultaneously. Contact is effected by a rotation of the hand from the wrist in conjunction with the dropping of the hand onto the *puṛī*. The resulting sound is half-damped, half-resonating. In the tabla repertoire, *ma* appears only in *parans* which are pieces from the *pakhāwaj* and/or *kathak* repertoire.

Non-resonating strokes on the *dāhinā*

There are a number of *bols* where the pads of slightly rounded fingers strike the centre of the *siyāhī*, momentarily sticking to the drumhead in order to dampen the resonance. The essential difference between these *bols* is their fingering, which to a certain extent modifies the sound produced (see Figure 11). For example, *ṭe* (finger 1) and *ti* (2) are light strokes used

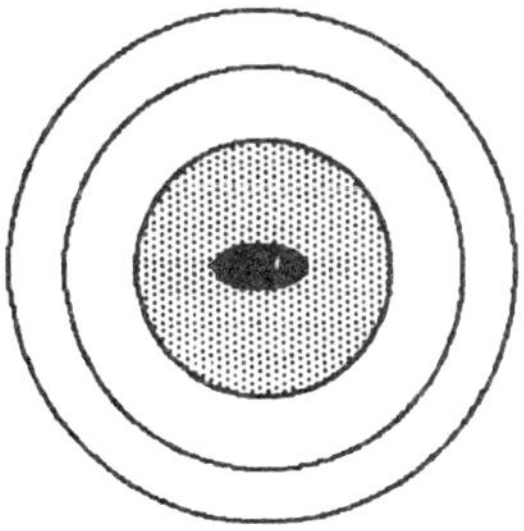

Name	Symbol	Alternative syllables
ṭe	1	te ti ra tak na
ti	2	te ṭe tit tī tak na
ti	23	te ṭe na
tak	123	
tak	234	ta tit

Figure 11

mainly in the Delhi style of playing, whereas *ti* (23) is a heavier stroke that commonly appears in the Lucknow, Farukkhabad and Benares styles. While these are all articulated by a downward striking of the fingers from the knuckles of a still hand, *tak* (123) and *tak* (234), which occur in Lucknow *gats* and *ṭukṛās*, both involve the use of the whole hand pivoting from the wrist. The use of three fingers helps to produce sharp, accented strokes.

Tit and *na* (see Figure 12) are both played on the line between the *siyāhī* and *maidān* at the point nearest the player. *Na* is a light stroke played by just the tip of a hooked and rigid third

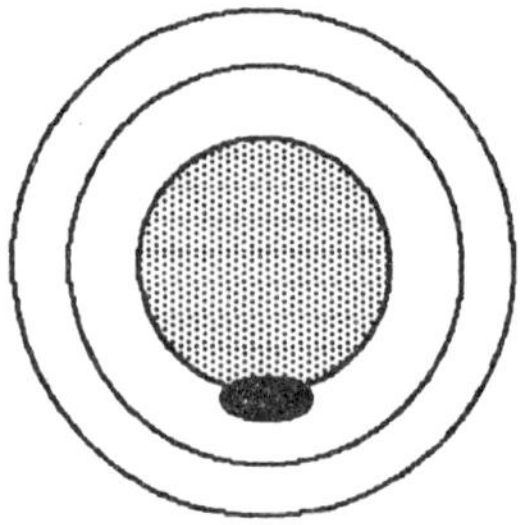

Name	Symbol	Alternative syllables
tit	∧	tet na ta tā
na	∨	ne ta ra ṛa ga

Figure 12

finger, which before contact is held higher than the first and second fingers. The stroke is then effected by a rotation of the hand from the wrist, causing the finger to strike down vertically onto the *puṛī*. *Tit* uses the pads of the second and third fingers. The action comes predominantly from the downward striking motion of the fingers themselves, though some leverage is added from the hand, which moves vertically up and down from the wrist. When represented by *tit* or *tet*, the stroke is intended as heavy and accented. When represented by *ta* or *na*, it is light and unstressed.

Ti and *ra* (see Figure 13) constitute an inseparable pair of damped strokes involving the use

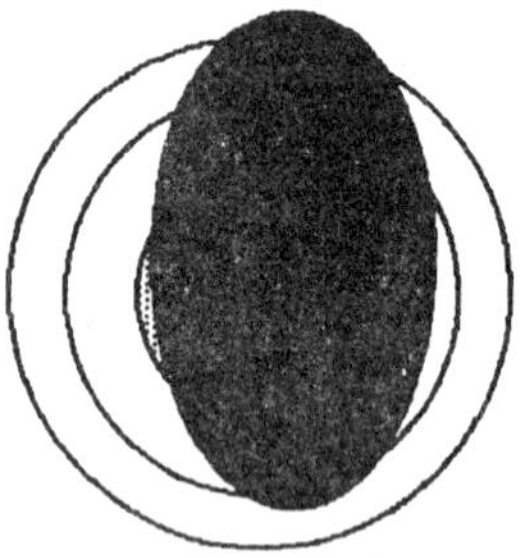

Name	Symbol
ti	>
ra	<

Figure 13

of the entire hand on the *puṛī*. The hand is divided into two parts: firstly, *ti* requires the slapping-down onto the *puṛī* of the third and fourth fingers and the outer edge of the palm; *ra* follows with a rotation of the hand from the wrist, causing the first and second fingers, the inner edge of the palm, and the ball of the thumb to strike.

Tak (see Figure 14) is a damped stroke used as a special sound effect to replace the

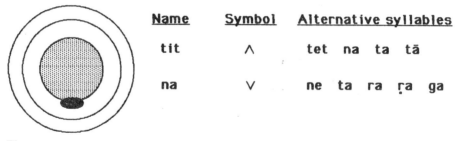

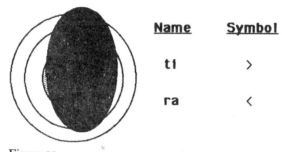

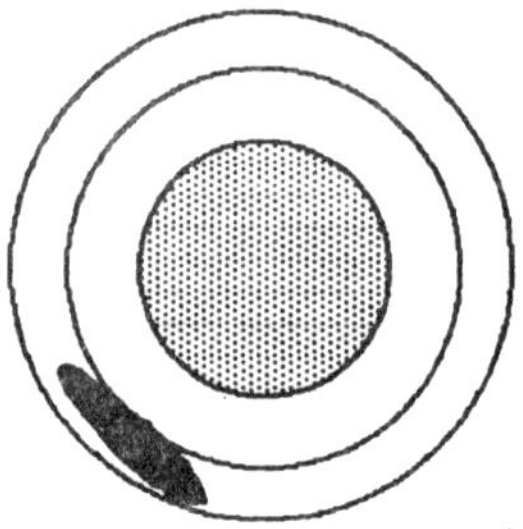

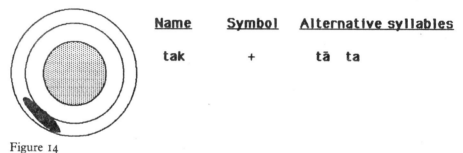

Name	Symbol	Alternative syllables
tak	+	tā ta

Figure 14

resonating *kinār tā*, particularly in *laggīs*. It involves the same motor movement as described for *tā*, but instead of ricocheting from the *puṛī*, the finger 'sticks' to the skin, resulting in a sound that resembles the sharp crack of a whip. It is often referred to as *capaknewālā tā*: 'the *tā* that sticks'.

Resonating strokes on the *bāyāṅ*

Unlike nearly all other styles of *bāyāṅ*-playing, the basic hand position requires very little pressure to be placed directly on the *puṛī*. The same reasoning behind the 'open style' of playing the *dāhinā* is applied to the *bāyāṅ*: it is felt that the full resonance of the drum may not be achieved if the heel of the hand applies pressure by digging into the skin, so preventing it from vibrating fully. Thus the forearm and underside of the wrist are in contact with the skin, but the heel of the hand is not. The forearm contact is light: just resting on the *puṛī*. The secret of maintaining this position in playing, and thus in maintaining an open, resonating sound, lies in the crooking and locking of the thumb in a backward position (see Plate 12). The fingers are held high, giving the hand the semblance of what Afaq Husain called a 'cobra, ready to strike'. The very base of the heel of the hand rests at the edge of the *siyāhī*, and the tips of the fingers strike down on the *maidān* on the opposite side of the *siyāhī*. All *bāyāṅ* strokes in the Lucknow style are characterised by their lack of exaggerated arm-and-shoulder movement.

Different fingerings may be used for strokes on the *bāyāṅ* (see Figure 15). All four fingers

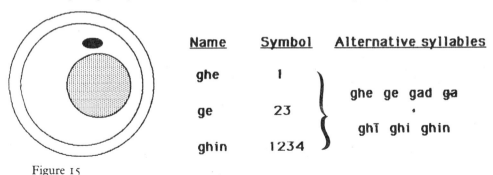

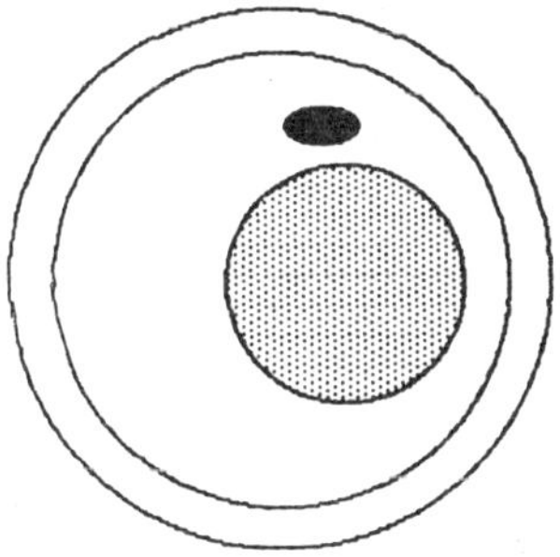

Name	Symbol	Alternative syllables
ghe	1	ghe ge gad ga
ge	23	
ghin	1234	ghī ghi ghin

Figure 15

may occasionally be used for heavy, accented strokes (*ghin*) when needed, but two strokes are mainly used: *ghe* (finger 1) and *ge* (23). The index finger is the main striking finger for the *bāyāṅ* in the Lucknow style, and consequently it is used to begin and end most phrases. This is in marked contrast to most other styles, where use of the second and third fingers predominates.

The position and pressure of the wrist and heel of the hand may be adjusted during or after striking, so modifying the pitch of the *bāyāṅ*. This adds inflexion to the 'voice' of the tabla, commonly referred to in India by the English word 'modulation'. There are numerous ways of 'modulating', but two deserve special mention as they are important to an understanding of Lucknow technique. The first device is a rising *mīṅḍ* (portamento) followed by a return to a low pitch which occurs when *ghe* and *ge* are played in succession. The first finger strikes the *puṛī* and immediately slides and straightens to end up pointing towards eleven o'clock. This causes the heel of the hand to dig lightly into the *puṛī* at the edge of the *siyāhī*, so causing the pitch to rise. The second and third fingers then return quickly to strike the *bāyāṅ* from the basic hand position, so producing a low pitch. The second device involves the striking of *ghe* with the first finger, following which the base of the heel of the hand is pushed directly forwards about one inch onto the *siyāhī*. The forearm moves swiftly, causing the sound to jump suddenly and thus rearticulating the stroke at a higher pitch level. This rearticulation has been notated with the symbol /.

An alternative *bāyāṅ* stroke *ghin* (see Figure 16) is played with the four fingers and the

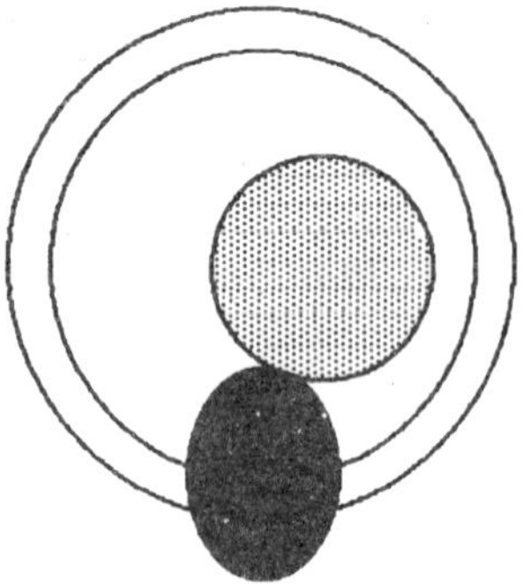

Name	Symbol	Alternative syllables
ghin	□	ghe ge gad ga ghī ghi dhu

Figure 16

upper portion of the palm on the part of the *puṛī* nearest the player. It involves a motor movement similar to that described for the resonating *dāhinā* stroke *dī*. The heavy downward striking motion of the whole hand from the wrist causes the sound of the *bāyāṅ* to boom in imitation of the *pakhāwaj*. It is regularly used in playing *dhumakiṭa*, and occasionally for effect in *gats* and *ṭukṛās*.

Non-resonating strokes on the *bāyāṅ*

In most styles, the commonest non-resonating *bāyāṅ* stroke is *kat* (see Figure 17), in which the whole hand is slapped onto the *puṛī* in a vertical movement from the wrist. In rapidly

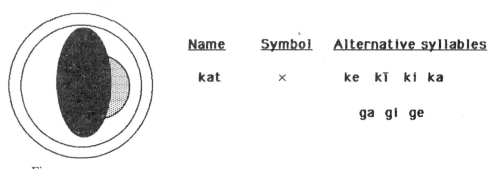

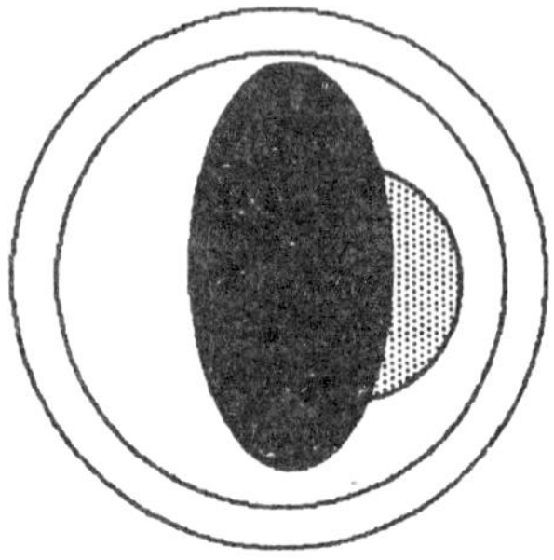

Name	Symbol	Alternative syllables
kat	×	ke kī ki ka ga gi ge

Figure 17

articulated passages, the hand may be curved so that just the fingertips, thumb and heel of the hand strike the *puṛī*. However, Lucknow *gharānā* musicians also use two other strokes, both called *ke*, (see Figure 18) that are considered as the non-resonating equivalents of *ghe* and *ge*. Their manner of articulation is identical to that for their resonating counterparts, with the exception that whereas for resonating strokes the thumb is held high, here it is lowered onto the drum. An alternative non-resonating stroke *ki* should also be mentioned, where the nail of

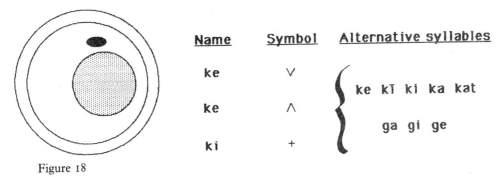

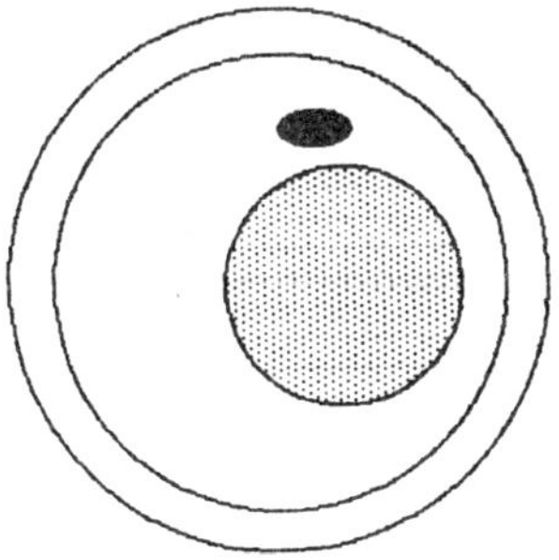

Name	Symbol	Alternative syllables
ke	∨	ke kī ki ka kat
ke	∧	ga gi ge
ki	+	

Figure 18

the first finger flicks from the side of the thumb onto the *puṛī*, which is damped by the heel of the hand, thumb and the other fingers. The sound produced resembles a sharp 'click'.

In this section, I have not discussed compound *bols* that result from the playing of *dāhinā* and *bāyāṅ* strokes simultaneously. This is because in teaching the basic technique of the tabla, or in analysing motor movement deficiencies at an advanced level, Afaq Husain usually broke down these elements and treated each in isolation. Once the two elements of a compound *bol* had been perfected separately, they could then be fused to create the new sound. The syllables of *dāhinā* strokes that are combined with non-resonating *bāyāṅ* strokes do not change their form, although their fusion with resonating strokes results in the phoneme *dh*, as in *dhā* (*ghe* plus *tā*), *dhin* (*ghe* plus *tin*), *dhi* (*ghe* plus *ti*), *dhī* (*ghe* plus *tī*), and so on.

Further aspects of technique

Any discussion of technique that goes beyond a brief explanation of its basic building blocks, as detailed above, might well resort to the use of movement notation in order to describe the complex series of motions governing transitions from one stroke or hand position to another in a string of *bols*. Much less ambitious, though not without value, would be a series of generalised statements pertaining to certain characteristics of Lucknow tabla technique. For instance, a Lucknow musician may be considered immediately identifiable by his relaxed, almost serene posture, by the absence of superfluous physical movement, and by the apparent effortlessness of his technique. But such a statement is comparative and requires equally generalised statements to be made concerning other styles of playing. Thus it may be better understood when compared with a description of Benares technique, which tends towards exaggerated physical movements and apparently uses strength and effort in the articulation of strokes. My aim in this section is neither to be too detailed nor too general, but instead to present a few specific instances of the ways in which Lucknow musicians adapt their technique to suit the requirements of particular musical situations. Many of these aspects of technique will no doubt be common to other styles of tabla-playing, but taken as a whole they represent many important features of the Lucknow style.

As a student of the Lucknow *gharānā*, one must learn a variety of techniques for the same spoken *bols*. Take, for example, the non-resonating *dāhinā bol* pair *tiṭe*, which was first introduced by Afaq Husain to his students as a component of many basic Delhi *qā'idas*. We were taught to play *ti* with the second finger and *ṭe* with the first. But later on we encountered *qāʿidas* of Lucknow origin in which *tiṭe* was fingered differently. Here *ti* was to be played with the first finger, and *ṭe* with the second and third fingers combined. Furthermore, as we progressed to other kinds of composition, we learned yet another fingering. In many fixed compositions such as *ṭukṛā*, *gat*, *cakkardār* and *paran*, *ti* with the second and third fingers combined, and *ṭe* with the first finger, were advocated. These different fingerings can be seen in the following three examples:

```
o 2  1 o       2 1   o  o
dhāti ṭedhā    tiṭe dhādhā...
1       23           1  23


o 1  23 1      23 ●      V
dhāti ṭedhi    ṭetā ghena...
1     23 1      23  1


23 1   ●         ■    ʌ
tiṭe katā      gadī gina...
       ×         1   23
```

The rationale for having so many different ways of playing *tiṭe* in Lucknow technique is based on the notion that each fingering evolved for a different style of playing. Therefore, when performing compositions of Delhi origin, one employed techniques that were created specifically for that style. Such techniques have their own motor movement logic and were no doubt originally developed with a particular aural image in mind. Different techniques were developed in Lucknow for similar reasons, although there seems always to have been something of a historical rivalry between the musicians of Lucknow and Delhi, and Afaq Husain believed that many of the techniques employed in the Lucknow style were simply the result of attempts by members of his family to be different from their rivals. The third manner of fingering *tiṭe* illustrated above appears to be closely modelled on *pakhāwaj* technique and *bol* phrases. Indeed, the vast *pakhāwaj* repertoire of fixed compositions appears to have been directly adapted for the tabla, or else has been a source of inspiration for new compositions.

Afaq Husain often told me that in order to discover which *gharānā* a composition originated from, one had to 'look closely at the *nikās*'. Whereas I found this to be a good general guideline, I soon discovered that he himself was not entirely consistent. He sometimes created a new piece which he claimed represented the Lucknow style, but which contained the Delhi fingering of *tiṭe*. When I questioned him regarding this, he replied that he preferred the sound produced by the Delhi technique in some instances, but that one might equally well apply Lucknow technique to the same piece if desired. What this discussion reveals, however, is the existence of different subtechniques within one overall technique. Each subtechnique is designed for its own specific set of circumstances. Whereas many other *bols* change their form in a similar way, I chose *tiṭe* to illustrate the point because it is the variable most visually conspicuous to the observer, and anyone who closely observes the tabla-playing of a Lucknow musician will certainly find examples of each of the three different fingerings illustrated above.

The spoken *bols* of tabla are drawn from the phonemic repertoire of North Indian languages such as Urdu, Hindi, Punjabi and Bengali. But only a very restricted number of phonemes are actually used to describe tabla strokes: *t*, *ṭ*, *d*, *dh*, *n*, *ṅ*, *r*, *ṛ*, *k*, *g*, *gh* and *m*, and the vowels *a*, *ā*, *i*, *ī*, *u*, *ū* and *e*. In whatever combination, they form syllables whose articulation is relatively uncomplicated (for the native speaker at least). To put it another way, tongue-twisters are avoided. In fact, all syllables (except *ma*, which is directly derived from the *pakhāwaj bol* phrase *dhumakiṭa* and is, in any case, rarely used) may be articulated without the movement of the lips or jaws. Only the tongue, which is far more versatile, is required to flick from one position to another. But even within a system so evidently designed for the easy articulation of syllables at high speeds, changes do occur in order to make phrases easier to say. Consequently, in very slow speeds *tiṭe* may be pronounced *teṭe*. At higher speeds the vowels may shorten to form *tiṭi*. Another common example is *teṭekeṭe*. Speeded up, this is transformed into *tirakiṭa*, which at even greater speeds may change to *tirakira*. The general tendency is for vowels to shorten as speed increases, although some may remain long if a particular *bol* within a phrase is to be stressed.

In the same way that spoken *bols* may change as the speed of articulation varies, so the positioning of strokes, and even their form, may be altered to make them easier to play, particularly if the speed is increased. Some musicians have expressed their opposition to this practice. Ustad Inam Ali Khan of the Delhi *gharānā* believed that it was wrong to play any piece at a speed that entailed changing the positioning or fingering of strokes. But as Bhupal Ray Choudhuri explained, the practice in the Lucknow *gharānā* was markedly different: 'There are places where you have got to change your fingers. The balance is different, otherwise you can't do it at that speed with that *bol* . . . without sacrificing the sound effect.' In other words, not only does changing a stroke at a higher speed of articulation make the technique easier, but it is also sometimes necessary to change it in order to retain the same overall sound picture of the piece. In Lucknow, then, greater concern is often shown for keeping the quality of the sound intact than for retaining unchanged the precise fingering of a piece. I shall now describe a number of changes that are made in Lucknow technique.

Firstly, there is the substitution of one stroke for another that uses the same fingering and produces approximately the same sound. Take, for example, the *bols dhā-na dhitiṭe dhā*. Played slowly, the right hand must make a relatively large movement in order to get from the bol *na*, played on the edge of the *siyāhī*, to *dhi*, played in the middle. This is impractical when the speed is increased, and therefore both strokes are placed on the centre of the *siyāhī*:

```
o     ^          1  ^  1       o
dhā - na         dhi ti ṭe     dhā...
1                23            1
```

```
o     23   1  23 1      o
dhā-na dhitiṭe          dhā...
1          23           1
```

Secondly, by retaining the same musical example, it is possible to illustrate further changes in the fingering of strokes. Should the speed of this string of *bols* be increased, it becomes physically impossible to follow the final *ṭe* with *dhā* as both *dāhinā* strokes involve the use of the first finger: for *ṭe* on the *siyāhī*, and for *dhā* on the *kinār*. In this case, the fingering of *nadhitiṭe* is reversed so that the final *ṭe* is played with the second and third fingers:

o 1 23 1 23 o
dhā-na dhitiṭe dhā...
1 23 1

Thirdly, there is the alteration of hand positions which results in changes being made to the actual placement of fingers. For instance, in slow speeds each stroke in the phrase *dhā tiṭe giṛa* naga, frequently used in *qāʿida-relā* and *relā* structures, is placed as indicated in the diagrams given earlier in this chapter. Yet in higher speeds there is a tendency to minimise movement, so allowing the player to cut down, by a split second, the time normally required to move the fingers across the drumhead. These differences are illustrated in Figure 19, with the black areas marking the finger placements.

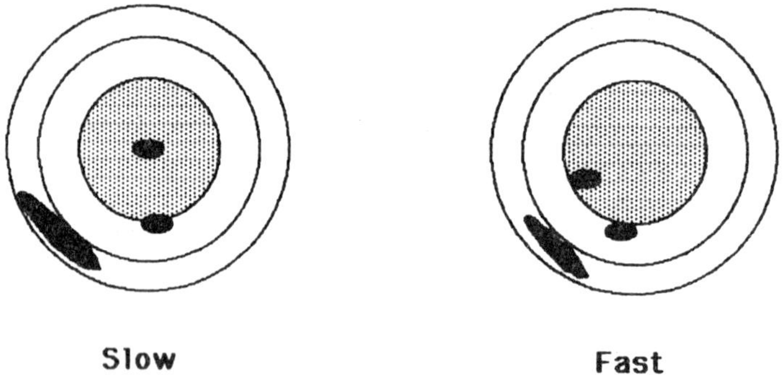

Figure 19

Fourthly, there is the substitution of one stroke for another that produces a completely different sound. The rearticulation of *kinār tā* in the sequence *dhāgenadhāgetiṭe* can be difficult at very high speeds. Attempting it may lead to the creation of physical tension in the hand, which may in turn distort the sound or change the balance of the musical phrase by putting an unwanted accent on the third *bol na*. These technical and musical problems can be easily overcome by substituting *na* with the non-resonating stroke of the same name as played on the line between the *siyāhī* and *maidān* with the third finger:

o o o 1 23
dhāgenadhāgetiṭe
1 23 1 23

o V o 1 23
dhāgenadhagetite
1 23 1 23

Fifthly, the practice of omitting *bols* from a phrase when doubling the speed is commonly encountered in the Lucknow style. For example, the fingering of the phrase *dhā– – ghinā–takiṭa ghinā–*, which appears frequently in *gats*, presents considerable technical problems when its speed of articulation is doubled. Consequently, the single, accented *bol tak* (played either with fingers 234, as given here, or else with 1) replaces *takiṭa*:

```
 ●              ●            1  Λ          ●
dhā - -       ghi nā -     ta ki ṭa     ghi nā -
 1             23              ×         23
```

```
 ●    ●          234   ●
dhā ghinā-       tak ghinā-
 1   23              23
```

But although the second version now becomes easier to play at high speeds, another problem becomes evident: the accents represented by *nā* (*tā* on the *sūr*) occur on divisions of the beat that are naturally unstressed, and so the higher the speed the more difficult it becomes to maintain the correct rhythm. In cases like this, the rhythm itself is modified to facilitate ease in playing by simply shifting *na* to the stressed divisions of the beat:

```
 ●      ●         234    ●
dhā-gi nā        tak-gi nā
 1     23              23
```

Lastly, in contrast to situations where *bols* are omitted or altered, it is important to note that there is an extremely important *bol* in the Lucknow style that is played, despite the fact that it is arguably unnecessary (although the fact that its use must modify the sound of other *bols* may be important). Normally, whenever *ghe* or *ge* appear alone in phrases that are *khulī* ('open', i.e. where all *bāyāṅ* strokes are resonating), they are replaced by *ke* in corresponding *band* ('closed', with non-resonating *bāyāṅ* strokes) repetitions of that phrase. However, Lucknow musicians substitute *ke* for every occurrence of *ghe*, even when found in combination with *dāhinā* strokes. In the following two illustrations, the *khulī* phrase has been given first followed by its *band* counterpart:

```
o 2  1  o      2 1  o  o            o 2  1 o      2 1  o o
dhāti ṭedhā    tiṭe dhādhā    →     tāti ṭetā     tiṭe tātā
1       23           1  23          V      Λ             V Λ
```

```
o   2 1   V o                       o  2 1   V o
dhā tite giṛa naga            →     tā tite kiṛa naga
1     1     23                      V      V      Λ
```

8 *The repertoire*

It is impossible, in one short chapter, to give a fair reflection of the extent and variety of musical forms present in the repertoire of the Lucknow tabla *gharānā*. My intention here is to present notated examples and brief analyses of each category of composition, and, where possible and appropriate, to indicate some of the varieties of form that fall within one category.

Western methods of analysis have so far been based on the close scrutiny of transcribed examples from the repertoire (see Stewart 1974; and Gottlieb 1977). Such an approach may tell us much about the structural outline of compositions, but it does not necessarily reflect the perceptions of the musicians who created them, for such methods focus essentially on the product of a musical process and consequently tell us little about the actual process itself. In contrast, I have attempted to identify the processes involved in creating tabla music. By learning and studying pieces as a tabla player within the tradition, I realised that a much deeper understanding of their structure could be achieved from an analysis based on folk perceptions. I have therefore tried to incorporate these perceptions into my analyses, and hope to reflect what musicians themselves believe to be of importance when composing or improvising.

Stewart (1974) and Gottlieb (1977) have both tended towards an ideal system of classification in which categories of composition are delineated and compartmentalised. However, in my experience this approach does not correspond to the real situation, which is never so clear-cut and unequivocal as to allow for singular definitions and classifications of pieces. The order of presentation I follow here is not based on the structure of a performance, for there are no fixed rules regarding the ideal sequence of types of composition. In general, however, there is a progression from compositions that provide a basis for improvisation to fixed forms. The former I have termed 'theme-and-variations' compositions, and the latter 'fixed' compositions. I shall firstly discuss the 'theme and variations' compositions, beginning with what many musicians hold to be the most important form: *qāʿida*. Once the rules for improvisation in *qāʿida* have been understood, the rules for improvisation in general have been mastered. Secondly, I shall concentrate on fixed compositions, which, it will be remembered, are usually dealt with much later on in traditional methods of training for students of the Lucknow *gharānā*. Separating these two sections is a short description of cadential pieces used either to terminate a series of variations or to bring most fixed compositions to a conclusion. Certain types may themselves develop into distinct fixed compositions, or alternatively they may provide formulae for improvised cadences.

I believe it is vitally important to understand that the repertoire presented here is weighted in a way that reflects Ustad Afaq Husain Khan's own interpretation of his musical tradition. Had I studied a generation earlier with his father, Khalifa Wajid Husain Khan, I might well have laid greater emphasis on different features of the repertoire, such as *relā* and *gat*, for which he had a personal preference. (This is supported by Gottlieb (1977), whose transcription of a tabla solo by Wajid Husain includes proportionately many examples of these forms.) Afaq Husain also likes and plays *relās* and *gats*, of which he has a vast knowledge. Yet his own personal preference is for *qāʿida* and *chand* because he is interested in, and very good at, methods of improvisation and *laykārī* (rhythmic play) as embodied in *chands*. What this amounts to is an example of the way in which a musical tradition evolves with each successive generation. It is not fixed: some elements are indeed maintained from past generations, but others are forgotten or omitted, and new developments constantly add different dimensions to the repertoire.

All notations given in this chapter are prescriptive: they represent a model for the performance of a piece and not any particular rendition of it. Many versions of each piece exist, and some performances even differ quite markedly from the model presented here. In some the spoken *bols* are varied, in others the strokes and their fingerings are altered, and sometimes even the rhythm of a piece may be changed in some minor way. Nevertheless, such versions are all considered representative of the same piece.

Theme and variations

Qāʿida

The origins of most categories of composition are obscure. Musicians tend to believe that each form represented in the repertoire is as old as the tabla itself, although it would seem much more likely that some forms were borrowed unchanged from instruments such as the *pakhāwaj*, while others were developed specifically for the tabla at a much later date. *Qāʿidas* are structurally unique to the tabla and are therefore probably among the latter, yet very little information is available on the subject. When exactly they first appeared is uncertain, but the earliest reference, along with a few notated examples, seems to be in Sadiq Ali Khan's *Qanun-e-Mausiqi* of 1895. What does seem certain, however, is that *qāʿida* originated in Delhi, for its performance has always been regarded as a speciality of members of the Delhi *gharānā*. Nonetheless, what I shall present here is very much a reflection of the Lucknow concept of *qāʿida*.

Qāʿida constitutes the very basis of composition and improvisation in tabla-playing. *Qāʿida* means 'rules' or 'system', and implies that variations (known variously as *palṭā*, *vistār*, *bal* or *peṅc* – Afaq Husain uses *peṅc*) on a fixed composition are created using systematic methods, such as the permutation, substitution and repetition of the original elements. It is the point at which all students begin, and to which they constantly return in order to develop both technical and mental facility. Owing to the repetitiveness inherent in their structure, they are natural exercises for developing motor movement skills. Afaq Husain indicated their importance in developing technical facility when he said: 'We give *qāʿidas* for the hand . . . they build the hand bit by bit, by concentrating on small aspects [i.e. the details] of playing.' Bhupal Ray Choudhuri assured me that 'Unless you master Delhi *qāʿidas*, your fingers will never be correct.' Furthermore, in developing techniques of composition and improvisation, Afaq Husain believed that the correct performance of a *qāʿida*, complete with a set of variations, indicated 'your strengths, and the extent of your knowledge'.

I collected a large number of *qāʿidas* from Afaq Husain during my training, and was fascinated by the ease with which he could make seemingly endless new variations based on the original composition. Whereas most musicians produce between six and ten variations in solo performances, Afaq Husain usually went far beyond this, and I have several recordings where he generates over fifty. I was encouraged to create my own variations too, and after about two years of trial and error in which I imbibed the rules of the compositional process both consciously and subconsciously, I began to succeed in producing spontaneous variations on completely new compositions. My experiences have led me to question Neuman's conclusion that 'In an ultimate sense a musical system is arbitrary, like language . . . [and] fundamentally irrational' (1974: 297), for I do not consider language or music to be, in any sense, arbitrary or irrational, but rather understand them to be primary modelling systems for human thought and action. Recent experimental research with tabla players on *qāʿidas* (Kippen and Bel 1984; Kippen 1985, 1987) has in fact indicated that a fundamental musical rationality governs each decision a musician takes when manipulating the elements of a musical system. However, it appears that this rationality cannot be understood in terms of verbal descriptions alone; rather, it may be best defined by means of dynamic models that represent formalisations of musical intuition. I do not intend to discuss the details of this research as it would necessitate a considerable amount of technical explanation. Nevertheless, it should be pointed out that experiments have both confirmed earlier suspicions and have afforded new insights about the ways in which *qāʿida* is organised.

Qāʿida is defined primarily by its structure and partly by its content. I say 'partly' by its content because there are no fixed rules concerning the kinds of *bols* that may be used in *qāʿida*, although musicians tend to say that the use of *pakhāwaj*-derived strokes and phrases that commonly appear in fixed compositions are not permissible in any theme-and-variations composition. A *qāʿida* may theoretically be set in any *tāl*, though in practice the vast majority appear in *tīntāl* and are then specially adapted to fit other *tāls* when required. The composition consists of a fixed pattern of *bols* which form a basic phrase, or 'sentence'. (For purposes of analysis, I have used the symbol 's' to represent the basic sentence of a *qāʿida*.) This sentence is then repeated according to certain conventions which may vary from *gharānā* to *gharānā*. In its most elementary form, as practised in the Delhi *gharānā*, the basic phrase is repeated once, and thus the *qāʿida* comprises two lines. This may be illustrated by the famous Delhi *qāʿida* of Natthu Khan (1875–1940), which is given in Example 1. Yet it can be seen that the second line (s2) is not an exact repetition of the first (s1): rather, s2 is subject to transformations which render certain *bols* or phrases either *khulī* or *band*. *Khulī*, meaning

Mātrā = mm.84–120

	o 2 1 o	2 1 o o	2 1 o	▼ o o
X	**dhāti ṭedhā**	**tiṭe dhādhā**	**tiṭe dhāge**	**tīna kīna**
	1 23	1 23	1 23	V Λ
	o 2 1 o	2 1 o o	2 1 o	▼ o o
2	**tāti ṭetā**	**tiṭe dhādhā**	**tiṭe dhāge**	**dhīna ghīna**
	V Λ	1 23	1 23	1 23

Example 1. Delhi *qāʿida* (*tīntāl*)

'open', refers to *bols* or phrases in which left-hand strokes are resonating, while *band*, meaning 'closed', refers to *bols* or phrases in which left-hand strokes are non-resonating. (Incidentally, the feminine form *khulī* is not used with the masculine noun *bol* in general speech, but I retain its use here because for the open/closed distinction musicians say *khulī/band*, not *khulā/band*.) The corresponding *khulī/band bols* of the *qā'ida* in Example 1 may be listed as follows:

khulī	*band*
dhā	tā
dhī	tī
ghī	kī

Tiṭe and *na* remain unchanged.

When merely referring to this *qā'ida*, Afaq Husain recited the composition in its elementary two-line form as given above. Of course, with four *bols* to the *mātrā* (*caugun*) the composition fills only half the *āvartan* and must therefore be played twice. Yet in performance he changed this structure radically and presented it as a four-line piece comprising three repetitions of the basic sentence. This I have called the Lucknow version, set out in Example 2. S1 and S4 are performed *khulī*, while S2 undergoes a partial transformation in which the

Mātrā = mm.84–120

	o 2 1 o	2 1 o o	2 1 o	▼ o o
X	**dhāti ṭedhā**	**tiṭe dhādhā**	**tiṭe dhāge**	**dhīna ghīna**
	1 23	1 23	1 23	1 23
2	**dhāti ṭedhā**	**tite dhādhā**	**tiṭe dhāge**	**tīna kīna**
				V Λ
0	**tāti ṭetā**	**tiṭe tātā**	**tiṭe tāke**	**tīna kīna**
	V Λ	V Λ	V Λ	V Λ
3	**dhāti ṭedhā**	**tiṭe dhādhā**	**tiṭe dhāge**	**dhīna ghīna**
	1			

Example 2. Delhi *qā'ida* (Lucknow style; *tīntāl*)

final four *bols* are played *band*. S3 is performed *band*, and includes *tāke*, the *band* transformation of *dhāge*. The resulting *khulī/band* structure may be represented in the following way:

S1	*khulī*	*khulī*	*khulī*	*khulī*
S2	*khulī*	*khulī*	*khulī*	*band*
S3	*band*	*band*	*band*	*band*
S4	*khulī*	*khulī*	*khulī*	*khulī*

It will be noticed that both the Lucknow and Delhi versions follow the *tālī/k͟hālī* structure of *tīntāl* in that their third quarters are performed *band*, thus corresponding to the *k͟hālī vibhāg* of that *tāl*. However, this is more easily demonstrated with the Lucknow version, which, when played in *caugun*, covers the full sixteen beats.

For the purposes of creating variations based on the *qāʿida*, the composition is divided into two halves, the first consisting of S1 and S2, and the second of S3 and S4. Whatever elements then change in the first half must necessarily be met with corresponding changes in the second. However, the *bols* continue to be subject to the *khulī/band* structure of the *qāʿida*. Therefore, only the first half need be known for a minimum description of any variation. This may be illustrated by the following example, a variation in which S2 undergoes a minor permutation causing a similar change to take place in S4. The *bols* that change are italicised:

S1	dhāti ṭedhā	tiṭe dhādhā	tiṭe dhāge	dhīna ghīna
S2	*tiṭe dhā*dhā	tiṭe dhādhā	tiṭe dhāge	tīna kīna
S3	tāti ṭetā	tiṭe tātā	tiṭe tāke	tīna kīna
S4	*tiṭe dhā*dhā	tiṭe dhādhā	tiṭe dhāge	dhīna ghīna

The majority of the rules governing the process of improvisation are learned by example or by trial and error, and only a very few are ever verbalised. Most prominent among these is one dictating that any improvisation should be limited to the *bols* of the original composition. For example, when broken down into indivisible components, the *bols* of this *qāʿida* are *dhā*, *tiṭe*, *dhāge*, *dhīna* and *ghīna* (plus their *band* transformations), and therefore the introduction into a variation of extraneous *bols*, such as *tit*, *tirakiṭa*, *dhāgena* or *dhiradhira*, is not permissible. A further rule stipulates that the structure of the *tāl* must not be violated by the addition or subtraction of beats. Once established, the *tāl* should be strictly maintained.

There are a number of different methods for rearranging the *bols* of a *qāʿida*. I shall demonstrate these using the Delhi composition of Natthu Khan as played in its Lucknow version (see Example 2). It is important to remember that this *qāʿida* owes its particular character to the *bols dhā* and *tiṭe*, and therefore the variations will usually involve the development of these *bols* to the virtual exclusion of *dhāge*, *dhīna* and *ghīna*, which function primarily as a kind of cadence to each sentence. Firstly, there is permutation. Take, for example, the opening *dhātiṭe* string of S1:

dhāti ṭedhā tiṭe dhādhā tiṭe . . .

Without changing any of the *bols*, it is possible to permute the elements in many ways to obtain different results. The following are just two:

dhāti ṭedhā dhāti ṭedhā tiṭe . . .

dhādhā tiṭe tiṭe dhādhā tiṭe . . .

Secondly, there is substitution. For example, a *tiṭe* may be substituted for two *dhās*:

dhāti ṭedhā tiṭe tiṭe tiṭe . . .

or conversely two *dhās* may replace a *tiṭe*:

dhādhā dhādhā tiṭe dhādhā tiṭe . . .

Thirdly, there is the repetition of short phrases. In the following example, the cadence has been suppressed and *dhātiṭe* appears four times in succession:

dhāti ṭedhā	tiṭe dhāti	ṭedhā tiṭe	dhādhā tiṭe

Here, *dhādhātiṭe* is appended to fill the sixteen units needed to complete S1. Lastly, gaps may be introduced into the string:

dhādhā –dhā	tiṭe dhādhā	tiṭe . . .
tiṭe –dhā	tiṭe –dhā	tiṭe . . .

Many variations in fact contain combinations of some or all of these methods of rearranging the *bols* of a *qāʿida* composition, and sometimes the same rearrangement may be described as having been achieved by more than one method.

In order that sense can be made of these newly formed strings, they must be incorporated into the structure already established. There are several ways to construct variations depending upon where in the original structure one wishes to insert new strings. There are three main methods: firstly, to vary S1 either in part or in full, while maintaining the original S2; secondly, to maintain S1 and to vary S2, remembering that its cadence must not be suppressed because here it signals the end of the first half of the structure; and thirdly, to vary both S1 and S2. In practice, a musician is unlikely to jump from one type of structure to another randomly, just as he is unlikely to generate new strings of *bols* without some overall design; rather, he is apt to pick one or two characteristics from the basic composition and develop them from one variation to the next. In other words, variations tend to display a continuity of thought. However, in the following examples I have chosen a broad sample of variations in order to display the variety of methods a musician can draw on. These may be heard on the accompanying cassette following Example 2.

1.	dhāti ṭedhā	tiṭe dhādhā	tiṭe dhāge	dhīna ghīna
	dhādhā tiṭe	dhādhā tiṭe	tiṭe dhāge	tīna kīna
	tāti ṭetā	tiṭe tātā	tiṭe tāke	tīna kīna
	dhādhā tiṭe	dhādhā tiṭe	tiṭe dhāge	dhīna ghīna

S1 remains unchanged, while S2 retains its cadence but undergoes a simple permutation of the *dhātiṭe* string, which could also be interpreted as a repetition of *dhādhātiṭe*. Note the corresponding changes in S4.

2.	dhāti ṭedhā	tiṭe dhādhā	tiṭe dhāge	dhīna ghīna
	dhā– –dhā	tiṭe dhādhā	tiṭe dhāge	tīna kīna
	tāti ṭetā	tiṭe tātā	tiṭe tāke	tīna kīna
	dhā– –dhā	tiṭe dhādhā	tiṭe dhāge	dhīna ghīna

S1 again remains unchanged. Gaps are introduced into S2 that merely replace one *tiṭe* from the original string, which otherwise remains unchanged. Afaq Husain said that this *peṅc* was one often performed by Natthu Khan, the composer of the original *qāʿida*.

3.	dhāti ṭeti	ṭedhā tiṭe	tiṭe dhāge	dhīna ghīna
	dhāti ṭedhā	tiṭe dhādhā	tiṭe dhāge	tīna kīna
	tāti ṭeti	ṭetā tiṭe	tiṭe tāke	tīna kīna
	dhāti ṭedhā	tiṭe dhādhā	tiṭe dhāge	dhīna ghīna

S1 undergoes partial variation, so leaving its cadence intact, while S2 remains unchanged. Two *dhās* are replaced by a *tiṭe* and the string is permuted. This could also be construed as a repetition of *dhātiṭetiṭe*. Note the corresponding changes in S3 where the *bols* appear in their *band* transformation.

4.	dhāti ṭedhā	tiṭe dhāti	ṭedhā tiṭe	tiṭe tiṭe
	dhāti ṭedhā	tiṭe dhādhā	tiṭe dhāge	tīna kīna
	tāti ṭetā	tiṭe tāti	ṭetā tiṭe	tiṭe tiṭe
	dhāti ṭedhā	tiṭe dhādhā	tiṭe dhāge	dhīna ghīna

In this *peṅc*, the cadence to S1 has been entirely suppressed. *Dhātiṭe* is repeated four times and the remaining four units of the sentence are filled with two *tiṭes*. S2 remains unchanged.

5.	dhāti ṭedhā	tiṭe dhādhā	tiṭe dhāge	dhīna tiṭe
	dhāti ṭedhā	tiṭe dhādhā	tiṭe dhāge	tīna kīna
	tāti ṭetā	tiṭe tātā	tiṭe tāke	tīna tiṭe
	dhāti ṭedhā	tiṭe dhādhā	tiṭe dhāge	dhīna ghīna

Only part of the cadence of S1 is varied. A *tiṭe* is substituted for the final *ghīna*. S2 remains unchanged.

6.	dhāti ṭedhā	tiṭe dhādhā	tiṭe dhāge	tiṭe dhāti
	ṭeti ṭedhā	tiṭe dhādhā	tiṭe dhāge	tīna kīna
	tāti ṭetā	tiṭe tātā	tiṭe tāke	tiṭe tāṭi
	ṭeti ṭedhā	tiṭe dhādhā	tiṭe dhāge	dhīna ghīna

This represents a far more complex construction in which both S1 and S2 undergo variation. As with the previous *peṅc*, only part of the cadence of S1 is replaced with the phrase *tiṭedhātiṭe*. However, this is longer than the phrase it replaces and must therefore run into the following sentence, so displacing the first *bol* of S2 and masking the first beat of the second sentence (i.e. the accented *tālī* of the second *vibhāg* of *tīntāl*). Note the corresponding changes in both S3 and S4.

7.	dhāti ṭedhā	tiṭe dhādhā	tiṭe –dhā	tiṭe dhādhā
	tiṭe –dhā	tiṭe dhādhā	tiṭe dhāge	tīna kīna
	tāti ṭetā	tiṭe tātā	tiṭe –tā	tiṭe tātā
	tiṭe –dhā	tiṭe dhādhā	tiṭe dhāge	dhīna ghīna

Both S1 and S2 undergo changes, though a substantial part of their sentences remains intact. Gaps are introduced, and part of S1 is repeated.

The last *peṅc* I shall describe involves the expansion of the whole *qāʿida* structure to double its original size, thereby occupying two cycles of *tīntāl* instead of one. Here, two variations are incorporated into one. This practice appears to be peculiar to the Lucknow *gharānā*, whose members have traditionally preferred and specialised in longer and structurally more complex *qāʿidas* (see Example 4).

8.	S1a	dhāti ṭedhā	tiṭe dhādhā	tiṭe tiṭe	dhādhā tiṭe
	S2a	dhāti ṭedhā	tiṭe dhādhā	tiṭe dhāge	tīna kīna
	S1b	tiṭe dhādhā	dhāti ṭeti	ṭedhā tiṭe	dhādhā tiṭe
	S2b	dhāti ṭedhā	tiṭe dhādhā	tiṭe dhāge	tīna kīna
	S3a	tāti ṭetā	tiṭe tātā	tiṭe tiṭe	tātā tiṭe
	S4a	dhāti ṭedhā	tiṭe dhādhā	tiṭe dhāge	tīna kīna
	S3b	tiṭe dhādhā	dhāti ṭeti	ṭedhā tiṭe	dhādhā tiṭe
	S4b	dhāti ṭedhā	tiṭe dhādhā	tiṭe dhāge	dhīna ghīna

Beginning with the first variation, the cadence of S1a is replaced by the phrase *tiṭedhādhātiṭe*, which may also be conceived of as a repetition of the six *bols* immediately preceding it. S2a remains unchanged. The first half of the second variation then follows. S1b is a permutation of S1a, a feature which provides a link between the two variations. S2b remains unchanged, thereby concluding the first half of the structure. The second half is a repeat of the first, although the convention for performing *khulī/band* transformations is slightly different here. S3a and S4a are performed *band* and *khulī* respectively, although the cadence of S4a is *band* as, according to Afaq Husain, 'the *peṅc* has not yet finished'. S3b and S4b are then performed *khulī* because together they function as the fourth quarter of the overall structure, a quarter which is by convention always *khulī*. This need to balance the variation as a whole overrides the *khulī/band* structure of the second variation, in which S3b would otherwise have been played *band*.

From the foregoing descriptions of the methods used to rearrange the *bols* of a piece, and of the various constructions which these may be fitted into in order to form variations, some idea may be gained of the huge potential for improvisation based on *qāʿida* structures. Theoretically, many thousands of 'correct' variations may be generated for any *qāʿida*, and this is reflected in musicians' statements to the effect that the scope for variation in *qāʿida* is limitless. Even greater variety is possible with *qāʿidas* which, unlike the one in Example 2, provide in their basic form a wider variety of *bols*. But improvisation is not a game of chance. It is a highly structured operation governed not only by theoretical rules, such as those I have already described, but also by aesthetic rules. The most essential aesthetic rule taught by Afaq Husain (by example, not verbally) was that the individual character of a *qāʿida* must be maintained during improvisation. Thus, at least with the first few variations, he tended to retain large chunks of the basic sentences as reference points, and varied only a few elements at a time. As the variations progressed, he altered the phrases and the structure more radically, yet they always retained something of the character of the original composition by relying on internal symmetries and repetitions, as instanced in some of the variations given above.

Even after taking into account restrictions imposed by what is aesthetically viable, players are still left with literally thousands of potential variations to choose from. Yet, in reality, they limit themselves to a comparatively small number of variations and it is possible to predict, to a certain extent, which these may be. This is possible because musicians have their own repertoires of formulae, which they usually rely on to help them to improvise. A formula may consist of arithmetical subdivisions of the beats into which groups of *bols* are fitted. It may constitute a fixed order in which the permutation or substitution of *bols* is performed. It may be a system for introducing gaps into variations. It may even be a system for repeating phrases derived from the basic *qāʿida*. These repertoires of formulae appear to be built up gradually during training and practice, for not only are pupils encouraged to create their own variations, but they must also memorise dozens of variations for each *qāʿida*, as dictated to them by their teacher. Thus a tabla player may spontaneously create entirely new variations for a new *qāʿida*, although he may have used the same formula many times before when improvising on other *qāʿidas*. These formulae are rarely conceptualised in words; rather, they appear to exist more as musical instincts.

Before ending this section, I should like to refer briefly to two *qāʿidas* which are unique to Lucknow, and which demonstrate special features commonly found in the Lucknow style.

Mātrā = mm.96–132

	O 1 23 1	23 ● V	O 2 V	▼ O V
X	dhāti ṭedhi	ṭetā ghena	dhāti ghena	dhīna ghena
	1 23 1	23 1	1 23	1 23
2	dhāti ṭedhi	ṭetā ghena	dhāti ghena	tīna kena
				V Λ
0	tāti ṭeti	ṭetā kena	tāti kena	tīna kena
	V ΛV	Λ V	V Λ	V Λ
3	dhāti ṭedhi	ṭetā ghena	dhāti ghena	dhīna ghena

Example 3. Lucknow *qāʿida* (*tīntāl*)

The use of *tā* on the *sūr*, and the Lucknow fingering of *tiṭe* is clearly shown in Example 3. (Being a Delhi *qāʿida*, Example 2 retained the Delhi fingering of *tiṭe*.) So too is the use of the non-resonating stroke *na* where one would ordinarily expect to find the resonating *kinār tā*. Also worthy of mention is the very active use of the *bāyāṅ* in both *khulī* and *band* sections of this *qāʿida*, although this feature is not reflected in the spoken *bols*. Structurally, this piece is identical to that shown in Example 2, and variations are therefore derived in the same manner as described above.

Example 4 displays the extended *qāʿida* structure peculiar to Lucknow. Here, each sentence comprises thirty-two units, twice as many as the sentences described above. Additionally, S2 differs from S1. Another noteworthy feature is the frequent use of *dhīnaghīna*, which is used extensively during the generation of variations. This device is common in Lucknow, although according to Inam Ali Khan its use is strictly disallowed in the Delhi *gharānā*, where *dhīnaghīna* is employed only as a cadential device to mark the end of each half of the *qāʿida* structure.

Qāʿida-relā

The name *qāʿida-relā* suggests a form that combines features of both *qāʿida* and *relā*. Although definitions differ from *gharānā* to *gharānā*, Lucknow musicians believe that the *qāʿida-relā* is technically a *qāʿida* that incorporates *bols* which lend themselves to rapid articulation, such as *tirakiṭataka*, *tiṭegiṛanaga* and *dhiradhira*, and which therefore form the natural stroke repertoire of *relās*. It should be noted that *tiṭegiṛanaga* is most commonly found in the Lucknow style because the phrase incorporates resonating *bāyāṅ* strokes, unlike its non-resonating counterpart *tirakiṭataka*. Examples 5 and 6 display only the first sentences of two common

Mātrā = mm.100–144

	o 1 23	▼ o o		
X	dhāge tiṭe	dhīna ghīna	dhāge tiṭe	dhīna ghīna
	1 23	1 23		
2	dhāge tiṭe	dhāge tiṭe	dhāge tiṭe	tīna kīna
0	dhāge tiṭe	dhāge tiṭe	dhīna ghīna	dhāge tiṭe
	o o o	1 23 1 23		
3	dhāge nadhā	tiṭe dhiṭe	dhāge tiṭe	tīna kīna
	1 23 1	23		
X	tāke tiṭe	tīna kīna	tāke tiṭe	tīna kīna
2	dhāge tiṭe	dhāge tiṭe	dhāge tiṭe	tīna kīna
0	dhāge tiṭe	dhāge tiṭe	dhīna ghīna	dhāge tiṭe
3	dhāge nadhā	tiṭe dhiṭe	dhāge tiṭe	dhīna ghīna

Example 4. Lucknow *qāʿida* (*tīntāl*)

qāʿida-relās; both undergo processes of repetition and transformation identical to those described for Example 2, and variations are derived in the same manner.

Chand

Chand is a much less well defined concept than *qāʿida*. It has two meanings: it is both a 'rhythm' and a particular kind of theme-and-variations composition. Afaq Husain explained

Mātrā = mm.96–132

```
     o 2 1  V o
X    dhā tiṭe giṛa naga      dhā tiṭe giṛa naga
     1      1      23

                                   ▼ o  V o
          dhā tiṭe giṛa naga       dhī na giṛa naga
                                   1      1      23
```

Example 5. *Qāʿida-relā* (*tīntāl*)

Mātrā = mm.96–132

```
     o 2 1  V o                > < > <  V o
X    dhā tiṭe giṛa naga        dhira dhira giṛa naga
     1      1      23          1    -     1      23

                                   ▼ o  V o
          dhā tiṭe giṛa naga.      dhī na giṛa naga
                                   1      1      23
```

Example 6. *Qāʿida-relā* (*tīntāl*)

that, as a rhythm, there were four *chands* in practical tabla-playing, by which he meant that there were four common ways of rhythmically dividing the beat: *jhaptāl chand*, *dādrā chand*, *rūpak chand* and *kaharwā chand*. *Jhaptāl chand* was the name he gave to the rhythm resulting from the division of one, two or four beats into five equal parts. *Dādrā chand*, *rūpak chand* and *kaharwā chand* denoted divisions of six, seven and eight respectively.

When taken to mean a type of composition, the word, but not the form (cf. *bāṅṭ* in the Benares *gharānā*) is peculiar to the Lucknow *gharānā*, though Inam Ali Khan claimed that *chand* was sometimes used in the Delhi *gharānā* as an alternative term for a *qāʿida* set in anything other than duple or quadruple time. A glance at the three notated examples of *chand* (Examples 7, 8, 9) is enough to suggest that no equally simple definition is possible for the Lucknow *chand*.

In its simplest form, *chand* is a rhythm articulated with a short string of tabla *bols* that is repeated over and over again, as is shown in Example 7, which is set in *rūpak chand*. There is little scope for improvisation, which at best would be restricted to the interplay of the phrases *dhāgenadhagetiṭe* and *dhāgenadhā– – –*. Set in *tīntāl*, these phrases are governed by the same *khulī/band* transformations that apply to *qāʿida*.

In its more complex form, *chand* is much more difficult to label. When Afaq Husain first taught me the piece notated as Example 8, he called it a *qāʿida*. The following day he referred to the same piece as a *chand*, and on yet another occasion he called it a *calan*. When I pressed him to settle for just one descriptive term he laughed at my concern for clarity and said that it

Mātrā = mm.66–84

```
     o    V o     1 23
X   dhāgenadhagetiṭe       dhāgenadhagetiṭe
     1 23     1 23

                    dhāgenadhagetiṭe       dhāgenadhā---
```

Example 7. *Chand* (*tīntāl*)

Mātrā = mm.84–108

```
      o        o          2 1            o             2 1   2 1
X    dhā-   gadhā     -ga  tiṭe     kadhā  -ga      tiṭe  tiṭe
      1 /    23  1     / 23           ×   1   / 23

        o               2 1      o            o               ▼    V
2    kadhā  -ga       tiṭe  kadhā     -ga  dhā-        gadhī  -na
      ×   1   / 23            ×   1     / 23   1  /      23   1
```

Example 8. *Chand* (*tīntāl*)

hardly mattered what it was called since the name did not affect the piece itself. In classifying it I have therefore decided to use the word Afaq Husain most frequently used. Furthermore, the piece is clearly modelled on another piece he always referred to as *chand* (Example 9), which consists simply of the rhythmic skeleton of Example 8. Complex *chands* have two main characteristics. Firstly, they tend to rely heavily on a limited range of *bols* that form short phrases which comprise an odd or irregular number of units; secondly, this irregularity causes stressed or accented *bols* to fall on the off-beats. This is clearly demonstrated in Examples 8 and 9. In every other way, the complex *chand* functions like *qā'ida* and is subject to the same rules for the derivation of variations.

Mātrā = mm.84–108

```
      o               ●
X    dhā  -dhā     -  dhin       -dhin  -      dhā  dhin


2    -dhin  -      dhā  -dhā     -  dhin       -dhin  -
```

Example 9. *Chand* (*tīntāl*)

I originally conjectured that a major difference between *qāʿidas* and complex *chands* lay in their cadential phrases. In other words, except for a number of elementary *qāʿida* compositions such as

dhā dhā ti ṭe dhā dhā dhī na

and

dhā tit dhā tit dhā dhā dhī na

qāʿidas seemed always to end with the *bols dhīnaghīna* although *chands* never did. There are, however, exceptions to most rules in tabla. I later learned a number of special *qāʿidas* (generally called *gat-qāʿidas* by Afaq Husain) from the Lucknow repertoire which were rhythmically complex and irregular, and which did not conclude with *dhīnaghīna*.

Calan

I indicated in the discussion of *chand* that it is frequently difficult to distinguish between certain *qāʿidas*, *chands* and *calans*. To compound further the problem of identification, the similarities between the *calan* given in Example 10 with the opening sentence of the Lucknow *peshkār* (Example 12) only serve to emphasise the fact that folk categories are often fluid, and therefore precise analytical definitions are virtually impossible.

Calans are not as common in the Lucknow repertoire as they may be in other styles, particularly that of Farukkhabad. The *calan* shown in Example 10 was composed by Afaq

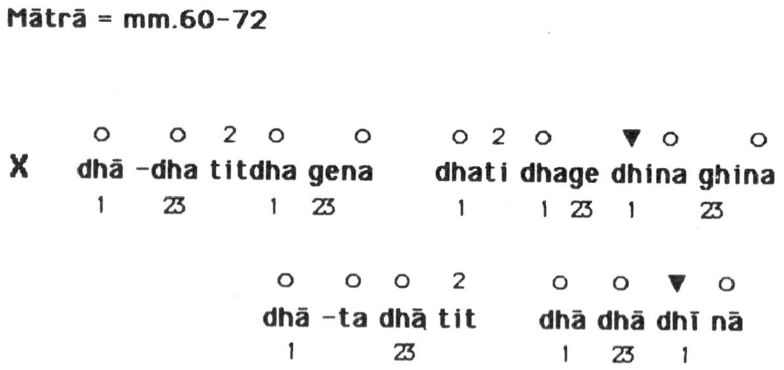

Example 10. *Calan* (*tīntāl*)

Husain's son, Ilmas, in 1983. It could not be termed a *chand* for, firstly, it comprises too great a variety of strokes and, secondly, it is rhythmically regular. Furthermore, despite the fact that it functions structurally like a *qāʿida* in that it uses the same derivation rules for its variations, it could not be termed a *qāʿida* because, as Ilmas Husain pointed out, its basic sentence contains phrases of different densities: the first two *mātrās* in *āṭhgun*, and the third and fourth in *caugun*. Therefore, it seems likely that in order for a *qāʿida* to be termed a *calan*, it should, like *chands*, display some form of rhythmic peculiarity.

Peshkār

Like *qāʿida*, *peshkār*, meaning 'presentation', originated in the Delhi *gharānā*, where its performance is considered to be a speciality. In solo tabla performances, it is usually the first theme-and-variations composition that is played, though it may be preceded by an introductory *mukhṛā*, *mohrā* or *uṭhān*. As the meaning of the word implies, *peshkār* is where a player 'presents' both his technical and musical ability to his audience. Through *peshkār*, he can immediately demonstrate his mastery over basic techniques, and can alternate between fast and slow passages to show off his virtuosity and his quality of sound production respectively. It is also permissible to introduce *laykārī* into variations and this offers the tabla soloist an early opportunity to exhibit his control over different rhythmic divisions. As a basis for improvisation, *peshkār* offers greater latitude than *qāʿida* in that a player is not necessarily restricted to the *bols* that constitute the original composition. According to both Afaq Husain and Ustad Ramzan Khan of the Ajrara *gharānā*, this is a relatively recent development, and is due almost entirely to the influence of Ahmadjan Thirakwa, who was particularly successful in interpreting quite liberally the rules for the derivation of variations. Before Thirakwa, they claimed, the common practice was to restrict the range of strokes used in variations to that presented in the basic composition.

Peshkār appears almost always in *vilambit* (slow) *tīntāl*, although theoretically any classical *tāl* may be used. Essentially, it consists of a four-*mātrā* phrase from which a second phrase of equal length is derived. These two phrases are then repeated to complete the sixteen *mātrās* of the *tāl*, as illustrated in Example 11a. As with *qāʿida*, and indeed all theme-and-variations compositions, the *khulī*/*band* transformations that correspond to the structure of *tīntāl* apply.

Example 11a is a famous Delhi composition that is widely known and performed by

Mātrā = mm.48–56

	● V ● O	O ▼ O	O 2 O 2	O O ▼ O
X	**dhī -kṛa dhī nā**	**- dhā dhī nā**	**dhā tit dhā tit**	**dhā dhā tī nā**
	1 23) 1	1 23	1 23	1 23 ×
	2 O O O	▼ O O 2		
2	**tit -dhā -ta dhā**	**dhī nā dhā tit**	**dhā -kṛa dhā tit**	**dhā dhā tī nā**
	1 23	1 23		
	V			
0	**tī -kṛa tī nā**	**- tā tī nā**	**tā tit tā tit**	**tā tā tī nā**
	×)			
3	**tit -dhā -ta dhā**	**dhī nā dhā tit**	**dhā -kṛa dhā tit**	**dhā dhā dhī nā**

Example 11a. Delhi *peshkār* (*tīntāl*)

members of many tabla *gharānās* in India. The principal idea behind improvising in *peshkār* involves substituting parts of the basic composition with short variations of the duration of two or four *mātrās*. Afaq Husain was quite consistent when demonstrating which parts of the *peshkār* were to be retained unchanged, and which could be replaced. For example, he always left the first four *mātrās* intact to serve as a reference point, and varied only the first half of the second four *mātrās*. The remainder of the piece he replaced either in part or in full. Example 11b shows how the first two *mātrās* of the third *vibhāg* have been replaced by *bols* derived from

o o   o ▼ o

0 - tā - tā   - tā tī nā   tā tit tā tit   tā tā tī nā

Example 11b

the basic composition, while Example 11c displays the introduction of the unrelated *bols ne* and *tiṭe*. Example 11d builds a longer phrase of four *mātrās* by developing and adding to the material presented in the previous cycle. Here, *tirakiṭa* is the only new string, for *kiṛanaga* may be viewed merely as an alternative pronunciation of *kīnatake*.

▼∧ ▼o V o   1 23 ▼∧ ▼o V

0 tīne tīna kīna take   tiṭe tīne tīna kīna

× × × ×   × × ×

tā tit tā tit   tā tā tī nā

2 o o o   ▼ o o

3 tit -dhā -ta dhā[ge]   tī nā ghe nā

1 1 23   × 23

o ▼ o

dhā tī nā ghe   nā dhā tī nā

1 ×

Example 11c

Variations in the final four *mātrās* of the composition tend to be rather *tihā'ī*-oriented. The *bols* in the final *vibhāg* of Example 11c are grouped to form a sort of pseudo-*tihā'ī* designed to create the same cadential sensation as a real one. A real *tihā'ī*, however, would normally mark the end of the improvisation. The *tihā'ī* in the final four *mātrās* of Example 11d was said to have been used frequently by Ahmadjan Thirakwa. It is derived from basic components of the original *peshkār*, and is set in *chegun* (six divisions of the *mātrā*), a good example of the way in which different rhythms may be incorporated into the variations.

Example 12 shows one variation taken from a Lucknow *peshkār* composed by Afaq Husain. The basic composition is closely modelled on the previous Delhi *peshkār*. For instance, it retains unchanged the important phrase

dhā -kṛa dhā tit   dhā dhā tī nā

V O ▼ O V O ▼ Λ ▼ O
0 kiṛa naga tī nā kiṛa naga tīne tīna
+ Λ V + Λ V ×

V O 2 1 V O 1 23 ▼ O O
kīna take tira kiṭa take tiṭe tīna kīna
× × × × × ×

O ● ● O 2 O O
3 dhāgedhin dhindhātit dhā(gena) dhāgedhin
1 23 1 23 - 1 23

dhindhātit dhā(gena) dhāgedhin dhindhātit

X dhā...

Example 11d

as a kind of cadence to each group of four *mātrās*, a phrase Afaq Husain felt to be a distinguishing feature of most *peshkārs*. When generating variations based on his own compositions, Afaq Husain, unlike Thirakwa, tended to limit his improvisations to the use of *bols* present in the original composition. This is especially noticeable at the beginning of the second, third and fourth *vibhāgs*, where the new material is derived entirely from the first two *mātrās* of the original composition (including *tākena*, which is the *band* transformation of *dhāgena*). The lively use of resonating *bāyāṅ* strokes is also noteworthy, particularly in phrases such as *dhā –dhā gena dhāge* and *dhā dhā[ge] tī nā*. This Lucknow *peshkār* tended to be played faster than its Delhi counterpart, thus helping to create the impression of a more sustained and vocalised bass to the tabla's sonority.

Laggī

The word *laggī* implies continuity, like that of an unbroken chain. The form is probably derived from the repertoires of the *naqqāra* and *ḍholak* (Stewart 1974: 142), and *laggī bols* are characteristically performed very rapidly. In tabla, *laggīs* are very short compositions commonly used in accompanying light and semi-classical vocal forms such as *ghazal* and *ṭhumrī*, and, in Lucknow, *kathak* dance. The tendency is for the composition to be repeated over and over again, although improvisation is possible by simple permutations and repetitions of the basic elements of the original composition.

The Lucknow repertoire contains a large number and variety of *laggīs*; most were developed in the nineteenth and early twentieth centuries for the specific purpose of accompanying the songs and dances of *ṭawā'ifs*. *Laggīs* are designed primarily to be played in *kaharwā tāl* (eight *mātrās*), though most may be modified to fit *dādrā* (six *mātrās*) while a few

Mātrā = mm.60-66


```
        O  ◡ O    O  O                    ▼  O  O  2
  X     dhā -dhā gena dhāge          dhī nā dhā tit
        |   |   ℥     |  ℥               |     ℥


                 O      V  O  2              O   O    ▼  O
                 dhā -kṛa dhā tit          dhā dhā[ge] tī nā
                 |   ℥)    |                 |   |   ℥   X


        O  ▼  O  O                     O      ▼  O  2
  2     dhā dhī nā dhā                 dhā[ge] dhī nā tit
        |   -     |                    |    ℥    |


             dha -kṛa dhā tit               dhā dhā[ge] tī nā


        O   O O  O    O                 O      ▼  O  2
  0     tāke natā -tā kena              tā[ke] tī nā tit
          X        X                     ∧   V


             tā -kṛa tā tit                 tā tā[ke] tī nā


        O   O  ▼                        O   O  2
  3     dhā dhā dhī                     nā dhā tit
        |   ℥  |                          ℥


             dhā -kṛa dhā tit               dhā dhā[ge] dhī nā
```

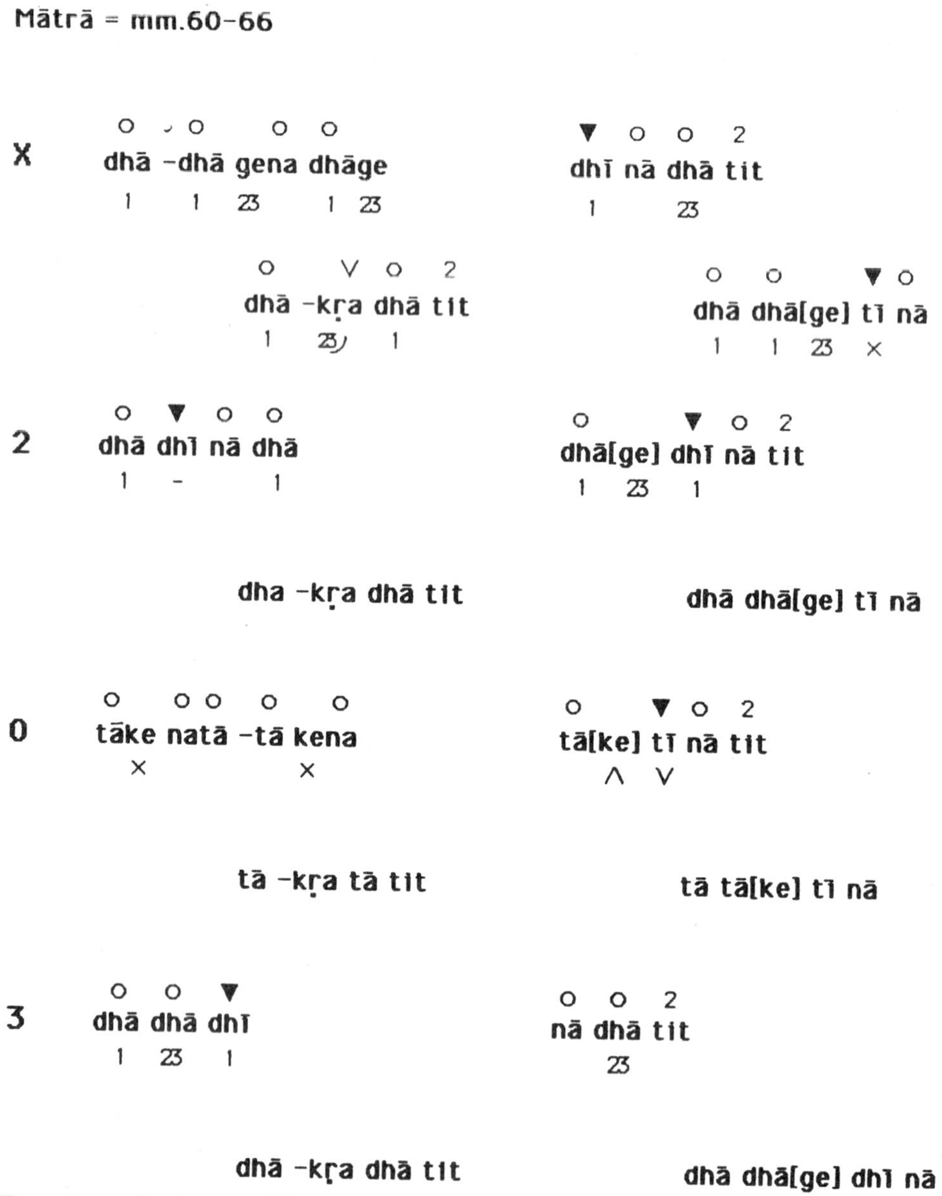

Example 12. Lucknow *peshkār* (*tīntāl*)

can be adapted for *rūpak tāl*. *Kaharwā* may be represented in many ways, the following being the most common:

x	dhā	ge	na	tī
o	na	ka	dhī	na

In general, though there are exceptions, *laggī* compositions follow this *khulī/band* structure, and most return to accented resonating *bols* on or just before the seventh *mātrā*. Example 13 is used in the accompaniment of *kathak* dance at the point where the tabla player is required to

Mātrā = mm.132–160

```
      o   1      23  o      o   ●       o
X    dhā ti      ṭe dhā     dhā tin   - ta
      1              1      23  ×

O    tā  ti      ṭe dhā     dhā dhin  - ta
                                 1
```

Example 13. *Laggī* (*kaharwā*)

accompany certain *cāls* at specific moments during the story-telling *gat bhā'o* sections of *ṭhumrīs* and *bhajans*. A *cāl* is a manner of walking used by the dancer to introduce a character from the story he or she is telling in dance and gesture. Afaq Husain used this *laggī* for the character of Radha, the consort of Lord Krishna. Example 14 is a slightly elaborated version that may be used both as a *cāl* and in accompanying *ghazals*. Example 15, however, would only be used for *ghazals* where, between sung verses, attention is focused on the tabla player, who reels off a number of *laggīs* in swift succession before concluding with a short *tihā'ī*. The

Mātrā = mm.144–160

```
      o    V        +      V        o   ●         ●
X    dhā  kiṭa     taka  ghina     dhā tin     - tin
      1    ×         23    1        1    ×         ×

O    tā   kiṭa     taka  ghina     dhā dhin    - dhin
                                        23         23
```

Example 14. *Laggī* (*kaharwā*)

Mātrā = mm.240–288

```
      1   23      o   o       1   23      1   23
X    dhi  ṭe     dhā dhā     ti  ṭe      ti  ṭe
      1           1   23      ×

O    ti   ṭe     dhā dhā     dhi ṭe      dhi ṭe
                              1           23
```

Example 15. *Laggī* (*kaharwā*)

tempo normally increases during these interludes, so allowing the accompanist to display great virtuosity. Once over, he must drop back to the original tempo in preparation for the next verse.

Relā

No consensus of opinion exists concerning the precise nature of *relā* (lit. a torrent or rushing stream), though musicians and scholars do agree that, at the most general level, it is a theme-and-variations composition played at great speed. The two main schools of thought are represented by the Delhi and Ajrara *gharānās* on the one hand, and the Purab *gharānās* on the other. Purab, meaning East (i.e. east of Delhi) is a collective term for the Lucknow, Farukkhabad and Benares *gharānās*.

Inam Ali Khan claimed that in the Delhi tradition a *relā* is defined as a string of *bols* which, when played unchanged at double speed, form a continuous stream of rapidly articulated strokes. Stewart (1974: 149–56) defined *relā* similarly and gave several examples, one of which corresponds to the *qāʿida-relā* I notated earlier as Example 6. Structurally, then, Delhi *relās* are viewed as *qāʿida-relās* by Lucknow musicians. By contrast, the Lucknow tradition (as well as the Benares – see Gottlieb's (1977 vol. 2: 149–54) transcription of a performance by Kishan Maharaj) defines *relā* as a rapidly articulated and elaborated development of a short phrase usually containing eight, but no more than sixteen, *bols*. There are a number of similarities between many of these phrases and *laggīs*, from which they may have developed. A basic phrase, sometimes referred to as *ṭhā* (but never as *laggī*), provides a skeletal framework for the elaborated version and is not, as Gottlieb (1977 vol. 1: 170) has mistakenly implied, an 'abbreviated form' derived from it.

Example 16 shows a typical and commonly played Lucknow *relā* in *tīntāl*, in which the *ṭhā*

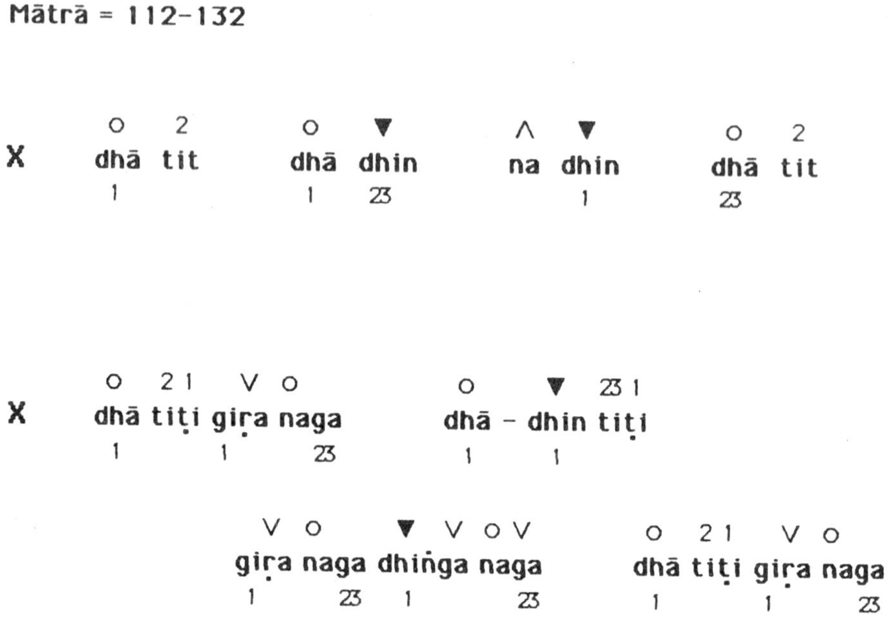

Example 16. *Relā* (*tīntāl*)

comprises eight *bols* played over four *mātrās*. Its subsequent repetitions are subject to the usual *khulī/band* transformations appropriate for the *tāl*. The *ṭhā* marks out a rhymthic profile

dhā dhādhin –dhin dhā

which must be maintained in the *relā* over the same number of beats, except that the spaces in between are filled with a great many rapidly articulated strokes played lightly so as to avoid obscuring the profile. The components of the *relā* may be thought of as simple transformations of parts of the *ṭhā*, so that

dhā tit	*becomes*	dhā tiṭi giṛa naga
dhin na	*becomes*	dhin tiṭi giṛa naga
dhin	*becomes*	dhiṅga naga

while *dhā* alone remains unchanged. When each transformation has been implemented, we are left with the *relā* given in Example 16.

In performance, Afaq Husain played the *ṭhā* several times in order to establish its rhythmic profile firmly in the minds of the listener before unleashing the *relā*. The basic phrase was occasionally subject to variation by means of simple permutations and repetitions of its elements. The new rhythmic profiles resulting from this process were similarly transformed into the *relā*. However, Afaq Husain frequently chose to create variations in the *relā* alone. Perhaps the common method he used to generate variations involved the dividing-up of the *relā* pattern into a number of large blocks of material which were then permuted and repeated. Here three blocks suggest themselves:

dhā tiṭi giṛa naga	dhā –
dhin tiṭi giṛa naga	dhiṅga naga
dhā tiṭi giṛa naga	

Rang

Rang, meaning 'colour', is structurally identical to *relā*, but is distinguishable owing to its exclusive use of *tā* (*sūr*) and *tene* (*dhene*), as illustrated in Example 17. I have listed it as a separate category from *relā* because Lucknow *gharānā* musicians think of it as a different kind of piece, evidently because it is a speciality of their *gharānā*. It is thought to have been invented by Salari Khan, a disciple of Miyan Bakhshu Khan.

Rang-rela

As its name suggests, *rang-relā* is a cross between a *relā*, in which rapidly articulated *bols* are mainly non-resonating, and *rang*, in which they are resonating. This is illustrated in Example 18.

Endings

Mukhṛā

Mukhṛās (lit. face) are rarely taught directly in the Lucknow *gharānā*; rather, they are absorbed gradually into a student's repertoire, almost without his realising it, for after years

Mātrā = mm.66–76

● ▽ △ ▽ △
X dhā[ge] dhene dhene dhā[ge] dhene dhene
1 23 1 23

dhā[ge] dhene dhene dhā[ge] dhene dhene

● ▽△ △ ▽△ V
X dhā[ge] dinagina dinagina dhā[ge] dinagina dinagina
1 23 1 23 1 23

dhā[ge] dinagina dinagina dhā[ge] dinagina dinagina

Example 17. *Rang* (*tīntāl*)

Mātrā = mm.192–224

O 2 O 2 ▽ △
X dhā tit [ge] dhā tit [ge] dhe ne
1 23 1 23 1

O 21 V O 21 V ▽△ V
X dhā tira kiṭa dhā tira kiṭa dina gina
1 23 1 23 1

Example 18. *Rang-relā* (*tīntāl*)

of observation he begins to imitate these patterns during practice or performance. *Mukhṛās* are short, improvisatory strings, or flourishes, that may comprise all kinds of strokes used to end a cycle of *ṭhekā*, the embellished articulation of the strokes representing a *tāl*. Sometimes patterns are derived from the *ṭhekā* itself. Essentially, they are designed to draw the listener's attention to the *sam* of the *āvartan*, as demonstrated in Example 19, where in the final *vibhāg* of *tīntāl* a sequence of regularly spaced accents leads the ear to the final *dhā*.

Mātrā = mm.48–72

	o 1 23	● ● o	1 23 o	o o o Λ
3	**tāke tiṭe**	**dhin dhindhā**	**tiṭe dhāge**	**nadhā dhātit**
	+	1 1 23	1 23	1 23
	o			
X	**dhā...**			
	1			

Example 19. *Mukhṛā* (*tīntāl*)

Mukhṛās are sometimes used in the Lucknow *gharānā* as short, simple, improvised introductions to tabla solos in place of fixed *mohrās* or *uṭhāns*. They are also used during accompaniment, and are especially important in vocal music, where the opportunities for improvisation are few, being restricted mainly to flourishes heralding the *sam*. Example 20 shows a *mukhṛā*, often played by Afaq Husain, that fills the last two *mātrās* of *ektāl* (twelve *mātrās* divided into six equal *vibhāgs*).

Mātrā = mm.48–54

	▼o Vo o 21 Vo	21 V o o o Λ
4	**dhīnā kiṛanaga tā–tiṭi kiṛanaga**	**tirakiṭa takadhā– –dhā tit–**
	1 x x x x	x 23 1 23
	●	
X	**dhin...**	
	1	

Example 20. *Mukhṛā* (*ektāl*)

Tihā'ī

Tihā'ī, meaning 'a third part', is a cadential formula for the threefold repetition of a phrase. In most cases, the final *bol* of the final repetition is designed to coincide with the *sam* of the *āvartan*, but in vocal and instrumental music there are instances where *tihā'īs* lead into melodic compositions which may commence from any point within the *āvartan*.

In its simplest and most skeletal form, the *tihā'ī* may be represented by a series of three evenly spaced *bols*, such as the following, which begins on the eleventh *mātrā* of *tīntāl*:

o	–	–	dhā	–
3	–	dhā	–	–
x	dhā			

Mātrā = mm.108–132

o 2 1   V o 2 1 V

0   – – dhā tira   kiṭa taka tira kiṭa

1   × × ×

o

dhā – – –   – – dhā tira

1

3   kiṭa taka tira kiṭa   dhā – – –

– – dhā tira   kiṭa taka tira kiṭa

X   dhā...

Example 21. *Tihā'ī* (*tīntāl*)

Example 21 is based on this formula: each *dhā* is preceded by a *mukhṛā*-like flourish *dhā tira kiṭa taka tira kiṭa*. Indeed, the pattern may really be seen as a kind of elaborated *mukhṛā*.

One of the main functions of a *tihā'ī* is to bring to an end improvisations on theme-and-variations forms by setting to a cadential formula one or more of the patterns employed. This may best be demonstrated with reference to the Lucknow version of the Delhi *qā'ida* (Example 2). A *tihā'ī* may be derived either from the basic phrase of the *qā'ida* or from a variation. The following illustrates the former:

x	dhāti ṭedhā	tiṭe dhādhā	tiṭe dhāge	tīna kīna
2	dhā –	– –	dhāti ṭedhā	tiṭe dhādhā
o	tiṭe dhāge	tīna kīna	dhā –	– –
3	dhāti ṭedhā	tiṭe dhādhā	tiṭe dhāge	tīna kīna
x	dhā . . .			

Furthermore, *tihā'īs* are also used to conclude most fixed compositions, where they may either be derived from, or be completely independent of, the piece to which they are appended. This will be demonstrated later.

Importantly, *tihā'īs* may be self-contained pieces displaying considerable variety of form. As such they deserve quite separate analysis. Example 22 shows a simple *tihā'ī*, written out in full for added clarity, set in *jhaptāl*. The phrase *tiṭe kata gadi gina dhā tit dhā* covers three and a half *mātrās* which, played three times, adds up to ten and a half: the ten *mātrās* of *jhaptāl* plus

Mātrā = mm.96-120

```
          23 1     ●          ■    ∧
X         tiṭe kata           gadi gina
              ×               1    23

          ●    ∧              ●
2         dhā tit             dhā tiṭe            kata gadi
           1                  23

0         gina dhā            tit dhā

3         tiṭe kata           gadi gina           dhā tit

X         dhā...
```

Example 22. *Tihā'ī (jhaptāl)*

the first half of the first *mātrā* (i.e. the *sam*) of the following cycle. More complex formulae are demonstrated in Examples 23 and 24, where a phrase played three times is itself repeated three times. The former spans two *āvartans*. These pieces are known as *tihā'ī kī tihā'ī* (the *tihā'ī* of a *tihā'ī*), although Afaq Husain sometimes used the alternative term *nau kī tihā'ī* (a *tihā'ī* of nine).

Mātrā = 96-132

```
         ○  1  23 ○        ○   ○           ▼○     ○        ○
X   [ | dhāti ṭedhā      gena dhāge      tīna kīna       dhā | - ]
         1      1        23     1 23      ×    ×          1
```

Example 23. *Tihā'ī kī tihā'ī (tīntāl)*

Mātrā = 52-60

```
          ○      ∧           ●
X   [ | dhā - tit -         dhā - - | -        - ]
          1                  23
```

Example 24. *Tihā'ī kī tihā'ī (tīntāl)*

Another form regarded by Lucknow musicians as distinct from other types of *tihā'ī* is the *tihā'ī-bandīsh*. *Bandīsh* is a general term for something that is 'bound'; it is sometimes used in tabla as a non-specific term for a fixed composition. In its simplest form, a *tihā'ī-bandīsh* consists of the threefold repetition of a short introductory phrase followed by a *tihā'ī*, as illustrated in Example 25. The optional parenthesised strokes are essentially embellishments

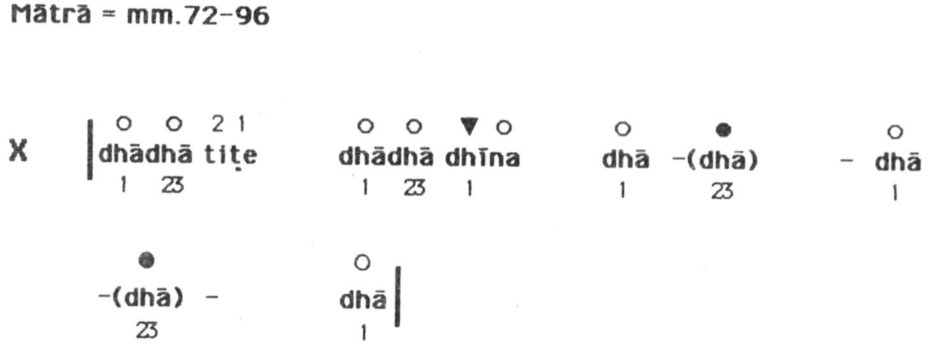

Example 25. *Tihā'ī-bandīsh* (*tīntāl*)

which, unlike the three main *dhās*, are not accented but which serve instead to fill the long gaps between the three main *dhās*. Such options are common features in Lucknow *tihā'ī* and *tihā'ī-bandīsh* structures. Example 26 shows a more complex *tihā'ī-bandīsh* set in *rūpak tāl*

Example 26. *Tihā'ī-bandīsh* (*rūpak*)

(seven *mātrās* divided 3+2+2). This time an introductory phrase followed by a *tihā'ī kī tihā'ī* is repeated in full three times. Afaq Husain conceived of this as a *farmā'ishī* piece tailored to the specification that it should contain twenty-seven repetitions of the *bol dhā*. Therefore, to avoid confusion *dhā* does not feature in the introductory phrase.

A noteworthy stylistic feature of all kinds of *tihā'īs* in the Lucknow repertoire, but rare in the repertoires of other *gharānās*, is a high incidence of single, repeated strokes (usually *dhā*). Here the influence of *kathak* is evident, for in dance numbers are frequently used instead of *bols* to indicate repetitions of a step, movement or gesture. A simple, numerically based Lucknow *kathak tihā'ī* (which Afaq Husain would classify as a *tihā'ī-bandīsh* – it corresponds to Example 25) is given below:

X	| tigdhā digdig	tigdhā digdig	1 -2	- 3
2	-4 -	5 |		

When based on numerical formulae, these pieces are known as *gintī tihā'īs*, or 'counting' *tihā'īs*. Example 27 exhibits a *tihā'ī* which toys with the number nine. Here the numbers from one to nine are performed in three different rhythms, and the whole piece is then repeated three times without intervening pauses, a device known as *bedam* (lit. without breath or pause). Once the structure has been fixed, *bols* may replace these numbers, in this case *ti ṭe ka tā ga di gi na dhā*.

During training, a large number of *tihā'īs* displaying many different structures designed for all *tāls* in common use must be memorised. These function as a reserve of formulae from which patterns may be drawn and remoulded to form the bases of new formulae. As with improvisations in *qā'ida*, manipulating these formulae eventually becomes instinctive, and it is stressed that when required a player must be able to improvise new *tihā'īs* with ease in performance.

Fixed compositions

Gat

The knowledge and performance of *gat*, meaning 'composition', is widely recognised to be a speciality of the Lucknow *gharānā*. Of all categories it is probably the most difficult to define, for there are so many varieties, each with its own distinct features. Stewart (1974: 203–30) has notated many examples of *gat*, though by no means all varieties are covered in her work. Here I am restricted to a description of just the main types, partly because to cover the form thoroughly would necessitate a separate chapter and partly because I did not receive permission to notate or describe certain pieces. *Gats* have always been highly prized, and the more choice compositions in a musician's repertoire have not been given away lightly. Indeed, so valued were these pieces that they were bestowed as important parts of dowries in the past.

Mātrā = mm.320–400

X	∧ ti	–	1 ṭe	kat ×
2	–	● ta	ga 1	–
0	■ di	gi 23	–	∧ na
3	● dhā 1	∧ ti	ṭe	ka
X	ta	ga	di	gi
2	na	dhā	23 1 tiṭi	kata
0	gadi	gina	dhā	

Example 27. *Gintī tihā'ī (bedam; tīntāl)*

Even now they are reserved for only the most refined and select of audiences. This is still the predominant sentiment among members of the Lucknow *gharānā*.

Gats exhibit great variety of form, and so not surprisingly musicians had difficulty in explaining their structural ingredients for purposes of identification. Afaq Husain suggested that one could identify a *gat* more accurately from its constituent *bol* phrases, of which

dhā ghinā-
takiṭa ghinā-
dhā-na dhitiṭe
ghinā -dhā -ṛa
tiṭe giṛa naga
dhiṅga naga

dhene ghene taka
ghin nan naga tiṭe

were the most common. It may be seen that resonating *bols* predominate throughout these phrases, especially *tā* as played on the *sūr*.

One of the oldest and simplest *gats* in the Lucknow repertoire is shown in Example 28, a

Mātrā = 120–132

X	● dhā - - 1	● ghi nā - 23	1 ∧ ta ki ṭa ×	● ghi nā - 23
2	○ 1 23 dhā ti ṭe 1	1 23 1 dhi ti ṭe 23	● ka ta ga × 1	■ ∧ di gi na 23
0	▽ △ na gi na ×	▽ ∧ na gi na ×	ta ki ṭa	ghi nā -
3	dhā ti ṭe	dhi ti ṭe	ka ta ga	di gi na

Example 28. *Gat* (*tīntāl*)

piece usually attributed to the founder of the *gharānā*, Miyan Bakhshu Khan. It is constructed in two parts: the first part is a statement of two phrases, each of four *mātrās* (A B), while the second is a repeat in which A is modified (A^{I} B). Performance convention requires the whole to be repeated, with those *bols* occupying the first *vibhāg* transformed into their *band* counterparts. Thus the two parts together span two *āvartans*, although the piece is not considered complete until both have been rendered at double speed, sc compressing them into one *āvartan*.

The majority of *gats* are played in *madhya* (medium) or *drut* (fast) *lay*, especially short compositions such as Example 28. Longer compositions may theoretically be played in any tempo, including *vilambit*. Example 29, composed by Khalifa Abid Husain Khan, was taught to me in both *madhya* and *vilambit lay*, but I have chosen the latter for this notation. Once again, the *gat* comprises four phrases, of which the first and fourth are identical, while the second and third are closely related, the one being in part a permutation of the other (A B B^{I} A). A special feature of this *gat* is the identical two-*mātrā* phrase used to conclude each section, including the third, which undergoes a change of rhythm in order to incorporate *dhiradhira*. As with the previous example, the piece is repeated with its opening section played *band*, and the whole is then performed at double speed.

Mātrā = 60–66

● ● V ● V ●
X ghinā -dhā -ṛa dhā giṛa naga
1 23 1 1 23

V ● 1 23 1 V ●
giṛa naga taka tira kiṭa tā
1 23 × ×

23 1 V ●
2 tiṭe giṛa naga giṛa naga tiṭe
1 23

giṛa naga taka tira kiṭa tā

0 tiṭe tiṭe giṛa naga giṛa naga

> < > <
dhira dhira giṛa naga taka tira kiṭa tā
1 –

3 ghinā -dhā -ṛa dhā giṛa naga

giṛa naga taka tira kiṭa tā

Example 29. *Gat* (*tīntāl*)

Example 30 displays a very different kind of *gat* that involves the structured repetition of a simple composition similar to that given in Example 28 (indeed, the second halves of both pieces are identical). However, here the two parts of the *gat* are more distantly related (A B plus C B[1]). Example 30 is a *pāṅcpallī gat*, *pallī* meaning a 'step' or 'measure', and hence a *gat* which is performed five (*pāṅc*) times 'in ever increasing, but mathematically proportionate densities' (Stewart 1974: 222). Theoretically, any number of repetitions is possible, with two

Mātrā = mm.54-60

	○ ∧	1 ∧ 1	○ 1 ∧	1 ∧ 1
X	dhā – na	dhi ti ṭe	dhā ti ṭe	dhi ti ṭe
	1	23	1	23
	∧	1 ∧ 1	◐	■ ∧
2	kat – ta	dhi ti ṭe	ka tā ga	dī gi na
	×	1	× 1	23
	∇ △	∇ ∧	1 ∧	●
0	nā gi na	nā gi na	ta ki ṭa	ghi nā –
	×	×	×	23
	○ 1 ∧			
3	dhā ti ṭe	dhi ti ṭe	ka tā ga	dī gi na
	1			
	● ○			
X	dhā dhā	nadhi tiṭe	dhāti ṭedhi	tiṭe kat
	1 1			
2	tadhi tiṭe	katā gadī	ginā nagi	nanā gina
0	taki ṭaghi	nā dhāti	ṭedhi tiṭe	katā gadī
		○ 23 1 23 1	○ 1 23 1 23 1	
3	gina dhā	dhā-na dhitiṭe	dhātiṭe dhitiṭe	kat-ta dhitiṭe
				1 23 1 23 1
X	katāga digina	nāgina nāgina	takiṭa ginā-	dhātiṭe dhitiṭe
2	katāga digina		dhā – dhā nadha	

tiṭe dhati ṭedhi tiṭe   kat tadhi tiṭe kata

0 gadi gina nagi nana   gina taki ṭagi nā

dhati ṭedhi tiṭe kata   gadi gina dhā –

1 23 1 23

3 dhā–na dhitiṭi dhatiṭi dhitiṭi   kat–ta dhitiṭi kataga digina

1

nagina nagina tak–gi nā   dhatiṭi dhitiṭi kataga digina

O

X [dhatiṭi dhitiṭi kataga digina | dhatiṭi dhitiṭi kataga digina

dhā –]

Example 30. *Pāṅcpallī gat* or *uṭhān* (*tīntāl*)

and three being quite common, though four and five are more rare. But there are problems with this definition because, although Afaq Husain referred to this piece as a *pāṅcpallī gat* to avoid confusion, he claimed it to be nothing more than a *dūpallī* (two *pallīs*) as it was not the different densities of the strokes of each *pallī* that mattered but rather their different *chands*. Here the phrases are set in just two *chands*: *dādrā chand* (triple time and its multiples) and *kaharwā chand* (duple time and its multiples).

Afaq Husain occasionally played Example 30 at the beginning of a solo tabla performance, in which case he used the term *uṭhān*, not *gat*. *Uṭhān* literally means 'getting up' or 'rising', and is the name commonly given to any large, fixed composition played either as an introduction to the tabla solos of musicians in the Purab *gharānās*, or as the first piece in instrumental accompaniment that serves to introduce the tabla player to the audience. (Lucknow musicians also frequently use the shorter *mohrā* or *mukhṛā* as an introduction.) An *uṭhān* must contain a long *tihā'ī*, and so in order to 'convert' this *pāṅcpallī gat* into an *uṭhān*, a *tihā'ī-bandīsh* derived from the fourth phrase of the *gat* composition has been appended.

There are a number of *gat* structures that correspond to neither of the two described in

Examples 29 and 30. Most are *farmā'ishī* pieces composed in response to requests for the inclusion of specific technical features: among these are the *dūhattī gat* (two-handed), *mañjhe-dhār gat* (mid-stream), *fard* (individual), and *akāl gat* (untimely). Each type is well represented in the Lucknow repertoire. Permission was granted for the notation of one short *akāl gat* (Example 31) that is particularly remarkable for its conciseness. The characteristic feature of all *akāl gats* is their premature termination one or two *mātrās* before the *sam*. To emphasise their somewhat sudden ending, the *sam* of the following *āvartan* is invariably left silent, whether in spoken recitation or in performance. Furthermore, the final *bol* of the *gat* is never *dhā*, but instead may be either *kat*, as demonstrated here, or *dī*. Example 31 also incorporates some rare strokes played by the *bāyāñ* hand on the *dāhinā*, including one played at the same time as a *dāhinā* stroke.

Mātrā = 224-264

			∇		∇	B ∇	ℬ 1	
X	ghin	–	nan	–	na	ga	ti	ṭe
	ℬ							

	ℬ 1			1	ℬ 1			
2	kṛa	dhet	–	dhī	ki	ṭa	ghe	ge
	×⌣ 1			1			ℬ 1	

	ℬ 1				B A ∇			
0	ti	ṭe	ghe	ge	nā	–	–	–
			ℬ 1					

	▼		●					
3	dhin	–	tā	–	kat	–	–	–
	□				×			

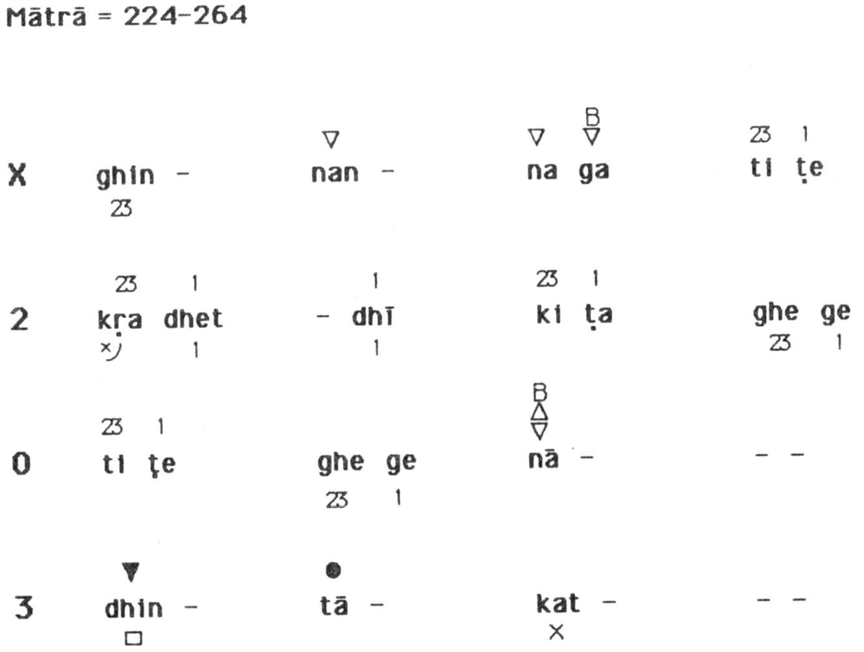

Example 31. *Akāl gat* (*tīntāl*)

Lastly, I have noted a *gat* which incorporates a *tihā'ī* (Example 32). The case for *tihā'īs* in *gats* is a contentious issue as many tabla players throughout India believe that any set composition which ends with a *tihā'ī* should not, by rights, be termed a *gat* at all. Inam Ali of Delhi called this piece a *ṭukṛā*, while others settled for a compromise and entitled it *gat-ṭukṛā*, a term with no meaning according to Lucknow musicians. Afaq Husain's immediate response to this kind of criticism was simply to reel off a dozen or so *gats* that included a variety of *tihā'ī* structures. *Tihā'īs*, he claimed, were a feature of some Lucknow *gats* and this was yet another of the main differences between the Delhi and Lucknow traditions, whose historical rivalry has been the underlying cause of many innovations in technique and composition.

Example 32 exhibits a wide range of *bols* and apparently unrelated phrases. In fact, it is perhaps difficult to identify the logic behind the structure of this piece without analysing it in

Mātrā = mm.120–132

X	▼ dhī –kṛa 1 ♪	▼ ● dhin dhā 1 —	∧ – tit	● dhā – 1
2	∧ kat ti ×	I ● ṭe ta	△ ▽ ghin tarā 1234	∧ ● –na dhā 1
0	▽ △ ▽ nagi nana ×	△ ▽ gina naga × ×	∧ I ● tite kata ×	△ ▽ ghin tarā 1234
3	∧ ● –na dhā 1	▣ tī ghin 1234	∧ – ta	● dhā – 1
X	● ∨ ● dhā kṛadña 1 ♪ 1	▼ ● ● dhintā kata — ×	△ ▽ ghin tarā 1234	∧ ● ▼ –na dhāti 1
2	∧ I kat tiṭe ×	● dhā – 1	∧ ● kṛa dhā ×♪ 1	▣ tī ghin □
0	∧ – tā	○ dhā 1		

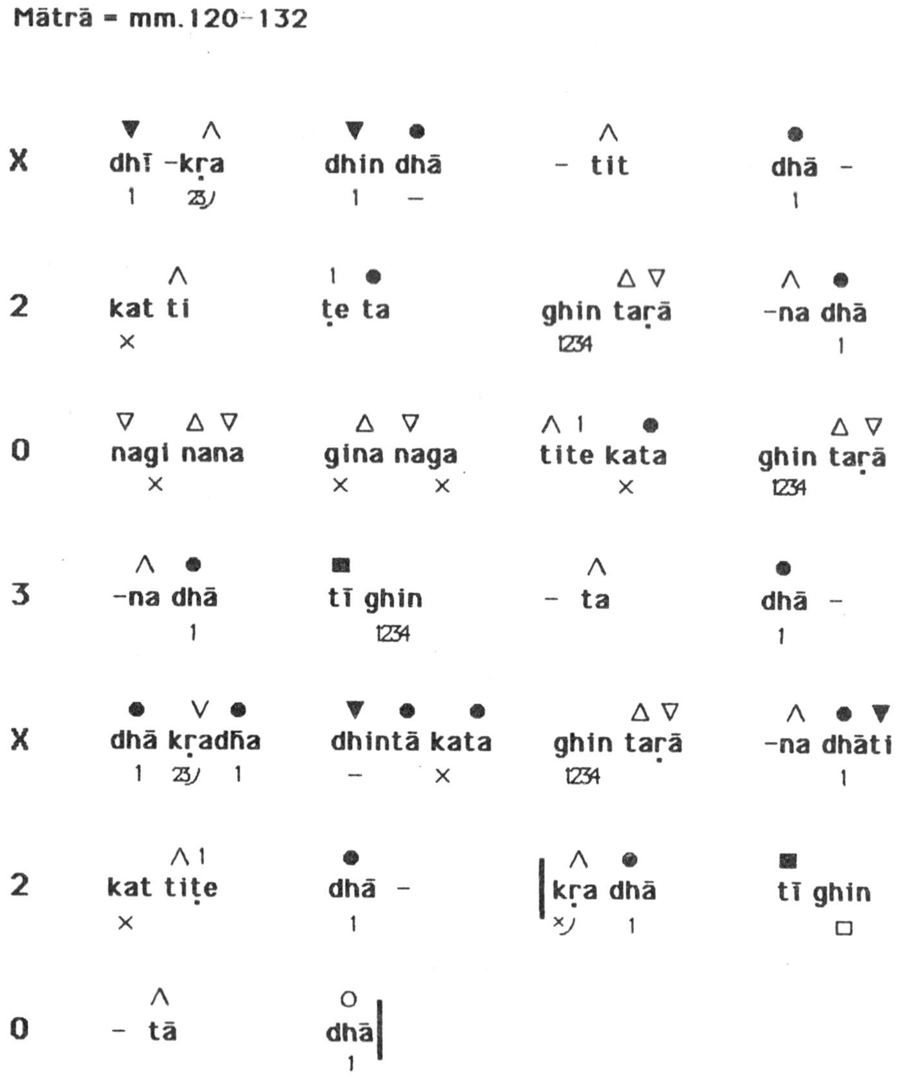

Example 32. *Gat* (*tīntāl*)

some detail. It is important to note that most compositions fall into 'families' within the confines of a particular form. This *gat*, attributed to Abid Husain, is one of a number of *gats* derived from a 'parent' *gat* whose phrases have been arranged and rearranged in many different ways. Some of these arrangements have resulted in simple, two-part *gats* similar in structure to Example 28, while others have developed into more complex pieces, including *akāl gats* and *gats* with *tihā'īs*. At one level, the musical material presented in the first *āvartan* of Example 32 may be broken down into compound phrases covering four, four, two and six *mātrās*. What then follows in the second *āvartan* is a concise summary of the first: for example, the essence of the opening four-*mātrā* phrase has been compressed into two *mātrās*, while elements from other phrases are similarly fused. The concluding *tihā'ī* is derived from the last phrase of the first *āvartan* prefixed by the *bol kṛa*, which is one of the characteristic touches in this family of *gats*.

Ṭukṛā

Ṭukṛā, meaning a 'piece' or 'morsel', is a fixed composition whose *bol* repertoire derives largely from *pakhāwaj* strokes and phrases, such as *tiṭe katā gadī gina dhā* and *dhiṭe dhiṭe*. Non-resonating strokes are more prominent here than in *gats*, in particular *tiṭe*, *dhit* and *kat*, while the resonating stroke *tā* is almost always played on the *sūr*.

Structurally, *ṭukṛās* are quite straightforward. They consist of an arrangement of blocks of material followed by any manner of *tihā'ī*, which need not be derived from the preceding material. In theory, therefore, *ṭukṛās* are relatively easy to compose. Afaq Husain taught his disciples (by example, not verbally) to devise a sequence of blocks and then to add a *tihā'ī* formula. Either the blocks or the *tihā'īs* (sometimes both) could then be adjusted to make the piece fit the *tāl*. An exercise he often set his disciples was to give an established *ṭukṛā* which they had to rearrange to fit *tāls* other than that in which the parent *ṭukṛā* was based.

Example 33 shows a *ṭukṛā* which concludes with a simple *tihā'ī*, while Example 34 ends with a *tihā'ī kī tihā'ī*. Both are old compositions from the Lucknow repertoire, and Afaq

Mātrā = mm.240–264

X	23 1 dhi ṭe 1	23 1 dhi ṭe –	● dhā ge 1 23	23 1 ti ṭe
2	23 1 kṛa dhi ×/ 1	23 1 ti ṭe	● dhā ge 1 23	23 1 ti ṭe
0	● dhā ge 1 23	∨ ● na dhā 1	■ ga dī 23	∧ gi na 1
3	▽ nā ge ×	∧ 1 ti te	● ka tā ×	● | ka tā ×
X	● ka tā ×	● – dhā 1	▼ ● dhin dha – –	∧ ka ṭa ×
2	● dhā – | 1			

Example 33. *Ṭukṛā* (*tīntāl*)

Mātrā = mm.132-160

X	∧ 1 dhi ṭi 1	● tā kat ×	● – tā	dhi ṭi
2	tā kat	– tā	▽ ghe nā 23	∧ 1 ti ṭe
0	● dha – 1	● – dhā 1	∧ 1 ti ṭe	∧ 1 ti ṭe
3	● dhā – 1	■ ga dī 23	∧ gi na 1	● dhā – 23
X	[○ 1 23 1 dhāti ṭedhi 1 23	23 1 ● tiṭe kata ×	■ ∧ gadi gina 1 23	● ∧ dhā tit 1
2	● dhā – | 23	– –	– –]	

Example 34. *Ṭukṛā* (*tīntāl*)

Husain no longer remembered their originators. The second is interesting in that it was evidently designed to deceive the listener into thinking that the *tihā'ī* had fallen short of the *sam*, for the first time it appears the phrase ends on the fifteenth *mātrā*. Only when the *tihā'ī* is repeated does the listener realise that he is listening to a *tihā'ī kī tihā'ī*.

Uṭhān

I have already noted, when commenting on Example 30, that *uṭhān* is the name given to any large, fixed, introductory composition. Although these pieces are frequently similar in nature to *ṭukṛās*, any kind of fixed composition can be used. Thus the word *uṭhān* describes the function of the piece and not its form; it affords the tabla player a dramatic entry into a performance, and so the tendency is for the composition to be fairly extensive and for the *tihā'ī* to be long and complex. All manner of strokes and phrases may be incorporated into the composition, a feature which tends to give the *uṭhān* a variegated complexion. For instance, Example 35, composed by Afaq Husain in 1983, includes a mixture of technical styles which

Mātrā = mm.44-52

```
      ●    ●    1   ∧           ●
X   dhā -dhā -ta kiṭa          dhā -ta kiṭa taki
     1    23       ×             1

                              V ●     23 1   23  1    ●  23 1   V
        ṭadhā -ta kiṭa dhā    kiṛanaga tirakiṭa takatā- tirakiṭa
                               ×       ×       ×       ×      ×

      ●    ∧ 1 ●                 ∧ 1  ●
2   tā  -  tiṭe tā             - dhiṭe dhā  -
                                   1    –

                  ▼ o            V o     2 1   V  o   o
        tiṭe tā - dhīnā          kiṛanaga tirakiṭa takatā-  -
                   1              ×       ×       ×       ×

    ∧ 1  ●  ∧  1   ●
0   tiṭe tā dhiṭe dhā             tiṭe tā dhiṭe dhā
             1     –

        kati ṭetā -dhi ṭidhā    kati ṭetā -dhi ṭidhā
         ×

    o
3   nāna nanā nana nāna          nāna nanā nana nāna
     ×      ×      ×

         o        o              ■        ■           ■
        tātā tā dhādhā dhā    |dhin- [ge]dhin  -[ge]  dhin
         ×        1             1 /  23     1   / 23     1

      V ●     23 1   V ●  234   23 1   V        ●    ●
X   kiṛanaga tirakiṭa takataka tirakiṭa      dhā -tā kiṛanaga tirakiṭa
     ×        ×        ×      ×  ×      ×         1

      takataka tirakiṭa dhā -tā     kiṛanaga tirakiṭa takataka tirakiṭa

2   dhā  -  -  -  |
```

Example 35. *Uṭhān* (*tīntāl*)

may best be illustrated by the three different fingerings of the phrase *kiṛanaga tirakiṭa takatā-*. It may be seen that the bulk of the material in this *uṭhān* is derived from just a few phrases, and yet these are presented in a number of different guises which help create considerable variety within the piece. The treatment of *tiṭetā* is a good illustration as it not only appears in both its *khulī* and *band* forms but it is also used to accentuate different fractions of the beat. The repetition of *nā* in the third *vibhāg* is curious because it appears to be a way of 'marking time' before the beginning of the *tihā'ī*. But Afaq Husain did not see it this way. He liked the sound effect, which he enhanced by stressing certain strokes in order to group the string rhythmically into three plus three plus two.

Mohrā

Mohrā literally means the 'front'. In the Delhi tabla *gharānā* it is traditionally the first piece to be performed, and hence it stands at the 'front' of a tabla solo. It is also occasionally used by Lucknow *gharānā* musicians.

Mohrā is structurally identical to *ṭukṛā*, but is distinguishable by three factors: firstly, it is very short, occupying no more than a single *āvartan*; secondly, it relies mainly upon rapidly articulated non-resonating *bols* prevalent in phrases such as *tiṭekiṛanaga* (or *tirakiṭataka*); and thirdly, *tā* as performed on the *kinār* is invariably used, in contrast to *ṭukṛās*, where the *sūr* predominates. Example 36 is set out as it would be played in *drut tīntāl*. Should this piece appear at the beginning of a tabla solo performance, it would fill only the final *vibhāg* of *vilambit tīntāl* (*mātrā* = mm. 48–52).

Mātrā = mm. 192–208

	▼ o	V o	o 2 1	V o
X	dhī nā	kiṛa naga	tā tiṭe	kiṛa naga
	23	V Λ	V	V Λ
	2 1 V	o o	2 1 V	o
2	tira kiṭa	taka tā	tira kiṭa	tā -
	×	×	×	
	o o		Λ	o
0	tā dhā	- | ghin	- ta	dhā - |
	1	23		1

Example 36. *Mohrā* (*tīntāl*)

Cakkardār

The word *cakkardār* means 'having circles'. It describes a fixed composition with appended *tihā'ī*, the whole of which is in turn played three times. Thus, figuratively speaking, it 'goes round in circles' until it finally resolves onto the *sam* of an *āvartan*.

One feature distinguishes *cakkardārs* in the Lucknow repertoire from those of all other *gharānās*. Lucknow musicians believe that it is compulsory for a *cakkardār* to undergo at least one change of *chand*, changes which may clearly be seen in Examples 37 and 38. Any structurally similar piece displaying a single *chand* is not a *cakkardār*, according to Afaq Husain. His term for such a piece was a '*cakkardār*-style *ṭukṛā*' or a '*cakkardār*-style *gat*'.

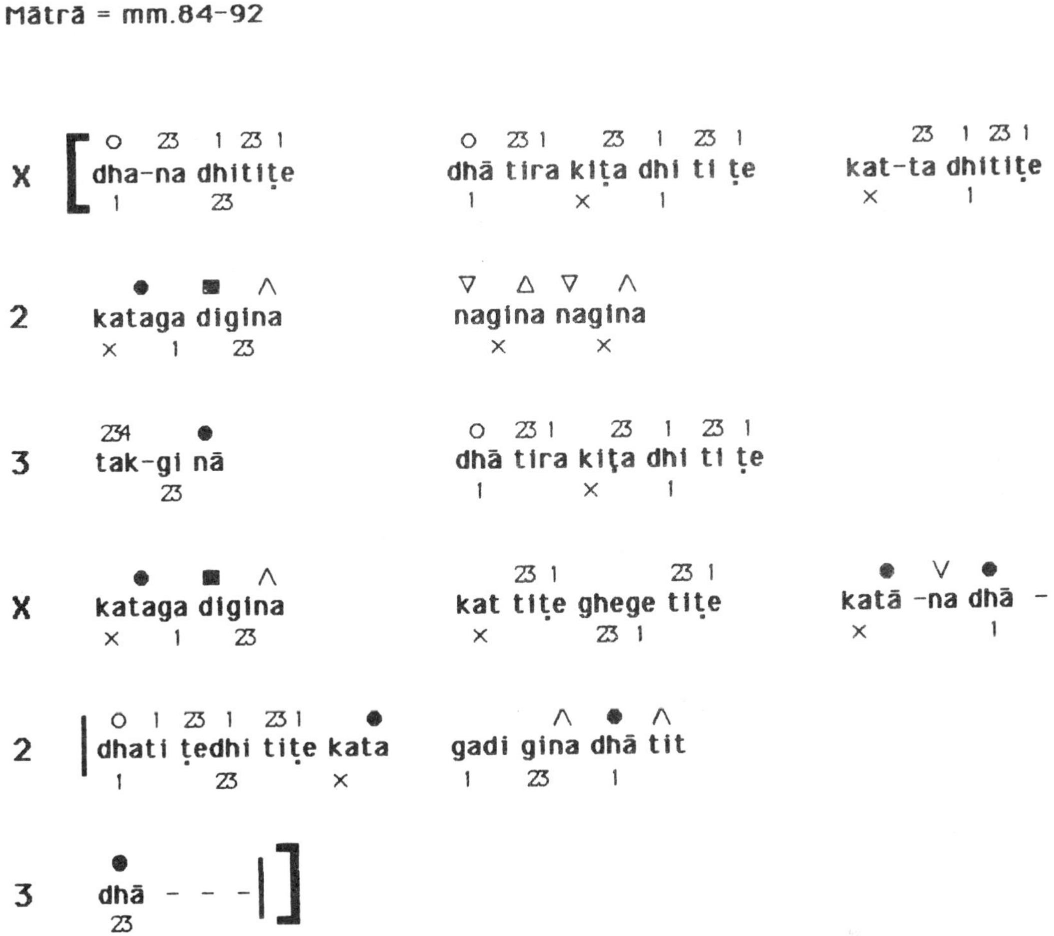

Example 37. *Cakkardār (rūpak)*

Example 37 is a simple *cakkardār* set in *rūpak tāl*. The phrases presented in *dādrā chand* in the opening eight *mātrās* of this piece are derived directly from those given in the basic *gat* of Example 30. To these have been added two phrases in *kaharwā chand* covering two and three *mātrās* respectively. The latter provides a link with the *dādrā chand* material while also functioning as the *tihā'ī* phrase. This is an excellent example of the way in which established compositions are manipulated to fit the structures of other *tāls*.

Example 38 displays a more complex structure based once again on the now familiar material of Example 30 that not only fills the first *āvartan* but is rearranged and repeated at double speed during the course of the second. It was composed by Afaq Husain. The

Mātrā = mm.112-120

X	dhā – na	dhi ti ṭe	dhā ti ṭe	dhi ti ṭe
2	kat – ta	dhi ti ṭe	ka tā ga	dī gi na
0	nā gi na	nā gi na	ta ki ṭa	ghi nā –
3	dhā ti ṭe	dhi ti ṭe	ka tā ga	dī gi na
X	kat tiṭe	ghege tiṭe	katā –na	dhā –
2	katī ṭetā	kata dhit	taghiṅ –na	dhā –
0	kat-ta dhitiṭe	kataga digina	dhatiṭe dhitiṭe	kataga digina
3	nagina nagina	tak-gi nā	dhatiṭe dhitiṭe	kataga digina
X	dhā –	– –		

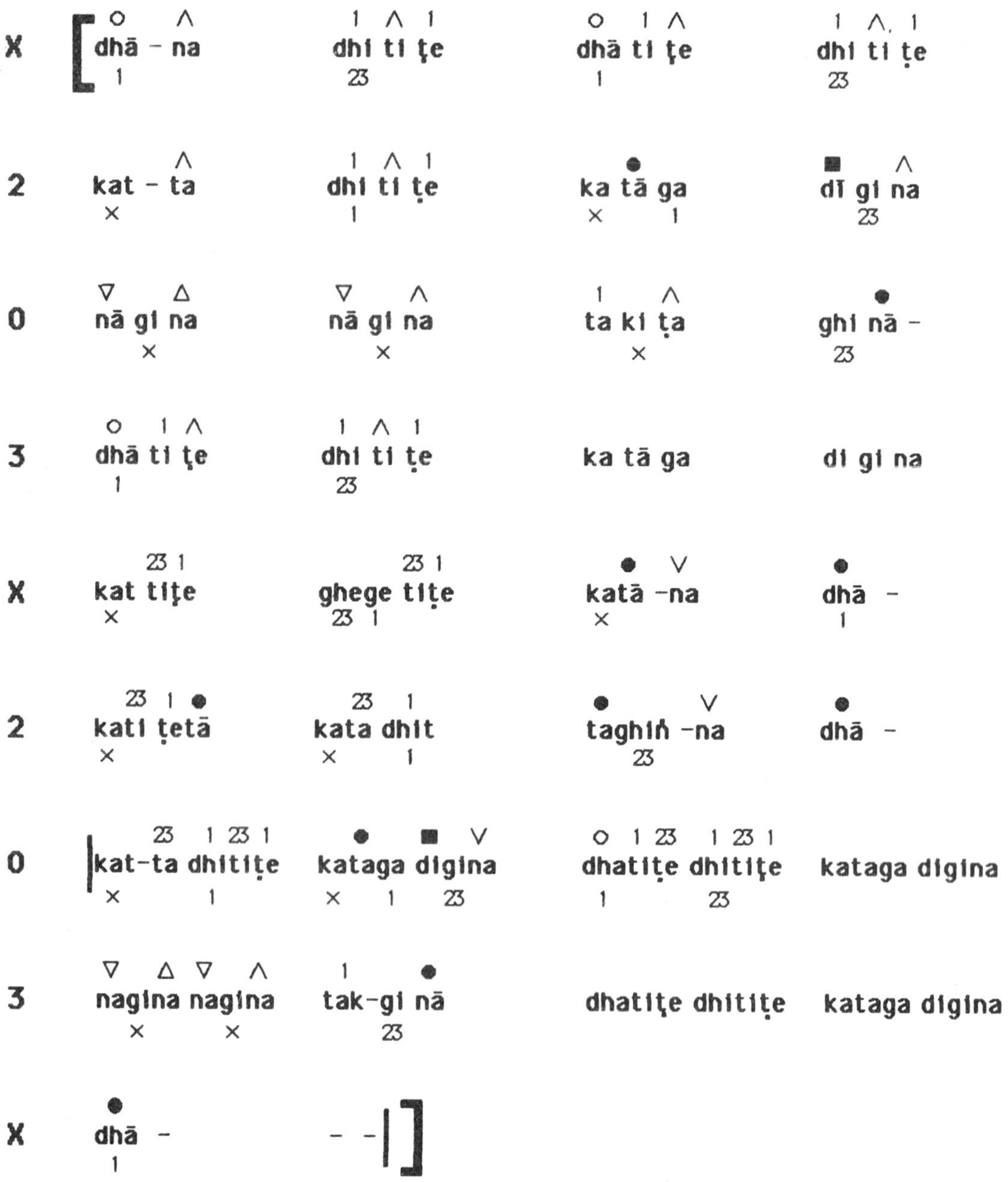

Example 38. *Farmā'ishī cakkardār* (*tīntāl*)

farmā'ishī structure displayed here is commonly referred to as *kamālī*, meaning a skilful feat, or a perfect and wonderful thing. The requirements for a *kamālī cakkardār* are as follows: when the *tihā'ī* first appears, its first phrase should end on *sam*; when played a second time, its second phrase should end on *sam*; lastly, on the third and final appearance of the *tihā'ī*, its third phrase should end on *sam* and so conclude the piece. Although Example 38 has been notated as it would be played in medium tempo, it may be played in slow (*mātrā* = mm. 56–60) or fast (mm. 224–40) tempo without destroying its special *farmā'ishī* feature.

Paran

The meaning of *paran* is obscure, although it may be derived from the Hindi *par* meaning 'a wing', and so would be taken to imply something that 'flies' in quick time. It is a composition that belongs to the *pakhāwaj* tradition, where it appears in a great variety of forms. Few of these have been incorporated into the repertoires of tabla *gharānās*, although the Benares repertoire contains by far the greatest variety of *parans*.

Most *parans* came into the Lucknow repertoire by way of *kathak* dance. Many *kathak parans* are themselves based on *pakhāwaj* compositions and it is therefore the *kathak* versions of these pieces that are known to Lucknow tabla players. Consequently, the tabla strokes used to articulate them do not necessarily represent the spoken *bols* but follow a different aesthetic, that of dance movements and gestures. This is clearly illustrated in Example 39,

Mātrā = mm. 160–184

X	● dhā - 1	● ● dhā tā 23	■ kā thuṅ 1	● gā - –
2	● dhā ge 1 23	■ dhīṅ ge – 1	● tā -	● ■ dhā dhin 1 23
0	● tā -	∧ ● dhet tā 1	∧ ● kiṛa dhā × 1	234 ● tak kā –
3	■ ● thuṅ gā –	1 ta ki ×	∧ 1 ṭa ta	● kā - –
X	ta ki	ṭa ta	kā -	ta ki
2	ṭa ta	kā -	∧ tā -	● dhā - 1

	^	1	●	
0	ti -	ṭe ka	- ta	gā -
		×		1
	■	^	●	23 1
3	di gi	- na	dhā -	ti ṭe
	23		1	
	●	■	^	●
X	ka ta	ga di	gi na	dhā -
	×	1	23	1
	23 1 ●	■ ^	● ^	●
2	| tiṭe kata	gadi gina	dhā tit	dhā -
	×	1 23	1	23
0	- |			

Example 39. *Paran (tīntāl)*

where *gā* and *kā*, which usually correspond to resonating and non-resonating *bāyān* strokes respectively, are both played as *tā* on the *sūr*. However, some *pakhāwaj* strokes not normally used in tabla-playing, such as *dhumakiṭa* (see Example 40), are maintained intact.

Mātrā = mm.288–320

	●	●	■	●
X	| dhā	dhā	dhin	tā
	23	1	23	
2	-	dhā	dhin	tā
0	-	dhā	dhin	tā
	^			
3	kṛa	dhā	dhin	tā
	×)			

X	1 taki ×	23 ṭata	kiṭa	1 dhit 1
2	● tagin 23	23 -na	1 dhit 1	● tā
0	∧ kra ×ⱼ	1 dhit 1	● tā	–
3	⊗ dhuma □	23 kiṭa ×	1 taka ×	● dhā 1
X	–	∧ tā	● dhā 1	–
2	23 1 tiṭe	● kata ×	■ gadi 1	∧ gina 23
0	● dhā 1	tiṭe	kata	gadi
3	gina	dhā	tiṭe	kata
X	gadi	gina	● dhā 1	● dhā 23
2	● dhā 1	– |		

Example 40. *Paran* (*tīntāl*)

Afaq Husain identified a *paran* either by its use of *bols* such as *dhumakiṭa*, or by recognising established *pakhāwaj* phrases such as *dhātā kāthuṅ gā* and *kiṭa taka thuṅ thuṅ*. The structure of any piece was thereafter irrelevant to him; they were all *parans*. Example 39 somewhat resembles a *ṭukṛā* in structure, whereas Example 40 is almost a *cakkardār* except that the short *tihā'ī* phrase has been modified to end with three *dhās* instead of one. Afaq Husain would of course also argue that Example 40 could not be termed a *cakkardār* as it is based on a single *chand*.

Parans such as these are rarely used in Lucknow tabla solos. Afaq Husain taught them to disciples who were training to accompany *kathak* dance recitals. His purpose was to prepare them for the different demands on technique and musical interpretation imposed by the nature of *kathak*.

Conclusion

The main conclusions arising from this study of a musical tradition in the specific socio-cultural context of Lucknow, as well as in the wider context of North Indian musical life, may best be set out as a series of four points.

Firstly, I have identified and documented something of the uniqueness of the music of the Lucknow tabla *gharānā*, a tradition shaped both by the artistic rivalry it enjoyed with the Delhi tradition and by the stylistic exigencies of accompanying *ghazal*, *ṭhumrī* and *kathak* dance. I have described many features of performance technique, and have notated examples from the repertoire of the *gharānā*. I have also explained some of the methods used to compose and improvise in an attempt to demystify these processes. I have observed that they involve logical and highly systematised procedures, an understanding of which has led me to question Neuman's (1974: 297) conclusion that 'a musical system is arbitrary . . . and fundamentally irrational'. As a musical entity, the tradition of the *gharānā* is not fixed. What I have presented is essentially Ustād Afaq Husain Khan's version of the Lucknow tradition: the inevitable result of his own personal preferences for certain musical forms and techniques. There are indeed compositions in his repertoire whose origins stretch back about two hundred years to his forefather and founder member of the *gharānā*, Miyan Bakhshu Khan, but I have shown that *ta'līm* is not static; rather, it is specifically designed to incorporate musical and technical evolution. Had I studied thirty years ago with Khalifa Wajid Husain, I might have learned a rather different Lucknow tradition. And no doubt in thirty years time Ilmas Husain will have developed new ideas according to his own musical tastes, and will teach some new techniques, compositions and methods of improvising alongside many of those developed by his forefathers. The musical tradition, then, is really a reservoir of knowledge from which each individual may draw selectively, and to which each may contribute new ideas that result from varying interpretations of the tradition. In other words, the material presented here is the musical tradition of the Lucknow tabla *gharānā* largely as interpreted by Afaq Husain during the first half of the 1980s.

Secondly, my data has shown that, as social entities, *gharānās* do exist as units of social organisation for certain groups of tabla players. What is more, I would argue that from the evidence pertaining to social organisation presented in this study, *gharānā* is the predominant concept among tabla players. This is contrary to the findings by Neuman, who, by imposing his own analytical model of social structure in an attempt to explain a particular situation he encountered in Delhi, failed to account for the fact that different people at different times and in different places appear to hold ideas that are greatly at variance with those he chose to emphasise. In particular, I have questioned Neuman's insistence that it is the *birādarī* which constitutes the primary unit of social organisation for tabla players. My own approach has focused upon the folk view of social structure and organisation, and consequently I have found that for most tabla players, especially those of Lucknow, the word *gharānā* is polysemic and is valid both as a technical and as a colloquial term for their social groups and their styles of playing. *Birādarī*, on the other hand, is never used except, it seems, by certain tabla players in Delhi for whom, I would argue, it is secondary to notions of the *gharānā*.

Thirdly, there is a need to reappraise certain kinds of information. There has been a tendency with scholars of Indian music to treat genealogical and historical data as factual statements. In many cases they may indeed be just that. But what my studies have suggested is that it is often more valuable, not to say frequently more accurate, to treat information concerning the genealogy and history of musicians and their families as statements about present-day situations. Thus, rather than representing a real event in history, or a real relationship between musicians or families, 'facts' such as these may be political statements of pedigree or allegiance which have considerably greater relevance to contemporary issues. These findings confirm the social anthropological view that culture is neither fixed nor inflexible. Rather, it is a floating resource which may be manipulated by individuals or groups to suit their own special interests at any given time.

Lastly, my data has shown that studying a particular music in the traditional manner within the *gharānā* and under the guidance of *gharānedār* musicians, whom Maitra has called 'the real custodians of the cultural heritage of Indian Music' (1977: 23), is a process involving much more than simply learning a musical system. Learning music is in fact a total system, the musical and social aspects of which are fully integrated. Indian musicians are not willing to divest themselves of their tradition unless pupils first prove themselves worthy of receiving it. A student's initiation or acceptance into discipleship is therefore an important rite of passage to a musical and social situation in which the very best training may be received. Not only does Afaq Husain teach his disciples techniques and compositions; equally important for him is the development of their characters. In short, disciples learn to adopt sets of musical and social values that inevitably reflect the values of their *ustād* or *gurū*.

Afaq Husain's values were largely incompatible with the modern world of North Indian classical music. They were more suited to a bygone age of princely patronage in which musical knowledge and skills were evidently highly prized by select and sophisticated audiences. It was the abundance of this patronage and enthusiasm that made Lucknow a major centre for music and the arts from the late eighteenth to the early twentieth centuries. The city's decline has been dramatic, and now it may justifiably be thought of as little more than a musical backwater. During many a conversation, Afaq Husain compared and contrasted past situations with those of the present, and we can see from several of his statements that he perceived there to be many parallels between the decline of Lucknow and the decline in popularity of musical traditions such as his own. He knew that his playing, though highly acclaimed by other musicians and connoisseurs, was seldom appreciated by modern mass audiences. However, he did not personally wish to make compromises with his art despite believing that a certain degree of compromise was a necessary ingredient of success in the modern era. The modern patrons of music constituted a largely unsophisticated audience that responded not so much to knowledge and skill, but rather to musical trivia, superficial gimmicks, and even to the appearance and demeanour of artists on stage. To cater to those tastes was anathema to him.

The socio-cultural climate that is needed to sustain the kind of musical tradition that Afaq Husain believed in and wished to perpetuate has long since disappeared. But if, as I have suggested, *gharānās* are essentially about individuals who remould their musical traditions according to their own particular preferences, then it very much depends on how the next generation of practitioners can cope with, and adapt to, the modern world of North Indian classical music. Afaq Husain wanted his musical tradition to survive because he believed it had something very valuable to offer, not only to other musicians and scholars, but also to the general listening public. This was the basis of his teaching. Yet, in practical terms, the survival of such a tradition, and others like it, may well depend upon the willingness of future generations to make significant musical compromises.

Glossary

Indigenous terms are explained when they first appear in the text. Only words used more than once are listed here.

akāl 'Untimely'. A variety of tabla *gat*, particular to the Lucknow *gharānā*, that ends before the *sam*

ālāp Exposition of the *rāg* without rhythmic accompaniment

āṭhgun 'Eight times'; the division of the beat into eight equal parts

āvartan One complete cycle of a *tāl*

azān The call to prayer for Muslims

baddhī A thong of uncured buffalo hide, used for tying and tightening the drumheads of the tabla

bāj Style of playing

band 'Closed'. Denoting that a tabla *bol*, string of *bols*, or section (i.e. *vibhāg*) is played using non-resonating strokes on the *bāyāṅ*

bandīsh Something that is 'bound'. A 'set composition' in tabla

bandīsh-ṭhumrī A style of *ṭhumrī* cultivated in Lucknow (syn. *bol-bāṅṭ ṭhumrī*)

bāṅṭ Theme-and-variations tabla composition common in Benares and not dissimilar to the Lucknow *chand*

barābar Equal rhythm or time (syn. *ṭhā*)

bastanī Cloth tied round the waist for holding the tabla when playing in a standing position

bāyāṅ The 'left-hand' drum, or bass drum of the tabla drum set (lit. left)

bedam Without a pause or gap

bhā'ī Brother

bhajan Hindu devotional song

bīn North Indian plucked stick zither with resonating gourds at each end

birādarī A 'brotherhood', from the Persian *birādar* meaning brother

bol A syllable representing drum strokes, or the stroke itself

cakkardār A fixed composition in tabla

cāl 'Gait'. A manner of walking or moving in *kathak* dance that often introduces a character being portrayed in a *gat bhā'o*. Also used for a *laggī* played in accompaniment to the *cāl*

calan A theme-and-variations tabla composition

capaknewālā 'The one that sticks'. Used to describe a particular stroke in tabla

caugun 'Four times'; the division of the beat into four equal parts, or quadruplets

chand A theme-and-variations tabla composition. Also a rhythm or repeated rhythmic device

chegun 'Six times'; the division of the beat into six equal parts, or sextolets

choṭā khayāl See *khayāl*

cillā A period of forty days. The discipline of organised musical practice over a period of at least forty days
dādrā The name of a *tāl* of six beats. Also a light vocal style employing that *tāl*
dāhinā The 'right-hand' drum of the tabla drum set (lit. right)
dangal A wrestling match. Sometimes used for a musical competition between two or more musicians
darbār Royal court, hall of audience
da'wat A feast
ḍe'oṛhī 'One and a half times'; the division of two beats into three equal parts
ḍhāṛī A community of musicians (low caste)
ḍholak Barrel-shaped, two-headed drum
dhrupad The most classical vocal style. Also a composition in that style
dom A community of musicians (low caste)
drut Fast tempo
dūgun 'Two times'; the division of the beat into two equal parts, or duplets
dūtāra Bengali (usually) four-stringed short-necked lute used in folk genres
ektāl A *tāl* of twelve beats
farmā'ish An order or request. Traditionally, a request made of a musician for a specific musical item
farmā'ishī That which has been requested, thus 'special'
gajrā The outer ring of the tabla drumhead
ganḍā bandhan 'Thread-tying' ceremony initiating a student into his teacher's close circle of disciples
gat Set composition in tabla. Also an instrumental composition set in *tāl*
gat bhā'o A section falling within a *kathak ṭhumrī* or *bhajan* in which the dancer tells a story in dance and gesture
gaṭṭā Wooden block for tuning the *dāhinā* (plural *gaṭṭē*)
ghar House
gharānā 'Of the house'. A group of hereditary specialists and their prominent disciples with a body of musical knowledge and a distinct style
gharānedār Of the *gharānā*
g͟hazal A poetic form in Urdu. Also a light vocal style sung to the words of the poetry
gintī 'Counting'. Used for tabla compositions (usually *tihā'īs*) that are numerically based
gīt Song
grūp-bāzī 'Group-play'. Another word for 'politics'
gurū A Hindu teacher or master
gurū-bhā'ī 'Brothers under one *gurū*'. Fellow disciples studying under the same *gurū* or *ustād*
gurū-pūrnamā The annual festival day in honour of one's *gurū* or teacher
Hajj The pilgrimage to Mecca
hathauṛī Hammer. Used for tuning the tabla
imāmbāṛā A religious meeting place for members of the Shiah sect. A building in which the festival of Muharram is celebrated, and in which services are held in commemoration of the death of Ali and his sons Hasan and Husain. Also used as a *nawābī* burial place
īṅḍwī Ring on which a drum is placed to keep it steady
jhālā The final section of the *ālāp* or *gat* in instrumental music (usually plucked instruments), characterised by the fast interplay of melody and *cikārī* strings

jhaptāl A *tāl* of ten beats
jor The second section of an *ālāp*, in which a pulse is introduced
joṛā 'Pair', especially a tabla piece composed as a pair for another (plural *joṛē*)
kaharwā The name of a *tāl* of eight beats
kāṭ Wooden, partially hollowed shell of the *dāhinā*
kathak Classical dance of North India. Also a Hindu caste (Kathak) of musicians and dancers hailing from eastern Uttar Pradesh
khālī 'Empty' beat or *vibhāg* of a *tāl*, marked by a wave of the hand
khalīfa The head of the *gharānā*. The oldest performing authority on a *gharānā*'s repertoire and style
khāndān Family, lineage
khāndānī Of the *khāndān*
Khāṅ Sāḥib A polite form of address for a Muslim musician
khayāl The most prevalent classical vocal style in North India. Compositions in that style (*baṛā khayāl*, a slow composition; *choṭā khayāl*, a fast composition)
khulā bāj 'Open style'. Style of tabla-playing found in Lucknow which utilises mainly open, resonating strokes where the fingers do not remain in contact with the drumhead after striking
khulī 'Open'. Denoting that a tabla *bol*, string of *bols*, or section (i.e. *vibhāg*) is played using resonating strokes on the *bāyāṅ*
kinār The outer portion of the three sections of the *puṛī*
kiṅgrī A folk fiddle
koṭhī Large house, mansion
laggī A theme-and-variations tabla composition, frequently used to accompany *ghazal*, *ṭhumrī* and *kathak*
lahrā A melody lasting one cycle of a given *tāl*, used to accompany drum solos
laṛant 'Fighting'. A style of tabla accompaniment in which the tabla player plays compositions or improvises simultaneously with the soloist
lay The concept of rhythm. Commonly, pulse or tempo
laydār Used to describe a musician who has good rhythmic facility
laykārī Rhythmic play, especially complex divisions of the beat
madhya Medium tempo
madhyam The fourth note of the scale, *mā*
maḥfil An intimate gathering, especially for the performance of music
maidān The middle portion of the three sections of the *puṛī*
majlis Assembly, congregation, especially for a religious meeting
mann A measure of weight of about 80 lb
marṣiya A poetic form in Urdu
mātam A chant of mourning performed by Shiites in small or large groups. Performers beat their breasts in rhythmic accompaniment
mātrā The unit of time. One beat or the duration between two beats
mīrāṣī Muslim 'caste' of musicians (low status)
miṭhās Sweetness. A quality of sound production recognised as a trait of the Lucknow tabla *gharānā*
mohalla A residential quarter of a city

mohrā A fixed composition related to *ṭukṛā* in the tabla repertoire
mu'azzin One who recites the call to prayer for Muslims
Muharram 'The sacred month'. The first month of the Muslim year (held sacred particularly by Shiites on account of the death of Husain, son of Ali)
mujrā A session of music and/or dance in the house of a courtesan
mukhṛā A short, often improvised flourish of tabla *bols* to herald the *sam* of the *āvartan*
muqābala Competition
mushā'ara Poetic symposium
nāl Barrel-shaped, two-headed drum used in folk genres
naqqāra A pair of hemispherical drums played with sticks
nau kī tihā'ī 'A *tihā'ī* of nine'. A *tihā'ī* set within another *tihā'ī*
nawāb Governor or viceroy. Also, a king
nazrāna A gift of money to one's teacher
nikās Technique
pakhāwaj Large, barrel-shaped, two-headed tuned drum of North India, used both to accompany *dhrupad* and as a solo instrument
pakhāwajī A *pakhāwaj* player
pallī 'Step' or 'measure'. Refers to a statement of a phrase in a tabla *gat* which is then repeated a number of times at different speeds
palṭā A variation derived from any theme-and-variations tabla composition. In vocal music, or melodic instrumental music, a kind of *tān* based on exercise patterns
pān Betel nut and leaf
pancam The fifth note of the scale, *pa*
paran A fixed composition found in *pakhāwaj* music and in *kathak* dance. Sometimes played on the tabla, particularly in the Benares tradition
parda A curtain, or the veil. The seclusion of women
paune-dūgun 'One and three-quarter times'; the division of four beats into seven equal parts
peṅc A variation derived from a theme-and-variations tabla composition
peshkār 'Presentation'. A type of theme-and-variations tabla composition
puṛī The drumhead
qā'ida A theme-and-variations tabla composition from which variations are derived by permuting, repeating and substituting elements of the original composition
qā'ida-relā A *qā'ida* that utilises rapidly articulated strokes such as those commonly used in playing *relā*
qawwālī Muslim devotional song
rabāb 1. Indian *rabāb*: a long-necked, unfretted lute with wooden top (now extinct). 2. Afghan *rabāb*: a short-necked, fretted lute with skin top
rabābiya A *rabāb* player
rāg The melodic system of Hindustani music as a whole. Also a particular melodic 'mode' (fem. *rāginī*)
Ramadan The ninth month of the Muslim year, the month of fasting
rang 'Colour'. A theme-and-variations tabla composition similar to *relā* in structure. Peculiar to the Lucknow *gharānā*
rang-relā A theme-and-variations tabla composition which is a cross between a *rang* and a *rela*

relā 'Torrent', 'rushing stream'. A theme-and-variations tabla composition which uses rapidly articulated strokes

riyāẓ Musical practice

rūpak A *tāl* of seven beats

sam The first *mātrā* of an *āvartan*

santūr North Indian (Kashmiri) dulcimer, struck with light hammers

sāraṅgī The main bowed instrument of North India

sarod A lute with skin top and steel plate fingerboard. Possibly developed from the Afghan *rabāb*

sātgun 'Seven times'; the division of the beat into seven equal parts

sāth saṅgat 'Together accompaniment'. A style of tabla accompaniment in which the tabla player plays compositions or improvises simultaneously with the soloist (syn. *laṛant*)

sawā'ī 'One and a quarter times'; the division of the beat into five equal parts

shaḍj The first note of the scale, *sā*

shāgird Disciple

shauq Enthusiasm, passion

sherwānī Long tailored coat with high collar

shijrā A genealogical tree

shishya Disciple

sīdhā Straight, plain

sitār Long-necked lute of North India

sīyahī A black spot, made of paste and iron filings, placed on a drumhead to give it pitch and resonance

soz A lament, set in a *rāg*, and 'read' (i.e. sung) by Shiites during the month of Muharram

soz-k͟hwān A 'reader' of *soz*

soz-k͟hwānī *Soz* 'reading'

sūr Sound. A musical pitch. Also a collective term for the *maidān* and *siyāhī* portions of the *puṛī*

surbahār A bass *sitār*

surshriṅgār A bass version of the Indian *rabāb* (now extinct), with a wooden top

tak͟ht Raised wooden platform or bed

tāl The system of rhythm in Indian music as a whole. Also a particular metric cycle

tālī 'Clap'. An accent or stress, marked by a clap, which signifies the first beat of each *vibhāg* (excepting the *k͟hālī* or *k͟hālīs* of a *tāl*)

ta'līm Education. Musical instruction

tāluqdār (*ta'alluqadār*) Landlord or tax-collector

tān A rapid, melismatic sequence of notes, usually of equal duration

tānpūrā Long-necked, plucked lute with gourd resonator. Used as a drone instrument throughout India

tarāna A fast vocal composition employing meaningless syllables

ṭawā'if A courtesan

ṭhā Equal time (syn. *barābar*). Also, the basic phrase of a *relā*

ṭhekā The articulation of drum strokes representing a *tāl*. Usually improvised and often elaborate

ṭhumrī Light vocal style (often copied by instrumentalists), in which love and devotion are interwoven

tīgun 'Three times'; the division of the beat into three equal parts, or triplets

tihā'ī A musical structure that involves the threefold repetition of a phrase. It is usually used cadentially, in which case the last *bol* or note of a repeated phrase falls on *sam*

tihā'ī-bandīsh A variety of *tihā'ī*

tihā'ī kī tihā'ī 'The *tihā'ī* of a *tihā'ī*'. A *tihā'ī* set within another *tihā'ī* (syn. *nau kī tihā'ī*)

tīntāl A *tāl* of sixteen beats. The most commonly used *tāl* in Hindustani music

ṭopī Indian hat

ṭukṛā A fixed composition in tabla

ūpaj Improvisation

ustād Teacher, master (Muslim). A title and term of address (Ustad) for a mature, knowledgeable and accomplished Muslim musician

uṭhān 'Rising', 'getting up'. A fixed composition used to begin a tabla performance

vibhāg A structural subdivision of a *tāl*

vilambit Slow tempo

zamīndār Landlord

Select Bibliography

Agarwala, Viney K. 1966 *Traditions and Trends in Indian Music*. Meerut: Rastogi

Ahmad, Imtiaz 1973 'Introduction'. In Imtiaz Ahmad (ed.), *Caste and Social Stratification among the Muslims*. Delhi: Manohar Book Service

Anon 1981 'Tabla solo by Afaq Husain Khan'. Review in the *Calcutta Statesman*, Calcutta, 4 March 1981

Anon 1984 'Interview with Latif Ahmed Khan', *Indian Music Newsletter* (Amsterdam), 10, pp. 4–5

Ansari, Ghaus 1960 *Muslim Caste in Uttar Pradesh*. Lucknow: Ethnographic and Folk Culture Society of Uttar Pradesh

Bailey, F. G. 1969 *Stratagems and Spoils: A Social Anthropology of Politics*. Oxford: Blackwell

Baily, John 1974 *Krishna Govinda's Rudiments of Tabla Playing*. Llanfynydd: Unicorn Bookshop

Baruah, U. L. 1983 *This is All India Radio*. New Delhi: Publications Division, Ministry of Information and Broadcasting (Government of India)

Bhatkhande Sangit Vidyapith n.d. *Prospectus and Syllabus for 1981 to 1983*. Lucknow: Bhatkhande Sangit Vidyapith

Bhatnagar, G. D. 1968 *Awadh under Wajid Ali Shah*. Varanasi: Bharatiya Vidya Prakashan

Bor, Joep 1984 'Baijis: Female Performers of the Past', *Indian Music Newsletter* (Amsterdam), 10, pp. 1–3

Chandra, M. 1973 *The World of Courtesans*. Delhi

Cowell, E. B. (ed.) 1895 *The Jataka, or Stories of the Buddha's Former Births*, vol. 2, translated by W. H. D. Rouse. Cambridge: Cambridge University Press

Deshpande, V. H. 1973 *Indian Musical Traditions*. Bombay: Popular Prakashan

Dumont, Louis 1972 *Homo Hierarchicus*. London: Paladin

Edwardes, Michael 1960 *The Orchid House: Splendours and Miseries of the Kingdom of Oudh 1827–1857*. London: Cassell

Evans-Pritchard, E. E. 1978 *The Nuer*. New York and Oxford: Oxford University Press

Firth, R. 1967 *Tikopia Ritual and Belief*. London: George Allen and Unwin

Gottlieb, Robert S. 1977 *The Major Traditions of North Indian Tabla Drumming*, 2 vols. Munich: Emil Katzbichler

Hasan, Amir 1983 'Starry-eyed Nawabs of Oudh', *Northern India Patrika*, Lucknow, 9 January

Hay, Sidney 1939 *Historic Lucknow*. Lucknow: Pioneer Press

Heber, Bishop Reginald 1828 *Narrative of a Journey through the Upper Provinces of India from Calcutta to Bombay 1824–1825*, 2 vols. London

Higgins, Jon 1976 'From Prince to Populace: Patronage as a Determinant of Culture Change in South Indian (Karnatak) Music', *Asian Music*, 7 (2), pp. 20–6

Husain, Mirza Jafar 1981 *Qadeem Lucknow ki Akhiri Bahar* (in Urdu). New Delhi: Bureau for the Promotion of Urdu

Imam, Hakim Mohammad Karam 1959 'Melody through the Centuries', translated by Govind Vidyarthi, *Sangeet Natak Akademi Bulletin*, 11–12, pp. 13–26, 33

Joshi, Narayan 1981 *Adital: Thirakwan Shaili* (in Hindi). Dombivli: Narayan Joshi

Kaufmann, Walter 1967 *Musical Notations of the Orient*. Bloomington: Indiana University Press

Keskar, B. V. 1967 *Indian Music: Problems and Prospects*. Bombay: Popular Prakashan

Khan, Sadiq Ali and Aijaz Raqm Khan 'Dihlavi' 1895 *Sarmaya-[e]-Ishrat: Qanun-e-Mausiqi* (in Urdu). Delhi: Munshi Muhammad Ibrahim

Kippen, James 1985 'The Dialectical Approach: A Methodology for the Analysis of Tabla Music', *Bulletin of the International Council for Traditional Music* (UK Chapter), 12, pp. 4–12

1987 'An Ethnomusicological Approach to the Analysis of Musical Cognition', *Music Perception* (University of California at La Jolla), 5 (2), pp. 173–95

Kippen, James and Bernard Bel 1984 'Linguistic Study of Rhythm: Computer Models of Tabla Language', *International Society for Traditional Arts Research (ISTAR) Newsletter*, 2, pp. 28–33

Knighton, William 1855 *The Private Life of an Eastern King*. London

Kripalani, Krishna 1975 'Medieval Indian Literature'. In A. L. Basham (ed.), *A Cultural History of India*. Oxford: Clarendon Press

Llewellyn-Jones, Rosie 1985 *A Fatal Friendship: The Nawabs, the British and the City of Lucknow*. Delhi: Oxford University Press

Maitra, Radhika M. 1977 'Musing on the Muse'. In the Foundation Day Souvenir of the Ramakrishna Mission Institute of Culture, Calcutta, pp. 20–6

Manuel, Peter 1986 'The Evolution of Modern Thumri', *Ethnomusicology*, 30 (3), pp. 470–90

Meer, Wim van der 1980 *Hindustani Music in the Twentieth Century*. New Delhi: Allied Publishers

1984 'Thats and Murcchanas; An Analysis of Tone Materials', *International Society for Traditional Arts Research (ISTAR) Newsletter*, 1, pp. 15–19

Miner, Allyn 1981 'Hindustani Instrumental Music in the Early Modern Period: A Study of the Sitar and Sarod in the Eighteenth and Nineteenth Centuries'. Unpublished Ph.D. thesis, Benares Hindu University

Misra, Susheela 1977a 'The Two Balis – Rai Umanath Bali and Rai Rajeshwar Bali', *National Herald*, New Delhi and Lucknow, 23 January 1977

1977b 'Khalifa Abid Husain Khan', *National Herald*, New Delhi and Lucknow, 3 April 1977

1981 *Great Masters of Hindustani Music*. New Delhi: Hem

1984 *Lucknow ki Sangeet Parampara* (in Hindi). Lucknow: Uttar Pradesh Sangeet Natak Akademi

Neuman, Daniel M. 1974 'The Cultural Structure and Social Organisation of Musicians in India: The Perspective from Delhi'. Unpublished Ph.D. thesis, University of Illinois at Urbana-Champaign

1978 'Gharanas: The Rise of Musical "Houses" in Delhi and Neighbouring Cities'. In Bruno Nettl (ed.), *Eight Urban Musical Cultures: Tradition and Change*. Urbana: University of Illinois Press

1980 *The Life of Music in North India: The Organisation of an Artistic Tradition*. New Delhi: Manohar

Oldenburg, Veena Talwar 1984 *The Making of Colonial Lucknow, 1856–1877*. Princeton, NJ: Princeton University Press

Owens, Naomi 1983 'The Dagar Gharana'. In Bonnie Wade (ed.), *Performing Arts in India: Essays on Music, Dance, and Drama*. Lanham, MD: University Press of America

Paine, Robert 1970 'Information Communication and Information Management', *Canadian Review of Sociology and Anthropology*, 7, pp. 172–88

Pemble, John 1977 *The Raj, the Indian Mutiny and the Kingdom of Oudh 1801–1859*. Hassocks, Sussex: The Harvester Press

Pettigrew, Joyce 1975 *Robber Noblemen*. London: Routledge and Kegan Paul

Platts, J. T. 1977 *A Dictionary of Urdu, Classical Hindi and English*. New Delhi: Oriental Books Reprint Corporation

Qureshi, Regula 1969 'Tarannum: The Chanting of Urdu Poetry', *Ethnomusicology*, 13 (3), pp. 425–68

Ratanjankar, S. N. 1961 'A Comparative Study of the Old Traditional Methods of Musical Training and the Modern Music Classes'. In G. J. Ambardekar *et al.* (eds.) *Commemorative Volume in Honour of Dr S. N. Ratanjankar*. Bombay: K. G. Guide

Roach, David 1972 'The Benares Bāj – The Tablā Tradition of a North Indian City', *Asian Music*, 3 (2), pp. 29–41

Roy Choudhury, M. L. 1957 'Music in Islam', *Journal of Asiatic Society* (Bengal), 23 (2), pp. 46–102

Roy Chowdhury, H. K. 1929 *The Musicians of India*, Part 1. Calcutta: Kuntaline Press

Russell, Ralph 1969 'The Pursuit of the Urdu Ghazal', *Journal of Asian Studies*, 29 (1), pp. 107–24

Russell, Ralph and Khurshidul Islam 1969 *Three Mughal Poets: Mir, Sauda, and Mir Hasan*. London: George Allen and Unwin
Russell, William 1957 *My Indian Mutiny Diary*, edited by Michael Edwardes. London: Cassell
Ruswa, Mirza M. H. n.d. *The Courtesan of Lucknow (Umrao Jan Ada)*, translated by Khushwant Singh and M. A. Husaini. Delhi: Hind Pocket Books
Saxena, D. N. 1973 *Differential Urban Fertility: Lucknow*. Lucknow: Demographic Research Centre, University of Lucknow
Sethi, Sunil 1983 'Madame Sings her Blues', *India Today*, 15 March 1983
Shankar, Ravi 1966 'Listening and Learning', *Indian Music Journal*, 6, pp. 44–8
Sharar, Abdul Halim 1975 *Lucknow: The Last Phase of an Oriental Culture*, translated and edited by E. S. Harcourt and Fakhir Hussein. London: Paul Elek
Sharma, Bhagwat S. 1981 *Taal Prakaash* (in Hindi). Hathras: Sangeet Karyalaya
Shepherd, Frances 1976 'Tabla and the Benares Gharana'. Unpublished Ph.D. thesis, Wesleyan University
Silver, Brian 1976 'On Becoming an Ustad: Six Life Sketches in the Evolution of a Gharana', *Asian Music*, 7 (2), pp. 27–58
1984 'The Adab of Musicians'. In B. Metcalf (ed.), *Moral Conduct and Authority*. Berkeley: University of California Press
Solis, Theodore 1970 'The Sarod: Its Gat-Tora Tradition with Examples by Amir Khan and Three of his Students'. Unpublished M.A. thesis, University of Hawaii
Solvyns, F. Baltazard 1810 *Les Hindous, ou description de leurs mœurs, coutumes, et cérémonies*, vol. 3. Paris
Sorrell, Neil and Ram Narayan 1980 *Indian Music in Performance: A Practical Introduction*. Manchester: Manchester University Press
Spear, Percival 1978 *A History of India*, vol. 2. Harmondsworth: Penguin
Srivastav, G. C. 1982 *Tal Parichaya* (in Hindi). Allahabad: Sangit Sadan Prakashan
Stewart, Rebecca 1974 'The Tabla in Perspective'. Unpublished Ph.D. thesis, University of California, Los Angeles
Vashishtha, S. 1982 *Taal Martand* (in Hindi). Hathras: Sangeet Karyalaya
Wade, Bonnie 1971 'Khyal: A Study in Hindustani Classical Vocal Music', 2 vols. Unpublished Ph.D. thesis, University of California, Los Angeles
1979 *Music in India: The Classical Traditions*. Englewood Cliffs, NJ: Prentice-Hall

Appendix: items on the cassette

The recorded items illustrate the notated examples given in Chapter 8. They were recorded in Lucknow during September and October 1987 and feature a number of different musicians. Each item will be announced separately on the tape.

Side A Examples 1–37

Example 1	Delhi *qā'ida*
Example 2	Delhi *qā'ida* (Lucknow style)
Example 3	Lucknow *qā'ida*
Example 4	Lucknow *qā'ida*
Example 5	*Qā'ida-relā*
Example 6	*Qā'ida-relā*
Example 7	*Chand*
Example 8	*Chand*
Example 9	*Chand*
Example 10	*Calan*
Example 11	Delhi *peshkār*
Example 12	Lucknow *peshkār*
Example 13	*Laggī*
Example 14	*Laggī*
Example 15	*Laggī*
Example 16	*Relā*
Example 17	*Rang*
Example 18	*Rang-relā*
Example 19	*Mukhṛā*
Example 20	*Mukhṛā*
Example 21	*Tihā'ī*
Example 22	*Tihā'ī*
Example 23	*Tihā'ī kī tihā'ī*
Example 24	*Tihā'ī kī tihā'ī*
Example 25	*Tihā'ī bandīsh*
Example 26	*Tihā'ī bandīsh*
Example 27	*Gintī tihā'ī (bedam)*
Example 28	*Gat*
Example 29	*Gat*
Example 30	*Pancpallī gat* or *Uṭhān*
Example 31	*Akāl gat*
Example 32	*Gat*
Example 33	*Ṭukṛā*
Example 34	*Ṭukṛā*
Example 35	*Uṭhān*
Example 36	*Mohrā*
Example 37	*Cakkardār*

Side B Examples 38–40 and two tabla solos

Example 38	*Farmā'ishī cakkardār*
Example 39	*Paran*
Example 40	*Paran*

Performers. Khalifa (Ustad) Afaq Husain Khan: Examples 1, 3, 4, 5, 6, 17, 18, 28, 32, 33, 34; Ilmas Husain Khan: Examples 7, 10, 12, 13, 14, 15, 16, 20, 23, 25, 29, 30, 35, 36, 37, 38, 39, 40; James Kippen: Examples 2, 8, 9, 11, 19, 24, 27, 31; Pankaj Kumar Chowdhury: Examples 22, 26; Probir Kumar Mittra: Example 21.

1. A short tabla solo in *tīntāl* by Ilmas Husain Khan (duration 9'30"). *Sārangī* accompaniment: Ustad Dildar Khan.

0'00"	*Sārangī* introduction, followed by *ṭhekā* with *mukhṛās*
0'36"	*Uṭhān (ṭukṛā)*
1'06"	*Peshkār* (see Example 11)
1'37"	*Qā'ida*
2'58"	*Qā'ida*
4'16"	*Relā*
5'56"	*Qā'ida-relā*
7'09"	*Relā*
8'05"	*Gat*
8'40"	*Qā'ida*
9'15"	*Ṭukṛā*

2. Excerpts from a tabla solo in *tīntāl* by Khalifa (Ustad) Afaq Husain Khan (duration 14'02"). *Sārangī* accompaniment: Ustad Dildar Khan.

0′00″	*Sāraṅgī* introduction, followed by *ṭhekā*
0′34″	*Peshkār* (see Example 12)
3′27″	*Calan*
4′44″	*Relā*
5′34″	*Qāʿida-relā*
6′25″	*Relā*
7′19″	*Qāʿida*
8′22″	*Qāʿida*
9′13″	*Chand*
9′26″	*Rang*
10′13″	*Ṭukṛā*
10′37″	*Akāl gat* (played twice)
11′06″	*Akāl gat* (played three times)
12′01″	*Gat* (played once)
12′12″	*Ṭukṛā*
12′30″	*Qāʿida-relā*
13′44″	*Ṭukṛā*

Index

Note: Performers are entered under their first names.